Words Onscreen

Words Onscreen

The Fate of Reading in a Digital World

Naomi S. Baron

OXFORD
UNIVERSITY PRESS

OXFORD
UNIVERSITY PRESS

Oxford University Press is a department of the
University of Oxford. It furthers the University's objective
of excellence in research, scholarship, and education
by publishing worldwide.

Oxford   New York
Auckland   Cape Town   Dar es Salaam   Hong Kong   Karachi
Kuala Lumpur   Madrid   Melbourne   Mexico City   Nairobi
New Delhi   Shanghai   Taipei   Toronto

With offices in
Argentina   Austria   Brazil   Chile   Czech Republic   France   Greece
Guatemala   Hungary   Italy   Japan   Poland   Portugal   Singapore
South Korea   Switzerland   Thailand   Turkey   Ukraine   Vietnam

Oxford is a registered trade mark of Oxford University Press
in the UK and certain other countries.

Published in the United States of America by
Oxford University Press
198 Madison Avenue, New York, NY 10016

Library of Congress Cataloging-in-Publication Data
Baron, Naomi S.
Words onscreen : the fate of reading in a digital
world / Naomi S. Baron.
p.   cm.
Includes bibliographical references and index.
ISBN 978-0-19-931576-5 (hardcover : alk. paper) —
ISBN 978-0-19-931577-2 (ebook)
1. Reading—Technological innovations.
2. Educational technology—Computer-assisted instruction.
3. Tablet computers.   4. Computer-assisted instruction.
5. Interdisciplinary approach in education.   I. Title.
Z1033.E43B37 2015   028'.90285—dc23
2014018512

9 8 7 6 5 4 3 2 1

Printed in the United States of America
on acid-free paper

For
Phyllis Peres, the Stanford Center for Advanced Study
in the Behavioral Sciences, and Todos 2012–2013

There would be no book without you.

Contents

nl;pr
Not Long; Please Read

A Preface

The headline in the *New York Times* ran "For Better Social Skills, Scientists Recommend a Little Chekhov." Social psychologists at the New School for Social Research had just documented what many of us have long believed: Reading serious fiction makes you more empathic and socially perceptive than reading light fiction—or not reading at all.[1]

The topic of reading is on many people's minds. A perennial question is whether we are reading enough. The National Endowment for the Arts periodically reports on the state of American reading habits, with the verdict vacillating from crisis to improvement to status quo. Another issue is what we read. Is it OK if adolescents go for graphic novels in place of Dickens? Can *Twilight* substitute for Tolstoy? Emanuele Castano and David Comer Kidd (the researchers at the New School) argue no. A fast-paced plot doesn't compensate for lack of complex character development. Writers like Chekhov provoke readers to take an active role in fathoming the psyches of their characters, nurturing emotional intelligence in the process.

But there is another concern these days. Does it matter what medium we use for reading: print or digital text? During the 1990s, we became increasingly comfortable reading on computer screens. Sometimes the amount was small—an email, a web page. Other times the text was longer—a magazine article or even an out-of-copyright book from Project Gutenberg. We still relied on hardcopy books, though newspapers and periodicals were finding their way online. Mobile phones ignited the texting revolution but were hardly seen as places for reading actual books.

That world changed in 2007, when Amazon introduced its first Kindle. Other eReaders had arrived a bit earlier in the United States but were met with a tepid response. The Kindle had superior technology, backed by a bookseller providing content both easily and at an attractive price. eReading took off. Three years later came the debut of Apple's iPad. While the tablet wasn't positioned as a replacement for eReaders, its buyers began downloading a profusion of books. Meanwhile, as mobile phone technology improved and smartphones proliferated, the phone morphed into a device not just for personal communication and not only for downloading apps. It became a reading platform.

One more piece of the puzzle. The educational establishment (especially in the United States) became increasingly concerned about the high cost of textbooks. Whether school districts or students were footing the bill, prices were often beyond their budget. The Great Recession made the financial crunch particularly painful. Equally troubling was the size of student loan debt, which in the United States was fast approaching $1 trillion. Expensive textbooks were one more fiscal albatross, and eTextbooks were promoted as a solution.

And so the migration began from reading in print to reading onscreen. I watched with curiosity—and concern.

My academic training is in linguistics. A cardinal tenet of the field is that our job is to observe and analyze, not judge. During the bad old days of linguistic prescriptivism, grammarians spent their time instructing others on the fine points of proper usage, spelling, and punctuation. But then descriptive linguists in the early twentieth century, followed by transformational grammarians several decades later, commanded those studying language to abandon the misguided prescriptivist past.

Among the new corollaries were that no language is better or worse than any other, and that all people (unless disadvantaged by a physical or mental condition) had the same fundamental linguistic competence. I understood the rationale. The late nineteenth century was laced with talk of "primitive languages" and "primitive peoples," justifying conquest, expropriation of resources, and enforced servitude. While I didn't question our equity of human genetic endowment (a cornerstone of Noam Chomsky's theories), experience convinced me that not all languages have equally rich vocabulary and syntax, and that some speakers indeed lack the linguistic sophistication found in other members of their tribe. I also believed such lacunae were generally remediable but needed intervention.

Then there was the issue of medium. For more than a century, linguists have taken speech as constituting "real" language and hence their quintessential object of study. Writing was just a handmaiden to talking. Since I was already risking my union card by passing judgment on languages and language users, why not go a step further? I began exploring written language—how writing arose, what it was used for, and how it evolved. Because writing necessitates some form of technology (a stylus, a quill, a telegraph, a computer), I went on to investigate the effects of technology on the way we use language, both written and spoken.

At the time I was writing my last book (*Always On: Language in an Online and Mobile World*), a question whirling about in public discussion was whether email, instant messaging, and texting were harming language. (Short answer: Whatever is happening with language, we can't lay much of the blame on computers and mobile phones.) Another concern was how the growing obsession with digital technologies affected face-to-face encounters.

In the back of my mind were a few added worries. The first was how much computer manufacturers, broadband carriers, and the mobile phone industry were fueling behaviors that were not particularly healthy, either socially or psychologically. We know that supersized orders of french fries make money for fast-food companies but are nutritional disasters. Were all-you-can-text plans driving Americans to addictive communication?

A second apprehension—but even harder to wrap my arms around—was whether all this communication-at-a-distance might alter the very nature of human interaction. Sherry Turkle had already begun arguing that we care more about our technologies than about one another. (*Alone Together* would come out in 2011.) Her analysis resonated with me.

One more quandary. As a university professor, I do a lot of reading—for my own research, as a reviewer for journals and academic publishers, and as a colleague participating in personnel evaluations. When doing research, I nearly always go for printed text (as do many professionals). I underline, write notes, draw arrows, attach Post-its. I also cover the desk and even the floor with pages and volumes to get a panoramic view of the materials literally at hand. And I tend to remember where to find what I have read by physical signposts: about halfway through, on the upper right-hand side; on the page with a grease stain from that late-night brownie.

The documents people send me for doing reviews inevitably arrive electronically. Should I read them onscreen or print them out? The answer is easy for a thirty-page manuscript: print, read and mark up, write the review, recycle. But what about for an entire book manuscript or the lengthy dossier of an assistant professor seeking promotion?

I'm no stranger to dealing with words onscreen. I have been doing "word processing" for more than thirty years. I regularly edit at the computer. Gamely, I have tried undertaking a couple of reviews onscreen. But immediately I know I'm cheating the hopeful author or applicant. Despite the thousands of hours logged reading and writing digitally, I cannot perform a careful analysis this way. I need to see the work as a whole, cross-reference back and forth, keeping multiple passages in view.

If I have trouble doing serious analysis when reading online, what about my students? As my research would subsequently show, many undergraduates treat online academic articles the same way I do: They print the pieces out. But what happens with textbooks or complex novels? When they are consumed online, what are the educational and psychological consequences?

Words Onscreen asks if digital reading is reshaping our understanding of what it means to read. The question sounds amorphous, but it has tangible substance and equally real fallout. I will argue that digital reading is fine for many short pieces or for light content we don't intend to analyze or reread. However, if eReading is less well suited for many longer works or even for short ones requiring serious thought, what happens to reading if we shift from print to screens? Will some of the uses of reading (and, for that matter, writing) fall by the wayside? If so, with what implications for education, culture, and ourselves?

These questions involve judgment and action—neither of which my linguistics training sanctioned. But the challenges are real, and so I broke ranks.

At the time I began actively working on this book, I routinely encountered skepticism—even veiled pity—when I described the venture. Did I fail to understand that technology marches on? That cars supplanted horses and buggies? That printing replaced handwritten manuscripts, computers replaced typewriters, and digital screens were replacing books? Hadn't I read the statistics on how many eReaders and tablets were being sold? Didn't I see all those people reading eBooks on their mobile devices? Was I simply unable to adapt?

The gauntlet was down, and I took up the challenge. If anyone was going to love (and be adept at) eReading, it should be younger readers. I needed to survey them, and so I did, beginning in 2010. Focusing on university students, I collected data from three cohorts in the United States, along with a group in Japan and another in Germany. Although the questions evolved over the years, in each case I inquired about habits and preferences when it came to reading in print versus onscreen. I'll save my findings for the chapters ahead, but suffice it to say I was roundly vindicated.

Empirical data from a sample of readers are just one part of the story. Achieving a balanced assessment of the print-versus-screen debate requires weighing a host of variables. You need to begin with reading itself. And since people can read only if someone is writing, you actually have to start there. As historians of reading (and writing) have shown, what is being written and read, who is doing the producing and consuming, and what people hope to get out of the experience alter with time. It is no surprise that the same issues resurface in the digital age.

Reading and writing are intertwined in another vital way. If reading habits change, so do the ways authors tend to write. Computers, and now portable digital devices, coax us to skim rather than read in depth, search rather than traverse continuous prose. As a result, how—and how much—we write is already shifting.

Digital reading is undeniably popular. Companies like Amazon and Apple are investing millions in tempting us to buy their readers, tablets, and phones, but customers are willingly flocking to websites and stores. Reading onscreen has many virtues, including convenience, potential cost savings, and one that consumers in wealthy countries don't often think about: the ability to bring reading tools and texts to people who might otherwise not have them. Open access to materials online. Free eReaders and eBooks distributed in places like Africa and India.

Yet the virtues of eReading are matched with potential—along with incontrovertible—drawbacks. Take environmental issues. People often praise eReading as more environmentally friendly than reading on paper. But are they right? Once you tally up the environmental costs of producing digital devices (including depletion of rare earth elements and creation of hazardous waste), the final winner becomes less clear. What we know for sure about eReading is that users are easily distracted by other temptations on their devices, and multitasking is rampant.

Your purpose in reading—to kill time, for relaxation, for work—is also relevant when sizing up the pros and cons of different reading platforms. People often say they like using eReaders or tablets for travel so they don't have to lug books in hardcopy. When you probe, you commonly find that what's being loaded on the mobile devices is light reading. The type of reading matters, because casual fare is generally read only once—what I call one-off reading. Since the emergence of print culture in the eighteenth century, and particularly with the rise of the novel and later the detective story, much of our reading has been one-off. The trend continues today. Think of all the books we read when traveling but toss when we arrive, the books we truck out to the beach, the newspapers and popular magazines we peruse and then scrap. That said, obviously some books are worth reading slowly, carefully, and more than once. (Just ask a Jane Austen fan.) Incidentally, it is these other books that tend to be the kind Castano and Kidd would say require you to wrestle with character complexity.

For one-off reading, digital devices may be every bit as good as print. But what about more serious reading? What about books that objectively merit keeping—and rereading? To the extent we shift our reading from print to screens, we become less likely to reread. A decline in rereading would mark a critical shift in the way at least some types of readers have encountered books for centuries.

Reading onscreen raises another question about the nature of reading: Is it an individual encounter with a text or essentially a social experience? The explosive growth of online social networking has triggered online reading groups. (Goodreads is but one example.) Historically, if you were literate, reading was typically an individual act. Is reading onscreen tipping the balance from a solitary enterprise to a social one? And if so, with what consequences?

A topic some eBook advocates dismiss as nostalgia is the physical side of reading: holding books in your hands, navigating with your fingers through pages, browsing through shelves of volumes and stumbling upon one you had forgotten about. Are we back to longing for buggies and typewriters? Or by going exclusively digital, would we lose some physical anchors that have been essential to the reading process for almost two millennia?

Other relevant data come from cognitive and neuropsychologists investigating how our brains behave when we use digital devices. Especially relevant is research on multitasking and distraction. We're not nearly as good at multitasking as many of us think we are. The consequences for mixing driving with texting are painfully self-evident. But there are also troubling outcomes when it comes to distracted reading, especially if we assume that appreciation for writing style or complex content matters.

If you live in the United States or the United Kingdom, it is easy to conclude that the continuing advance of eReading onto print's turf is a fait accompli. These are the two countries with the highest penetration of eBooks. If you look across the English Channel or to the Far East, the picture changes. Yes, eBooks are selling, but the percentage of sales is a small fraction of that among the Yanks and the Brits. Some of the difference has to do with marketing, but there is also the cultural question: Do the French or Germans or Japanese want eBooks? And if not, why?

There are all sorts of readers—and reasons for reading. Some people thrive on an exclusive diet of murder mysteries or biographies or romance. We find avid readers and those who read sparingly. Bibliophiles and college graduates who gather no books (print or electronic). Those who read only for school or a job, people who read out of boredom, and some who burrow in their books to avoid social contact. Add in the spectrum of ages and levels of reading ability, and it becomes obvious that "the fate of reading in a digital world" must be viewed through multiple lenses.

This book considers a spectrum of readers and motivations. We will talk about young children (and the parents who read to them), about teenagers, and about adults who flock to physical or digital reading groups. The biggest emphasis will be on young adults, since that is the cohort for which I have gathered data. While they are all university students, I probed their reading habits and preferences both for doing academic work and when reading for pleasure.

Recently, it has been interesting to watch prognostications shift regarding the fate of print in the face of digital reading. The growth rate of eBooks has slowed substantially. Surveys conducted by the media and by companies committed to selling the public on eBooks are reporting that sizable numbers of readers (especially teenagers and young adults) aren't sold.

This is not to say eBooks will—or should—recede. For the foreseeable future, they will provide a major platform for reading in growing parts of the world. For the same future, it seems probable that print will persist.

We need to dig beneath the hype on both sides of the discussion if we want to understand how technology is affecting the way we read, for good or for ill. *Words Onscreen* is my take on the debate.

Before we begin, one obvious note. Digital technologies evolve quickly, generating ever more new applications and statistics. I finished drafting this book in February 2014. By the time you read *Words Onscreen*, you won't find the next new thing. But the principles of what it means to read—and whether medium matters—stand firm.

Words Onscreen

1 | "I Hate Books"

Words Go Digital

E-books resemble motel rooms—bland and efficient. Books are home—real, physical things you can love and cherish and make your own, till death do you part. Or till you run out of shelf space.

—*Michael Dirda*

How are you reading this book? Holding a physical volume? On an eReader, a tablet, a mobile phone?

Does the medium matter? Michael Dirda, book critic for the *Washington Post*, thinks it does. Others—like the person I am about to introduce—disagree.

It was June 2012 when I met the young man in question. He was on a panel at the International Digital Publishing Forum's Digital Book conference, held in the Javits Center in New York. The session's title was "Case Study: A Window into the E-Future of the World's First School to Go Full E-Only."

South Kent is a small private high school in northwestern Connecticut. In fall 2011, the curriculum went digital. No heavy textbooks to carry. Just iPads loaded with eBooks. Delano Williams, who had just graduated from South Kent, effused about "e-only" learning. During the Q&A, I asked whether there was any book—any book at all—he would prefer to read in hardcopy. His lightning-fast retort: "I hate books!," meaning anything in paper with a binding.

Delano didn't hate reading. Just printed books.

In less than a decade, the book trade, along with personal reading habits, has transformed dramatically. eBooks are now a multibillion-dollar business for Amazon, while Borders has shuttered its doors and the fate of Barnes & Noble remains uncertain. By 2012, more books were purchased online in the United States than from brick-and-mortar stores.[1] A growing number of those were eBooks. Students continue selling textbooks back to campus stores at the end of the term, but they now exercise new options, including buying or renting electronic versions.

Publishers of reference books are acknowledging the shift. The *Oxford English Dictionary* announced in summer 2010 it would not be publishing its next edition in print. *Encyclopedia Britannica* followed suit in March 2012. Macmillan ceased publishing physical dictionaries as of 2013.[2]

Even entire libraries are backing away from print. In 2005, the University of Texas at Austin caused a stir by removing nearly all books from its undergraduate library.[3] Then San Antonio caught the no-book fever. UT San Antonio's Applied Engineering and Technology Library houses more than 400,000 volumes—but all virtual.[4] Bexar County, Texas, which includes the city of San Antonio, next joined the digital club. BiblioTech, a book-free library, opened in late 2013, with its collection housed entirely on computers, tablets, and eReaders.[5]

Why the shift?

The earliest ripples of change began with increased reading on computer screens in the 1980s and early 1990s. The waves strengthened with the proliferation of email, instant messaging, electronic versions of newspapers and magazines, and efficient online search tools by the end of the 1990s. Once eBooks began really selling (following the arrival of Amazon's Kindle), a growing number of people turned to consuming book-length text onscreen. With the coming of the iPad in 2010, a tidal wave ensued. The paradigm was changing, and reading in hardcopy was depicted as old-school. The explosion of online academic courses (usually complete with online readings) has become a sign of the times. And one more sign: In June 2014, a US ambassador took the oath of office on an eReader for the first time.[6]

There has been a lot of talk about the future of printed books: scholarly works (like Geoffrey Nunberg's *The Future of the Book*), organizations (such as Bob Stein's Institute for the Future of the Book), and conferences (including a 2012 meeting at MIT, "Unbound: Speculations on the Future of the Book").[7] But an even deeper issue is whether new digital technologies will upend our understanding of what it means to read in the first place. If so, will we be better off, worse off, or about the same when it comes to learning or enjoyment?

The answers are hardly obvious. And they will probably keep shifting as technology evolves and as our experience (and comfort level) in using digital devices for reading increases. Change is likely on other fronts as well. Just as growth of the novel in the late eighteenth century was advanced by the expansion of print technology, new literary forms might well emerge that are tailor-made for screens.

But what do we mean by "reading"?

DEFINITIONS

READING AND TEXTS

At its most basic level, the word "reading" has something to do with deciphering written text. OK, so what is a "text"?

Most simply, a text is a stretch of written words. How long a stretch? The answer is something of a moving target. If you read the word "STOP" on a road sign, technically you are reading. The same goes for deciphering words on a billboard or your electric bill. But what we have in mind in this book is more continuous prose—say at least a page or two, with an unbounded upper limit. You can also read poetry or plays, but we will be focusing on prose.

BOOKS AND EBOOKS

We know what books are. Today they are compilations of pages bound together and covered by a stiffer (or at least different) material. Books used to come in other forms, including scrolls (in the Middle East, and then Rome) and even palm leaves joined together (in India and Southeast Asia).

"eBooks" (no surprise) are books available in electronic form. In principle, they can be read ("eReading") on any digital device, including a desktop or laptop computer, an eReader, a tablet computer, or a mobile phone. eBooks themselves come in two basic varieties. The first are digitally formatted versions of print originals, made either from PDFs or through digital adaptations using software publishing tools like HTML5 or EPUB. These days, an increasing number of books are initially published digitally, perhaps with a later print run.

The second kind of eBooks are "digitally native," meaning they are designed to capitalize on the special possibilities digital technology offers.[8] Visual images (stills or video) are increasingly common. Digitally native books are made for user interaction: rotating images, connecting with web pages or other readers, and maybe completing quizzes and getting feedback on performance. In the publishing industry, digitally native eBooks will be an important development, though as a genre, they are still very much a work in progress, partly because they are expensive to produce and partly because we need to figure out what we want digitally native books to accomplish. What it will mean to "read" them remains to be seen (and is not a question we will be tackling in *Words Onscreen*).

A final note on the word "eBooks": Because of the surge in sales of eReaders and book-length texts in digital format, it has become common to let actual eBooks dominate the conversation about reading on digital screens. Of course, there is more involved: newspapers, Facebook updates, movie reviews, blogs, scholarly articles. Since this book is about text that is at least a page or two long, we will focus on reading that has some linear heft, while keeping in mind that short spans of text may shape how we read longer ones.

eTEXTBOOKS

When the world of education talks about digital textbooks, they are called eTexts. The term is a bit confusing, since in principle you would think an eText is any kind of writing—a novel, a newspaper, a tweet—that appears on a screen. When we get to talking about uses of digital textbooks in education, we will call them eTextbooks, though that's not the term you will find when most people discuss education and eBooks.

eREADING BY THE NUMBERS

How prevalent is eReading? The answer depends on what activities you include. Anyone with a computer, eReader, tablet, or smartphone is reading electronically. You're browsing the top stories from the *Los Angeles Times* on your iPhone. The woman next to you on the bus is absorbed in a novel on her Kobo, while the guy just ahead is checking out upcoming Black Friday sales on his tablet. When you reach the office, you keep Gawker.com minimized on your desktop as potential relief from your day job but devote most of your time to reading reports on political unrest in the Middle East. Do these all count?

When number crunchers tally up eReading, they first pare away anything that doesn't meet the "continuous prose" and "at least a page or two" criteria. The ads are out; for the *LA Times* stories and Gawker.com, it depends upon the length; the novel on that Kobo and reports on your desktop are both technically in. However, in reality, the critical numbers tracked by industry (and nonprofits such as the Pew Research Center's Internet & American Life Project) involve eBooks and the devices on which people read them.

Start with eBooks.

EBOOK SALES

If publishing industry hype is to be believed, eBooks are poised to bury the print market. Understandably, publishers are looking to turn a profit. Once acquisition, editing, and setup are expensed, the cost of producing and distributing eBooks is negligible, especially compared with bound books. Vast resources are being plowed into making eBooks attractive alternatives to what some are now calling "p-books" or just plain "p."

The efforts are paying off. On Christmas Day 2009, Amazon's sales of eBooks in the United States surpassed hardcover sales for the first time (presumably thanks to new eReading customers eager to fill those Kindles found under the tree that morning). Other landmarks confirm how big the eBook footprint is becoming:

- By January 2011, Kindle eBook sales moved ahead of paperbacks.[9]
- eBook sales for 2011 rose 117 percent over 2010. (In 2010, the rise was 164 percent, and in 2009 it was 177 percent.)[10]
- In 2008, eBook sales accounted for only 1 percent of American publishers' revenues. In 2012, these sales made up nearly 23 percent. By 2013, the number had risen to 27 percent for adult trade books.[11]

While sales of eBooks have kept rising, the fate of print has been a different story. Between 2010 and 2012, American sales of print books fell nearly 16 percent.[12] The United States was not alone, as print sales also slumped internationally. Is that a sure sign that ePublishing is eating print's lunch? The answer is not so simple. The Great Recession affected economies around the globe, with print book sales just one victim of consumer retrenchment. Take continental Europe, where penetration of eBooks hasn't risen above the single digits (as we will see later on). Simple logic says that digital publishing there was hardly responsible for the decline in print sales. Two examples: In Italy (which has negligible eBook sales), the book market declined 8 percent in value in 2012 from the previous year. In France, where eBook sales are not much higher, the market also declined, though not as steeply.[13]

eReaders and Tablets: Shifting Sands

To do digital reading, you need an appropriate electronic device. You can read eBooks on desktop or laptop computers (and, as we'll see, university students commonly do). However, the most popular platforms for the general public have been eReaders and tablets.

The explosion in eBook sales was initially driven by success of the Amazon Kindle (launched in late 2007) and then Barnes & Noble's Nook (two years later). As of mid-2010, only 4 percent of American adults owned eReaders. By January 2014, ownership had jumped to 32 percent.[14]

In April 2010, Apple released the iPad. Initially the tablet was largely marketed as a terrific device for organizing (and displaying) photos, as well as handy for accessing the internet on the go. Composing text has never been its forte. And although there is a Newsstand app and a shelf for iBooks, the iPad wasn't designed to replace the Kindle or Nook. In fact, Steve Jobs had not initially been impressed with the concept of eReaders. When asked in January 2008 for his take on the Kindle (that is, soon after its release), Jobs was flatly dismissive: "It doesn't matter how good or bad the product is, the fact is that people don't read anymore."[15]

Up through 2011, dedicated eReaders remained the primary digital tool for accessing eBooks. Technophiles were buying both tablets and eReaders (along with smartphones), but functions tended to be divided up between devices.

What is so attractive about eReaders? Generally they cost less than tablets and are lighter to carry. But their primary virtue (at least for the early eReaders, and now for the Kindle Paperwhite or Kobo Touch) has been minimizing distraction. As Jen Doll wrote in *The Wire*,

> People who read e-books on tablets like the iPad are realizing that while a book in print or on a black-and-white Kindle is straightforward and immersive, a tablet offers a menu of distractions that can fragment the reading experience, or stop it in its tracks.[16]

Single-function eReaders sometime even trump print when it comes to aiding concentration. Author Alan Jacobs reports that he finds reading on a Kindle even less distracting than reading a print book: "The technology generates an inertia that makes it significantly easier to keep reading than to do anything else."[17] (For the record: Jacobs' Kindle was an early, non-internet-enabled model.)

As with so much else in the technology realm, the world turned. Jobs proved wrong about reading (or at least about downloading eBooks). And market researchers were wrong about the growth trajectory of eReaders.

In late 2011, Juniper Research had projected that by 2016, sales of eReaders would reach 67 million.[18] Yet by 2013, acquisition of dedicated eReaders—despite the internet access provided by newer models—had begun to taper off as tablet revenues rose. The *Wall Street Journal* reported estimates that global eReader shipments, which peaked in 2011 at about 25 million, would fall to 8.7 million by 2014.[19] As of January 2014, the Pew Internet & American Life Project reported that 42 percent of American adults owned a tablet, compared with 32 percent owning eReaders.[20]

The publishing industry began worrying that rising sales of tablets (at the expense of eReaders) might put a damper on the eBook business. In the words of Kelly Gallagher, then vice president of publishing services at Bowker Market Research (a major data source for the publishing industry),

> The tablet is a multifunction device and will therefore draw the reader into non-book activities and therefore cause them to consume books slower and therefore buy fewer books versus a single function e-reading device.[21]

Those in the publishing world are acutely aware of the distractions tablets offer. In fact, they have run seminars on how to create eBooks with "enriched content...designed and built to compete" in a tablet environment crowded with "applications and activities, from Angry Birds to e-mail."[22]

Distracted or not, people are buying eBooks and report reading them on tablets. A 2012 study found 43 percent of tablet users in the United States saying they read books at least weekly on their tablets. Yet to put this statistic into perspective, reading books was in fifth place for tablet use, after email, news, games, and social networking sites.[23] People are also increasingly reading eBooks on mobile phones. In the same study, 15 percent of respondents said they used smartphones weekly for reading books, though again, the numbers significantly trailed email, news, games, and social networking. Given the explosion in smartphone use worldwide—a billion smartphones shipped in 2013[24]—we must not underestimate the role of phones as a digital platform of choice.

Age makes a difference in how people access eBooks. Young adults are more likely to read eBooks on their mobile phones than those over age 30. These "older" readers do more of their eBook reading on tablets.[25]

DO READERS LIKE eREADING?

People are buying digital devices they use for reading. In January 2014, 28 percent of American adults reported having read an eBook over the past year.[26] Millions of eBooks are selling. The publishing industry, along with hardware distributors, is pressing us to buy even more.

But what do readers themselves say about eReading? Do they like it? To contextualize that question, it makes sense to ask how much reading they are doing in the first place.

WHO IS READING HOW MUCH

Long before the proliferation of eReading devices, America had been worrying if reading was "at risk." A scary 2004 study by the National Endowment for the Arts said yes, reporting that between 1982 and 2002, there was a 10 percent decline in the number of adults reading literature.[27]

A follow-on NEA study released in 2007 expanded "reading" to include nonfiction of all sorts—not just books but magazines, newspapers, and online reading. This time the study added adolescents as well. The results were just as gloomy. While 15-to-24-year-olds watched TV almost two hours a day, they devoted only seven minutes to leisure reading. Moreover, reading scores on standardized tests given to 12th graders in the United States had fallen significantly since 1992.[28]

The picture seemed a bit rosier in 2009 when the NEA issued *Reading on the Rise*. Adult reading of literature had risen 7 percent, with the most rapid gains among 18-to-24-year-olds. But before we get too excited, keep in mind what these figures represent. The survey had asked, "During the last 12 months, did you read any a) novels or short stories; b) poetry; or c) plays?" That's "any" as in "even one." When the survey asked about reading books of any sort for pleasure, there had been a drop between 2002 and 2008.[29] A recent survey, this time by Nielsen Book, reported that a whopping 41 percent of the teenagers they surveyed don't read for fun. That number had been a comparatively benign 21 percent in 2011. And the US Bureau of Labor Statistics found that of the nearly 6½ hours that 20-to-24-year-olds devoted to leisure or sports activities each day on weekends and holidays, on average barely 10 minutes were spent on leisure reading.[30]

Measuring how much people are reading is a bit like judging levels of happiness. There is the problem of self-reporting, a research technique plagued with inaccuracies. There's also the question of what "counts" as reading (much less happiness). For reading, do we include comic books? Online newspapers? And does just starting a book qualify?

Writing in the *Atlantic*, Alex Madrigal tried to debunk the notion that the internet killed (or at least wounded) book reading. Using data from Gallup surveys, he pointed out that between 1957 (definitely pre-internet) and 2005 (definitely post-), the number of people who said they were presently reading a book had doubled from less than 25 percent to almost 50 percent. Looking at Gallup's press release for its 2005 survey, there was even more encouraging news. When pollsters asked adults whether the internet was affecting their book-reading habits, 73 percent responded no. Another 6 percent said the internet led to their reading more books, while 16 percent reported a negative effect. (The remaining 5 percent had no opinion.)[31] Remember these data are pre-Kindle and pre-iPad.

The Pew Internet &American Life Project has post-Kindle/post-iPad findings, collected in late 2011. Adults (age 16 and older) who read eBooks reported doing more book reading overall (eBooks plus print) than those who only read printed books: an average of 24 books per year versus 15 books. Those who owned eReaders or tablets were more likely, on any given day, to have done book reading—onscreen or in hardcopy—than readers who didn't have a portable digital device (56 percent versus 45 percent).[32]

A caveat about the Pew study, as well as most others: It is not clear whether "reading a book" means finishing it. For what it's worth, when the digital library service Oyster needs to decide if you have "read" one of its books, the threshold is 10 percent. At that point, Oyster—which can track where you stopped—needs to pay the publisher's fee.[33] A mere 10 percent counts (at least for financial purposes) as having read a book? Were I a Twitter denizen, I'd tweet that number.

Another Pew analysis focused on readers ages 16–29. Among those who indicated they read long-form digital content (defined here as books, newspapers, and magazines), 40 percent said they were spending more time reading now because they could access material onscreen.[34]

Reading onscreen is undeniably growing. You might think that is because readers increasingly prefer digital books.

Do they?

THE PREFERENCE QUESTION

Reading on screens is a bit like anchovies: Some love them, some hate them, some tolerate them, and some change their minds. Throughout this book, the issue of user preferences—print or onscreen—will engage us. Here is a flavor of what is to come.

For over two decades, psychologists and reading specialists have been comparing how we read on screens versus in print. Studies have probed everything from proofreading skills and reading speed to comprehension and eye movement. Nearly all recent investigations are reporting essentially no differences.

But a second finding is also consistent: When asked, the majority—sometimes the vast majority—say they prefer reading in print. (Later on we will review the data.) They comment that print is more pleasant to read, that it is less taxing on the eyes, that they just like hardcopy. Some report they learn better with paper. When we talk about the eTextbook movement in higher education, we will see recurring mismatches between administrators' attempts to save students money by moving to electronic books and many students' beliefs that hardcopy makes for better education, at least when doing long-form reading.

What about eBooks for kids?

CHILDREN'S BOOKS GO DIGITAL

Start with the money trail.

eBooks for children (from babies to adolescents) has become a new frontier for publishers. With sales revenue for adult eBooks cooling off from earlier triple-digit growth, attention to the children's market paid off: 2012 eBook revenues in the "children's/young adult" category rose 121 percent over the previous year.[35] Conferences and webinars are focusing on children's eBooks, and annual book fairs—from New York to Frankfurt and London—are brimming with new digital offerings for kids. In the words of Andi Sporkin, a spokesperson for the Association of American Publishers, "It's the fastest growing category in the trade."[36] Data out in early 2014 indicate that two-thirds of American children ages 2 to 13 are now reading eBooks.[37]

Yet look more closely, and the picture blurs. In 2011, Pew interviewed adults who had read both eBooks and printed books in the past 12 months. Of these, 81 percent said print was a better format for reading with a child. Data from a year later documented parents' belief that having children read print books themselves is "very important."[38] Matt Richtel and Julie Bosman, reporting in the *New York Times*, found that even "die-hard downloaders of books onto Kindles, iPads, laptops and phones" wanted their children to be reading print (and having it read to them). Why? Parents were concerned their kids would get distracted by the "bells and whistles" of the devices and not focus on the reading part.[39]

I am reminded of another Richtel piece, this one about Silicon Valley parents sending their children to the Waldorf School of the Peninsula, where digital technologies are out and paper, pen, and knitting needles are in. Parents included the chief technology officer of eBay, along with employees of Google, Apple, and Yahoo. These folks were hardly technophobes. But they believed there is a time and place for using digital tools, and early schooling isn't one of them. In the words of one father, whose experience at Google included writing speeches for Eric Schmidt, "If I worked at Miramax and made good, artsy, rated R movies, I wouldn't want my kids to see them until they were 17."[40]

Data from the publishing industry confirm that parents—and children—are not fully sold on eBooks for younger readers. A study conducted by Bowker in fall 2012 found that 69 percent of parents preferred print books for children under age 6 and that 61 percent preferred print for children 7–12. When asked why, the parents talked about hardcopy helping children focus—not get distracted—along with preference for the look and feel of print.[41] A spring 2013 survey by Harris Interactive reported that 76 percent of parents with children up to age 8 favored reading printed books to their children.[42] Similar findings have been reported by the children's publisher Scholastic.[43]

Data on 13-to-17-year-olds came from the teenagers themselves. In the Bowker study, preference for print over eBooks rose from spring 2012 (61 percent) to fall 2012 (66 percent), equaling the level previously reported for fall 2011. Bowker referred to this shift as "snapping back" to print. When teenagers were asked why they didn't want to read eBooks, answers included preference for the experience of a printed book, cost of getting a digital device, and not seeing a need for reading onscreen.

In thinking about eBooks for children, it is one thing to look at sales figures and personal preference. It's another to ask whether eBooks are good for kids. The question is on many people's minds.[44] The American Academy of Pediatrics continues to urge parents to restrict the amount of time children under age 2 are exposed to media, including not just television but digital screens of any sort. The Academy's 2011 report advised that "unstructured playtime is more valuable for the developing brain than any electronic media exposure." Or, as Frederick Zimmerman at UCLA put it, "Kids need laps, not apps."[45]

WHAT AUTHORS SAY

If college students generally prefer reading in print, and children (and their parents) are leaning toward hardcopy, what about authors? Book critic Michael Dirda described eBooks as being like motels rather than "home." In a similar vein, novelist and travel writer Paul Theroux had this to say:

> [With eReaders] something certainly is lost—the physicality of a book, how one makes a book one's own by reading it (scribbling in it, dog-earing pages, spilling coffee on it) and living with it as an object, sometimes a talisman.[46]

Mohsin Hamid, who also loves technology, finds that reading print offers him more of the solitude he craves (including freedom from distraction). Anna Holmes speaks of how challenging it can be to get deeply engaged in reading an eBook—and how she encouraged people not to buy the electronic version of her own second book.[47]

At the same time, other authors are (or have become) digital screen devotees. Farhad Manjoo reflected that once he got an iPad, he

> pretty much stopped reading on paper altogether. . . . When I do page through print newspapers and magazines, I feel something novel—the sensation that I'm experiencing an inferior product.[48]

Even William H. Gass, known for his 1999 essay "In Defense of the Book," did an about-face in 2012 by writing a long essay (accompanied by Michael Eastman's photographs) that could be read only on an iPad running iBooks 2. In contrast to his earlier declarations that digital words "have no materiality, they are only shadows, and when the light shifts they'll be gone," Gass now concluded that over the past ten years the internet had improved, and electronic publishing finally made sense.[49]

Science fiction giant Ray Bradbury also eventually made his peace with eBooks. In 2008, Bradbury had memorably dismissed digital books, telling the Associated Press, "There is no future for e-books because they are not books" and "E-books smell like burned fuel." A year later, he described the internet as "a big distraction."[50] Yet in 2011 (the year before he died), Bradbury was convinced by his publisher, Simon & Schuster, that he had no choice but to allow ePublication of his work. As his literary agent explained, "A new contract wouldn't be possible without ebook rights. [Bradbury] understood and gave us the right to go ahead."[51] Not exactly a resounding conversion.

THE "CONTENT VERSUS CONTAINER" DEBATE

Much of the controversy over digital reading revolves around how we view the relationship between "content" and "container." Are the words themselves fundamentally what readers are after, or does the form they take (in a printed book or on a digital screen) matter? Admittedly, not all screens are created equal. Some have better resolution than others; some screens have more physical real estate—though for that matter, printed works hardly assume a uniform shape. But the fundamental point remains: Are there readers who reject digital screens just because they are not physical objects?

Appeals not to confuse text with how it is bound up echo up to us from the mid-eighteenth century, when Philip Dormer, the Earl of Chesterfield, advised his son:

> Due attention to the inside of books, and due contempt for the outside is the proper relation between a man of sense and his books.[52]

English professor Leah Price reminds us that Victorian readers of novels were focused on stories, not bindings.[53] Today, eReading advocates urge us to focus on content. Brian O'Leary cautions that

> the way we think about book, magazine, and newspaper publishing is unduly governed by the physical containers we have used for centuries to transmit information.[54]

Others go even further, suggesting eBooks themselves are only a transitional phase, with the next transformation being into web-based content and then apps.[55]

Yet sometimes the container matters more than the content.

BOOKS AS OBJECTS

In seventeenth-century England (and New England), there were those who owned Bibles, though no one in the household could read. The Good Book itself had totemic value. An early eighteenth-century traveler in Scotland was asked to use his Bible to fan the face of an illiterate sick man because of the book's presumed curative powers. At the end of the nineteenth century, a woman in Hampshire, England, "ate a New Testament, day by day and leaf by leaf, between two sides of bread and butter, as a remedy for fits."[56]

OK, you say, but that was the Bible. Are there other cases where books are used as objects, not for their content? Lots.

A prime example is the books sold by the yard to the burgeoning middle class in nineteenth-century England. Bindings were coordinated with the decor, and such owners rarely picked up a volume to read. An article in *Fraser's Magazine* described books as the new fashion for "furnishing" a home:

> We live in an age that…spends a vast deal of money upon books. It does so, however, apparently very much as it scatters its abundance in the purchase of crackle china, mediaeval carvings, Louis Quinze furniture, or fictitious Turners—simply because it is the fashion to do so.[57]

The tradition of text-as-decor traces back at least to the time of Seneca, who rebuked "those who displayed scrolls with decorated knobs and colored labels rather than reading them."[58] In early modern England, with the rise of a new gentry class, Daniel Defoe included this dialogue in his guide for the socially mobile, *The Compleat English Gentleman*, composed in the early 1700s:

Gentleman: "What should I do with books? I never read any…."

Friend: "O but Sir, no gentleman is without a library. 'Tis more in fashion now than ever it was."

…

Gentleman: "I hate any thing that looks like a cheat upon the world. Whatever I am, I can't be a hypocrite. What should I do with books that never read half an hour in a year I tell you?"

Friend: "But, Sir, if a gentleman or any relation comes to your house to stay any time with you, 'tis an entertainment for them…; besides 'tis a handsome ornament."[59]

Before you dismiss such behavior as eighteenth- or nineteenth-century foolishness, check out modern services specializing in helping you judge a book by its cover. Book Décor offers handsome leather-bound volumes for beautifying your home. As its website explains,

> The books we feature are used almost exclusively for ornamental purposes. While all of our products contain rich texts, *they are all imported from Europe and therefore printed in foreign languages.*

Books by the Foot has prices starting as low as $6.99 per foot. For more money, you might select books bound in earth tones or "luscious creams."[60] For the do-it-your-selfer, there are a host of guides on decorating with books.[61]

Books also assume value as rare objects on the market. Volumes often fetch high prices not on the basis of their content but because they are first editions, are signed by the author, or have a special binding. Stephen Crane's *Red Badge of Courage*, with the original dust jacket, recently sold for $10,625. A copy of the Fourth Folio edition of Shakespeare's plays, printed in 1685, can be yours for only $247,500.[62]

If you are feeling creative, you might repurpose books or make them into works of art. Here is an example (taken from Lisa Occhipinti's *The Repurposed Library*) of a cookbook given "new life" by transforming it into a kitchen tool bin.

Graphic artists such as Cara Barer make sculptures out of physical books, while Kara Witham hollows out books to form safes.[63] A company called Litographs uses book text to decorate clothing (see next page):

"Tool Bin," Lisa Occhipinti. From *The Repurposed Library* (New York: Stewart, Tabori & Chang, 2011), 139. Used with permission.

Alice's Adventures in Wonderland T-Shirt. Litographs. Used with permission.

You'll need to get out a magnifying glass, but printed on the T-shirt (front and back) are about 75,000 words from *Alice's Adventures in Wonderland.*[64]

As eBooks have begun to encroach upon the print market, one real possibility is that hardcopy books will increasingly become boutique items. Horses—for centuries a basic means of human transport—are now largely relegated to racetracks and personal recreation. Motorized ships replaced sail for commercial travel, though the America's Cup still attracts a strong following and sailing remains a wonderful summer pastime.

AFFORDANCES OF PRINT AND SCREEN

By this point you may be asking, Why such an either-or approach to the media we use for reading? Can't we just recognize that print might be well suited to some purposes and digital text preferable for others?

Of course. There is even a name for talking about what a particular object is good for: affordances. One of the affordances of paper is that it can be folded. An affordance of grass is that it's edible to cows (though not to people). These days, the notion of affordances is commonly invoked when talking about information and communication technologies such as computers or mobile phones. An affordance of computers is their ability to store large amounts of data. An affordance of mobile phones is that, unlike landlines, the telephone number is personal.[65]

One important affordance of digital screens is their convenience. They lighten the load. (Consider twenty books on a Kindle versus twenty in your suitcase.) They also help clear floor space. Alex Halavais, a professor of communication and social computing, made news in 2010 for systematically scanning most of his 3,000-volume personal library and then disposing of the hardcopy originals. The books, he said, were taking up too much space in his small New York City apartment.[66]

Print has its own affordances, chief among them being the very physicality of a book, newspaper, or magazine. When reading printed text, you have a literal sense of place. You also have a sense of touch. In the words of Andrew Piper, a literature professor, "Reading isn't only a matter of our brains; it's something that we do with our bodies."[67] And assuming you bought a printed work or received it as a gift, you own it: You can mark it up, lend it to friends, sell it, or will it to your heirs. Not so with eBooks you acquire from Amazon. It turns out you are essentially leasing them, though at least now Amazon grants limited rights to lend a Kindle book you "bought."[68]

Then there are the trade-offs. For many readers, short texts seem fine for eReading but long ones tend to work better in hardcopy. Digital devices are tailor-made for searching and consuming gulps of information, while print is arguably better suited for "deep reading" of complex texts. Similarly, when reading on a digital device with an internet connection, you can check out a reference on the web—but you are also more likely to get distracted.

Affordances are properties of objects. But what about the properties of readers themselves? A popular (though far too categorical) hypothesis is that adults cling to print while younger people gravitate toward eBooks. In talking about children's books, we have already seen eBook-reading parents wanting print for their children. We also observed that not all teenagers are making a beeline for digital. And when we get to looking at data from young adults, we'll see a strong preference for hardcopy.

Then there is the question of habit. Do we favor reading on one platform or another simply because we have done so in the past? And when we are doing eReading, are there affordances of print that we miss?

It's time to start tackling these issues. The first step: getting a handle on what we mean by reading, including how it has changed with time.

2 | Reading Evolves

> Reading has a history. It was not always and everywhere the same.
>
> —*Robert Darnton*

Why do we read?

Seriously, why do we? Answering that question will go a long way toward figuring out if reading is different when done on digital screens than on paper and, if so, whether encountering words onscreen alters the very nature of reading.

READING AND READERS

He was sitting in Ahmednagar Fort in Maharashtra, imprisoned by the British for his role in India's independence movement. Jawaharlal Nehru wrote:

> Why does one read books? To instruct oneself, amuse oneself, train one's mind... certainly all this and much more. Ultimately it is to understand life with its thousand faces and to learn to live life.... [B]ooks give us the experiences and thoughts of innumerable others, often the wisest of their generation, and lift us out of our narrow ruts.[1]

Books can educate. They can entertain or extend our horizons. And they can provide relief from boredom or distract us in times of woe. During the First and Second World Wars, England experienced an explosion in light reading that helped take people's minds "off the war."[2]

The word "reading" hardly refers to just one kind of activity. What are some of the possibilities?

TYPES OF READING

Begin with the physical act of reading. Are you reading aloud or silently? Alone or with others?

Historically (at least in the West), reading used to be done aloud. True, "aloud" was relative, since in most cases it meant "with moving lips" and essentially mumbling to yourself. The fact that Saint Ambrose actually read silently (a feat observed by Saint Augustine) is generally taken as evidence that silent reading was rare through at least late antiquity.[3]

Manuscript expert Paul Saenger argues that in early medieval Europe, it was introduction of spaces between written words that helped make silent reading possible. The shift, he says, occurred sometime between A.D. 600 and 800.[4] Before that, the words in texts—portable or monumental—ran one after another in a continuous stream known as *scriptio continua*, as in these words inscribed on Trajan's Column in Rome:

SENATVSPOPVLVSQVEROMANVS

While *scriptio continua* may be fine if you are reading aloud in a language you already know, spaced words make it easier to decode in your head, particularly in a language you don't. In the British Isles, spacing started showing up in manuscripts written in Latin, apparently to help members of the clergy who, popular lore notwithstanding, had considerable difficulty understanding the language. Later, spacing found its way into vernacular texts as well.

Even if you know how to read silently, you don't always keep quiet. In the Middle Ages, much of what was read was read aloud. Think of those storied monks gathered for the evening meal, listening to the Bible being intoned, or of Chaucer, reading his work aloud in court. Reading aloud remained common for centuries to come. The reasons are many. We read to others who do not know how, whether the scene is twenty-first-century parents with toddlers on their laps or an eighteenth-century gentleman reading the newspaper to a cluster of illiterate citizens gathered around him. We read aloud to people who are otherwise occupied, as happened in early twentieth-century cigar factories in Key West, Florida.[5] Poets and novelists hold "readings."

The list goes on. But since this book focuses on reading in print versus onscreen, and since the lion's share of digital reading is done silently and alone, we will concentrate on silent, solitary reading.

Reading specialists traditionally identify an assortment of ways we might approach a written work. Familiar categories include skimming (getting the gist of things), scanning (searching for specific information), reading extensively (say, reading novels for fun), and intensive reading (really concentrating on the text). In the eighteenth century, Samuel Johnson laid out a rather similar set of distinctions:

- Hard study (done with pen in hand)
- Perusal (searching for particular information)
- Curious reading (when engrossed in a novel)
- "Mere reading" (browsing and skimming)[6]

Doing a bit of regrouping, we will distinguish between "reading on the prowl" and "continuous reading."

Reading on the Prowl

You are browsing in Barnes & Noble for a book on Elizabeth I. After selecting a prospect in the English history section, maybe you glance at the back cover to check out the author's bio and blurbs from distinguished-sounding sources saying complimentary things about the book. You might skim the table of contents and even the bibliography, then thumb through some pages to confirm if the volume seems worth a real read (and your money).

Now imagine you are looking online for information on the Virgin Queen. If you google her name, the first hit (at least in the United States) is likely to be the Wikipedia article, which you breeze through to get some basic orientation. Say your memory for history is a bit hazy, and you don't remember who Elizabeth's mother was. Forget about scanning through the piece, which you would need to do if it were in hardcopy. Instead, just gin up the FIND function, type in "mother," and up pops "Anne Boleyn."

Skimming and scanning are tried-and-true methods for getting the gist of what is in a text or finding something in particular. Tables of contents and indexes obviously help as well. In that book about Elizabeth you found at Barnes & Noble, you probably didn't start reading the chapter on her early years to identify her mother. More likely, you went to the index, found "mother," and turned to the first page listed. Not as spiffy as FIND on your computer, but the method worked.

In the digital age, reading on the prowl has become increasingly common. In fact, researchers at University College London, in analyzing how academics approach text on digital screens, describe the activity not as reading but as "power browsing." Their study goes on to suggest, "It almost seems that [readers] go online to avoid reading in the traditional sense."[7]

Continuous Reading

This time you are looking to pick up a mystery story to read on an upcoming trip. Again, in the Barnes & Noble scenario, you select a couple of options, skimming the synopses on the back and checking out the blurbs. Maybe you read an opening paragraph or two. But when you settle into your plane seat, you start at the beginning, working through to the end.

When do we read from start to finish? One common occasion is reading for enjoyment. It could be a self-help book, a story in *Time*, or perhaps an essay we come across in *Slate*. The other prime context is for education—in Nehru's words, to "train one's mind." Maybe an authority figure (like a professor) asked you to read Robert Putnam's *Bowling Alone*. You might have decided to work through Robert Caro's multivolume biography of Lyndon Johnson because you're a presidential history buff. Whatever the text, there is a story line to pursue.

Of course, the same written material can be read continuously either for enjoyment or for intellectual enlightenment. Take Swift's *Gulliver's Travels*. Perhaps you read the book on a lark in your teens after seeing the 1996 TV miniseries. But then in college you read it again, this time more carefully and with historical context provided in the English literature course you were taking. (As we will see, your brain doesn't behave the same way for these two types of reading.)

Continuous reading provides the opportunity for what is sometimes called "deep reading"—the kind you were asked to do in literature classes. Reading specialists Maryanne Wolf and Mirit Barzillai define deep reading as

the array of sophisticated processes that propel comprehension and that include inferential and deductive reasoning, analogical skills, critical analysis, reflection, and insight.[8]

More than a century ago, Edith Wharton had this kind of reading in mind when she derided those who only read mechanically, without independent thought:

If the book enters the reader's mind just as it left the writer's—without any of the additions and modifications inevitably produced by contact with a new body of thought—it has been read to no purpose.[9]

How much of our reading is "prowling" and how much is continuous? Intuitively, we might assume that power browsing and the like are new phenomena, and that before the digital revolution, people read books (or articles or treatises) from start to finish. Not so, says Peter Stallybrass, a historian of the book. In fact, Stallybrass argues that while continuous reading characterizes the way we approach novels or detective stories, what I call reading on the prowl has been closer to the norm for practically everything else since the development of the book form (the codex) in the early centuries of the Common Era.[10]

TYPES OF READERS

"To instruct oneself, amuse oneself, train one's mind…understand life with its thousand faces and to learn to live life": Nehru's notions about why we read books are inspiring. But if you are feeling that your own motives for reading don't measure up, keep in mind that Nehru wrote these words while in jail, much of the time in solitary confinement. He also went on to lead India as its first prime minister.

What about the rest of us?

Readers come with all manner of temperaments, education levels, and motivations. Some are just learning to read, whether as children or as adults becoming literate for the first time. There are those who read slowly and those who are speed-readers. Students are made to read, while professionals generally are paid to do so. There are people who read only for pleasure and those who never do. Some regularly read with a pen or pencil in hand, while others never mark up a text.

Categories of readers don't end there. There is, for instance, a long history of reading to impress. Listen to Jean-Jacques Rousseau, writing in 1761 in *La Nouvelle Héloïse*:

The Frenchman reads a lot, but only new books; or to be precise, he leafs through them, not in order to read them, but in order to say that he has read them.[11]

In early twentieth-century America, bevies of women (and a few men) sought to "read up" by following advice proffered by Hamilton Wright Mabie in the *Ladies'*

Home Journal. From 1902 until 1912, ten times a year, Mabie counseled his flock on which books they should read to increase their social cachet.[12]

Reading to impress has hardly faded with time. Much as a left-wing college student in the 1960s might carry around *The Communist Manifesto* and an intellectual wanna-be later toted *Gödel, Escher, Bach*, there are social circles in which displaying a particular bestseller on your blanket at the beach is hardly a casual move. The irony today, of course, is that as books increasingly make their way onto eReaders and tablets, your choices are camouflaged.

Types of reading—how we read, why we read, what we read—come in a cornucopia of shapes and sizes. The variety reflects not only reader motivations but what is being written.

READING AND WRITING ARE JOINED AT THE HIP

We know a lot about the history of writing.[13] By about 3200 B.C., early cuneiforms were being used for administrative purposes in Sumeria, perhaps originating from an even earlier numerical accounting system.[14] Religious texts appeared on Egyptian pyramids somewhere between 2400 and 2300 B.C.[15] In Mycenaean Greece (roughly 1400 B.C.), the purpose of writing (here, in Linear B) was to keep track of the palace bureaucracy's accounts.[16] The earliest writing in China arose by around 1200 B.C. as incised marks on oxen or sheep bones or on turtle shells for use in divination (so-called oracle bones).[17] Writing in the New World is more of a Johnny-come-lately, not debuting (in this case, among the Olmec) until about 650 B.C.[18]

Other than being decorative (or strictly for the author's personal use), writing is largely useless if no one reads it. And so the story of new writing genres is equally the saga of new types of reading. While tracking property, managing bureaucratic affairs, and engaging in religious practices were the earliest uses of writing, they were also the first reasons to read. Literary writing (and reading) came later, including setting down oral tales such as the *Iliad* and the *Odyssey*. The writing (and reading) of history is usually dated to Herodotus in the fifth century B.C., though his line between history and legend is sometimes wiggly.

Once people possessed the know-how for committing words to a durable medium, all manner of other sorts of writing (and reading) appeared. We find Babylonian letters etched on clay tablets by at least the early third century B.C.[19] Old English texts offered up riddles and medicinal recipes.[20] The list goes on.

Translations also shape what people read—even whether they learn to read in the first place. The classic example is Martin Luther's translation of the Bible into

German (beginning with the New Testament, rendered from Greek, in 1522, and then the Old Testament, from Hebrew, in 1534). Familiar assumptions credit Luther's biblical translations with fueling growth in literacy. But the actual history is more complex.[21]

Luther had initially been enthusiastic about putting the Word of God (and the apostles) directly into the hands of the populace, believing the meaning of the text was transparent. All you needed to be was literate. Thanks to availability of the newly invented printing press, Luther churned out thousands of short religious pamphlets between 1520 and 1523 (written in German so people could read them). In the early years of the Reformation, Luther urged "that every Christian study for himself the Scripture and the pure Word of God."[22]

Luther was to change his mind. During the German Peasant Wars of 1524–1526, in which peasants, townspeople, and laborers rose up against the feudal structure run by the iron hand of the aristocracy, the rebels were seen to be drawing inspiration from their reading of Scripture: There was no feudal structure described in the Bible. Another of Luther's concerns was the possibility of heresy. If individual readers arrived at differing interpretations of what they read, how could Reformation doctrine be kept pure?

In the aftermath of the wars, Luther did a conceptual about-face. He began writing catechisms—essentially doctrines to be learned by rote—that he wanted widely distributed. Instead of counseling people to read the Bible themselves, Luther declared that "the catechism is the layman's Bible."[23] The task of teaching from the Bible was now left exclusively to preachers. The populace should read, yes, but not the Bible.

As the modern world unfolded, new literary forms emerged. These included the essay (developed by Michel de Montaigne in the sixteenth century) and the short story, a genre with many precursors, including the Bible, the *Decameron*, and the *Canterbury Tales*, but commonly seen as beginning with Nathaniel Hawthorne's *Twice-Told Tales*, published in 1837.[24] Another innovation was the novel, usually dated (at least for Western literature) as 1740, the year Samuel Richardson's *Pamela* appeared.[25] As we will see, the novel would revolutionize not just what people read but how they read.

The rise of new forms of writing, along with growth in readership for newspapers and periodicals, naturally shifted the balance in the kinds of materials being printed. In England as well as on the Continent, religious works had dominated booksellers' shelves up through the seventeenth century. By the end of the eighteenth century, the subject matter shifted, along with the language in which books were written.

Statistics from Germany chronicle the change. In German book fair catalogues, the supply of "modern" books such as works on geography, politics, education, and belles lettres rose from 6 percent in 1740 to a bit more than 21 percent in 1800. In these same catalogues, the percent of books written in Latin fell from 28 percent to 4 percent.[26]

READERS AS WRITERS

In the act of reading, many readers become writers. They underline passages, draw arrows, and doodle. They write in margins, revealing their own thoughts or objecting to what authors have said.

Marginalia has a long history.[27] A favorite examples of mine shows up in the Gutenberg Bible owned by the Harry Ransom Center at the University of Texas at Austin. While the value of a Gutenberg Bible today runs into the millions of dollars, some early owner apparently felt no compunction about taking a hand to the pages.[28]

Historically, marginalia has played an integral role in learning. Students mark up their textbooks with highlighters. Librarians complain about patrons defacing library property. And scholars and writers make meticulous notes for future reference.[29] Edgar Allan Poe explained:

> In getting my books, I have been always solicitous of an ample margin; this not so much through any love of the thing in itself, however agreeable, as for the facility it affords me of pencilling suggested thoughts, agreements, and differences of opinion, or brief critical comments in general.[30]

Alan Jacobs counsels that the effort is worth it:

> Writing...comments [in a book's margins] is enormously time-consuming. It slows you down. It allows you to read fewer books. To those complaints I reply, Yes. It is, it does, and it does. And those are good things.[31]

Samuel Coleridge also wrote in books, but his habit spilled over into annotating works friends lent him—sometimes for this express purpose. It was Coleridge who introduced into English the word *marginalia* (from Latin) in 1819.[32]

Once upon a time, students were instructed to write in their books. An English schoolmaster named John Brinsley published a handbook, *Ludus Literarius* (1612), to help students make sense of what they read. One piece of advice was to mark up the text:

mee tues. Nunquid irasceris in perpe-
tuū? aut pseuerabis in sinem? Ecce lo-
cuta es et secisti mala: z potuisti. Et dixit dominus ad me i diebus iosie regis.
Nunqd vidisti que secerit auersatrix
israhel? Abijt sibimet super omnem
montem excelsum et sub omni ligno
srondoso: et sornicata est ibi. Et dixi
cum secisset hec omnia · ad me reuerte-
re: et nõ est reuersa. Et vidit puaricatrix soror ei⁹ iuda qa pro eo q mechã-
ta esset auersatrix israhel dimisissem
eam z dedissem ei libellũ repudij: z nõ
timuit puaricatrix iuda soror ei⁹ · sed
abijt z sornicata est etia ipã. z sacilita-
te sornicationis sue cõtaminauit ter-
ram: z mechata e cum lapide z ligno.
Et in omnibz hijs non est reuersa ad
me-puaricatrix soror eius iuda i toto
corde suo: sed i mendacio ait dns. Et
dixit dns ad me. Justificauit animã
suã auersatrix isrl cõparatõe puari-
catricis iude. Vade z clama sermones
istos contra aquilone et dices. Reuer-
tere auersatrix israhel ait dns et non a-
uertam facie meã a vobis? qa sanct⁹
ego sum dicit dns: et non irascar in
petuū. Verūtamen scito iniquitatem
tuã: quia in dnm deū tuū puaricata
es. Et disisti vias tuas alienis sub
omni ligno srondoso: et vocem meã
non audisti ait dns. Couertimini silij
reuertentes dicit dns:quia ego vir ve-
ster. Et assumã vos-vnũ de ciuitate z
duos de cognatione:et introducã vos
in syon. Et dabo vobis pastores iu-
xta cor meū: et pascent vos scientia et
doctrina. Cunqz multiplicati sueritis
z creueritis in terra in diebz illis ait dominus nõ dicent ultra archa testame-
ti dni?neqz ascendet sup cor neqz recor-
dabutur illi? nec visitabitur nec siet

ultra. In tempore illo vocabūt iherusa-
lalē soliũ dni? et cõgregabūtur ad eã
omnes gentes in nomine dni in iherusalē: z nõ ambulabūt post prauita-
tem cordis sui pessimi. In diebus illis
ibit domus iuda ad domũ israhel: z
veniet simul de terra aquilonis ad terrã
quã dedi patribz vestris. Ego aut dixi.
Quomõ ponã te in silios?et tribuã ti-
bi terrã desiderabilē hereditatē prclarã
exercituū gentiū? Et dixi. Patrē voca-
bis me: z post me ingredi nõ cessabis.
Sed quomõ si cõtemnat mulier ama-
torē suũ: sic contempsit me domus isrl
dicit dns. Vox in vijs audita est plo-
ratus z ululatus silioz israhel:quoni-
am iniqz secerūt viam suã:obliti sunt
domini dei sui. Couertimini silij reuer-
tētes:z sanabo auersiones vras. Ecce
nos venimus ad te. Tu eni es dns de-
us noster. Vere mendaces erãt colles
et multitudo mõtiū. Vere in domino
deo nostro salus isrl. Confusio comedit
laborē patrũ nostroz ab adolescen-
tia nrã? greges eoz et armeta eoz:sili-
os eoz et silias eoz. Dormiem⁹ i con-
fusione nrã et opriet nos ignominia
nostra? quoniã dno deo nro peccaui-
mus nos et patres nostri ab adolescen-
tia nostra usqz ad diem hanc: et non
audiuim⁹ voce dni dei nostri.   IIII.
Si reuerteris ad me israhel ait dominus: ad me cõuertere. Si abs-
tuleris offendicula tua a facie mea nõ
commouebereis. Et iurabis viuit dominus in veritate z in iudicio et in iu-
sticia: z benedicent eũ gētes ipmqz lau-
dabūt. Hec eni dicit dns viro iuda z ha-
bitatori ihrlm. Nouate vobis nouã-
le: z nolite serere sup spinas. Circucidi-
mini dno: z auserte prpucia cordiũ vro-
rum viri iuda et habitatores iherusalē:

Gutenberg Bible (Harry Ransom Center, University of Texas at Austin). Used with permission.

Difficult words, or matters of speciall obseruation, [which] they doe reade in any Author, [should] be marked out.

Brinsley went on to say that annotations are an aid to memory. But most important, they further understanding, helping put what we read to good use:

To read and not to vnderstand what wee read, or not to know how to make vse of it, is nothing else but a neglect of all good learning, and a meere abuse of the means & helps to attaine the same.[33]

Writing in the twentieth century, Mortimer Adler (almost channeling Brinsley) argued in his classic *How to Read a Book* that reading is serious business:

The most direct sign that you have done the work of reading is *fatigue*. Reading that is reading entails the most intense mental activity. If you are not tired out, you probably have not been doing the work.

How to Read a Book offers detailed steps for "doing the work." Key among them is writing as you read:

One of the reasons why I find reading a slow process is that I keep a record of the…thinking I do. I cannot go on reading the next page, if I do not make a memo of something which occurred to me in reading this one.[34]

Granted, the kind of reading Adler is talking about centers on books designed to educate rather than entertain. This is the Adler who, along with University of Chicago president Robert Hutchins, created a list of the "Great Books of the Western World," which included works by the likes of Aeschylus, Aristotle, and Thomas Aquinas. But for Adler, the central principles of thinking about what you read and writing about it extend across genres.

Of course, you don't have to be reading "great books" in order to do the work that Adler advocates. Studs Terkel, the popular American historian who wrote about jazz, the Great Depression, and World War II,

was known to admonish friends who would read his books but leave them free of markings. He told them that reading a book should not be a passive exercise, but a raucous conversation.[35]

A raucous conversation between reader and author.

Annotating what you are reading makes sense only if you assume that you (or maybe another person) will return to the text. Maybe you conceive of annotations as a sort of personal intellectual diary. Perhaps you are a student who is writing a paper or knows there will be an exam at the end of the course. (It's easier to study from annotated text than from pristine pages.)

But do we revisit texts these days? Several factors mitigate against return engagements. If college students sell their books at the end of a term (or rented them), there is literally no going back. What is more, books are heavy, and postage is expensive. Even when I talk with students who are avid readers (and sometimes on the cusp of entering PhD programs), they increasingly say they don't plan to build much of a personal library until they are "settled" (a notoriously indefinite point in time). At the other end of the career spectrum, empty nesters who are downsizing to smaller living space often deaccession not just furnishings but books.

What about digital annotations? Comparatively speaking, eBooks are harder to annotate than print. In the memorable words of John Dickerson, chief political correspondent at *Slate*, "marking up text [on an iPad] is...like eating candy through a wrapper."[36] Admittedly, annotation continues to become easier on digital devices, especially for those who practice. Yet as of late 2013, the Book Industry Study Group reported that 84 percent of American college students still said that ease of bookmarking and highlighting was either a "somewhat important" or "very important" reason for preferring print textbooks over digital.[37]

There are other issues with electronic annotation. At one extreme is the danger of annotations not being preserved. The marginalia of Mark Twain, Charles Darwin, and Thomas Jefferson are highly prized today. We have them because they were written in hardcopy books. What if Jefferson's annotations were on his computer and he died without leaving his password?

At the other extreme, we have the privacy challenge. What if you accidentally turned on "Public Notes" on your Kindle, enabling the vast sea of Kindle readers to access your personal thoughts?[38] While your name is not attached to your annotations (only Amazon knows whose account they came from), you might not be the kind of person who wants to share, even anonymously. And what if you're a student taking a class in which all your online reading is being monitored by the person running the course? CourseSmart, a major distributor of electronic textbooks and course materials, offers teachers the ability to see which pages of electronic textbooks students have accessed and what annotations they have made.[39] Shades of Big Brother.

Books didn't always work this way. In fact, the book as we know it is not all that old as a physical container.

ENTER THE CODEX

What today we call a book is technically known as a codex. The origins of the codex (rectangular covers, clasped or tied together, and a place to write in between) trace back to writing tablets that contained a waxed surface for inscribing messages. Such tablets were actively used in classical Greece, though their roots are even earlier.

The Romans are credited with producing the earliest codexes in which the writing surface was parchment, probably by the early first century A.D. However, these initial volumes were personal notebooks, not "published" works of the sort we think of today when we talk about books. It would take several centuries before the codex became the accepted format for literary and religious works.

Early Christians were among the first to embrace the innovation. Why? Codex scholars have identified some possibilities:

- *Cost.* Because you could write on both sides of a page (unlike with a scroll), you needed only half the papyrus or parchment, making it cheaper to create a volume.
- *Compactness.* Smaller in size than a scroll containing the same amount of text, the codex was easier to carry and store. You could also fit more into a single volume, compared with the several scrolls needed to record the same amount of text.
- *Ease of use.* Logically, it seems easier to read a codex (since you can easily flip the pages) than a scroll (where you have to keep rolling and unrolling). While this reasoning makes sense to modern readers, we can't flat-out assume that readers at the time—who were accustomed to reading scrolls— would have agreed. What is clear is that finding your place in a text is in- credibly easier with a codex than with a scroll.[40]

It is hard to know which of these advantages was most important to the early Roman Christians, though portability was probably crucial. Often Christians of the time needed to practice their religion in hiding, and a codex of the New Testa- ment would be much easier to carry—and conceal—than a scroll.

Over time, the codex developed other useful affordances, especially for helping readers find their way in the text. This evolution makes for interesting and relevant history, since navigation within digital text brings its own advantages and challenges.

FINDING YOUR WAY IN A BOOK

Open any Western book, and one of the first right-hand pages will contain the title and author, along with the name of the publisher and maybe place and year of publication.

It didn't used to be that way.

If you look at manuscripts before the days of printing, such niceties as title and author were generally nowhere in sight. (The issue of a publisher was obviously moot.) Producing parchment was labor-intensive work, and you did not waste those precious sheets. The text began on the first page, always on the right-hand (recto) side. If you wanted to know what the book was about, you needed to start reading.

The coming of printing (and increased use of paper, which was less costly than animal skin) brought a new idea. That first page tended to get dirty, and so printers introduced an extra sheet in front to keep the initial page of text clean. But why waste even paper? By the late 1470s, printers had begun putting handy information like title, author, and publisher on the new recto piece. (The back—or verso—of the new page would come to be used as well.) By the end of the fifteenth century, almost all printed books had title pages.[41]

Tables of contents are another tool for orienting in a text. The earliest tables seem to date back to Pliny the Elder, whose hefty *Naturalis Historia* (*Natural History*) appeared shortly before he died in A.D. 77. Pliny's table contained short descriptions of the subjects that would be discussed in each of the 37 "books" (meaning "sections") that followed, a custom that persisted for Western tables of contents even up through the nineteenth century. A favorite example of mine, from my earlier incarnation as an English grammarian, is the table of contents of Richard Mulcaster's *The First Part of the Elementarie Vvhich Entreateth Chefelie of the Right Writing of Our English Tung*—in other words, a grammar of English—published in London in 1582. Chapter titles in the table of contents include (this time with modern English spelling) "That this five branched Elementarie is warranted by general authority of all the greatest writers and the best commonweals" and "That this Elementarie seasons the young minds with the very best and sweetest liquor."

What about indexes, which are usually a speedier way of finding what you are looking for? They didn't appear in a form we would recognize until after the development of printing.[42] There are a couple of important reasons for the delay. For starters, in antiquity (before the shift from scrolls to codexes), the continuous nature of the book offered few anchor points to reference.

Next is the issue of how you would organize items in an index. Alphabetization seems to have been invented in the third century B.C., probably in Alexandria by

Callimachus to catalogue the Great Library (estimated to contain over half a million rolls).[43] The technique didn't make its way to western Europe for many centuries.[44] As late as 1604, Robert Cawdrey felt the need to counsel readers of his *Table Alphabeticall* (the first English dictionary) that

> to profit by this Table...then thou must learne the Alphabet, to wit, the order of the letters as they stand,...as (b) neere the beginning, (n) about the middest, and (t) toward the end.[45]

But the third reason was a general lack of page numbers: Even if you had an alphabetical index, what would the index refer you to? Pages numbers are significant because of their historical role in reshaping how readers interact with writing. Equally important is the status of page numbers in an online world and what that status portends for the future of reading.

Numbering pages started out not as a tool for readers but a guide for those who physically produced books. In Latin manuscripts copied in the British Isles as far back as the eighth or ninth century, numbering was sometimes used to ensure that individual sheets of parchment were collated in the correct order. In some cases, numbers appeared on both the recto and verso pages, but other times, only one side of the leaf (page) bore a number. Use of numbering was sparse. It has been estimated that around 1450—just before the birth of printing in the West—less than 10 percent of manuscript books contained pagination.[46]

Fifty years later, the proportion of now-printed works with pagination was much higher. Part of the change reflected the new role page numbers were coming to play. Rather than strictly being tools for compiling leaves in the proper order, by the 1510s scholars were starting to "refer to folio numbers of specific editions to designate loci within printed texts."[47] Since the early sixteenth century, readers have relied on page numbers to find their way in books.

With the rise of digital technology, the lure of random access could end up undermining page numbers. A decade ago, I began noticing a change in my students' attitude toward page numbers: Most students were no longer inserting them into written assignments, no matter how explicit my requests or how much I threatened. Yes, I knew that page numbers are not inserted by default in Microsoft Word. Yet my students were otherwise quite savvy regarding Word's functionality. What was going on?

Here is what I have been able to deduce. Given students' wealth of experience reading onscreen, page numbers for documents created on a computer (in this case, their written assignments for me) seem irrelevant to them. When readers access newspapers online, there are no page numbers (and more people read newspapers online than on newsprint—especially in this age group). Some of the scholarly articles they are assigned still come as unpaginated PDFs. Documents native to the web are overwhelmingly unpaginated, and the page numbers on eBooks generally bear no relationship to their print counterparts. Since the assignments in question were created on computers—and sometimes submitted electronically—surely (so the logic apparently goes) if I, the reader, want to locate a word or passage in students' texts, I should use the FIND function, not revert to the apparently antiquated convention of pagination.

With the initial emergence of print technology in the mid-fifteenth century, the way people read began to change. Just so, with FIND now available for navigating online reading, the notion of reading is potentially being redefined from a linear activity (continuous) to a random-access process (reading on the prowl).

Finally, a confession. In writing this book, I repeatedly faced the dilemma of whether to expend the effort needed to track down original page numbers for the natively print newspaper and magazine articles I had accessed online (most websites don't indicate pagination) or to say the heck with it. I generally took the latter tack. My justification: In the age of the internet, bibliographic conventions have changed.[48]

MORE READING EVOLUTION: THEN AND NOW

Navigation tools like tables of contents and page numbers are a big help in finding your way through a text, but what if there is too much to read in the first place? There's too much to read when the amount people are writing mushrooms.

TOO MUCH TO KNOW, TOO MUCH TO READ

Over the past 500 years, surges in how much people were writing have resulted from the coming of printing, rising literacy rates, declines in the price of paper (and of taxes on paper and newsprint), universities demanding that scholars publish or perish, and arrival of the internet. And here are two more sources: the information explosion in early modern Europe and increased readership in the late eighteenth century, largely triggered by the rise of the novel. As we will discover, a profusion of written material and subsequent growth in readership also helped trigger a new approach to reading itself.

To get started, I invite you to think (oddly enough) about shoes.

Suppose you own seven pairs of shoes. To use them equally, you wear each pair fifty-two times a year. Now say you possess 365 sets of shoes. (Imelda Marcos, wife of a disgraced president of the Philippines, is reputed to have accumulated well over 1,000.) If you wear a different pair each day, at the end of the year you have only managed to use each pair once.

The same principle applies to information. As Ann Blair explains in *Too Much to Know*, early modern England experienced a dramatic rise in new information and knowledge.[49] Forays into science, geographic exploration, and discoveries of other cultures generated a wellspring of data—and books. Intellectuals of the time devised strategies for making their way through the deluge, including creating encyclopedias and compendia of selections. But the most obvious solution was simply not to read everything. As Francis Bacon memorably wrote in his 1625 essay "Of Studies,"

> Some books are to be tasted, others to be swallowed, and some few to be chewed and digested: that is, some books are to be read only in parts, others to be read, but not curiously, and some few to be read wholly, and with diligence and attention.

Over time, the challenge of "too much to read" increased. By the mid-eighteenth century, western Europe saw the rise of what came to be known as print culture.[50] The literate population expanded, as did book production. About 400 different titles were published in England between 1500 and 1510. By 1790, that figure had risen to about 60,000.[51] The first English novel, Samuel Richardson's *Pamela* (published in 1740), launched a new genre that would generate a prolific writing—and reading—industry.[52] Between 1750 and 1770, about 600 different novels were published. That number rose to about 1,400 by 1770–1780.[53]

Periodical literature was also expanding. The *Tatler* and then the *Spectator* offered new reading opportunities. (More on those in a bit.) Newspaper sales in England flourished. England's first daily paper, the *Daily Courant*, appeared in 1702. Estimated sales in 1704 were 43,000 copies per *week*. By 1753, these numbers had risen to 23,673 copies per *day*.[54] By the early nineteenth century, the volume of publications had soared. Even authors complained, as when Charles Lamb wrote in 1825 (in "Readers Against the Grain"), "No reading can keep pace with the writing of this age."

Readers needed a way of managing this profusion of print. The answer reminds us of Bacon's advice.

Historian Robert Darnton speaks of the distinction between "intensive" and "extensive" reading in describing how readers coped with the new abundance of printed material. Intensive reading had been characteristic of literate Europe before the middle of the eighteenth century. With the flowering of print culture, intensive reading began yielding to extensive reading:

> [Rolf] Engelsing has argued that a "reading revolution" (*Leserevolution*) took place at the end of the eighteenth century [in Germany]. From the Middle Ages until some time after 1750...men read "intensively." They had only a few books—the Bible, an almanach, a devotional work or two—and they read them over and over again....By 1800 men were reading "extensively." They read all kinds of material, especially periodicals and newspapers, and read it only once, then raced on to the next item.[55]

A similar transition took place in America.[56]

Even if you were going to read extensively—reading many things but only once—you still needed strategies for sorting through the mountain of possibilities. A host of solutions emerged between the eighteenth century and now, such as abridgments, anthologies, encyclopedias, serialization, and condensation. Later we will look at all of these shortening techniques. But before getting to that story, let's return to reading revolutions, this time in the digital world.

READING IN THE AGE OF DIGITAL SCREENS

The digital reading revolution predates the internet. It began in 1971 with Michael Hart. Then a student at the University of Illinois, Hart launched a digital project to make available for free thousands of books and documents that already lived in the public domain—but in print. To enter that archive, all you needed was access to ARPANET (progenitor of the internet). The undertaking, which Hart dubbed Project Gutenberg, was highly labor-intensive, since all the texts needed to be typed into files, which were then uploaded. Only in the late 1980s were image scanners and optical character recognition software sufficiently developed to make for easier input.[57] As of 2014, Project Gutenberg offered free access to over 46,000 eBooks, along with links to more than 100,000 additional titles available through other organizations or affiliates.[58]

By the 1990s, readers' access to online material had begun to surge. The internet had became a public tool, and personal computers gave everyone with an internet connection the ability to read—and write—online. Libraries were already starting to digitize their collections, and in 2002, Google undertook the venture that came to be known as Google Books. A growing number of newspapers and periodicals began going digital. Universities increasingly asked students to use computer-based "learning management systems" (such as Blackboard or Canvas), where faculty can post assigned readings online. eReaders, eBooks, and tablets have since proliferated, and the stage is potentially set for replacing the physical codex.

Is a total switch likely? In weighing the prospects, it helps to think about the affordances of reading onscreen. Here are four of them.

MEDIA OPTIONS

Aside from pop-up books, *Pat the Bunny*, and the luscious art books of publishers like Skira Rizzoli, the majority of printed books are known for their text. Illustrations and photographs? Sometimes. What would *Alice's Adventures in Wonderland* have been without John Tenniel's wondrous illustrations, or a modern travel guide without pictures? But mostly text.

Digital technologies open up far more possibilities. Besides photographs, you can include video and sound. There are options for manipulating text, including font size (a favorite for many eBook users). Video and audio can be sped up or slowed down.

Multimedia and scaling features lead to the larger question of whether changing the medium for content transforms the work itself. Earlier, we talked about the "container versus content" debate over written work appearing in print or onscreen. But the issue has broader ramifications. Think about audiobooks. Does the medium alter what it means to read if we encounter the same words with our ears rather than eyes?

The roots of audiobooks are far removed from the container/content discussion. Putting aside the first literal audiobooks (reading books aloud to others—whether the listeners were medieval monks or are modern two-year-olds), the physical audiobook grew out of sound recordings made by England's Royal National Institute for the Blind for use by blinded soldiers returning from the front in World War I. The service officially launched in 1935 and included titles by Agatha Christie and Joseph Conrad. By 1942, the Library of Congress in Washington began a similar project.[59] Audiobooks became an option for the non-visually-impaired public with development of portable cassette tape recordings in the 1960s, followed by the likes of the Sony Walkman, CDs, the iPod, and now downloads. Audiobooks have become a huge business. Millions of commuters, joggers, and elliptical machine users swear by them.

But are they books? In the audio version of his book *America*, Jon Stewart opens with the words, "Welcome, nonreader."[60] Is Stewart right?

Audiobooks are now a subject for scholarly analysis.[61] Some of the issues in comparing listening to a book with reading it are reminiscent of questions raised about the pros and cons of reading in print versus on a screen. Common challenges to the "bookness" of audiobooks are that listening is a passive activity, that audiobooks don't require the same level of concentration as print, and that audiobooks lack form.[62]

A study at the University of Waterloo lends empirical support to the notion that it is easier to remain focused when reading a written text than when listening to an audiobook. Researchers compared how much our minds wander when we are reading a text passage aloud, listening to someone else read a passage, or reading a passage silently. It turned out that subjects (here, university students) had the least amount of mind wandering when they were reading aloud and the most when listening to someone else read, with reading silently falling in between. On a subsequent memory test, those who read aloud did best, following by the silent readers, with those listening to someone else read coming in at the bottom of the heap. The authors suggest that lack of physical engagement in the reading process leads to diminished attention and memory performance when someone else is doing the reading for you.[63]

Like Jonathan Swift's Big Enders and Little Enders in *Gulliver's Travels*, even highly educated academics disagree over the pros and cons of listening to books. The choice, especially for pleasure reading, seems to come down to a matter of individual choice. Howard Gardner, a professor at the Harvard Graduate School of Education, eschews audiobooks ("To me, reading is something I do with my eyes"). His wife, Ellen Winner, a psychologist at Boston College, is an audiobook aficionado, listening to "great literature, classics that I would not have the time or patience to read if they were in print."[64]

SEARCH

Ability to search a stretch of text (or the internet itself) is clearly a virtue of reading onscreen. While writing this chapter, I tried to track down a comment Mortimer Adler had presumably made in *How to Read a Book* about the importance of marking up books as a way of making them your own. As I scanned through all 371 pages of the original edition, I grumbled, "If only I could do a search on the words 'mark up' or 'make your own' in a digitized version." I never did find the passage.[65]

I even began to empathize with one of my students who had bitterly complained that an article I had uploaded to our course online site was the "wrong" version. The problem? Since my library did not have an electronic subscription to the relevant journal, I had gone to the trouble of scanning my own copy and then posting the file. But here's the rub: While the FIND function works on digitally native texts, it is useless with scanned files. In essence my student was saying she had no intention of reading the whole article. Instead, she looked to do what she always did when reading for class: search for some key words, read a few lines above and below, and be finished. Was she short on time, attention span, or both?

This snippet approach to reading, enabled by online search tools, is one of the downsides of digital reading's search affordance. But the snippet frame of mind also pops up in the way students use print sources. The Citation Project, which studies issues relating to the teaching of writing (with a special eye toward plagiarism), offers worrisome findings about the way today's university students are making use of reference sources (books, journals, online materials, and so on) in their research papers. In the student papers the project reviewed,

- 46 percent of citations were to the first page of the source
- 23 percent were to the second page
- 77 percent were to the first three pages

For the record: Of the works that students cited, 63 percent were indeed longer than three pages, some much longer.[66]

As we have already hinted (and will hint again), one of the major effects of digital screens is to shift the balance from continuous reading to reading on the prowl. While it is hard to unbundle the chicken-and-egg problem (did habits with reading in hardcopy influence reading onscreen or vice versa?), reading on the prowl in both media is mutually reinforcing. The result? The meaning of "reading" increasingly becomes "finding information"—and often settling for the first thing that comes to hand—rather than "contemplating and understanding." Adler would hardly approve.

One more observation about search. It's actually another confession. For many years, I have been skeptical about my university library's decision to purchase eBooks instead of print. Initially the eBooks were awkward to access, clumsy to read, and a challenge if you wanted to print more than a couple of pages. The technology has since improved, though the number of hardcopy purchases seems to have shrunk in inverse proportion.

In the throes of finishing this book, I frequently made a beeline for my library's catalogue, only to find that many of the books I most needed were e-only. I was willing to take what I could get. This time, the books opened like a charm, and tracking down what I was looking for was generally easy. Mission accomplished—sort of. My search was successful. But I didn't linger over a book the way I would have with a hardcopy of the same text, stumbling upon intriguing topics I wasn't expecting. I didn't discover alongside the targeted volume those library shelfmates that might have proven even more useful.

Score one for efficiency, not for careful reading. Print books may not be easily searchable, but their sheer physicality encourages productive happenstance.

CONNECTION

Most digital reading has the affordance of allowing readers to be "connected" because of access to the internet. Travis Alber and Aaron Miller write:

> To us…the Web offered endless possibilities for a new kind of reading experience, something that was not possible offline, and not possible with printed books…[:] connections to other readers, a sense of communal experience, a window into other people's reactions, the chance to respond or add our own thoughts.[67]

Later on, we will examine the degree to which reading was a social experience in the past and whether digital reading will inevitably make it yet more so.

A second kind of connectivity is between the individual and resources on the web: pages revealed by hyperlinks, online foreign language dictionaries, Wikipedia. The benefits of such connectivity get mixed reviews. On the one hand, a quick look at related information (like translation of the word *Gemütlichkeit* into English) can be handy—not much different from using a physical copy of the *Duden*. But on the other, there is always the danger of becoming distracted. What was intended as a fast look at Wikipedia to find out when the Russian Revolution began might end up as a detour into Russian literature or Russian roulette.

AVAILABILITY

The last affordance is availability. A profusion of material (free or paid) is available to read in digital form. Yes, the Library of Congress has its 838 miles of bookshelves, but most people don't live in Washington, DC, and not everyone qualifies for a reader's card.

Availability, like search and connectivity, is Janus-faced. So much to read. So little time. How do we cope? One solution in the digital age has been for writers and publishers to slim down the amount of text they offer readers, particularly digital readers. In turn, reducing length reshapes assumptions about how (and how much) we might expect to read.

Let's see how.

3 | tl;dr

Readers Reshape Writing

tl;dr: Literally, "Too long; didn't read." Said whenever
a nerd makes a post that is too long to bother reading.

—*Urban Dictionary*

How long do you spend on a web page? Estimates vary. As of January 2013, Nielsen.com pegged the average in the United States at 1 minute 12 seconds.[1] Remember, that is an average. Many "visits" are much briefer. An earlier study found almost 50 percent of users lingered less than 12 seconds.[2]

If you are breezing through web pages, are you actually reading them? Jakob Nielsen (a different Nielsen, this one a cognitive psychologist) says you're not:

> People rarely read Web pages word by word; instead, they scan the page, picking out individual words and sentences. In research on how people read websites we found that 79 percent of our test users always scanned any new page they came across; only 16 percent read word-by-word.[3]

Nielsen estimates that given the amount of time readers average on a web page, they only have time to read at most 28 percent of the words, though he thinks 20 percent is probably a more accurate figure.[4]

If web users are scanning rather than reading, what kind of scanning are they doing? Using eye tracking studies, Nielsen analyzed how people read online. His answer: "The dominant reading pattern looks somewhat like an F."[5] Readers tend to start in the upper left-hand corner, chugging all the way across the page to the right (assuming we are talking about scripts written horizontally from left to right). As they work their way down the page, people tend to view less and less of what is on the right-hand side. By the time they reach the bottom (assuming they get that far), essentially they are only processing what is in the lower left-hand corner.[6]

What about scanning patterns on subsequent pages (or, to use a newspaper analogy, "below the fold")? Not a particularly relevant question, since most readers don't get there. Nielsen's data show that web users spend about 80 percent of their time reading what is on the initial page ("above the fold"). That leaves only about 20 percent of their attention for what follows the initial screen.[7]

Nielsen cares how readers tackle web pages because the Norman Nielsen Group (a partnership with Donald Norman, another cognitive psychologist) advises companies how to create websites that maximize the chance consumers will actually read the companies' messages. While not everyone processes all web pages using an F pattern, it is pretty clear that most people, most of the time, don't see web pages as meriting continuous reading.

tl;dr.

JUST BROWSING

When I think about how so many of us read on the web, analogies about shopping come to mind. You are at Macy's, ambling through the kitchen wares section, when a salesperson comes up asking if you need help. "No thanks," you say, "just browsing." If you happen upon a food processor that looks interesting, you might linger and check out the features, maybe even asking a few questions or comparing prices on your mobile phone. Otherwise, you keep on cruising.

As with the not-really-needed Cuisinart (there is already a perfectly adequate older model at home), we pay only glancing attention to much of the writing we encounter. Sometimes our rationale is that we aren't sufficiently interested anyway. Another common justification is that we're too busy: "Just browsing now. When I have more time, I'll be back to take a closer look." But we rarely return. Often that is the utterly sensible decision. Much of what is written doesn't merit our sustained attention.

At least since the nineteenth century, time has been a Western obsession. The notion of a clock is hardly new. Sundials and water clocks go way back.[8] But the nineteenth century brought the railroad and the pocket watch, along with standardization of the twenty-four-hour time cycle.[9] "Running on time" became a matter of good business practice and, in the case of the railroads, a practical necessity (you needed to keep trains from crashing into one another).[10] Lest anyone try to convince you that time pressures are an affliction of just the late twentieth or early twenty-first century, remember the White Rabbit in *Alice's Adventures in Wonderland* or watch *Modern Times*, Charlie Chaplin's 1936 film about industrialization.

Browsing rather than actually reading is sometimes a response to limited time. But there are also people who intentionally read as little as possible. Here is the story of Jeremy Spreitzer, whose reading habits headlined a piece in the *Washington Post*, aptly entitled "The No-Book Report: Skim It and Weep":

> A graduate student in public affairs at Park University in Kansas City, Mo., Spreitzer, 25,...skims required texts, draws themes from dust jackets and, when he absolutely, positively has to read something, reaches for the audiobook.
>
> "I am fairly lazy when it comes to certain tasks," says Spreitzer. "Reading is one of them."[11]

Spreitzer is not alone. According to a report published in 2000, on any given day only about one-third of the undergraduate and graduate students surveyed had completed their reading assignments. That number had dropped from over 80 percent in the early 1980s.[12] How much reading students do probably reflects the number of hours they spend studying. That number has shriveled over the past half century, from about 24 hours a week in the early 1960s to about 15 hours per week now.[13]

A different option for coping with text overload is speed-reading. Literary critic Harold Bloom is reputed to zip through 400 pages an hour,[14] while the rest of us mortals are more likely to plod along at the rate of maybe 30-ish to 60-ish pages per hour, depending upon the nature of the text and type of reader.[15] While speed-reading has a longer and broader history (and has counted among its practitioners Theodore Roosevelt and John Kennedy), the technique gained wide traction when a Salt Lake City high school teacher and her husband launched Evelyn Wood Speed Reading Dynamics in 1959. The popularity of speed-reading crested before the end of the twentieth century, though sporadic moves to resurrect it keep popping up. An article in *Forbes* asks, "Do You Read Fast Enough to Be Successful?"[16] There is also the World Speed Reading Council, which sponsors a World Champion Speed Reader contest. In 2007, the record holder, Anne Jones, zipped through *Harry Potter and the Deathly Hallows* at an average rate of over 4,000 words per minute.[17]

A new speed-reading tool is called Spritz. This digital app flashes one word on the screen at a time, with the company claiming the tool can accelerate your reading speed from a basic 250 words per minute to 400 words per minute without compromising comprehension. Yet the CEO, Frank Waldman, distinguishes between what Spritz is good for (like mobile news) and what it's not: "You wouldn't really want to read classic lit or Shakespeare on [Spritz]."[18]

Speed-reading is not just for literary critics, presidents, and contest winners. For many of us it's also a common practice in our professional lives. Granted, sometimes it's more skimming than speed-reading, but in either case we make short shrift of longer text. A recent discussion of how professional recruiters review resumés noted that readers averaged only six seconds with each document.[19] Hint to applicants: Formatting is all.

Of course, there is yet another option: shortening the length of what we write. We can abridge, condense, or anthologize selections from more protracted works. We can produce reviews. We can write abstracts and executive summaries. We can also set limits—the dozen or so syllables in a haiku, the maximum 140 characters in a tweet.

Short—and shortened—written materials have been important ways of crafting text for centuries in the modern West. We will look at a number of these shortening techniques, roughly in chronological order. This historical excursion has an ulterior motive: demonstrating that limits on readers' time, interest, or both often shape the length of works that writers (and publishers) produce. As we have said, reading and writing are joined at the hip.

COPING WITH TOO MUCH TO READ IN A PRINT WORLD

Say you are a resident of London, about Shakespeare's time. You're literate, but not to the manor born. What might you be reading? Yes, the Bible. But what else?

A common—and cheap—option is broadsides. Made from a single sheet of paper, a broadside might contain ballads, rhymes, and news, sometimes accompanied by woodcut illustrations. A publication you probably consult rather than read through is an almanac. Here you can check on weather forecasts (sorry, no guarantee of accuracy), tables of tides, times for planting, and dates of religious festivals—all in a single volume.

There are also chapbooks. These small books (made by folding one piece of paper multiple times) were the seventeenth- and eighteenth-century workingman's reading mainstay both in England and in the American colonies. What was in chapbooks? Anything from abridged versions of medieval romances of knights and maidens, tales of monsters and fairies, songs, jokes, riddles, fortune-telling, and weather forecasting to maybe some theology.[20] Chapbooks were sold in bookstores but also hawked on the street and by itinerant peddlers. (The word "chap" comes from Old English *ceap*, meaning "barter" or "purchase.")

Now move up the social ladder a bit and settle comfortably into the eighteenth century. Here we find several new writing genres, along with ramped-up efforts to boil down text into smaller packages.

PERIODICALS

There is a British magazine called *Tatler*, whose pages are filled with "glamour, fashion, society, features and fun."[21] Stories in the May 2013 issue include "Chelsea Uncovered: Jumping into Bed—and into the Bath—with the Cast of *Made in Chelsea*" and "Meet the Family: All You Need to Know About the Clan of Cressida Bonas, the Golden-Haired Girl Flying High with Prince Harry."

The masthead says "Established in 1709." Condé Nast, publisher of today's *Tatler*, is stretching the truth a bit. The original *Tatler*, started by Richard Steele, closed down in early 1711. What both publications do have in common is a dual focus on gossip and news.

The first *Tatler* launched a 300-year tradition of periodical publications. Steele's original foray was promptly replaced by a new venture (though also short-lived), this time published jointly with Joseph Addison. The *Spectator* sought to replicate the kind of lively conversation going on face-to-face in coffeehouses and clubs. Wit and humor were the stylistic order of the day. The range of topics included "religion, men, women, love and marriage, family, education, literature, business, [and] the proper use of wealth." To spice things up, there were also pieces on "the genealogy of humor," "grinning and whistling for prizes," "beards," and even "a day watchman who has a pet goose that helps him call the time."[22]

It was not until 1731 that Edward Cave founded the *Gentleman's Magazine* in London, giving the periodical genre lasting footing. (The magazine ran continuously until 1922.)[23] The publication was created as a monthly summary of news and observation on issues that the educated reader might find interesting. Notice that Cave called his publication a "magazine." He was, in fact, the first publisher to use the term, which he took from the French word *magazine*, meaning "a place to store things" (as in a gunpowder magazine).

A historical aside: In 1738, Samuel Johnson began working as a writer for the *Gentleman's Magazine*. It is hardly coincidental that in his monumental 1755 *Dictionary of the English Language*, Johnson included the following in his entry for "magazine":

1. A storehouse, commonly an arsenal or armoury, or repository of provisions.
2. Of late this word has signified a miscellaneous pamphlet, from a periodical miscellany named the *Gentleman's Magazine*, by *Edward Cave*.[24]

Magazines were to become a flourishing enterprise. They enabled readers to keep abreast of the news (near and far), as well as read literary pieces, find recipes, or get advice for the lovelorn, depending upon the type of publication. In practically all instances, the stories were brief enough to be read in a single sitting.

In America, the roots of the genre trace back to Benjamin Franklin's *Pennsylvania Gazette*, which he began (essentially as a newspaper) in 1728. The publication was renamed the *Saturday Evening Post* in 1821 and evolved into a popular family-oriented magazine, complete with cartoons and with covers painted by Norman Rockwell.[25] Other important American magazines include *Scientific American* (1845), *Harper's Magazine* (1850), the *Atlantic Monthly* (1857), *Ladies' Home Journal* (1883), and *Time* (1923).

ENCYCLOPEDIAS

Back to Europe.

In his "Precepts for Advancing the Sciences and Arts," Leibniz wrote in 1680 of the "horrible mass of books which keeps on growing," calling for academies to extract the best parts of the best books, and then add comments by experts.[26] One approach was encyclopedias.

The first major step was John Harris' *Lexicon Technicum*, published in England in 1704. But it was Ephraim Chambers' *Cyclopaedia, or Universal Dictionary of Arts and Sciences*, appearing in 1728, that set the model for subsequent encyclopedias. The work was translated into French and provided impetus for the Enlightenment project known as *Encyclopédie, ou dictionnaire raisonné des sciences, des arts et des métiers* (*Encyclopedia, or a Reasoned Dictionary of the Sciences, Arts, and Trades*). Edited by Denis Diderot and Jean d'Alembert, the project's 28 volumes appeared piecemeal between 1751 and 1772.

Across the Channel, some Scotsmen were troubled by the godless cast of the *Encyclopédie*. Their response was to produce a new English work whose sources included writings by Francis Bacon, David Hume, and John Locke, along with pieces from Chambers' *Cyclopaedia*. The result, completed in 1771, was grandly called the *Encyclopedia Britannica*.

ABRIDGMENTS

Encyclopedias are practical syntheses, lumping together summary information on a wide swath of topics. The goal is to educate, either intellectually or practically. And the entries are all nonfiction. Literary works, particularly fiction, present a different kind of challenge. If the author carries on too long, you might want an abridgment.

The novel as a literary genre entered English with a weighty presence. Samuel Richardson's first novel, *Pamela*, qualified as a "long read." (The 1981 Penguin Classics edition runs to 544 pages.) Yet Richardson's *Clarissa*, which appeared in 1748, might serve as a doorstop. (Penguin Classics' 2004 edition has 1,536 pages.) By some estimates, *Clarissa* contains around a million words.[27]

When working on *Clarissa*, Richardson expressed concern to his friend Aaron Hill, a writer and dramatist, that the book might become too lengthy. Richardson sent Hill some initial chapters, soliciting Hill's assistance in reducing the verbiage. Hill declined. Writing to Richardson in January 1744, Hill explained his decision:

> I see no modest possibility of [shortening your prose]; since precision, in so natural a flow of drapery, would only serve to stiffen, what you bid me shorten. You have formed a style, as much your property as our respect for what you write is, where verbosity becomes a virtue.[28]

And so Richardson wrote on—and on. *Clarissa* was published in stages, totaling eight volumes.

Not all would-be readers relished slogging through long-form Richardson. Abridged versions and excerpts sprouted up within a few years of *Clarissa*'s appearance. For the next century, abridgments regularly abandoned the letter format in which the original was cast in favor of narrative.[29] Richardson was popular on both sides of the Atlantic, but with an interesting twist: While eighteenth-century English readers seem to have preferred the unabridged version, in America, abridged editions of Richardson's works were more popular. When *Pamela* appeared in Philadelphia in 1792, it totaled only about 27,000 words (compared with the original quarter million). And the abridged *Clarissa*? The American version, appearing in 1795, was slimmed down to about 41,000 words.[30]

Richardson himself was aware that *Clarissa* readers might have a rough time keeping all the pieces of the novel straight. And so in 1749—just a year after *Clarissa* appeared—the author added a table of contents to the second edition, in which he summarized each of the letters constituting the novel.

ANTHOLOGIES

An alternative solution to abridging a single lengthy text is selecting shorter portions of several works. Wrap up the extracts in a single book, and you have an anthology.

The idea of gathering together different pieces of writing into one book is hardly new. Look at bound volumes containing manuscripts from the English Middle Ages, and you often find a potpourri of independent items essentially stuck together. A prime example, known as MS Cotton Vitellius A.xv (once the property of Sir Robert Cotton and now housed in the British Library), contains the only known copy of the *Beowulf* manuscript. But collected together in the same volume are the "Soliloquies of St. Augustine," a "Debate Between Solomon and Saturn," and the "Life of St. Christopher." With the development of printing, more "planned" miscellanies appeared, containing, for example, selections of poetry or translations of classical works.[31]

The later decades of the eighteenth century saw a proliferation of anthologies. Growth of the genre was facilitated by changes in British copyright law. The 1774 ruling in the case of *Donaldson v. Beckett* was especially critical in reducing copyright protection for authors whose works were being anthologized. Producers of these anthologies were now free to publish (and profit from) such collections without legal threat from the original authors or publishing houses.[32]

Anthologies enabled readers to read extensively, concentrating on the selections that were included (in principle, reading them carefully), without the burden of plodding through entire works. Leah Price, in her study of anthologies and the rise of the novel, explores the tension emerging from the mid-eighteenth century to the end of the nineteenth between anthologizing (which entails wrenching sections from their larger context) and abridging (which may yield little more than plot lines).[33] Either way, you shorten the reading time, though abandoning the reading experience the author intended.

Yet anthologies continue to be in hot demand. The publisher boasts that the *Norton Anthology of American Literature* has been read over the past 30 years by more than 2½ million students.[34]

BOOK REVIEWS

Still trying to cope with too much to read? Another possibility is to let someone preview books for you. You can get the gist of what a book is about from a reader with credibility, helping you judge if the volume is worth your time. There is also the matter of money. You don't want to shell out cash for a work that doesn't pan out.

And so the book review was born.

Exactly when book reviews first appeared is a matter of debate. Some scholars trace the roots back to the second half of the seventeenth century. On the Continent, book reviews of sorts appeared in French scholarly publications such as *Journal des Sçavans*, though the audience for such reviews was extremely small. In England, publications like the *Intelligencer; Published for the Satisfaction and Information of the People* previewed the contents of books and brought their existence to potential readers' attention. Sometimes the information came in the form of advertisements or summaries provided by publishers.[35] (Think of postings from publishers that you find today on Amazon.)

What everyone agrees is that book reviews as a modern genre began in 1749, when Ralph Griffiths started publishing the *Quarterly Review*. This new periodical, Griffiths promised readers, would provide "some idea of a book before they lay out their money or time on it."[36] A piece in the *London Advertiser and Literary Gazette* effused that

> it certainly is of the highest Utility to the Public to have a just and judicious Criticism upon the modern Productions, whereby Works of Merit may not only be rescued from Oblivion, but much Expense, and what is of infinite more Concern to Mankind, their Time may be saved.[37]

More review journals soon followed, such as Tobias Smollett's *Critical Review*, begun in 1756. The contributors were no intellectual slouches. Among them were Samuel Johnson, David Hume, and Oliver Goldsmith.

Book reviews became a staple in the tool kit we use for selecting what we want to read. Today's offerings run the gamut from highbrow publications such as the *Times Literary Supplement, New York Review of Books,* or *New York Times Book Review* to user-sourced reviews in online social reading groups like Goodreads.

SERIALS

The coping strategies we have been looking at so far generally involve reducing the amount you end up reading. Another approach is to break the whole into smaller chunks to consume seriatim.

Reading on the installment plan was at first financially driven. Up through the seventeenth and eighteenth centuries, books were still generally expensive items. Readers sometimes could not afford an outright purchase. A solution from publishers was to issue books in loose sheets, which readers could have bound after purchasing all the segments. This system was used for distributing serial portions of the Bible, along with Milton's *Paradise Lost,* Smollett's *History of England,* and Chambers' *Cyclopaedia.*[38]

Serial production, particularly of novels, became wildly popular in the nineteenth century. Installments ran in newspapers and magazines. Each piece could be read in a relatively short time, and the price of the publication in which it appeared was affordable to a wide audience. Once the serial was complete, publishers issued the whole collection for sale as a single volume.

The best-known examples of novels that began as serials are surely works by Charles Dickens, including *The Pickwick Papers* and *The Old Curiosity Shop.* But there were scores of others, including Harriet Beecher Stowe's *Uncle Tom's Cabin,* Alexander Dumas' *The Count of Monte Cristo,* Leo Tolstoy's *Anna Karenina,* and Arthur Conan Doyle's Sherlock Holmes stories.[39] In America, it became prestigious for novelists to have their work first appear in a highbrow magazine. In the words of an article in *Scribner's Monthly,*

> Formerly, the best writers of fiction never appeared in the magazine....Now it is the second or third rate novelist who cannot get publication in a magazine, and is obliged to publish in a volume, and it is in the magazine that the best novelist always appears first.[40]

Serials also enabled authors to build an audience for a book they had not completed. What if an author died before producing the final chapters? Again, Dickens is a perfect example. The first installments of *The Mystery of Edwin Drood* appeared in serial format, beginning in April 1870. But then Dickens died in June, leaving the work unfinished. It remains a mystery how Dickens intended to conclude the novel—assuming he had already decided.[41]

Newspaper serialization also became a hook for attracting new readers and subscribers. Cunning strategies were exploited in nineteenth-century France. While Balzac's *La Vielle Fille* was serialized (with daily installments appearing in 1836 in *La Presse*), it was serialization of Eugène Sue's writing that both reshaped the way serials were presented and made for quantum jumps in readership:

> Unlike Balzac's narration, which tended to end each installment of his novels at a point of *dénouement*, Sue's narrative strategy...purposely does not achieve closure; rather, he ended each installment at a point of unresolved narrative tension, precisely in order to leave his readers in suspense. If they wished to know the outcome of the events narrated, they would simply have to purchase the next installment.[42]

Serialized fiction has continued as a literary form. Modern examples include Tom Wolfe's *The Bonfire of the Vanities* and Michael Chabon's *Gentlemen of the Road*, both later appearing as traditional bound volumes. Yet the modern genre came nowhere close to matching the nineteenth-century fervor—until the explosion of online publishing. As we'll see a bit later, onscreen options are giving serialized fiction new life.

CONDENSED BOOKS

Two final approaches to lightening the reader's load are twentieth-century innovations. Both are versions of abridgment, but each with its own twist.

For the first, step back to 1922 and the origins of DeWitt and Lila Acheson Wallace's *Reader's Digest*.[43] DeWitt was the mastermind of the operation. His concept was to collect together in a smallish magazine (about the dimensions of a paperback book, though thinner) articles that would appeal to lowbrow and middlebrow audiences. These were not just any articles. Rather, each was a "condensed" version of a presumed original. ("Condensation" was not meant to be the same thing as "abridgment.") Some of Wallace's originals had been published in other magazines, though over time, the majority of pieces originated with *Reader's Digest* writers.[44]

The idea had come to Wallace years earlier, while he was working for his uncle in Colorado. Later Wallace fought in World War I and was injured in the Meuse-Argonne offensive, ending up in the hospital for several months at Aix-les-Bains. There he spent hours reading American magazines and "trying out his theory that many of their better articles could be reduced in length without losing the point and flavor."[45] Several years after returning home, he put his scheme to the test.

The condensation process at *Reader's Digest* seems to have been a blend of common sense, editorial consensus, and Wallace's keen eye. Samuel Schreiner, who spent many years working for Wallace, provides some examples:

> The basis of [the cutting process] is deciding what point the article to be cut is trying to make and eliminating anything extraneous to this point. If, for example, an author uses three anecdotes to show that his subject is a generous man, it's obvious that the best of them is enough to get that point across

When the *Digest* published condensations of *Time* cover stories that interwove the subjects' policies with their personal lives,

> if the Digest's intent in reprinting the piece is to inform its readers about policy, the cutter may drop the personal details entirely.[46]

I am reminded of Sergeant Joe Friday in the old television series *Dragnet*, who would say to the loquacious women he always seemed to be interviewing, "Just the facts, ma'am."

Reader's Digest went on to become enormously popular. Over time it came to be published in multiple languages and distributed across the globe. For many years it was the best-selling magazine in the world.

Later Wallace had another idea: Why not condense entire books? The venture got under way as "book supplements" to the *Digest*. Then followed the series that came to be known as Reader's Digest Condensed Books, offering potted versions of works Wallace believed people would want to read. These hardback but affordable volumes were marketed using the book club model already familiar from the Book of the Month Club (which began in 1926). Every month Wallace sent subscribers a new volume, typically containing four or five condensed books. (You can imagine the degree of condensation.)

The book condensation process was a mix of art and science. While there doesn't seem to be a published formula, Evert Volkersz extrapolates this description:

> An extended hierarchical editorial process of abridging and summarizing text by retaining both style and substance..., omitting quotation marks from verbatim passages, replacing deletions with transitions made in the manner

of the author, and toning down or excising excessive violence and explicit sex scenes, without changing vocabulary other than inserting dashes following the first letter of a profanity.[47]

The resulting condensations were guaranteed to be G-rated. Most books were recent fiction (such as Alan Paton's *Cry, the Beloved Country* or Michael Crichton's *The Great Train Robbery*), though there was the occasional nonfiction account (like Thor Heyerdahl's *Kon-Tiki*) or biography (Coretta Scott King's *My Life with Martin Luther King, Jr.*).

In its heyday, the series attracted both aficionados and naysayers. Some critics complained that violence was being done to the authors' original texts. Other celebrated bringing literature to the masses. What we know is that Wallace's series based on brevity sold well. Theodore Geisel (aka Dr. Seuss) captured the joy of such concision in 1980 in "A Short Condensed Poem in Praise of Reader's Digest Condensed Books":

It has often been said
There's so much to be read,
you never can cram
all those words in your head.

So the writer who breeds
more words than he needs
is making a chore
for the reader who reads.

That's why my belief is
the briefer the brief is,
the greater the sigh
of the reader's relief is.

And that's why your books
have such power and strength.
You publish with *shorth!*
(Shorth is better than length.)[48]

CLIFFSNOTES AND THEIR PROGENY

Reader's Digest Condensed Books were designed for leisure reading. What if you have real work to do, like taking a test on *Macbeth* in high school or writing a paper on *War and Peace* in college? Teachers would love to believe that in preparation, everyone actually reads the works in question. But let's not be naive. Not when there are CliffsNotes and SparkNotes offering tidy plot summaries. As SparkNotes says on its website, "Sometimes you don't understand your teacher, your textbooks make no sense, and you have to read sixteen chapters by tomorrow."[49] Study guides are fine, but it is the "read sixteen chapters by tomorrow" part that resonates with most of the clientele.

Apparently not all of the clientele are students. Some are members of book clubs. In the words of Justin Kestler, then editorial director for SparkNotes, "Nobody's going to read that 500-page John Adams book [by David McCullough], but people still want to know what they missed and what they should retain."[50] No, there hasn't been a SparkNotes version of McCullough's book, though SparkNotes has a book on John Adams. Book club readers who are short on time (or sustained interest) might have to make do with that.

To be fair, publications in this genre are billed as study guides, not shortcuts. Back in the 1950s, Clifton Hillegass decided to produce study materials on Shakespeare for an American audience. (He had previous experience creating these kinds of works, published in Canada.)[51] Beginning with the Bard's writings, Hillegass came out with sixteen guides in 1958. Several hundred more slim volumes followed, including guides to other literary masterpieces, as well as aids for studying foreign languages, math, and accounting.

The CliffsNotes website suggests how their guides should be used:

Most people use CliffsNotes by reading a chapter of the book or an act of the play, and then reading the corresponding section in the CliffsNotes. Alternatively, read the entire book or play, and then review with CliffsNotes.

"Read the entire book or play." Good counsel, but I'll bet a year's supply of Red Bull that the majority of students who have used these guides were not heeding this advice.

Other study guide companies followed. In the 1960s, Monarch Notes proved a strong competitor. Now the main player is SparkNotes. The company began online but for print-minded readers offers hardcopy versions of some of its literary guides. For the visually inclined, you will find free videos on the site, offering the lowdown on works such as *1984* and *Othello*. (It's like comic books but with voice-over instead of text.) There is also the No Fear Shakespeare series, which "puts Shakespeare's language side-by-side with a facing-page translation into modern English— the kind of English people actually speak today."[52]

Devising techniques for truncating text. Helping readers decide what books actually to tackle. Publishing collections of short essays or fiction. Offering novels as serials. Producing extended plot synopses. There is a long history of saving readers time and money, especially when there is too much to read.

How are these techniques now playing out onscreen?

COPING WITH TOO MUCH TO READ IN A DIGITAL WORLD

He was all over the news in late March 2013. Nick D'Aloisio, a British high school student, had just become a multimillionaire. No, he didn't win a lottery. Rather, he sold to Yahoo! a news-reading app named Summly. The app takes longer news stories and shortens them to fit neatly on a mobile phone screen. And I do mean *a* screen. In the words of the *Washington Post* story on D'Aloisio, the teenager "has expressed disdain for scrolling down a smartphone screen, which readers of full-sized articles must do repeatedly to reach the end."[53]

Summly goes to the heart of tl;dr. But it takes the principle a step further, addressing the problem of "too long; didn't scroll." Most people are guilty, at one time or another, of tl;dr. Ask yourself: When you are doing a Google search, how often do you bother scrolling down to the bottom of even the first screen?

As more and more reading takes place on screens, publishers and users are creating products and strategies for shrinking the amount of continuous text we confront. Note I said "continuous." While our eyes are probably encountering at least as many words as ever (even more, according to a study done at the University of California, San Diego),[54] digital screens are leading us to consume them in small, bite-sized chunks.

Here is how.

SNACK READING

Taking the long view, trends in today's digital publishing are, to invoke Yogi Berra, déjà vu all over again. Our historical recounting of publishing strategies for coping with too much to read might itself have felt too long. Yet the enumeration helps us understand that some of today's seemingly novel approaches to shrinking continuous text are either carryovers or improvisations on older themes.

The two biggest carryover growth areas are online book reviews and serialization. Each comes with its own digital character.

Book reviews by "credentialed" writers (generally themselves authors or professionals in the field) continue to be published online and off. What's new is the surge of user-generated reviews. Want to be a book reviewer but no one has requested your services? No problem. Start your own blog. These days, there is even an online compendium (BookReviewBlogs.com) made of up links to scores of book review blogs. Add in social networking reading sites, along with reader reviews on the likes of Amazon.com, and you have a vast array of opinions to help you decide if you actually want to read a particular book.

Serialization of longer works is also growing online. Today's general public is already familiar with radio serials (at least if you are older) and television series. Much as Americans purportedly waited at the docks in New York in 1841 to learn whether Dickens had killed off Little Nell in *The Old Curiosity Shop*, the buzz around water coolers and bars in 1980 was who shot J.R. (as in J.R. Ewing, the hard-driving Texan from the popular television series *Dallas*).

Digital serialization of full-length books (or books in the process of being written) is an obvious next step. In fall 2012, Amazon introduced Kindle Serials. As the website explains,

> Kindle Serials are stories published in episodes. When you buy a Kindle Serial, you will receive all existing episodes on your Kindle immediately, followed by future episodes as they are published. Enjoy reading as the author creates the story, and discuss episodes with other readers in the Kindle forums.[55]

Established authors such as Margaret Atwood and Joe McGinniss are among those signing contacts for digital serialized fiction as well. Similarly, Wattpad, a popular online fiction site, is filled with short installments of longer works.[56]

But the new—and biggest—development in digital publishing is creating new works that are short to begin with. On the commercial side, start with Amazon Singles ("Compelling Ideas Expressed at Their Natural Length").[57] Created in 2011, the enterprise offers inexpensive titles that run anywhere from about 5,000 to 30,000 words. Production turnaround is quick. Stephen King dashed off an essay on guns as an Amazon Single right after the December 2012 school shooting in Newtown, Connecticut, and the piece was available for sale almost immediately.[58]

The "short is beautiful" theme keeps building. In mid-2013, Nook Media introduced Nook Snaps: short fiction and narrative nonfiction works selling for under $2.[59] By the end of the year, Amazon had launched StoryFront, a new imprint of individual short stories.[60] Dozens of publishing initiatives are now creating standalone works that are intentionally short. Among the players are One Bite Reads and

SnackReads, which offers reading in portions "perfect for your lunch break, your commute, or right before bed."[61]

Make no mistake: Short-form reading can be both enjoyable and edifying. The essay is short-form, as (obviously) are short stories. The issue is whether today's surge in snack-sized texts also marks a move toward more lightweight reading.

Bringing more gravitas to the enterprise is Tim Waterstone, founder of the eponymous Waterstone's bookstore in the UK. Now he has embarked on a new venture, Read Petite. Waterstone had previously not been a fan of digital reading, describing his first reaction to the Kindle this way:

> I think I went through a crisis: [Was it] the end of Waterstone's and the end of the book trade? I was incredibly depressed. I pretended I wasn't, but inside I was churning: "Maybe I should die now."[62]

But then Waterstone decided, if you can't lick 'em, join 'em. If readers wanted digital works, he would provide them. One important difference between Waterstone's plan and sites such as SnackReads is that Waterstone will be offering writing by established, published authors.

Read Petite will bring short stories to readers, using a monthly subscription system such as Spotify uses for music. The service is aimed at helping adults readers who have too little time and have "got out of the habit" of reading. The stories will be short-form: about 9,000 words or even shorter.[63] In the same general vein, there is now a TED Talk book app. TED Books "are typically under 20,000 words—long enough to unleash a powerful narrative, but short enough to be read in a single sitting."[64]

For all their novelty, new digital shorts remind me of earlier incarnations of short works for time-strapped readers. Discounting the eighteenth-century language, the words of Vicesimus Knox, written in 1778, sound eerily modern:

> But what shall [one] read during the interval of half an hour, interrupted perhaps by the prattle of children, or the impertinence of visitors, or the calls of business. Not a long and tedious treatise, divided and subdivided, and requiring at least the unsuspended attention of half a day, fully to comprehend the whole … but the periodical essay satisfied.[65]

ACADEMIC WRITING AND PUBLISHING

In the academic world—at least in the humanities and social sciences—publishing only journal articles usually will not get you tenure. Scholarly books continue to be the coin of the realm. While hardly responsible for what happens in university tenure and promotion decisions, academic publishers have been responding to their own signs of the times: The sales market for "scholarly-length" monographs is shrinking. And so, therefore, is the size of what academic presses are looking to publish if they wish to stay financially afloat.

The trend began more than a decade ago, as academic publishers started encouraging authors to keep it short. To quote Walter H. Lippincott, then director of Princeton University Press, "If a manuscript is over 100,000 words, you have to start to think whether you can afford to publish it."[66] Libraries (with their own tightening budgets, especially for print) cannot be counted on to buy enough copies to cover publication costs. If you price a book too high, the public readership won't buy it. It is perhaps no surprise that at Princeton University Press, "the editorial board takes length into account before agreeing to publish a book."[67]

Recently, academic presses have taken a more dramatic step: creating whole series of "short" or "brief" books, designed as digital releases.[68] We now have

- Princeton Shorts ("brief selections taken from influential Princeton University Press books and produced exclusively in ebook format")[69]
- UNC Press Shorts (excerpted "compelling, shorter narratives from selected bestselling books published by the University of North Carolina Press and present[ed] ... as engaging, quick reads")[70]
- Stanford Briefs ("short e-originals—about 20,000 to 40,000 words—[focusing] on a variety of academic topics")[71]
- Chicago Shorts ("distinguished selections, including never-before-published material, off-the-radar reads culled from the University of Chicago Press's commanding archive, and the best of our newest books, all priced for impulse buying")[72]
- Oxford University Press' Very Short Introduction series ("concise and original introductions to a wide range of subjects")[73]

Presses such as Princeton are also experimenting with serial chapter releases, "hoping to build interest in the final book"[74]—a sentiment that would have resonated deeply with authors and publishers in the nineteenth century.

Academic publishers are not the only ones getting in on the act. Among the other contenders is the *New York Times*, whose E-Singles are

original short e-books featuring narratives in areas in which The Times has reporting expertise including culture, sports, business, science and health.

These e-books contain material that has not previously been published in The Times and are meant to be read in one sitting.[75]

The *Atlantic*'s new eBook series, The Atlantic Books,

will include both "original long-form pieces between 10,000 and 30,000 words, and curated archival collections that span the magazine's 155-year history and feature some of the best-loved voices in American letters."[76]

Amazon Singles, Kindle Serials, StoryFront: You have competition.

ACADEMIC READING

Academic publishers are upping their production of shorter scholarly works. We know from the University College London study that many scholars engage more in power browsing than in actual reading when they access texts online. What about the amount of text they are encountering in the first place?

The question applies to books but also to the journal literature. Each year, ever more academic journals are being published, resulting in increased demands on practitioners trying to keep up in their fields. How much of this literature are people reading?

Researchers from the University of Tennessee and the University of North Carolina have been studying the reading patterns of faculty members in science, technology, medicine, and the social sciences, going back over thirty years.[77] The goal is to see how much professors read the journal literature each year and how much time they spend reading each article. Between 1977 and 2005, the average number of articles scientists read annually increased from 150 to 280. However, the average amount of time (in minutes) spent on each article decreased from 48 minutes in 1977 to 31 minutes in 2005.

Curiously, participants in the study reported they were paying the same amount of attention to articles over the years, despite the decline in how much time they devoted to actually reading each piece. Were the faculty members now doing more power browsing than in years past? Had they become better readers? Had the scientific articles gotten shorter between 1977 and 2005?

The authors of the study don't say. However, at least in the field of psychology, "short" is a definite trend for journal articles. In January 2011, the incoming editor of the *Journal of Experimental Psychology: Human Perception and Performance*,

James Enns, decided to feature short reports as the first items in each issue. "The culture demands shorter reports and rapid publication," wrote Enns.[78] Psychologists at the University of California, Davis, report that for the past twenty years, there has been a decided move in psychology publications to "short and fast," causing concern about reducing research findings to what others have called "bite size" science.[79]

There's another potentially troubling trend in scientific scholarship that relates less to length than to breadth and seems directly linked to the move from hardcopy to electronic journal access. A sociologist at the University of Chicago surveyed the references cited in a database of 34 million scientific articles. He analyzed the citations with respect to whether the articles cited were available online. The more journals became digitally available, the more recent the references became, and the narrower their scope. The author suggests that

> the forced browsing of print archives may have stretched scientists and scholars to anchor findings deeply in past and present scholarship. Searching online is more efficient and following hyperlinks quickly puts researchers in touch with prevailing opinion, but this may accelerate consensus and narrow the range of findings and ideas built upon.[80]

Obviously short has its virtues, as readers, writers, and publishers have acknowledged for the past three centuries. Equally clear is that the internet and digital screens afford a wealth of new opportunities for creating and disseminating compact reading packages.

Reading onscreen has other virtues as well. It is time to explore some of them.

4 | The Appeal of Words Onscreen

A Magazine Is an iPad That Does Not Work

—Jean-Louis Constanza

That is the caption on a YouTube video posted by a father who filmed his 1-year-old daughter exploring an iPad and a magazine. Over 4 million viewers have shared in the girl's giggles and antics. "There!" you can almost hear viewers say. "Children are natural digiphiles. The age of print is over." The YouTube video also conjures up words spoken by Ben Horowitz (co-founder of Andreessen Horowitz Venture Capital) at the Association of Magazine Media conference in October 2012: "Babies born today will probably never read anything in print."

Will Horowitz be proven right?

Start with an advantage of eReading you might not have thought of. Did you read *Fifty Shades of Grey*? If so, on a digital screen or in hardcopy? The eBook came first—and sold millions of copies before appearing in print. Did readers just like the convenience of having the book on a portable device? Or were they grateful for the privacy? With an eBook, no one needs to know what you are reading. As one writer put it, "E-books brought erotica out of the bedroom and onto public transportation."[1]

Since digital devices (especially mobile phones) tend to be personal possessions, a book delivered digitally becomes more private than a print book, whose cover anyone can see. In describing short novels read on mobile phones in Japan (know as *keitai* novels), Jacob Lewis writes, "Delivered to a cellphone, a story is like a private email or text message: implicitly intimate by virtue of the distribution mechanism alone."[2]

Erotica and intimacy are hardly the only appeals of eReading. Other candidates include convenience, cost, environmental benefits, and democratizing access. We'll look at each in turn and then zero in on student reading, especially in universities.

CONVENIENCE

Convenience has been a selling point for all manner of digital devices used for reading. What is so convenient? There's the weight issue. Since they are light (and hold lots of stuff), you tend to carry the devices around with you, especially the smaller ones. Riding the subway, you pick up where you left off in a novel on your Kobo. You catch up on Facebook on your mobile phone while in line at the sandwich shop.

More conveniences: Adjust the size of the type font. Follow links for more information. Email a friend the funny line you just read in an article on your iPad. Always have something to read without planning in advance.

Goodreads, the online social reading community, polled 1,500 of its members to see where they do their reading.[3] Among those surveyed, 75 percent read books at least sometimes in an electronic format. Which format? For 37 percent of respondents, the answer was "cell phones." Among this group, 72 percent read eBooks while commuting or waiting in line. As for tablets, 68 percent of owners read on their tablets in bed.

Members of Goodreads are self-proclaimed "readers." They come in all ages and education levels, and many relish reading onscreen. Yet print still has traction. Of those surveyed, 23 percent read only in print, and 45 percent read a combination of print and eBooks.

COST

Cost has a long history of influencing choice of reading medium. By the fourteenth century in Britain, manuscript preparation was at a crossroads. Throughout the

Middle Ages, animal skins had provided the main writing surfaces. Paper, though known in the West, was initially expensive. That was to change. As paper prices gradually fell, the economics of manuscript preparation needed to be confronted. Scribes still favored the superior writing surface that hides provided, but money talked:

> Even as early as the close of the fourteenth century, a quire of paper (twenty-five sheets) cost no more than the average skin, but it gave eight times as many leaves of equivalent size.[4]

Paper won out.

Fast-forward several centuries to the dark years of the Great Depression. A new idea for book publishing was born that was all about cost. I pass on the story as told in *Smithsonian Magazine*:

> In 1935, Allen Lane, chairman of the eminent British publishing house Bodley Head, spent a weekend in the country with Agatha Christie. Bodley Head, like many other publishers, was faring poorly during the Depression, and Lane was worrying about how to keep the business afloat. While he was in Exeter station waiting for his train back to London, he browsed shops looking for something good to read. He struck out. All he could find were trendy magazines and junky pulp fiction. And then he had a "Eureka!" moment: What if quality books were available at places like train stations and sold for reasonable prices...?[5]

The story may be apocryphal, but there is nothing apocryphal about either the rise of Penguin as a paperback publisher or the broad proliferation of "quality paperbacks."

WHAT SHOULD eBOOKS COST?

Money talks for eReading as well. When Amazon launched the Kindle, it introduced an ingenious pricing scheme: All eBooks would cost $9.99. Considering that hardbacks (and most paperbacks) were generally priced higher on Amazon, consumers purchasing Kindles were getting a wonderful deal. Jeff Bezos knew he was losing money—even with the discounted prices he was paying publishers, $9.99 didn't always cover his costs. But as with any loss leader, he was selling an idea: Read books on Amazon's eReader.

Pricing continues to be a volatile issue in the eBook trade. As sales skyrocketed and other players entered the marketplace, customers hardly knew what to expect from one day to the next. Price wars sometime ensued. In fall 2012, Sony ran a promotion in the UK on the eBook version of James Herbert's *Ash* (retailing in hardcover for £18.99—roughly $30) for a mere 20p (about 30¢). Amazon.co.uk matched with similar discounts of up to 97 percent or more.[6]

What should an eBook cost anyway? Once the formatting is done, the expense of "manufacture" (no paper needed, no binding) and distribution (no postage to pay) is trivial. Obviously, preparation of the manuscript comes with an initial cost. But pricing itself is something of a conundrum. While 30¢ is probably too little, we might assume the price tag will always be lower than for a print copy, or at least less than for the hardback.

Not so. Take J. K. Rowling's *The Casual Vacancy*. In the UK, as of September 2012, Amazon was selling the hardback for £9 but the Kindle version for £11.99.[7] Why? You can bet Amazon has a complex pricing formula that rivals that of the airlines. But part of the answer must be convenience. If I want *The Casual Vacancy* right now—tonight, not tomorrow or next week—Amazon is betting I will shell out the difference.

THE LONG ARM OF THE LAW

Another costing issue has been legal. Many in the book distribution industry were incensed that Amazon was selling eBooks at a loss (and undercutting the competition). Since publishers and authors were getting paid at contracted rates, there was originally no case. But the situation was to change. This time it was other distributors of eContent—including five major American publishers and Apple—that were on the hook. In April 2012, the US Department of Justice filed suit that the six players had conspired to raise the price of eBooks.[8]

The case went like this. As Apple was preparing to launch the iPad in 2010, it worked out a pricing arrangement with HarperCollins, Hachette, Macmillan, Penguin, and Simon & Schuster. Apple would sell eBooks from the five publishers under an arrangement called "agency pricing," whereby the publishers received 70 percent of the retail price and Apple got a commission of 30 percent.[9] Under the traditional sales model, known as "wholesaling," publishers typically sell books to distributors for about half their cover price, and then distributors may charge whatever they choose. Amazon had chosen to charge $9.99. Using the agency model, Apple prices were between $12.99 and $14.99.

Three publishers immediately settled with the government. Two others later came to terms with the Department of Justice. Apple was the only holdout. The final ruling (against Apple) was handed down on July 10, 2013, when US district judge Denise Cote found Apple guilty of violating the Sherman Antitrust Act.[10] The Competition Bureau of Canada announced a similar limitation to agency pricing in February 2014.[11]

Legal battles are not limited to American shores. The European Commission (the executive part of the European Union) was also unhappy with Apple's agency model, charging in 2011 that the scheme violated EU competition rules by raising prices through collusion between Apple and four publishers selling in Europe. Settlement came in late 2012.[12] Since all the settlement conditions have time limits, the European pricing story is hardly over. (There are more European legal tussles with American eBook distributors, but we will save them for later when we talk about intersections between reading and culture.)

PUBLIC LIBRARIES

Another aspect of the American pricing story has been public libraries' battles for reasonable access to eBooks for their patrons. Many publishers placed excessively restrictive limits on library eBook purchases. Some constraints involved cost, but others ran the gamut from when the eBook could be purchased (for example, not until six months after the hardback had come out) to how many times the book could be lent out and whether a new "copy" needed to be bought each year.[13] While slow progress is being made in negotiating terms public libraries can afford—and that serve their readers—it continues to be a long slog.

AUTHORS

In looking at pricing, we have talked about consumers and publishers (or distributors). What happens to authors when competition drives down eBook prices? Kate Pool, deputy general secretary of the Society of Authors in the UK, worries that

> since before the inception of the Society 128 years ago, authors have fought long and hard to ensure that copyright properly protects their fundamental right to control and profit from their creations.... If books are perceived to have almost no value, that fight seems pyrrhic indeed, as are the chances of professional authors, of even the most sought-after books, let alone those

which are highly researched or costly to produce, making a living from their writing.[14]

Some indie (self-publishing) authors are prospering with digital-first books, setting their own prices (typically quite low) and profiting through volume sales. Many of these works are young adult or adult fiction produced fairly quickly. If readers become accustomed to books selling at bargain prices, will traditional works that take years to write and require serious research (or literary skill) continue to be valued?

ENVIRONMENTAL BENEFITS—OR NOT

Another way of considering cost is to look at the toll that publishing—of print or eBooks—takes on the environment. To introduce the issue, let me start with some personal experience.

I spent the fall semester of 2007 on a Fulbright fellowship at the University of Gothenburg in Sweden. Their Department of Linguistics kindly arranged an office for me, complete with computer, desk, and bookshelves. But where was the trash can? After a few minutes of searching, I concluded it must be that plastic bag attached to a wire frame—about the size of a small paperback.

Outside in the hall, I eyed the serried ranks of recycling containers: one for paper, one for cardboard (but you needed to deconstruct the boxes first), one for other recyclables, a place for spent batteries. In the kitchen was a compost bin. I had never seen recycling taken so seriously. (The United States would only catch up years later, but still sporadically.) Sometimes I felt like a postman walking his route, but instead of delivering letters and packages, I was distributing whatever I came to realize was not allowed in my miniature office bag.

Back home in Washington, DC, my university campus prides itself on its green initiatives, including LEED-certified buildings and an Office of Sustainability. We have an innovative Green Teaching Program encouraging faculty to conserve natural resources by the way they conduct classes.[15] Faculty earn "points" through such actions as posting course syllabi electronically rather than printing them, assigning eBooks rather than hardcopy, and having students submit written work electronically. Faculty holdouts who want assignments delivered in hardcopy can still be "green" by requiring the pages be printed double-sided, single-spaced, and with skinny margins.

Lots of paper saved, indeed. Yet are there consequences for higher education's primary agenda: teaching and learning? The first class of each semester, I go over the syllabus with my students. We talk, they ask questions, and most annotate the physical copies that, yes, I distribute (single-spaced and double-sided, I promise). Were I to say (as some of my colleagues do), "Go read the syllabus. It's online. Email me if you have questions," there would be no conversation and no "establishing shot" of what our time together during the term was going to be about.

Or take students' written work. Electronic submissions have all sorts of advantages: Besides saving paper and printer ink, students can share them online with classmates. Faculty with lousy handwriting can insert comments and do corrections with Microsoft Word's Track Changes function, Google Drive, or whatever.

But what if, as a faculty member, you prefer to grade papers by hand? Maybe it's because you can only stand so many hours a day on a computer. Maybe because you sometimes grade papers while waiting in a doctor's office and dislike typing on an iPad or mobile phone. Maybe because you feel you get a better grasp of the argument when you can see the entire thing at once without constantly scrolling or paging back and forth.

Or take that recommendation that students submitting hardcopy do double-sided printing, single-spaced, and keep margins to a minimum. Where am I supposed to put my comments? I need those margins. I need those spaces between lines. And yes, I often need the backs of pages for continuing my feedback. Squishing text into the smallest possible real estate might be penny-wise for tree conservation but pound-foolish for learning.

Many young people today have a heightened environmental consciousness. The Book Industry Study Group reports that 72 percent of college students they surveyed expressed preference for digital textbooks over print because digital was "more environmentally friendly."[16] But some readers also recognize that beliefs about how to preserve the environment may conflict with personal reading preferences. As a student wrote in one of the reading studies I have done, "I prefer hard copies, but think they're bad for the environment."

Are they?

PAPER VERSUS ELECTRONICS

One day when I was loading paper into my printer at home, I happened to notice these words on the wrapper of the Hammermill ream:

Enviro-Facts
Many forests are being replaced by development.
When you use paper, you help keep trees growing.

If we are not using land to grow trees, we're probably covering it with buildings and asphalt. The end result deprives our ecosystem of much-needed absorption of carbon dioxide and release of oxygen, making for bad environmental consequences.

Calculating environmental costs is a surprisingly complex exercise. The challenge applies when doing a cost-benefit analysis of printed materials and even more so when looking at the digital devices we increasingly use to replace paper.

How Green Is My iPad: Digital Devices from Cradle to Grave

Daniel Goleman and Gregory Norris wrote a provocative op-ed in the *New York Times*, asking "How Green Is My iPad?"[17] The piece walks us through the life cycle of an iPad or eReader, from the materials they contain and fossil fuels used in the manufacturing process to health consequences, transportation costs, and disposal problems. Did you know:

- It takes 33 pounds of minerals to make a single eReader compared with 2/3 of a pound to make a printed book.
- Those minerals for the eReader include rare metals such as columbite-tantalite, generally mined in African conflict-filled areas, where profits often support warlords.
- Producing an eReader requires 100 kilowatt-hours of fossil fuels, which produce 66 pounds of CO_2—compared with 2 kilowatt-hours and 100 times less in greenhouse gases for a book.
- "Recycling" an eReader (to extract its precious minerals) is generally done in poor countries, often by children, where workers are exposed to enormous health risks from toxins. For a book, assuming it goes to a landfill, the environmental impact is about double that of the book's initial manufacture.

Also remember that paper, unlike many components in digital devices, is a renewable resource.

Another source of concern surrounding digital technologies is the incredible amount of heat generated by servers bringing us the data, YouTube videos, newspapers, and eBooks we access on our devices. Reporting in 2012, James Glanz offered some troubling examples:

- About 30 billion watts of electricity are consumed worldwide by digital data warehouses, the approximate equivalent of the output of 30 nuclear power plants.

- Servers are backed up by generators, in case of power failure. In just one part of Virginia (where Amazon has many of its data centers), the power needed for these backup generators equals nearly the output of a nuclear power plant.[18]

You need one heck of a lot of fans to cool those data storehouses, and those generators produce one heck of a lot of pollution.

Measuring Environmental Impact

Given the environmental challenges posed by paper and digital reading devices alike, people are trying to calculate the impact of various forms of reading. The Swedes, for instance, have compared the effects on global warming and the potential for human toxicity of reading a paper newspaper versus a web-based newspaper. (The answer: It's complicated.)[19] Others have looked at eReaders. Writers toss out varying statistics on how many books you need to read a year to environmentally justify using an eReader. Is it 23? Maybe 40?[20] In some sense, the number is meaningless, since environmental impact depends upon how long the books are, whether you are a slow or fast reader, and whether you finish the books.

How about textbooks? One study found that the difference in greenhouse gas emissions for the lifecycle of a print text versus an eTextbook is small: for a printed text, 9 pounds of CO_2e (carbon dioxide equivalent) per student versus a bit less than 8 pounds for the eTextbook. But as usual, other factors come into play. If students sell their printed textbooks at the end of the course to someone else, the greenhouse gas emission per student drops by half. Traditional desktop computers consume far more electricity (generating more greenhouse gases) than laptops, while eReaders are the least polluting. There is also the issue of whether students print out pages from online materials, since you then need to factor in emissions resulting from paper production and distribution.[21]

Signs of Progress

On the digital front, Europe took the lead in the early 2000s by establishing the Waste Electrical and Electronic Equipment (WEEE) Directive. The goal: reducing electronic waste, including making manufacturers responsible for recycling goods they sell.[22] The United States, which probably produces the largest amount of such waste globally, has been slower in taking similar legal steps.[23]

Paper production is another area in which policy and practice can affect whether paper or eReading is more eco-friendly. By using both recycled paper and refuse from sawmills, newsprint could become a greener option than reading on digital devices.[24] Organizations such as the Green Press Initiative (in the United States) are looking for smarter ways to produce paper, and in the process preserve natural resources and reduce greenhouse gases. In Europe, the EU's European Cooperation in Science and Technology (COST) initiative has a project exploring new ways of combining the advantages of both print and digital media.[25]

Progress, yes. But at this point, the jury is definitely still out on whether digital reading or paper is now—or will become—more environmentally friendly.

DEMOCRATIZING ACCESS

One area in which digital texts are an incontrovertible blessing is broadening access to the written word. Public access to information and learning is a modern concept. In much of the world (and until recently in the West), if you want to send a child to school, there are fees that must be paid. The notion of a free public library is also fairly recent. (The first one in the United States was established in Peterborough, New Hampshire, in 1833.) Now both public schooling and libraries are ubiquitous in America.[26]

But free access to what? Not all public schools are created equal. Neither are libraries. What's available at the New York Public Library is light-years beyond what I can find in my local Little Falls Library in Bethesda, Maryland. Countries often have a national library with an embarrassment of riches, such as the Library of Congress in Washington. But at the Library of Congress, you need to be at least age 16 and have proper identification to apply for a reader's card. And almost no one gets access to the stacks.

OPEN EDUCATION, OPEN ACCESS, OPEN SOURCE

Centuries back, if you gathered in the town square, you could hear the news. By the nineteenth century, workingmen's groups were forming to help men better themselves.[27] In New York, Peter Cooper founded the Cooper Union for the Advancement of Science and Art in 1859, modeled after the École Polytechnique in Paris. Cooper Union was open to all—and no one paid tuition. In the same spirit, Hugh Chisholm, editor of the famous eleventh edition of the *Encyclopedia Britannica* (completed in 1911), saw the mission of the *Encyclopedia* to be "democratizing the means of self-education."[28]

With the coming of the BBC in England in 1922, anyone with access to a radio set could hear free educational programming. After television emerged (especially public broadcasting and cable options), you had your pick of free college-level courses running the gamut from chemistry to Chinese, not to mention the fruits of PBS. The recent emergence of university-based massive open online courses (MOOCs) continues in this tradition.

Options for free education are an important step toward equity of access. However, when it comes to published written materials that are under copyright, it's a different ball game. If you are the publisher of a commercial journal, you hesitate to make articles available to whoever wants them, given that you are charging substantial fees to libraries (and lesser ones to individuals) for annual subscriptions. If you are an author, you may be relying upon royalties to pay for groceries.

Grassroots movements have emerged offering the public greater access to written works. One is Creative Commons.[29] Begun in late 2002, the designers sought a middle ground between "all rights reserved" and "free" for material available online. Their solution was a tiered set of licenses from which authors might choose. Options run the gamut from letting others download and share your work (but not permitting changes or commercial use) to allowing people to modify your work and even profit commercially from it, as long as you are credited.

Another approach is open-access journals. Given how pricy online journal subscriptions have become, especially in the sciences, a group of prominent scientists forged a better solution. Academics were already sharing (online) preliminary versions of papers that were destined to go under the publisher's lock and key. The problem with the independent laissez-faire system was that anybody could upload anything, with no assurance of quality or even accuracy. What if you created an online journal whose submissions were subject to the same rigorous review process used by prestigious journals in the field, but you didn't charge for reading the contents? Academics were already serving as reviewers for those journals for free. Surely they would do the same for a publicly available enterprise.

The Public Library of Science (PLoS) grew out of an initiative begun by Harold Varmus (Director of the National Cancer Institute), Patrick Brown (at Stanford), and Michael Eisen (at the University of California, Berkeley).[30] With help from foundations (after all, there are real costs to putting out a journal, even if you are not looking to turn a profit), PLoS was created. It has been enormously successful. Now with more than half a dozen journals, PLoS commands strong respect in the fields of science and medicine. And it is free to anyone with an internet connection. This model of rigorous review and free access to journal content (even predating PLoS) can also be found, albeit sporadically, in other academic fields.

A LIBRARY OF EVERYTHING: COMMERCIAL OR FREE?

What about entire digital libraries?

In the late 1960s, a couple of graduate students from MIT told me about a project that sounded straight out of science fiction: digitizing all the books in the world, creating a comprehensive global library. This was at a time when "computer" usually meant a huge mainframe. When ARPANET (the precursor to the internet) was just being born. Even before Project Gutenberg. We all laughed.

But years later, along came a company named Google, which was serious. Here's how Google tells the story:

> In 1996, Google co-founders Sergey Brin and Larry Page were graduate computer science students working on a research project supported by the Stanford Digital Library Technologies Project. Their goal was to make digital libraries work.... Even then, Larry and Sergey envisioned people everywhere being able to search through all of the world's books.[31]

The rest, as they say, is history. Google Print formally debuted in late 2004, with books coming from Harvard, the University of Michigan, and the New York Public Library. Renamed Google Books, the scanning maw was soon consuming pages from additional libraries and making it possible for scholars (or the merely curious) to access a vast array of books.

Sort of. Depending on copyright issues and publisher preference, there were books available in their entirety, books from which you could view selected pages, and books entirely MIA. If you wanted to print pages, you couldn't, though there were links encouraging you to purchase books from online vendors.

There were more challenges. Publishers and authors weren't earning a dime. They sued, claiming copyright infringement. Cases were filed in both the United States and Europe. In the United States, after much wrangling, a proposed settlement fell through. In France, Google was judged in 2009 to have violated copyright and was ordered to pay a fine of €300,000, as well as remove infringing material from its site.[32] Google finally won the American case in late 2013.[33]

Beyond the question of copyright, there is the larger issue of who owns the world's written oeuvre. Google's plan appears to be to license its full collection (for a fee) to libraries, including those that freely offered up books to be scanned in the first place. Robert Darnton, historian and university librarian at Harvard, cried foul. In a series of pieces in the *New York Review of Books*, Darnton argued that commercializing knowledge violates the eighteenth-century Enlightenment principles upon which America was founded.[34]

The solution, said Darnton, was to create an alternative digital repository open to anyone. And that is what Darnton and his colleagues (along with support from foundations) are doing. On April 18, 2013, the Digital Public Library of America was launched—238 years to the day after Paul Revere made his famous ride to warn the American colonists that the British were coming.[35] While its initial holdings are still rudimentary, items from some of America's most important collections (including at Harvard, the New York Public Library, and the Smithsonian) are being added to the archive.

Other free digital archives are also available online. The American Memory project of the Library of Congress provides "free and open access through the Internet to written and spoken words, sound recordings, still and moving images, prints, maps, and sheet music that document the American experience."[36] In Europe, the EU funds Europeana, an internet portal offering open access to books, works of art, and archival materials from more than 2,000 European institutions.[37] And Norway is in the process of digitizing all holdings in its national library.[38]

"Free access" can be achieved in other ways as well. One is to donate digital materials to students in the developing world. Words onscreen are a critical part of the solution. Worldreader (a joint American and European nonprofit initiative) sends eBooks and eReaders to children in sub-Saharan Africa. In addition, more than half a million readers have free access to books on their mobile phones.[39] In the words of David Risher, one of Worldreader's co-founders,

> There's a huge difference between being able to read from a selection of the 10 books that you happen to have—or that somebody donated—versus being able to get your hands on a book that you are really interested in.[40]

Access and affordability are serious challenges for providing reading materials, especially to children, in the poorest parts of the world. While the scale of the problem is relative, affordability is becoming an increasing challenge for students in the United States. Textbook costs are up and family incomes (along with state budgets) down. Are eTextbooks the solution?

THE PRICE OF LEARNING IN AMERICA

Education in America is too expensive.

Over a 30-year period, college tuition rose 1,120 percent (compared with 600 percent for medical care and 275 percent for the Consumer Price Index).[41] The College Board estimated that during the 2012–13 academic year, students paid an average of about $1,200 for textbooks and supplies.[42] Meanwhile, the US Government Accountability Office found that over the past decade, the price of new textbooks had increased 82 percent.[43] It gets worse. By the time undergraduates collect their diplomas, seven out of ten are saddled with student loans, with an average indebtedness of nearly $30,000.[44]

How are students responding? One solution is not to buy the books. One study reports that seven out of ten students surveyed had not purchased at least one of their textbooks because they were too expensive.[45]

What counts as a textbook? In principle, anything faculty assign that's bound between covers and bears an ISBN number. The biggest financial challenge comes from those glossy, mostly hardbound productions typically used in introductory courses and carrying price tags in the triple digits. Other sorts of books obviously appear on reading lists, but their costs tend to be more tractable.

Many schools are concerned. Some are putting the most expensive or most widely used textbooks on reserve in the library. (University libraries don't usually purchase introductory survey textbooks, but a number of institutions are realizing this may be the surest way to help students have access to the reading.)[46] Electronic reserves are another possibility, though copyright restrictions on fair use (generally one chapter per book, one article per journal issue) mean that unless their institution is willing to pay a copyright fee, faculty cannot assume that all of what they want students to read will be electronically available.[47]

A third option is digital textbooks. For this story, we start in the Golden State.

eTextbook solutions

California had a budget problem. In November 2007, the state was anticipating a deficit of $11 billion over the next year. By early 2009, that projection rose to over $41 billion within the coming 18 months.[48] State employees were put on unpaid leave, hours for public services were curtailed, and education budgets were slashed. But Governor Arnold Schwarzenegger had an idea: free digital textbooks for students, beginning with high school classes:

It's nonsensical—and expensive—to look to traditional hard-bound books when information today is so readily available in electronic form. Especially now, when our school districts are strapped for cash and our state budget deficit is forcing further cuts to classrooms.[49]

In September 2012, a subsequent governor, Jerry Brown, signed into law a provision for making free digital versions of popular textbooks available to college students.[50]

California has not been alone in embracing eTextbooks, and cost hasn't been the only motivation. It is easier to update an electronic text than a printed one. (Just ask the producers of the *Oxford English Dictionary*.) There is also a general move in education to ensure that students can handle technology, and eTextbooks are perceived as helping that process along. The EU has its Digital Agenda for Europe.[51] In the United States, the Federal Communications Commission and the Department of Education set a goal of having every K-12 student use a digital textbook within five years.[52]

Digital textbooks are working their way into K-12 education.[53] Cities such as New York are setting up electronic storefronts for managing digital materials (including eTextbooks) across multiple schools.[54] The process is fueled in part by growth in online courses in lower education. But it is higher education in the United States that has witnessed the most organized and wide-reaching efforts to make eTextbooks standard fare.

ETEXTBOOK INITIATIVES IN HIGHER EDUCATION

Say you are a college student planning your textbook acquisitions for the coming term. You could buy or rent the print version. You might also snag a used copy.

Or you could go digital.

Price differentials can be enormous. Take a book like the 2012 edition of John Cutnell and Kenneth Johnson's *Physics*, a popular introductory text published by Wiley. In December 2013, Amazon was charging $203.27 for the hardcover, $89.50 for the eVersion, and about $65 to rent either the hardcover or Kindle edition. If you rent the book (print or digital), you only get it for one academic term. And if you rent the print version, Amazon lets you know (on its FAQ page) that annotation could mean you end up buying the book:

> As a courtesy to future customers, we ask that you limit your writing and highlighting to a minimal amount. If we determine that the book is no longer in acceptable rental condition when you return it, including because of excessive writing or highlighting, you will be charged the full purchase price, less any rental fees and extension fees you have already paid.[55]

Return to purchasing the digital version. Given reproduction and distribution costs, $89.50 sounds like a lot. Why so much? Because commercial publishers are in business to make money. The name of a conference that the Book Industry Study Group runs for the trade is telling: "Making Information Pay for Higher Ed Publishing."

Can anything be done to lower that price? A few years ago, Indiana University took matters into its own hands.

The IU, Internet2, EDUCAUSE Initiatives

Brad Wheeler, vice president for information technology and chief information officer at Indiana University, had an idea. Given the reality of textbook prices, plus advances in computer technology, how about developing a university-based eTextbook initiative? The school was already used to negotiating favorable software licensing agreements with Microsoft and Adobe. Why not negotiate with publishers to give better prices on eTextbooks than usually available? Students would win by paying less for their texts. And publishers would win, because the system—once fully implemented—guaranteed that every student would purchase a new text by building in the cost as a course fee.

The project got off the ground in 2009. IU worked with a company called Courseload to build a software platform on which students could access and also annotate their texts.[56] Each semester, more faculty signed on to use eTextbooks in their courses, and Wheeler and his colleagues negotiated with more textbook publishers. Additional education partners now include Internet2 (a computer consortium of colleges and universities) and EDUCAUSE (a major American force in developing the use of information technologies in higher education), along with a growing number of universities.[57]

Open Access

Another university-driven response to the high cost of textbooks has been encouraging faculty members to write open-access digital texts (especially for introductory college courses) and make them available for free. In many cases, the electronic books are also open source, meaning users are free to adapt the content to suit their individual course needs.

One of the most established initiatives comes from Rice University, under the direction of Rich Baraniuk. Debuting in 1999, the Connexions platform provides free access to digitally authored and published materials. Rice's OpenStax College offers open source course textbooks and materials through Connexions. All the contributions are peer reviewed, and print-on-demand copies are available for modest fees. The ultimate goal is to provide free textbooks to 10 million students around the world.[58] Rice is not alone in developing open-access (or open-source) materials. Temple University has been creating its own digital texts, and the University of Minnesota is compiling a database of publicly available peer-reviewed eTextbooks.[59]

ASK THE USERS: ARE WORDS ONSCREEN APPEALING?

Finances are driving many eTextbook initiatives. But one piece of the equation often neglected is what users themselves have to say about eBooks. Do they like them? If so, why? If they don't, why not? It is easy to assume that a generation spending so much time on digital devices will naturally prefer digital reading. But survey students, and you will be surprised what you find.

What kind of data are out there? Not a great deal, but enough to see clear trends.

One source is statistics gathered by publishing industry and market research firms. Next come studies carried out by universities engaged in eTextbook experiments. Third are my own studies of reading patterns and preferences in the United States, Japan, and Germany, complemented by some exploratory work done by colleagues around the world. Despite the disparity in samples and methodologies, there is considerable convergence in the findings.

INDUSTRY REPORTS

Student Monitor

Student Monitor is a college marketing research firm that surveys American students twice yearly on a range of topics, including their behavior surrounding textbooks. For fall 2013, they reported that cost was the main reason students in four-year colleges bought an eTextbook rather than a print copy. A number also said eBooks were good for the environment. For those who didn't purchase eTextbooks, the two biggest reasons were "I prefer printed textbooks" and "I don't like reading on a screen for a long period of time," followed by "I prefer to purchase used textbooks" and "I get distracted by other things... when I read an eTextbook."[60]

The issue of used books also surfaced in the spring 2013 Student Monitor survey. This time the question was, "If the price were the same, which textbook format would you prefer?" Not surprisingly, 59 percent went with a new print textbook. But 14 percent chose "used textbook."[61] Why? Perhaps because used texts typically have the underlining and marginalia of the previous owner, cutting down on the amount of time the new owner needs to expend identifying what may be most important in the book—and on the test.

Book Industry Study Group

The Book Industry Study Group conducts surveys of college student attitudes toward eTextbooks. According to BISG, between November 2011 and late 2012, student preference for print over eTextbooks dropped from 72 percent to 60 percent. (Translation: In late 2012, 60 percent of students preferred print.)[62] These numbers seem to be moving targets. In a survey administered in October 2013, when students were asked which format they thought they'd prefer for a textbook, 56 percent said "print textbook." But another 15 percent said "print textbook including online supplements," making a total of 71 percent.[63]

UNIVERSITY EVALUATIONS OF ETEXTBOOK INITIATIVES

Early in the game, Amazon began experimenting with electronic textbooks. In 2009, the company released the larger-screen Kindle DX. Would more screen real estate make the new Kindle suitable for reading college textbooks? Amazon arranged with several schools (including Reed College and Princeton University) to do some pilot testing. The answer was no. Students complained that page turning was too slow (making it difficult to locate relevant passages during class discussion), that they couldn't view multiple texts simultaneously, and, perhaps most important, that annotation was very cumbersome.[64]

In the world of digital reading technology, 2009 counts as ancient history. Millions of students were reading onscreen at the time, but overwhelmingly on computers, and the material was largely web pages or comparatively short articles. eReaders were not yet common (less than 5 percent of Americans owned them), and the iPad had yet to be born. A much better test of the viability of eTextbooks would come from the venture begun by Indiana University.

Evaluating the IU, Internet2, EDUCAUSE Initiatives

From the start, Indiana University recognized the importance of surveying students in classes using eTextbooks. As the initiative has expanded to other universities (facilitated by Internet2 and EDUCAUSE), assessment continues to be a critical theme. Here are a few snapshots of findings.

Start with IU graduate and undergraduate students enrolled in fall 2011 classes that used eTextbooks. Among the MBA (graduate) students polled, almost 20 percent said they read more in eTextbooks than they would have in hardcopy, though more than 40 percent indicated they read less with eTextbooks. Among undergraduates, two-thirds reported reading more with eTextbooks. But that's not the full story. While the MBA students said they completed, on average, three-quarters of the reading for the course, the average among undergraduates was only a bit over half.[65]

How much did students think they had learned? Among MBA students who largely did their reading onscreen, one out of ten felt they learned more by reading an eTextbook than reading a hardcopy book. But almost two-thirds said they had learned less. By contrast, among the undergraduates, a little more than half reported learning more from eTextbooks, and almost one-quarter felt they had learned less (again, compared with reading a hardcopy text). It's possible the younger (under-graduate) students were more adept with new technologies. Alternatively, the older (graduate) students may have taken their studies more seriously.

And now some data from spring 2012 classes (mostly undergraduate) using eTextbooks at Cornell, Indiana University, the University of Minnesota, the University of Virginia, and the University of Wisconsin:

- Lower cost and portability were the most important factors for students considering subsequent purchase of an eTextbook.
- Students reported doing a bit less than half the assigned reading in the eTextbooks. At Michigan, faculty found that students now using eTextbooks did less reading than those who used print texts in previous semesters.
- At Cornell, Indiana, Minnesota, and Wisconsin, students expressed a preference for print textbooks over eTextbooks.
- At Wisconsin, 54 percent said they learned more from print, while 25 percent indicated medium made no difference.[66]

As the initiative continues, look for updates on the EDUCAUSE and Internet2 websites.[67]

THE AMERICAN UNIVERSITY READING HABITS PROJECT

For all the hype in America about digital communication technologies, we continue to see stories about students and faculty preferring print.[68] Outside the United States, preference for physical books also appears strong.[69]

Yet much of the reporting remains anecdotal or impressionistic. It was time for some hard data. And so I began the American University Reading Habits Project.

For all the gravitas of the title, this was largely a one-person operation, made possible by several wonderful research assistants at my home university in Washington and the generosity of colleagues from Japan and Germany.

I began work in fall 2010, surveying 82 college students. The following fall, there were 203 more.[70] In spring 2013, another 47. All were undergraduates studying in the United States, and between ages 18 and 24. In summer and fall 2013, I gathered international data from 119 Japanese undergraduates (again, ages 18–24) and 82 Germans (including both undergraduate and graduate students, with the age range from 18 to 26).[71] Subjects were largely drawn from classes that my colleagues or I happened to be teaching, or in one case from volunteers looking to fulfill a requirement for a psychology course.

Random samples? Not by a long shot. What is more, I haven't (yet) run statistical tests of significance and make no claims that these findings reflect the behaviors and judgments of all American, Japanese, or German university students. Yet for all these caveats, the data give us much to think about.

The research (except in Japan) was done using online surveys. Specific survey questions evolved over the three-year period. The final iteration (used in the United States in spring 2013) was translated into Japanese and German for administration abroad.

The surveys contained two types of questions. In the first cluster, students selected an answer from among several choices. For instance, if the question was about rereading books, students were asked whether they reread "most of the time," "sometimes," "occasionally," or "never." Another group of questions were open-ended, including four "like most"/"like least" questions: "What is the one thing you like most about reading in hardcopy? On a digital screen? What is the one thing you like least about reading in hardcopy? On a digital screen?"

"Like most"/"like least" responses were coded using a scheme I devised with vital help from my research assistants. I also gave participants the chance to add whatever other comments they wished. Fluent bilinguals translated all the open-ended responses from Japanese and German. (The coding process for these translations was still in progress when I finished this book.)

Ownership, Annotation, and Rereading

Each semester, university faculty assign reading lists, anticipating that students will procure the materials. If the works are print books, students have several choices if they want their own copy: buy the book and keep it, rent it, or buy it but then sell it at the end of the course.

I became interested in book ownership because of two seemingly unrelated questions: How much annotation were students doing? And how much rereading? If you don't plan to keep a book, is it likely you will be doing much annotation—particularly when used books fetch higher prices if they are not marked up? As for rereading, annotation welcomes you back to a text you already know. If you haven't annotated, you may have less motivation to reread.

In my first study, I asked about ownership, annotation, and rereading of academic books. It turned out that 61 percent sold their textbooks at the end of the course "most of the time," that 48 percent made annotations only "occasionally" or "never," and that 59 percent said they reread academic works "occasionally" or "never."[72] Probing further, I found that medium mattered when it came to rereading. Two-thirds were more likely to reread if they had hardcopy.

For the 2013 studies, I again asked about rereading and medium, this time contrasting schoolwork with pleasure reading. For academic work, the American contingent did the most rereading (only 28 percent said they reread academic materials "occasionally" or "never"), followed by Germans (32 percent) and Japanese (41 percent). The discrepancy between the American figures in 2010 and 2013 may be an artifact of sampling. All the subjects in 2013 were psychology students, while the 2010 group came from a variety of disciplines. When it came to rereading for pleasure, the Japanese did the most (only 39 percent saying "occasionally" or "never"), Germans the least (67 percent), with participants in the United States at 56 percent. However, to be fair, we don't know what kind of pleasure reading they did: Comics? *Leaves of Grass*? *Divergent*?

Medium again mattered, both when rereading academic materials and rereading for pleasure. In each case, students were asked whether they were more likely to reread a book or article if it were in hardcopy or on a digital screen, or if rereading in the two media was equally likely. The results:

		United States	Japan	Germany
Rereading schoolwork				
	Hardcopy	57%	37%	54%
	Digital screen	24%	23%	8%
	Equal	19%	40%	38%
Rereading pleasure reading				
	Hardcopy	67%	47%	69%
	Digital screen	18%	24%	1%
	Equal	15%	29%	30%

In the United States and Germany, hardcopy still ruled among students in my sample when it came to rereading academic materials. (Japanese students showed less commitment to print.) But for all three groups (especially in the United States and Germany), when rereading for pleasure, print was the clear choice.

Memory and Medium

If medium matters for rereading, what about for memory of what you have read? Students in my first study were asked to evaluate their memory for what they read in light of the medium. About half (52 percent) said they remembered more if they read in hardcopy, 2 percent said onscreen, and the remaining 46 percent felt medium didn't matter. Obviously, we don't remember everything we read—and haven't, even before the coming of eReading. But it could turn out that the ephemeral nature of reading onscreen compromises memory more than print does. In the words of author Alain de Botton, "I found that whatever I read on my Kindle I couldn't really remember in the long term. It was as if I had never read it."[73]

Reading Practices: Print or Screen?

Do people prefer to read in print or on digital screens? In 2010, I asked students for their preferences by genre (serious fiction, light nonfiction, and so on). In all cases except academic journal articles (which at my university were generally only available online) and newspapers, the overwhelming choice was hardcopy for both academic and pleasure reading.

For the 2013 studies, the questions were slightly different: What percent of academic reading and pleasure reading were students doing in hardcopy versus on digital screens? In interpreting the results, we need to be mindful that personal preference is but one factor. If journal articles or PDFs are only available online, that is where you read them. If you own an eReader or a tablet, you are probably more likely to be doing digital reading than if you only have a laptop or desktop.

There is also the mobile phone issue. Japan started actively using the internet on mobile phones long before the United States or Germany, so I was not surprised to find that the Japanese in my study did a lot of reading on mobiles (both academic and for pleasure). A different survey question had asked which digital device students used when reading onscreen. For academic reading, 94 percent of my subjects in the United States and 88 percent in Germany said desktop or laptop, compared with 70 percent in Japan. Why? Because 26 percent of the Japanese said mobile phone. The discrepancies between countries were even greater when it came to reading for pleasure: 65 percent in the United States and 62 percent in

Germany said laptops or desktops were their digital tool of choice, compared with only 24 percent of the Japanese. The explanation: 70 percent were doing pleasure reading on their mobile phones.

Now back to the main issue: What percentage of their reading (for school and pleasure) did students do in hardcopy versus on digital screens (of whatever kind)? Here are the findings:

		United States	Japan	Germany
Schoolwork done using				
	Hardcopy	59%	75%	68%
	Digital screen	41%	25%	32%
Pleasure reading done using				
	Hardcopy	73%	76%	69%
	Digital screen	27%	24%	31%

For schoolwork, variation across countries probably reflects the written material involved. I'm fairly confident that much of the assigned reading in the United States entailed journal articles or book chapters only available online, hence the relatively high use of digital screens (41 percent). I don't have information about academic assignments in Japan and Germany. What is unambiguous is that when it comes to pleasure reading, students in all three countries favored print over digital.

Two more relevant notes. In 2010, I asked about students' reading and printing habits. If an academic assignment were available online, did students read it onscreen, print it and read it, or read it onscreen and then print it out? While 55 percent indicated they only read the piece onscreen, 39 percent printed it out and then read it (a practice common with many professionals). A small but noteworthy 6 percent of the students read the piece onscreen and then printed it out. And so 45 percent wanted a print copy, one way or another.

What happens if you dangle a printed copy in front of students? When I asked students if they were more likely to read an assigned article if it were available online or if they were handed a printed copy, 38 percent said it made no difference and 6 percent indicated they were more likely to do the online reading. But the rest—56 percent—found being handed a paper copy was the better motivator. If faculty want students to do assigned reading, we need to rethink whether blithely saying "You can find it online" is effective.

The Long and the Short of It

Does length matter when it comes to choice of reading platform? Absolutely. If the text is short, medium preference is not particularly strong—a mixture of hardcopy, digital screen, or no preference. This pattern held across samples in all three countries and applied to both academic and pleasure reading.

Reading longer texts is an entirely different story. Just looking at preference for hardcopy, these are the numbers when the text is long:

		United States	Japan	Germany
Long schoolwork text				
	Prefer hardcopy	92%	77%	95%
Long pleasure reading text				
	Prefer hardcopy	85%	74%	88%

Both for schoolwork and pleasure reading, the numbers in Japan are somewhat lower than in the United States and Germany. Possibly the dominance of mobile phones in the lives of Japanese students contains part of the answer, since these percentages closely mirror how much reading they do in hardcopy to begin with (school: 75 percent; pleasure: 76 percent).

Convenience, Cost, and the Environment

We've spoken about convenience, cost, and the environment being potential advantages of reading onscreen. What did the surveys reveal? While I didn't explicitly ask about any of these issues, students' opinions bubbled up in the open-ended questions (which asked what they liked most and least about reading in print or onscreen, and what other comments they would like to make).

When it came to what students liked most about reading onscreen, convenience won hands down each time I administered the survey. Students said things like:

"It's lighter to carry 1 device with many readings than a lot of books/papers."
"Easy access to the document."
"Saves space."

Looking at the 2013 results for the American sample, 57 percent of all responses to the question of what they liked most about reading onscreen involved something relating to convenience. Not surprisingly, 62 percent of what they liked least about reading in hardcopy related to inconvenience (such as "carrying the book").[74]

Yet "convenience" lives in the eye of the beholder. In her additional comments, one respondent wrote:

> "For those us of spending most of the time in a job, pulling out a book is unacceptable, while pulling up an article online is more acceptable."

Employers take note! Another student, in explaining what he liked most about reading digitally, said, "Accessibility and ease of multi-tasking." We will return to the multitasking issue.

Given the high cost of education—including textbooks—it's not surprising that many students commented on cost issues in the open-ended section of the surveys:

Liked most about reading onscreen:
   "Saves money not having to print."
Liked least about reading in hardcopy:
   "Having to buy expensive books you're only going to read once."

Or as one student said in her additional comments, "Cash rules everything around me." In the 2010 survey, 11 percent of the participants mentioned cost as what they liked least about reading in print.

It is one thing to worry about what is in your wallet (or on your credit card bill). It's another to ask what happens when you take cost out of the equation in deciding where you prefer to do your reading. And so for the 2013 surveys I asked, "If the cost were identical, in which medium would you prefer to do reading" for schoolwork or for pleasure? The results reveal a huge mismatch between the idea of going digital to save money and what students themselves seem to want:

		United States	Japan	Germany
If cost were the same, preferred medium for schoolwork				
	Hardcopy	89%	77%	94%
	Digital screen	11%	23%	6%
If cost were the same, preferred medium for pleasure reading				
	Hardcopy	81%	83%	89%
	Digital screen	19%	17%	11%

Yes, hardcopy may be less convenient to carry around, and hardcopy generally costs more. Yet if money is not a factor, students from all three countries voiced an overwhelming preference for print. The 89 percent American figure for academic materials tracks closely with the Student Monitor finding that if price were the same, 83 percent of those in their survey would prefer some version of print (new purchase, used purchase, or rental).[75]

A strong concern for the environment came through in the open-ended responses to the American surveys:

Liked most about reading onscreen:
  "Not wasting resources."
Liked least about reading in hardcopy:
  "Kills trees."

In my first survey, 21 percent of the answers regarding what students liked most about reading onscreen involved something ecological, as did 17 percent of responses to the question of what they liked least about reading in hardcopy.

Yet as with the cost issue, we find signs of internal conflict—here in balancing environmental concerns with personal preference. Take these additional comments from participants in my early studies:

  "I like that digital screens save paper but it is hard to concentrate when reading on them."
  "While I prefer reading things in Hard copy, I can't bring myself to print out online material simply for the environmental considerations. However, I highly, highly prefer things in Hard copy—just to clarify."

The Physical Side of Reading

Books are tangible objects. So are eReaders and tablets, though digital content is virtual. In their open-ended responses, participants in the various American surveys often commented on the physical side of reading. Generally, it was words of praise for hardcopy.

In a later chapter, we'll talk in more detail about the physicality of reading. Here is just a flavor of what students had to say:

Liked least about reading onscreen:
  "Lack of physical interaction with reading material."

Liked most about reading in hardcopy:
  "Having a tangible copy of the text."
  "Physically turning the pages."

For the 2013 study, about a quarter of all American responses to the question of what they liked most about reading in hardcopy involved the physical or emotional dimension of reading.

There is another physical side to reading, and that involves legibility of the text and eyestrain. Visual concerns surfaced over and again. In the United States, 30 percent of the complaints about reading onscreen involved eyestrain (comments such as "The screen hurts my eyes" or "Headaches").

Multitasking, Concentration, and Learning

At its core, reading is a mental activity. If our minds are to be engaged, it stands to reason that the greater the distractions, the lower the engagement. Later in the book we will be looking at reading as a cognitive enterprise. Some of that discussion builds on what students in these studies had to say about multitasking, concentration, and learning.

A surefire way to disrupt careful reading is to multitask. In 2010, I inquired if students were more likely to be multitasking if they were reading in hardcopy or onscreen, or if the amounts were about the same. The results were jaw-dropping:

More likely to be multitasking while reading in hardcopy: 1%
More likely to be multitasking while reading onscreen: 90%
Same amount of multitasking with each medium: 9%

The 2013 studies framed the question somewhat differently, asking if students multitasked "very often," "sometimes," "occasionally," or "never" when reading onscreen or in hardcopy. For rough comparability with the 2010 version, I have clumped together "very often" and "sometimes" responses:

	United States	Japan	Germany
Multitask when reading in hard-copy	26%	35%	31%
Multitask when reading on digital screen	85%	46%	79%

In each case, there was more multitasking when reading onscreen—in the United States and Germany, a lot more. I think there's an explanation for the relatively low amount in Japan. Both in the United States and Germany, the bulk of the students' onscreen reading took place on a computer, while in Japan, much more was done on mobile phones, especially when reading for pleasure. It is harder to multitask on a mobile phone than on a computer, where you can have multiple screens open simultaneously.

Another way of looking at mental activity when reading is to ask about concentration: Is it easier to concentrate when reading onscreen or in hardcopy? The answer in the surveys was crystal clear: Hardcopy won out everywhere (United States: 92 percent; Japan: 92 percent; Germany: 98 percent). As reading goes increasingly onscreen, if we want our students to concentrate, we will need to figure out how to cut down on digital distraction—be it hopping to another digital site or responding to a text message.

Besides specific questions about multitasking and concentration, the open-ended questions generated mounds of useful information about how students approach reading. Many sang the mental or educational praises of reading in hardcopy:

> *Liked most about reading in hardcopy:*
>   "I can write in it."
>   "Necessary for focus."
> *Liked least about reading onscreen:*
>   "I hate not being able to dog-ear pages and flip back and forth!!!!!!"
>   "It's harder to keep your place online."
>   "I don't absorb as much."
>   "I get distracted."

Or, as a student of mine put it more recently,

> "Reading [on] paper is active—I'm engaged and thinking, reacting, marking up the page. Reading a screen feels passive to me."

Other responses in my 2013 study pointed up educational or navigational advantages of reading onscreen:

> *Liked most about reading onscreen:*
>   "You can easily look up words you don't know."
>   "Easy to look up additional information."

Liked least about reading in hardcopy:
  "Ctrl+F [FIND] doesn't work for hardcopies!"

But my all-time favorite response was this:

Liked least about reading in hardcopy:
  "It takes me longer because I read more carefully."

Wasn't careful reading supposed to be a hallmark of higher education?

COST ACTION FPS 1104

Beyond my own data, there is a second important source of university-based research, this time courtesy of colleagues working on an EU-sponsored project. The European Union has a set of initiatives known as COST Actions. Essentially, they are projects designed to further European development in science and technology, though colleagues from other countries are sometimes invited to join. One of these Actions, FPS 1104, is called "New Possibilities for Print Media and Packaging—Combining Print with Digital." Players include the forestry industry, companies involved in producing paper or electronic forms, and researchers comparing the ways we read in print versus onscreen.

It is this last group that has been undertaking studies relevant to my own work. Their research agenda includes both student reactions to reading digitally or in hardcopy and also attitudes regarding word processing on digital devices versus writing by hand. Here, I will stick with the project's work on reading.

Scholars from Italy, Finland, the United Kingdom, Germany, Portugal, and Slovakia, as well as Russia, Hong Kong, and the People's Republic of China, have been asking university students to write short essays describing the differences they find between reading on paper and on a screen, along with explaining what they like and dislike about each medium. While the findings thus far have not been analyzed quantitatively, student responses complement what I have seen in my own studies. A few examples:[76]

Reading on paper: advantages
  "When I read on paper, I just read.... When I read on my iPhone I could be with my friends.... It cannot be the same concentration that it would be if the same message [were] on paper." (Italy)

"When I read on paper, I can count on the fact that there are no banner ads popping out that would irritate me when I am reading something that I am really interested in." (Finland)

"I like to watch how many pages I have covered and how many are left [by comparing the physical thickness of each]." (Russia)

"Encourage annotation and reflection." (Hong Kong)

Reading on paper: disadvantages

"I am so used to hypertexts that I miss this application when reading texts on paper." (Germany)

"Paper...cannot be easily shared." (Portugal)

"Too heavy." (Hong Kong)

"Not so environmentally friendly." (Slovakia)

Reading onscreen: advantages

"I like the fact...I can read in the dark." (Italy)

"More comfortable for browsing through text." (Germany)

"It is easier to transport." (Russia)

"More interactive and colorful." (Hong Kong)

Reading onscreen: disadvantages

"E-book readers...[are]...unnecessarily capable [of storing] thousands of books, when in principle one reads one or two at a time and one hardly needs to carry an entire library." (Italy)

"E-books have no atmosphere. Reading books...is an aesthetic pleasure." (Russia)

"The screen encourages skimming and a tendency to choose specific sections, rather than focus on the document as a whole." (UK)

"Easy to get lost in the ocean of information." (People's Republic of China)

There were recurring complaints about eyestrain when reading onscreen, but even more frequent were concerns about concentration:

"For me it is easier to focus on reading on paper." (Finland)

"When we read on paper we pay more attention to the words." (Portugal)

"Reading on screens causes problems in concentration, later also headache." (Germany)

"Better concentration [when reading on paper]." (Slovakia)

"Whilst reading on a screen I can be easily distracted or find it hard to focus on the content of the writing." (UK)

It should be obvious by now that reading onscreen is not a one-size-fits-all proposition. Whatever their drawbacks, there is much to like about eBooks. Undoubtedly they are more portable than hardcopy. Depending upon the country, they can be cost-effective. As the technology continues to improve, they will doubtless become easier to annotate and hopefully more environmentally friendly. The democratizing possibilities for digital texts are one of their most important contributions in the world of learning.

One dimension we have not talked about yet is the kinds of reading that may be particularly well suited to eBooks. In a number of countries (including the United States and the UK), the most popular reading genre for eBooks is fiction. By fiction, we are not primarily talking about the likes of *The Scarlet Letter*, but more about chick lit or erotic romance. While you might go back and reread Hawthorne some day, the prospects for *Fifty Shades* are presumably lower.

What if you only want to read a book once?

5 | The Web Ate My Print Option

One-Off Reading

Oprah Winfrey, speaking with Toni Morrison about her
book *Beloved*:

> "Do people tell you they have to keep going over the
> words sometimes?"

Toni Morrison:

> "That, my dear, is called reading."

How many books have you reread? There is a history to the question.

BRIGHTON BEACH READING

It's summer, and you are looking for a quick getaway from the city. The beach is not far off, less than 50 miles, so you decide to catch a train—a train from London to Brighton, on the south coast of England. It is the 1850s.

Brighton is one of the bustling seaside towns to which middle-class families are flocking for brief vacations. There is Chain Pier, originally built as a docking place for ships traveling to France, but now also housing a promenade and some amusements.

For women and children there are bathing machines, gently dragging bathers for a "dip" in the water (that's really what it was called), protected from the prying eyes of men. New hotels provide lodgings for your stay.

Before departing London, you want something to read on your journey. Thanks to the foresight of two booksellers, a plentitude of light reading is available. In 1848, WH Smith opened its first bookstall in London's Euston Station, the same year George Routledge began his Railway Library. With expansion of the railroad, which carried thousands of short-term vacationers to the seaside, Smith and Routledge seized a golden marketing opportunity. In contrast with the popular but pricey triple-decker novels dominating British fiction, the two entrepreneurs brought out cheap editions of books already published (generally without the nicety of paying royalties).

In the 1850s, the journey between London and Brighton took several hours—about the right amount of time to read one of the "yellowbacks," as they were known, since most had yellow covers. What to do with the book when you were done? Like a modern Long Island Rail Road commuter ditching the newspaper on the seat when the train pulls into Penn Station, you might leave your book on the train for a passenger making the return trip to London. If you haven't finished when your train arrives in Brighton, you can polish off the volume at night, then abandon it in your hotel room for the next guest.

Vacations then and now are tailor-made for inexpensive books we only read once. Just as it is unlikely you will be hauling *The Complete Pelican Shakespeare* to today's Brighton Beach in Brooklyn, Londoners off to Brighton in the mid-nineteenth century probably would not have packed books they treasured or planned on rereading.

Beach reading, whether at the beach or on the way there, reminds us that much of the reading most of us do is what I call one-off reading. It's reading we do for pleasure (like the latest John Grisham novel). Reading to keep up with what is happening in the world (say, the *San Francisco Chronicle*, whether in hardcopy or online). Or reading because we have to (think of school or professional assignments we need to trudge through so we can move on).

How much of our reading is a one-shot deal? It is hard to say, since these are not the kind of data people seem to collect. But anecdotes suggest it is a lot. Take my neighbor Sara, a retired real estate agent. She is college-educated, has traveled widely, and enjoys reading. We got to talking about the research I was doing for this book, and I mentioned that the university students I teach are not annotating their books very much and, in similar proportion, are not doing a lot of rereading.

Sara stared at me and with a wry smile proclaimed, "I've never reread anything."

Whether her declaration was literally true, I cannot say. But it did make me ask: If a sizable chunk of reading is one-off, how much does the platform on which we read it—hardcopy or digital screen—matter? If you are not planning to read something a second time, not intending to pass a book down to your children, not looking to mull over an author's argument or style, is there any reason not to read on an eReader or tablet? The editor and author Will Schwalbe, in a conversation with his mother (who was a voracious reader), captured the sentiment this way:

> "I can't see giving up real books," she said.
> "But electronic books are good for trips," I said.
> "Yes, I can see that. And maybe for books you don't want to keep."[1]

The historical roots of one-off reading reflect a confluence of developments in the seventeenth and eighteenth centuries. The printing press began generating a flood of words on paper. Costs fell, while the size of the literate population rose. Intensive gave way to extensive reading, and novels and newspapers increasingly became everyday fare. The appearance of paperbacks made it feel less odious to discard a book when you were done with it.

You could, of course, try selling some of those books you have already read. We know that students in the United States frequently take up this option, in part because many textbooks have become incredibly expensive. But there is a second motivation for divestiture: Once through (assuming you actually made it that far) was quite enough. How many students plan on reading about demand curves or Newton's laws after graduation?

NOW YOU SEE IT, NOW YOU DON'T: DIGITAL ENCOUNTERS

So much for hardcopy. What about digital?

ONE-OFF READING ONSCREEN

Digital devices are logical places for accessing texts we don't plan to read more than once. Like titles in the Routledge Railway Library, eBooks on eReaders (or tablets or mobile phones) are handy for travel. And although you can still access your books once you are done reading, since they are out of sight, they tend to go out of mind.

We have mentioned that you don't actually own the eBooks you have purchased; technically, you are leasing them—as with software. But for the moment, imagine they are legally yours. What does it mean to "own" something that lives in space? You can physically put your hands on your iPad or BlackBerry (much as you can a hardcopy of *Gone with the Wind*). Does the lack of physicality of eBooks make us think about these digital objects differently?

The ephemeral nature of digital texts puts us more in the role of visitor than proprietor. In the words of Microsoft researcher Abigail Sellen, people "think of using an e-book, not owning an e-book."[2] If we see ourselves as visitors, how much commitment should we rationally make in the encounter? Consider the difference between the vacation cottage you rent for a week and your own home. Sure, the cottage could use an extra lamp, and a plumber could stop that sink from dripping. You let these issues go for the rental, which you probably would not at home.

Entertaining the option of reading something more than once commonly leads to making an investment the first time around. You underline or make annotations. You pause to mull over the author's ideas or words. (As author Jhumpa Lahiri wrote, "In college, I used to underline sentences that struck me, that made me look up from the page.")[3] When the work has no tangible substance, are we less likely to expend the effort, to take the time, to look up from the page?

A group of computer scientists in the UK explored the question of digital ownership by asking about people's attitudes toward different types of possessions: physical possessions, digital materials they had under their own control, and digital materials that lived online. Subjects ranged from teenagers to adults in their 50s or 60s. The researchers found that material possessions were viewed as part of people's identity. By contrast, digital possessions under their control (like photos stored on their own computers) did not seem as "real" as physical equivalents (such as traditional photo albums). In the words of one middle-aged subject,

> The digital ones, they are my possession, but I don't know exactly what's in there anymore and that sense of not knowing, or not easily knowing, makes possessing them feel somewhat different.

That "sense of not knowing" reminds me of some research involving digital photography, this time assessing college students' memory for objects in a museum, depending upon whether they simply looked at the object or also took a photograph. Memory was worse when they took the photos. The students seem to have been relying on the camera to do the remembering for them.[4]

Content owners in the UK study felt even more estranged from digital materials living on the web. As one twentysomething put it,

> I have this fear that all of a sudden [Facebook is] going to get shut down and they're going to wipe [my content] and I won't be able to get it back. So it doesn't feel like I'm fully possessing it.

The researchers concluded that

> posting something online, in today's world, can mean *relinquishing control* over the things that you care about, but also *losing awareness* of what exists, where it is, who has access to it, who is accountable for it, and what is being done with it.[5]

Most of these digital examples pertain to content that users have generated themselves—digital photos, blogs, personal documents, their own presence on social networking sites. But the same logic applies to "possessions" that are digital books. Like banks having the right to call in mortgages (meaning to demand the outstanding amount in full, even if you have not defaulted on your payments), Amazon can wipe your digital bookshelf, and you have little recourse. These digital "possessions" are vacation rentals, not home.

REDEFINING THE KODAK MOMENT

Even if all our digital "possessions" were really ours, we tend to lose awareness of what we own. There is also a tendency to have less psychological investment in them than in their tangible counterparts.

Take digital photographs. Like one-off reading, digital photos are commonly one-off affairs. Granted, photographs are graphic, and this book is about reading. Yet understanding the way we use digital photography can help up grasp how proliferation of inexpensive objects (texts or photographs) ends up reducing the amount of time we spend with them.

Jonas Larsen, a professor at Roskilde University who studies tourists' use of photography, reminds us that digital photography enables us to snap more pictures than we reasonably could with film. Back in the days of "analog" (aka film) cameras, tourists were inclined to take photographs they might preserve as long-lived material objects. Such potential keepsakes justified spending ample time composing each shot. And because each frame had a price attached to it (in developing and printing), we tended to value quality over quantity.

Digital cameras changed the dynamics. We now take less time composing before we shoot. And why not? There is no added cost for snapping multiple photos of the same scene. In principle, we just delete what we don't want. In fact, Larsen reports that in his research "few tourists expressed any emotional difficulties about deleting photographs, even of loved ones." He suggests that the digital photos' "lack of material aura perhaps explains why they are so easy to delete."[6]

Of course, some of us don't bother deleting what we don't want. Many of our digital photos live forever on memory cards or mobile phones, never being sorted or viewed. Yes, they have a kind of permanence, but it is more like the clutter in our attics or garages than the physical photos we once selectively preserved.

A POWERPOINT STATE OF MIND

eBooks and digital photographs are but two examples of how electronic materials encourage one-off encounters, given their lack of, well, materiality. But this penchant for the ephemeral (now you see it, now you don't) has an earlier progenitor: PowerPoint.

These days, PowerPoint is everywhere: in lower-school classrooms, at city council meetings, at academic conferences, at military briefings.[7] Its roots, though, are strictly business. The inventor of PowerPoint, Robert Gaskins, lays out the whole story in a hefty book.[8] Here is the short version.

The presentation tool that today we know as PowerPoint started out in a company called Forethought. The idea was to build a program that could create the equivalent of overhead transparencies and flip charts. Who heavily used these tools? Businesses. Think of presenting quarterly earnings reports, setting goals for the upcoming fiscal year, or energizing the sales force to move more vacuum cleaners.

PowerPoint 1.0 launched on the Apple Macintosh in April 1987. Three months later, Bill Gates purchased Forethought, turning it into Microsoft's Graphics Business Unit. Note the word "business." Versions (and users) multiplied rapidly, and before long, PowerPoint was showing up at meetings around the world.

Why harp on the word "business"? Just as books might contain any manner of content, so can PowerPoint slides. The issue is this: What kind of presentations best fit into PowerPoint format? Given restrictions on how much text a slide can reasonably accommodate, and given the fact that slides are displayed seriatim, what makes sense for business data may not do justice to intellectual discourse. Data visualization expert Edward Tufte has written on the "cognitive style" of PowerPoint, maintaining it is ill-suited to logical argumentation.[9]

PowerPoint is quintessentially designed for one-off reading, to show an audience the contents of each slide just once. Think about the myriad slide shows you have seen. The probability of remembering specific material is low—unless you have access to a printed copy of the set or the speaker dwells on a particular slide. Yes, some PowerPoint slide sets are posted online, and yes, you can usually print them out. But how many of us actually go back for a return viewing? And how many of the presentations we experience ever make their way online anyway?

Back in the day, lectures and presentations were often accompanied by written handouts. True, many of them ended up on chairs, on the floor, or piled in the back of the room. But some were saved and reread, maybe for the quotations or references they contained, maybe for the broader ideas. Today, speakers who bring along handouts are often branded retrograde, tree-killers, or both.

Whatever the name-calling, PowerPoint has fundamentally redefined the relationship between speaker and audience, as well as our attitudes toward writing. The PowerPoint revolution has socialized millions of us to assume that much of the text we see on screens is meant to be viewed just once, and fleetingly at that.

How fast is "fleetingly"? Some professional conferences have introduced Power-Point-based events like Ignite, where the deck is automatically advanced every 10 or 15 seconds, compelling speakers to keep on track and allowing the audience only a glancing encounter with each slide. While designed to generate audience interest, a consequence of these speed performances is that we are further diminishing the value of the written word in the minds of readers.

PowerPoint has had a cumulative effect on how we read onscreen. Experience with the program is leading us to expect that text accessed on any digital device is ephemeral. But (you may be saying), if a person wants to preserve some of that online content in durable form, why not print it out? Too often my answer is, "Lots of luck."

THE WEB ATE MY PRINT OPTION: ONE-OFF AS A LIFESTYLE

We all have our own ways of exploring a subject. If I am serious about a project, I want to have written materials I can access on demand, including when there is no internet access or even no digital device handy. I like to be able to mark up sections, sort articles into piles, and stare at them again. Though I read an enormous amount onscreen, for me, professional work entails paper. I'm hardly alone in this sentiment, though for now I will focus on my own experience.

Online content providers don't always share my approach, even when they are reporting on quantitative findings that you would assume people might want to think about. Here's my story.

I subscribe to *DBW Daily*, a listserv run by Digital Book World, whose editorial director is Jeremy Greenfield. Opening my email, I can count on finding a wealth of the latest news relating to all things eBook (and sometimes hardcopy). Some are pieces written by Greenfield himself, while others are cross-postings or links to a wide array of sites. I could not have written *Words Onscreen* without these research leads. Thank you, Jeremy.

But here's the hitch. Many of those cross-posted or linked sites have adopted a restrictive definition of what it means to read. I am welcome to access their articles online. Invariably, I am invited to share the content with others through a myriad of social networking options, and sometimes email as well. But a "Print" option? Typically nowhere to be found.

I have gotten creative. Sometimes the site lets you print anyway. Other times, emailing the article to yourself allows you to print in the next iteration. Dragging the URL onto your desktop and relaunching the site sometimes works, but not always. The same goes for copying the URL and pasting it into Google: an option for some sites but not for others, where the "Copy" option on the "Edit" menu is grayed out. And there are occasions when I can print the first page of the piece, while the rest is MIA. In desperation, I have even resorted to doing successive "Print Screen" shots of the full text, clump by clump.

What kind of craziness is this? I understand why Google Books does not permit printing pages from its online database. There is a commercial issue at stake (though we could debate whose interests are being protected). I don't understand why a site that posts short, timely information and invites readers to share those tidbits with the world makes it so difficult to generate your own hardcopy for future reference.

When I'm feeling benevolent, I try telling myself that these "no print option allowed" sites are aiming for sustainability. We all have seen email signature tag lines saying something like "Think twice before printing this page." But since the sites in question have nothing to do with environmentalism, the only rational conclusion I have been able to draw is that their web designers didn't envision anyone actually wanting to print the pieces. Instead, read it now, maybe share with a colleague (a great form of free publicity), and move on. A PowerPoint state of mind.

In a digital world, once is seen as quite enough. And when that "once" involves reading, both the lack of a tangible object and the rush forward to the next online temptation tend to make for fast or unfocused reading.

Is there an alternative?

SLOW READING

Opening day near the Spanish Steps in Rome. On March 20, 1986, the first McDonald's in Italy began welcoming customers. But this was not your typical McDonald's—this one was housed in an old palazzo and bedecked with marble.

Carlo Petrini was not amused. A quiet revolutionary who had long been concerned about the growing disconnect between local farmers and large-scale food production, Petrini cried, *"Basta!"* What began as a protest against the fast-food giant staking its claim in such a historic spot soon turned into a slow food movement. In another three years, the movement became international, issuing a Slow Food Manifesto. Among its tenets:

- We are enslaved by speed and have all succumbed to the same insidious virus: *Fast Life*, which disrupts our habits, pervades the privacy of our homes and forces us to eat Fast Foods.
- Our defense should begin at the table with *Slow Food*. Let us rediscover the flavors and savors of regional cooking and banish the degrading effects of *Fast Food*.[10]

There is, of course, more to "fast" than just fast food. Canadian journalist Carl Honoré wrote a best-selling book in 2004, *In Praise of Slowness*, in which he argued we are running ourselves ragged by valuing speed and efficiency over quality, and that we need to reclaim our lives.[11] What is the problem? In the words of Klaus Schwab, business school professor and founder of the Davos World Economic Forum, "We are moving from a world in which the big eat the small to one in which the fast eat the slow."[12]

Incrementally, "slow" movements began arising. Beyond slow food we have slow media (also with its own manifesto) and even slow beer (for linking makers of craft beer with local agriculture).[13] And there is slow reading. We are not talking about reading done by young children, non-native speakers, or people with reading problems. We mean slowing down when you read because you choose to.

The idea of pacing reading speed to fit your purpose is hardly new. Neither is the notion that if you want to savor an author's language, if you are trying to work through a complex passage, if you want to reflect on what you have just read, slow is the way to go.

In discussions of slow reading, it has become almost *de rigueur* to cite Friedrich Nietzsche. In his preface to *Daybreak* (*Morgenröthe*), originally published in 1881,

Nietzsche counseled his audience that reading must be done slowly and deeply, not in a rush. This approach, he argued,

> is more necessary than ever today, by precisely this means does it entice and enchant us the most, in the midst of an age of "work," that is to say, of hurry, of indecent and perspiring haste, which wants to "get everything done" at once, including every old or new book.[14]

We can only imagine what Nietzsche would have said about reading habits today.

Others have emphasized the same theme: Take time in reading in order to understand (or enjoy). Mortimer Adler, in *How to Read a Book*, advised us three-quarters of a century ago to stop at the end of each page to process what we had read.[15] A few years later, Reuben Brower, from his perch at Harvard, began advocating reading in "slow motion."[16] Sven Birkerts' *Gutenberg Elegies*, published in 1994 at the dawn of widespread onscreen reading, reminded us of the importance of "deep" reading, by which he meant "the slow and meditative possession of a book."[17] More recently, he wrote that

> the reader who reads without directed concentration, who skims, or even just steps hurriedly across the surface, is missing much of the real point of the work; he is gobbling his foie gras.[18]

The subtitle to Birkerts' piece is "Notes on Why the Novel and the Internet Are Opposites, and Why the Latter Both Undermines the Former and Makes It More Necessary." While the internet, says Birkerts, is fine for analyzing information, the novel promotes contemplation.

Of course, contemplation is a worthy goal for reading most types of texts, not just novels. Stephanie Harvey and Smokey Daniels, both teachers of reading and writing, suggest some handy symbols that students might use in annotating their reading:

✓ = I knew that.
X = That contradicts my expectations.
? = I have a question.
?? = I am confused or puzzled.
! = That is surprising or exciting to me.
L = I learned something new.[19]

In the same vein, Harvard University Library has produced a six-step guide on how to read critically, intended for first-year students. Step two is on annotation, a process that takes time. The guide advises ditching highlighters and instead using the margins to write, in your own words, what you are thinking about.[20] Mortimer Adler would applaud.

Getting students to slow down when they read, even if they don't annotate, is hardly as simple as issuing an invitation. In the United States, these same students have been trained for years to take standardized tests that have strict time limits: Read this passage, answer the following questions, and then rush on to the next section. Students practice timing themselves, even taking cram courses to increase their accuracy while blitzing through exams. We have turned measurements of learning into horse races. Teachers and researchers know this move doesn't make sense. As developmental psychologist Howard Gardner put it,

> Few tasks in life—and very few tasks in scholarship—actually depend on being able to read passages or solve math problems rapidly. As a teacher, I want my students to read, write and think well; I don't care how much time they spend on their assignments.[21]

Regrettably, it is unlikely that the Educational Testing Service will unilaterally lift its time caps anytime soon.

Like fast food, slow reading now has its own movement. Actually several.

Start with John Miedema, who published a slim book, *Slow Reading*, in 2008. His themes are familiar: "Slow reading is not about reading as slow as possible at all times, but rather exercising the right to slow down at will" and "Slow reading increases literacy skills." Miedema is adamant that slow reading demands hardcopy: "Print is still the superior technology for slow reading anything of length, substance or richness."[22]

In 2009, author Alexander Olchowski was inspired by Carlo Petrini's slow food movement to launch the Slow Book Movement, looking to generate "a reawakening to the act of reading." Olchowski strongly implies that slow reading is equated with hardcopy:

> What constitutes a Slow Book? It is a book that has weight in the hands, with a cover that invites a prospective reader in, with a page layout that makes reading it a distinctly pleasurable experience for the individual.[23]

Better known is Thomas Newkirk's *The Art of Slow Reading*. For Newkirk, slow reading has to do with the relationship we have with what we read, with the quality of attention that we bring to our reading, with the investment we are willing to make.

Newkirk reminds us that while much of the interest in slow reading tends to be linked with works of literature, the lessons he offers (such as attending carefully to the language, listening to the text in our minds, and concentrating on following the author's train of thought) are "relevant to all texts we take seriously."[24]

The slow-reading procession continues. Another Italian, Antonio Tombolini, issued a Slow Reading Manifesto in 2012. While Tombolini sees digital devices as threatening slow reading with extinction, he argues we need to co-opt the technology. His reasoning goes like this. Digital reading tends to be fast reading, which is useful for finding information but often superficial. The reality in publishing is that the transition from print to eBooks is "inevitable and unstoppable." The solution is to engineer the way we read onscreen so that we can—and will—engage in slow reading.

What should a slow-reading eBook look like? Here are some of Tombolini's suggestions:

- It is not shorter, faster, or easier than a paper book.
- It is not an enhanced eBook (that is, it contains text, not sounds and images).
- It is meant to be read "alone by yourself, temporarily isolated from the rest of the world, and immersed in the world that the book creates for the reader at that moment."

Tombolini describes how slow eBook reading works for him, inviting others to follow suit:

- "I will mainly use an ereader…no online navigation, no colors, no interruptions and distractions."
- When reading on a tablet, computer, or cell phone, "I will deactivate the connection for the entire time I'm reading."[25]

In a similar vein, English professor David Mikics counsels that for deep or slow reading, we need to "shut down the Internet browser, avoid Twitter and text messages, turn off the television."[26]

Deactivate the connection? Shut down the internet browser? Tombolini and Mikics are both right—but is the advice realistic? I can hear most teenagers and young adults laughing at the idea.

Earlier when we talked about what it means to read, we emphasized that one size doesn't fit all—all texts or all readers. Skimming is fine for finding a name you're looking for. Getting only the gist is ample before deciding whether to buy a book. (As writer Henry Hitchings put it, "If I am reading…James Joyce, slow reading feels appropriate. If I'm reading the instruction manual for a new washing machine, it doesn't.")[27] There are works we enjoy ambling through; those that seem boring or more of a chore we sometimes take at a canter or gallop.

Speed-reading has its advocates, though current research suggests that speed-readers, while able to handle general comprehension questions, tend to fail on the details. This finding is hardly surprising, since one of the tricks to speed-reading is not reading every word. In fact, when you compare eye movements of speed-readers with those of readers instructed to skim, the results are similar.[28]

The challenge that reading onscreen raises for slow reading is whether the medium is sufficiently adaptable. In the days of the original Kindle, the internet was not a temptation—it wasn't available on the device (other than for downloading books). Tombolini's suggestion that we exercise self-discipline ("deactivate the connection") when reading on internet-connected tools is a bit like setting a bowl of potato chips before hungry teenagers and saying, "Don't ruin your appetite before supper." Like those adolescents racing to the bottom of the bowl, when we read onscreen, we often rush through the text. The irony is that in the early days of computer screens, the concern was that we read more slowly onscreen than in hardcopy.[29]

We have been talking about reading and genre. What about reading and text length? Do we behave differently when we read long texts versus short ones? And are we even reading long texts these days?

Time for another movement.

THE FUTURE OF LONG-FORM

Several months after Amazon's November 2007 introduction of the Kindle, Jeff Bezos had this to say in a letter to his shareholders:

> We hope Kindle and its successors may gradually and incrementally move us over [the] years into a world with longer spans of attention, providing counterbalance to the recent proliferation of info-snacking tools.[30]

Remember that at the time, Amazon's big business was selling print books. This was long before the evolution of eBooks as a genre unto itself—and years before Amazon introduced such "info-snacking tools" as Amazon Singles.

Reading with "longer spans of attention" nearly always means reading longer texts. For several decades now, we have seen a move—both in publishing and in education—toward shorter reading. The trend pre-dates contemporary screen-intensive reading. Ask seasoned university professors what has happened to their course reading lists over the past thirty years, and I'll wager they will tell you the lists have shrunk. Ten books became three or four. Books were replaced with chapters or articles. Thirty years ago, did students read everything on the syllabus? Often not. But at least at the better schools, they read substantially more than they do now.

Reading onscreen favors short-form reading. As we have seen, students in my studies consistently reported that for short pieces, reading onscreen may be fine; for longer texts, print wins hands down. There is a logic here. If the text is brief, maybe you can read it in one sitting (or one stroll across campus or one trip on the Metro). Maybe even without interruption. Probably you can remember the main points of what you have read without making annotations. Once the text becomes longer, the task grows weightier: more ideas to keep track of, notes you want to make to yourself. It is more taxing to keep all the pieces in your head.

Young adults are telling us that if we assign them longer texts, then medium matters. But they are also rebelling against long-form assignments. What to do? Institute a long-form movement? Actually, there already is one. And this time it is online.

Longform.org was founded in 2010 to recommend "new and classic non-fiction from around the web."[31] The basic rules are that pieces must be over 2,000 words and must be available for free online. In 2012, Longform Fiction was added, along with an app for the iPad. There is also Longreads.com, offering articles of varying length. Pieces are neatly categorized by number of words and estimated time for reading them, such as "Less than 15 minutes (Under 3,750 words)" or "More than 60 minutes (Over 15,000 words)."

Before protesting, "Didn't you just say that long-form reading and screens might not mix?" remember this: There are lots of people who love to read long-form. Particularly for one-off reading, medium may be less relevant for them. Committed readers sometimes consume vast numbers of volumes as eBooks. Highbrow magazines such as the *Atlantic*, the *New Yorker*, and the *New York Times Magazine* attract onscreen readers, even for their longer essays.[32] The appetite for online long-form might be lower on news-based sites, where, in the words of Josh Tyrangiel, then managing editor of Time.com, the goal "is to make people smarter by saving them time."[33]

Is there a connection between text length and reading speed? While it is obviously hard to generalize, I suspect studies might show that shorter texts tend to be read comparatively quickly (in the sense of words per minute), especially on devices with internet connections. With longer texts, it is true that some will be skimmed. But if you engage in the "slow reading" we have just been talking about, chances are you will slow down for the passages you care about—either because they are worth relishing or because it takes time to mentally work through them.

Longer texts have another attribute: If they are well written or contain complex (or significant) ideas, they invite rereading.

READING AND REREADING

Who rereads a book, an essay, or a story? Not my neighbor Sara. And not a number of the university students I surveyed, especially if they are accessing the text on digital screens.

If we are being generous, we might speculate that young adults are extensive rather than intensive readers, consuming the new rather than revisiting the old. Regrettably, the data don't back us up. While it's hard to accurately compare overall book reading across time (especially since many college assignments have shifted from books to shorter pieces), we can at least have a look at historical statistics on reading in America, courtesy of the National Endowment for the Arts.[34]

In 1982, roughly 57 percent of the adult population said they had done some literary reading (fiction, poetry, plays) in the past year. By 2002, that number had dropped to not quite 47 percent, though rallying in 2008 to 50 percent. For 18-to-24-year-olds (across the board, not just those in college) the figures were:

1982:	60%
2002:	43%
2008:	52%

The NEA's 2009 report, triumphantly entitled *Reading on the Rise*, celebrated the uptick by the late 2000s. But we still had not returned to 1982 levels.

Another way the NEA probed book reading was to ask how many people had read any kind of book (not just literary) in the past year. More specifically, the study inquired about reading that was not required for either school or work. Among 18-to-24-year-olds (again, not just college students), the answer in 2002 was 52 percent. By 2008, it had crept down a notch to just under 51 percent.

STARTS AND STOPS: ONE-OFF, SOME-OFF, NONE-OFF

Most research on how much reading people do asks something like, "Have you read a book this year?" or "How many books have you read in the past 12 months?" But there is a difference between starting and finishing. Does halfway through count? What about completing just the first chapter? Maybe those abandonments were wise decisions. In the words of Arthur Schopenhauer, life is "too short for bad books."[35]

There are countless reasons for stopping. We get bored with the plot. We don't like the writing style. We get distracted with other activities, including other books. The volume comes due at the library. We lose it. Some readers feel guilty when they halt partway through a book, like the woman from Seattle who describes herself as feeling "like a quitter."[36] Others enjoy their right to move on at will.

How commonly do readers not finish the books they start? There is a figure floating around on the internet that 57 percent of the books people start (presumably in the United States) are not read through to completion, though I can't corroborate the statistic.[37]

Does medium matter? Anecdotal discussion (again, floating around) suggests readers are more likely to finish print books than eBooks, though to my knowledge, no one has done comparative studies. We do have some hard data, courtesy of digital library services (which generally track your every move in an eBook), about what kinds of titles customers are likely to finish. Romance (especially erotica) seems to make for speedy (and presumably complete) reading. Oyster (one of these services) reports that by contrast, less than 1 percent of their clientele who start Arthur M. Schlesinger Jr.'s *The Cycles of American History* make it through to the end.[38]

It is one thing to abandon a book partway through. It's another not to begin in the first place. The late Hugh Amory, senior rare book cataloguer at Harvard's Houghton Library, once quipped that "perhaps the majority of the books ever printed have rarely been read."[39] I suspect all of us have purchased books we have never cracked open. That has been true for print, especially over the past century as books have become less expensive and incomes have risen. It is also true for eBooks. A study commissioned by Ricoh Americas Corporation reported that in the United States, 60 percent of all the eBooks downloaded are never actually read—though I don't have confirmation from the likes of Amazon and Kobo.[40]

Will none-off reading be more prevalent with eBooks than print? Two reasons for hypothesizing a yes answer are cost and lack of physicality. Think of the clothes in your closet. If you bought things on sale, are you less likely to care if you actually wear them than if you paid full price? And if your closet is so stuffed you can't even see what you own (out of sight, out of mind), you are unlikely to even go looking.

There is also the issue of impulse buying. Grocery stores strategically place candy bars alongside their checkout counters. When you walked through the food aisles, you never thought about grabbing some M&Ms. Waiting in line to pay, it's easy to yield to temptation. Just so with buying eBooks, especially if they are not particularly expensive. It's only one more click and a couple of dollars. But unlike that small bag of candy-coated chocolates, which you polished off before reaching the car, those eBooks require longer-term effort that may not prove worth expending.

One-off. Some-off. None-off. All of these are well-established approaches to reading. But what about those works we honor with return engagements?

WHY REREAD?

We opened this chapter with an exchange between Oprah Winfrey and Toni Morrison. The conversation took place in preparation for discussion of Morrison's book *Beloved* on Winfrey's show. A skilled reader (and show host), Winfrey gave voice to the question she knew would be on the minds of many in her audience:

"Do people tell you they have to keep going over the words sometimes?"

To which Morrison replied,

"That, my dear, is called reading."

"Going over the words." Rereading. At the simplest level, we reread when we review a passage immediately after having read it once. Or we reread a paragraph in Chapter 3 when something in Chapter 7 leads us to retrace our steps. More often, though, when we talk about rereading, we mean going through an entire work another time. Think of Jane Austen fans who read *Pride and Prejudice* every year or those of us who return to Sherlock Holmes stories we read years ago or to a Russian novel we really didn't understand in our youth.

Why do we reread? Probably for as many reasons as there are rationales for doing first reads. A prosaic possibility is that this is the only book we have around. A pedagogical rationale is that we will be tested on the book's contents. Yet another motivation is to revise or proofread what we have written. But let's put those aside and focus on more edifying motivations.

Vladimir Nabokov had this to say about rereading:

> Curiously enough, one cannot *read* a book: one can only reread it. A good reader, a major reader, an active and creative reader is a rereader.... When we read a book for the first time the very process of laboriously moving our eyes from left to right, line after line, page after page ... stands between us and artistic appreciation.... But at a second, or third, or fourth reading we do, in a sense, behave towards a book as we do towards a painting [which we take in with our eyes on first contact].[41]

Patricia Meyer Spacks, in her book *On Rereading*, echoes the sentiment:

> Less overwhelmed than she was the first time by the energy of plot and characters, [when rereading, the reader] may have psychic space now to evaluate, to analyze, to understand rather than only to feel.[42]

Rereading, as Spacks explains, is as much about ourselves as about the text, for the process evokes memories not only of the book from an earlier read but of who we were when we first encountered it:

> Rereading brings us more sharply in contact with how we—like the books we reread—have both changed and remained the same. Books help to constitute our identity.[43]

Or in the words of author Verlyn Klinkenborg,

> The real secret of rereading is simply this: it is impossible. The characters remain the same, and the words never change, but the reader always does.[44]

Or as newspaper columnist Danny Heitman put it,

> Maybe the best reading is the kind that merely sets the stage for rereading, so that the greatest books, like the best friends, become part of us only through regular and repeated intimacy.[45]

There's a delightful book called *Rereadings*, edited by Anne Fadiman. The volume is a collection of essays that appeared in the *American Scholar* while Fadiman was editor, drawn from a series she created called Rereadings. In each essay, a distinguished writer chose a book (or a story or a poem or even, in one case, an album cover) that had made an indelible impression on him or her before the age of twenty-five and reread it at thirty or fifty or seventy.[46]

Like others who write about rereading, Fadiman is fascinated with the way the act reveals how the relationship between a book and a reader shifts over time. How rereadings aid in reflection, help us understand who we have become, and perhaps make us who we are. (John Stuart Mill is reported to have read Alexander Pope's translations of the *Iliad* and the *Odyssey* at least twenty times.)[47]

Does medium matter for rereading? Patricia Spacks wonders what happens when you shift from print to onscreen:

> If you have read a book the first time in paper form and reread it on the screen, will the experience resemble that of reading a favorite Russian novel in new translation? How will the impermanence of words of a screen…affect what rereading feels like? Will people feel more tempted to reread, or less? Or will the medium fail to modify the degree of temptation?[48]

Spacks is a retired professor of literature. Her first readings were all done in bound books. I suspect that the relevant question for readers under the age of, say, 30 will be what happens when your first reading of a book is onscreen: Will you reread it onscreen? If you reread it in hardcopy, will the experience differ because of medium?

Why we reread depends heavily on genre and content. A lot of our discussion has focused on long-form literature—in particular, works we feel justify rereading. The thrillers we buy to kill time on a plane ride generally don't qualify. *The Brothers Karamazov* does. Poetry, which is typically short-form (I'm discounting the likes of *Paradise Lost*), invites rereading and even reciting.

What about nonfiction? Depending upon professional need and individual penchant, nonfiction might be a one-off affair or something we return to. Lawyers have traditionally held on to their books on case law (though admittedly they are missing the more recent cases). Roman history buffs might want to keep a copy of Gibbon's *Decline and Fall of the Roman Empire* handy for future reference. Those who annotate their books—fiction or nonfiction—typically do so in anticipation of return engagements.

Rereading is a time-honored practice. Admittedly, it is one that may entail trade-offs: Do I read a different work rather than returning to one I know? The decision should be not simply one of time management but also one of principle. Perhaps the most important gift rereaders can bestow on children and especially young adults is an understanding of why rereading matters—regardless of medium.

So far, we have been focusing on the individual reader. But there is another world of reading that is increasingly generating a strong buzz: social reading. If popular media are to be believed, reading is quintessentially a social activity.

Is it?

6 | How Social Is Reading?

> The real issue with the internet may be that it erodes,
> slowly, one's sense of self, one's capacity for the kind of
> pleasure in isolation that reading has, since printed books
> became common, been standard.
>
> *—Henry Hitchings*

> Books are one of the strongest social objects that exist.
>
> *—Otis Chandler*

Is Hitchings right? Is Chandler? The first is an author; the second, founder of Goodreads. As with many debates, the answer hinges on how you define your terms and individual practice. It also depends on when in history you ask the question.

It is the Middle Ages in England, say around 1250. You know how to read and are comparatively well-off, within the ranks of the minor nobility. You own a handful of books, largely religious. When reading (probably silently, though maybe with moving lips), you do it in private.

Next scenario. It's still the Middle Ages (now coming up toward 1400), but this time you are sitting in the court of Richard II, listening to Geoffrey Chaucer read aloud "Troilus and Criseyde" to the assemblage. This tableau was apparently for real, depicted in a manuscript illumination now residing in Corpus Christi College, Cambridge. Chaucer's audience was likely literate. But outside the castle walls, few people could read. Low rates of literacy continued for several hundred years, and so reading aloud to those who were not able to was a common occurrence. Robert Darnton suggests that "for most people throughout most of history, books had audiences, not readers."[1] A social activity? Yes, but essentially unidirectional.

Today, we both read alone and read (sometimes aloud) in the presence of others. There is even the scenario of reading alone to avoid social interaction. We get out books on planes to forestall conversation with our seatmates. The Japanese have perfected the art, whipping out their *bunkobon* (small paperbacks) or *keitai* (mobile phones) on the subway in Tokyo, encasing themselves in virtual cocoons—even though cultural constraints all but ensure that the stranger next to them won't strike up a conversation.

Contemporary technology has broadened opportunities for private and social reading alike. Tiny personal lights attached to our books (along with glowing eReaders and tablets) let us read in bed without disturbing partners or roommates. Online social reading tools, now breeding faster than rabbits, invite "conversation" with other readers and sometimes even authors.

If you are a Kindle owner, Amazon's "Popular Highlights" feature lets you see what other readers of the same eBook have chosen to mark. In the words of Amazon's FAQ,

> We combine the highlights of all Kindle customers and identify the passages with the most highlights. The resulting Popular Highlights help readers to focus on passages that are meaningful to the greatest number of people.[2]

Media guru Steven Johnson captures the essence of digital social reading this way:

> Even when we manage to turn off Twitter and the television and sit down to read a good book, there will be a chorus of readers turning the pages along with us, pointing out the good bits.[3]

By relying on the judgments of other readers to point out the "good bits," we crowd-source our construction of meaning. Do we really care which passages "are meaningful to the greatest number of people"? Mortimer Adler wouldn't. He would be urging us to judge for ourselves what is striking, significant, or memorable.

Novelist Cynthia Ozick sums up the interplay between solitude and the social in the world of reading:

Print first made possible the individual's solitary engagement with an intimate text; the Gutenberg era moved human awareness from the collective to the reflective. Electronic devices promote the collective, the touted "global community"—again the crowd.[4]

During the heyday of print culture, from about 1700 to the dawn of the internet, the growing literate (and increasingly affluent) population of the West largely did their reading in private. Today, in a world where more than a billion people are on Facebook, the pendulum has swung to literacy being a public act.

Online social media encourage all manner of discussion, including about books. The conversation might involve works we read in hardcopy or onscreen. An ever-larger cadre of readers are online and standing ready to talk about whatever they are reading. Given the explosion of online connectivity, digital technologies are poised to turn reading from a largely individual activity into a quintessentially social one.

The issue here is not so much whether we are reading in print or onscreen but whether we formulate our take on a book individually or collectively. At the same time, as eBooks increasingly build in features that let readers connect with others directly from the digital book, there are growing inducements to do that reading onscreen.

IN THE COMPANY OF OTHERS

What does it mean to say reading is social? Does mental conversation with the author count? What about reading someone else's annotations, borrowing a book from a friend, asking questions of an author at a bookstore event, or discussions at a book club? All are possibilities.

BETWEEN READER AND AUTHOR

In his essay "On Reading" ("*Sur la lecture*"), Marcel Proust has an eloquent discussion of the relationship between author and reader. For Proust, the reader's conversation with the author is conducted in solitude. When we allow another person into the discussion, our dialogue with the author "dissipates immediately."[5]

Proust's notion of reading is highly active: "We can receive the truth from nobody...we must create it ourselves."[6] He warns against the temptation to be a passive reader. What is more, we should not assume authors know all. Instead, to read is to have meaningful conversations with them, which might result in disagreements. Reading, says Proust, entails a friendship, but with a person either dead or otherwise absent. We can be bluntly honest in our responses. We never need ask of our authors, as we might of real-life friends with whom we discuss a book, "What did they think of us? Didn't we lack tact? Did we please?"[7]

ANNOTATION AS CONVERSATION

Another form of social reading stems from the markings we leave. Sometimes the interlocutors are none other than ourselves. You read a book ten years ago and made all kinds of notes in the margins. Returning to that book today, your conversation is with the younger you. As Patricia Spacks reminded us, one function of rereading is to help chart personal evolution.[8]

Anyone getting hold of our marginalia can enter into discussion with us as well, though at one remove. Used books sometimes present this prospect. Many works published up through the nineteenth century included their own printed marginalia, in essence highlighting what the author thought was most important in the actual text. And as we suggested earlier, these days some students may prefer purchasing marked-up used books less for the cost savings than for presumed time savings in not having to ferret out the "good bits" themselves.

BOOKS ON DISPLAY

Remember the social climbers who ordered books by the yard, selected to impress visitors or now beach books conspicuously left on our towels? Leah Price, a professor of English at Harvard, candidly describes some of her early reading habits: "In my college dorm, a volume of Sartre was spread-eagled across the futon when I expected callers."[9] A hilarious spoof by the *Onion* announces a (fictitious) new Kindle Flare, which solves the digital dilemma of not being able to show off your erudition when reading on a standard eReader. Using a built-in speaker, the Flare "loudly and repeatedly proclaims whatever high brow title you are reading at the moment."[10]

Bookshelves themselves offer opportunities for a version of social reading. Think of homes or offices you've been in where you scanned the shelves and, in the process, constructed a mental profile of the books' owner, maybe seeding conversation. Perhaps you asked to borrow a volume, generating more discussion when you returned it. Borrowing books from friends—or simply getting their recommendations—is a long-standing way of socially connecting through reading. Sometimes the sharing entails actual talk ("Did you think the ending was believable?"), while on other occasions what is silently shared is knowledge that you and another person have experienced the same reading space.

Digital technology has embellished the idea of what it means to share your bookshelves. Leaving aside what Amazon.com or Barnesandnoble.com might know about your physical or digital holdings (they have your spending history), online sites such as LibraryThing invite you to catalogue your collection and share it with other site participants.[11] (More on LibraryThing in a moment.) You will also find hundreds of "bookshelf tours" online (on blogs, on YouTube), in which book owners show off their collections through still shots or videos.

AUTHORS ON DISPLAY

It is one thing to have a ringside seat providing access to another reader's books. What about a seat at an event with an author? Say Charles Dickens.

Dickens wasn't only a talented writer. He was also a consummate speaker, a master of public readings.[12] Between 1853 and 1870 (the year he died), Dickens packed in 472 readings in Britain and the United States. Other literary figures of the time such as Thomas Carlyle lectured, but Dickens performed. It's no surprise that at the beginning of his career Dickens had considered becoming an actor.

Author book tours have become standard fare for writers (and their publishers) aiming to get the word out about a new book. The goal: driving sales. These events are social in the manner of Dickens' readings, but also in that these days, audience participation in the form of questions or discussion is usually welcomed. Most events are free, though some bookstores sell tickets (think "lecture fee"). The model is reminiscent of poetry readings, for which attendees pay the price of admission to hear poets intone works that may have been written years back.

Literary events, like so much of contemporary living, are becoming more casual. Writers are reading—and competing—in book slams that might combine "cabaret, comedy and club nights."[13] Todd Zuniga, editor of an American creative writing magazine, is the creator of Literary Death Match, a kind of literary talent show in which author readings are evaluated by a panel of judges.[14] Such "matches" are cropping up from Paris and London to Beijing. Other literary events (with or without judges) now dot the landscape, sometimes complete with a speakeasy environment, including alcohol and live music. Generally they are low-tech, not counting the sound system.

There are also high-tech solutions for putting authors on display. What if, as an author, you would like to go on a traditional book tour but no one is bankrolling a travel budget? These days you can go virtually.

One model is the blog book tour. The oldest and most established of the packagers is Kevin Smokler's Virtual Book Tour. Instead of visiting physical locations, the author makes "stops" at a number of websites (typically blogs). At each, authors might be interviewed, make blog posts, upload new material, or answer questions. The service can be purchased for different tour lengths (one day, five days, up to a month, or customized for just a few blogs). For the one-day tour, for instance,

> you'll spend a full day blogging and getting interviewed at 10–15 weblogs. Each of the tour stops will have a minimum traffic of 500 visitors a day. At least 2 will have a readership of more than 1,000 visitors a day. Your book reaches thousands of potential readers. You never leave your house![15]

A newer alternative is essentially a live video conference. Take Shindig. The company's beginnings were a far cry from virtual book tours. In 2011, Shindig was hosting online video tarot games (it still does) and making a splash with ShindigChess.com, enabling master chess players from around the world to compete in the first chess tournament held via video chat.[16] But the New York City venture had broader plans. The company now enables authors (or anyone else, for that matter—such as musical groups or press events) to "give an online reading, talk, or interview in front of an online group of 50 to 1000."[17]

Virtual book tours are hardly for everyone. Forget about writers who are camera-shy. There are sociable authors who want a physical connection with readers—and even with those who sell their books. In the words of crime writer Douglas Corleone:

> My author tour…is a learning experience. I want to meet my readers and make some friends. I want to talk to booksellers about what makes them fall so in love with a book that they decide to hand-sell. But most of all, I look forward to seeing how people react to me and my work.[18]

As musicians and actors who appear before live audiences will attest, real-life performances are a different animal from studio recordings or moviemaking.

GATHERING TOGETHER

What we have largely ignored so far is the discussions readers have with one another. Sometimes we chat with a stranger on the bus who is holding a book we just finished. We might check in with the friend to whom we gave a favorite book for Christmas. If you and I are listening in the car to an audiobook as we drive across the country, it's natural to share reactions when we stop for dinner.

Teachers structure book discussions all the time on works they have assigned their students. And then there are book clubs—formal or casual, face-to-face or virtual.

SOCIAL READING EVOLVES

It is hard to date the earliest organized gatherings of readers to talk about works appearing in print. A reasonable guess is that the practice began in the late seventeenth century. No guessing is needed about the participants: overwhelmingly men.

IN THE COMPANY OF MEN: MODERN ROOTS OF ORGANIZED READING

The first coffeehouse opened in London in 1652. Over time, coffeehouses became gathering places to hear the latest news. Initially the news was read aloud, but by the early eighteenth century, men congregated to drink coffee, read newspapers themselves, and discuss (among other things) their contents.[19]

One motivation for readers coming together was financial, though monetary interests cut two ways. For readers, it was sometimes the high costs of books or periodical literature (newspapers and later journals), leading readers to share copies.[20] For booksellers, setting up book clubs in their stores could lead to subsequent business. Robert Darnton describes how in the eighteenth century

> provincial booksellers often turned their stock into a library and charged dues for the right to frequent it. Good light, some comfortable chairs, a few pictures on the wall, and subscriptions to a half-dozen newspapers were enough to make a club out of almost any bookstore.[21]

Some of these clubs focused more on socializing, smoking, and drinking than intellectual activity.[22] The social dimension continues in many reading groups to this day.[23]

By contrast, there were special groups that took their reading quite seriously. Often the goal of the gatherings was overall self-improvement, with reading playing a role in the enterprise. Take Benjamin Franklin's Junto Society, founded in 1727 in Philadelphia. Franklin organized a group of friends (all male) that met each week to talk about issues ranging from morals to politics and natural philosophy, with business and community-oriented topics included as well. To help structure the society's discussions, Franklin devised a list of twenty-four questions, the first of which was

Have you met with any thing in the author you last read, remarkable, or suitable to be communicated to the Junto? particularly in history, morality, physics, travels, mechanic arts, or other parts of knowledge?[24]

Sixteen years later, the Junto Society became the American Philosophical Society, which continues to this day.

Franklin was hardly alone in bringing people together for the purpose of self-betterment. On both sides of the Atlantic, workingmen's associations and mechanics' institutes sprang up to help improve the working conditions—and education—of laborers. Often group meetings took the form of lectures, though many of the organizations had libraries attached to them.[25]

The list of organized gatherings goes on. On the popular end of the social spectrum was the lyceum movement, fueled by a traveling circuit of speakers and later entertainers.[26] Generally more exclusive was the Athenaeum movement—as in Athena, the Greek goddess of wisdom. In America, Boston was the first city to organize an athenaeum (1807), followed by Philadelphia and Providence. (London had its own version, founded in 1824.) Activities included concerts, lectures, and book discussions. In each case, a building housing a library collection provided space for events.[27]

Later in the nineteenth century, the Chautauqua movement arose in the United States. Initially designed to foster adult education among the working and middle classes (and run by the Methodists), Chautauquas later evolved into nonsectarian enterprises that included social activities as well.[28] Think of an earlier—and populist—version of Renaissance Weekend à la Bill and Hillary Clinton.[29]

Both genders were welcome in some of these later self-improvement programs. But it was largely women we have to thank for the growth of the phenomenon we know as the modern book club.

BROADENING THE BASE: WOMEN AND BOOK CLUBS

"For the past two hundred years, reading groups have…been predominantly women's groups." So writes sociologist Elizabeth Long.[30] While no one has definitive figures, she is probably correct. Here is a quick chronology of how book clubs developed in America, drawing on Long's work.

Act 1: Young women met informally to "improve their minds." By the late 1700s and early 1800s, New England was dotted with such groups. Reading lists included a wide swath of offerings, from the *Iliad* and issues of the *Spectator* to *History of Columbus*.[31]

Act 2: Following the Civil War, women became increasingly vocal about the need for social change. As political scientist Robert Putnam observes, postwar literary clubs formed by women had a hand in pushing for reforms during the Progressive Era.[32] More often though, women came together for intellectual and cultural fellowship, with books playing a key role. Among these organizations were the New England Women's Club (founded in 1868), Sorosis (a New York literary group, established the same year), the Ladies Reading Club of Houston (1885), and the Dallas Shakespeare Club (1886).[33]

The agenda of these groups was to discuss books. In the process, members could "cultivate a taste, which thus far has been wanting for [their] mental development."[34] And the clubs were for women only:

> Because they were pursuing their own self-development, women generally barred men from membership, feeling that they might be silenced by the men's presence.[35]

Act 3: Reading groups continue to meet to discuss books. But much has changed. The social reform element is largely gone. So, too, is the theme of self-development. While many groups end up predominantly (often wholly) female, gender composition tends to result from affinity, not fiat. Women's access to education has undergone a sea change over the past century. In fact, in the United States, there are now more females enrolled in college than males.[36]

CHOOSING AND SUPPLYING THE BOOKS

If you are going to have a book group, someone has to choose what to read. If the goal is to attract a really large audience (or even lots of smaller ones), first you need to cultivate the practice of reading for pleasure among the general public. In the twentieth century, two important subscription services aimed to do just that.

We have already talked about Reader's Digest Condensed Books—marketed to middle Americans, people who rarely if ever set foot in a bookstore but were open to trying preselected books that were short and not overly taxing. The other, even earlier service was the Book-of-the-Month Club, commonly referred to as BOMC.

BOMC wasn't actually a club. Rather, it was a business, launched in 1926 by one Harry Scherman, coming off a stint at the J. Walter Thompson advertising agency.[37] Scherman's idea was to combine the enticement of convenience with a play on reader guilt as engines for creating a new book distribution industry that would, in turn, fuel middlebrow reading.

The convenience factor? The books came to your doorstep. Particularly for those living in rural areas or small towns where there wasn't a bookstore within miles, direct delivery mattered. This was long before the days of shopping malls with a Walden Books, before the big-box bookstore like Borders or Barnes & Noble, before Amazon.

And guilt? An early advertisement for BOMC explains:

Think over the last few years. How often have outstanding books appeared, widely discussed and widely recommended, books you were really anxious to read and fully intended to read when you "got around to it," but which nevertheless you *missed*! Why is it you disappoint yourself so frequently in this way?[38]

Darn! Everyone is talking about a book I should have read but haven't. BOMC to the rescue! How? Because BOMC reviewed advance copies of new books about to be published and selected the ones that seemed destined for public buzz (and sales). If BOMC's Selection Committee said the month's selection was an important book, you trusted that recommendation. Maybe you even chose it for your book club.

This trust model would underlie other subscription "clubs" as well. A highbrow example is the Readers' Subscription, run from 1951 to 1963 by three literary luminaries: Jacques Barzun, W. H. Auden, and Lionel Trilling.[39] The books on offer each month were intended for an audience willing to work harder than your average Book-of-the-Month Club reader. Readers' Subscription selections included works by the likes of Günter Grass, Gustave Flaubert, and Claude Lévi-Strauss. You trusted Barzun, Auden, and Trilling that these were books worth reading—either by yourself or in the company of others.

In the company of others. The usual model we think of is face-to-face book clubs. But there are other options. Radio and television provide opportunities for what we might call armchair book clubs: You listen to an author and interviewer (think of *Fresh Air* on National Public Radio), sometimes having the opportunity to call in or text comments or questions (think of *The Diane Rehm Show*, also on NPR). Another armchair example is C-SPAN's *Book TV*.

And then there's Oprah.

THE MOTHER OF ALL BOOK CLUBS

In September 1996, Oprah Winfrey, the Chicago-based talk show phenomenon, announced she was starting a book club. Oprah? A book club? The move was not as oddball as it might have first seemed. Oprah has always been an avid reader. She also realized that from her television pulpit, she might accomplish what perhaps no one else could: get her audience to read, including reading serious works of literature.

Yes, face-to-face reading groups were going strong in America. However, the people attending them tended to be college-educated and often upper middle-class. Oprah's audience did not neatly fit the profile.[40] They were probably less likely to have completed higher education, less likely to be frequenting bookstores, and less likely to be reading mainstream book reviews. Which is precisely why Oprah decided to start her book club. As she explained to *Publishers Weekly*, "I want books to become part of my audience's lifestyle, for reading to become a natural phenomenon with them, so that it is no longer a big deal."[41]

All the works Oprah selected were comparatively recent publications. Some were fairly easy reads, while others were sufficiently challenging to qualify for graduate literature seminars. Oprah briefed her audience in advance about what to expect and how much time they would have to read the upcoming title.

Is it fair to call Oprah's Book Club "social reading" when most readers were at home in front of their television sets, watching Oprah interview an author on camera, and seeing pan shots of the studio audience? Probably. Oprah carefully laid the ground-work to help viewers feel like a part of the conversation. The show's website offered questions to think about beforehand. There were opportunities for online discussion, both before and after the show. Readers could write in (Oprah read some letters on the air), and audience members participated in the live conversation.

True, if you are watching TV, you are not directly part of the action. Yet let's be fair. If you are a member of a book group, do you always speak? When your college literature class discussed *Richard III*, did you pipe up? Or did you want to hear what the professor had to say? If the selection for Oprah's Book Club was a modern one (say Anna Quindlen's *Black and Blue*) and you were lucky enough to have the author present (a scheme Oprah typically used on her show), would you rather hear yourself talk or listen to Quindlen?

Like the literature professor maybe you wish you had had, Oprah is a skilled discussion leader. And she wears her excitement on her sleeve. If you didn't understand what Toni Morrison was saying in *Beloved*, hang on. Oprah feels your pain. And both she and Morrison are there to help.

Oprah's initial Book Club ran, with a hiatus, from 1996 to 2011.[42] Through her Club, Oprah succeeded in encouraging (sometime cajoling, sometimes enticing) millions of viewers to take reading seriously, to make it "no longer a big deal." Her TV Book Club redefined what a book club might look like. But yet another redefinition of reading in the company of others was waiting in the wings. This time the internet did the connecting.

JOIN THE CROWD: ONLINE SOCIAL READING

It started with Facebook. Technically, it began with Friendster, but it was Facebook that made social networking an everyday practice.

Launched in 2004 for students at Harvard, TheFaceBook (soon renamed Facebook) found its way onto other American college campuses, then high schools, and by 2006 was available to anyone with an email address. There are competitors these days: LinkedIn (for professional connections), Twitter (to build followings), and YouTube (check out the comments section on some videos), not to mention Foursquare, Orkut, Pinterest, and dozens of others. Add in the millions of blogs and websites that invite comments, plus the conversations users have been having for years in chat rooms and in back channels of multiplayer online games, and you see what living social on Web 2.0 is all about.

In this milieu, it is hardly unexpected that someone would think to bring conversations about books to social networking.

FIRST CAME LIBRARYTHING AND SHELFARI

It's 2005. Facebook has not yet opened itself to the whole world, and Kindle will not arrive for another two years. Yet the internet is already a lively place for posting, meeting, and sharing. Chat rooms, blogs, and MySpace are going strong. Newspapers, magazines, and journals are establishing their digital presence, and library catalogues are generally online.

What if you want to catalogue your own books? Tim Spaulding thought it would be fun doing so in cyberspace. Following the model of Flickr (for sharing digital photographs) and del.icio.us (for making social connections built around shared stops on the internet), Spaulding created LibraryThing, an online site for creating and sharing book collections.[43]

LibraryThing enables users to be as social or private as they please. If you don't want others to see what you have catalogued, just mark your account "private." Sort of like having an account on LiveJournal but adjusting your settings so only you can read your entries. Yet most people using LibraryThing have a more social bent. In addition to giving you a speedy way of tracking your own collection (automatically filling in such niceties as a picture of the book cover, date of publication, ISBN number, and list of alternative editions), the site encourages interaction with other readers. (As of 2014 there were 1.8 million of them.) Among the options are joining book groups to connect up with readers having similar tastes, getting book recommendations, accessing early reviews of new books, and linking directly to Twitter so you can tweet reviews.

Soon after LibraryThing entered the online book-lover landscape, a trio of developers created Shelfari in late 2006. Not quite two years later, Amazon bought it. In many ways similar to LibraryThing, today's Shelfari is "a community-powered encyclopedia for book lovers" that lets you "create a virtual bookshelf, discover new books, connect with friends and learn more about your favorite books—all for free."[44] And yes, since the site is "powered by Amazon.com," it is oh-so-easy to purchase books from guess who.

THEN CAME GOODREADS

A short fast-forward to January 2007, when Otis and Elizabeth Chandler were (also) looking for a way to help people discover and talk about books. Like their predecessors, they wanted to build a tool through which readers could share online their common love of books. And so Goodreads was born. By November 2012, there were 12 million members, of which 55 percent were in the United States, along with 15–20 percent in other English-speaking countries. A year later, there were 20 million.[45] And the number continues to grow.

Goodreads can be thought of as three kinds of aggregators rolled into one site: of individual readers, of the books they read, and of the book clubs they form.

Readers can post reviews of books, create catalogues of their own bookshelves (real or virtual), and form virtual groups. On Goodreads, there are thousands of book groups, ranging from The Sword & Laser (boasting over 18,000 members) to South African Romance Writers (which has just a handful). With all those readers, books often have many reviews—in fact, very many. *Twilight*, *The Hunger Games*, and *Harry Potter and the Sorcerer's Stone* all clock in at around 2 million.

There is also the author component. Authors (and their publishers, assuming the authors aren't self-publishing) are invited to give away some free books, a move that commonly generates Goodreads reviews, along with mentions on external blogs. Authors can blog with Goodreads members, a buzz gets created, there are links for where to buy the book, and sales potentially soar. Over 100,000 writers are part of the Goodreads author program.

Goodreads doesn't sell books. But Amazon does. In March 2013, Amazon swooped in and bought Goodreads. Chandler promptly assured his members that the acquisition was the right move.[46]

BUT WAIT, THERE'S MORE

If Goodreads is not for you but you'd like to connect with others online, there are scores of options, including 1book140, Avon Social Reader, Booksai, and WeJIT. Two of the newest ventures are Zola and Librify.

Zola is the brainchild of Joe Regal, onetime literary agent, who was looking to create a site for selling eBooks that was more about civility and community than cutthroat pricing. Unlike Amazon, which has driven out of business brick-and-mortar bookstores large and small, Zola is designed to support publishers, authors, and independent bookstores. And unlike most of the other social reading sites, Zola's book reviews come from professional reviewers, not customer/members.

Zola users can purchase eBooks that work on any eReader or tablet. The focus of the site layout is on authors, with each book having its own author photo and bio, along with those professional reviews. Independent bookstores are invited to set up storefronts. Readers find many of the social reading tools they have come to expect, and publishers, authors, and bookstores get a reasonable share of the financial take. For its content, Zola is publishing some new books, along with eEditions of earlier classics. In late 2013, Zola became the only eDistributor of works by Joan Didion such as *Slouching Towards Bethlehem*.[47]

Librify has a different strategy. Its goal is to create an online environment (complete with virtual easy chairs and wine bottles) that reminds visitors of book-lined libraries in which friends gather to talk about what they are reading. The sales model is a bit like that of Book-of-the-Month Club. Through a subscription ser-vice, each month members choose one eBook. (There is an option for making print purchases from local bookstores as well.)

But unlike the old BOMC, Librify is built for directly supporting book clubs. The site enables face-to-face groups to schedule meetings and select new books online, as well as share annotations other readers have made in their eBooks. People who are not members of physical book clubs are also welcome to subscribe to Librify.[48] (The platform was still in Beta form as of mid 2014.)

And then we have Bob Stein's approach. Stein has never been a man to think small about technology or the written word. Using money from a 2005 MacArthur Foundation grant, Stein started the Institute for the Future of the Book. Viewing books not as closed, completed physical things but rather as places "where people congregate to hash out their thoughts and ideas," Stein argues that

> the reification of ideas into printed, persistent objects obscures the social aspect of both reading and writing, so much so, that our culture portrays them as among the most solitary of behaviours. This is because the social aspect traditionally takes place outside pages.[49]

It comes as no surprise that Stein's newest venture is Social Book.[50] As Stein said in an interview with the Canadian Broadcasting Corporation in its documentary *Opening the Book*, "This idea that we read by ourselves is a relatively recent idea and is going to go away."[51] People using Social Book are able to congregate with friends on their personal digital networks. Users can let one another know what they're reading and engage in conversation. They can also write in the digital margins, make highlights, and pull out content for other purposes.

Is Stein right in predicting that solitary reading "is going to go away"? Not if you listen to some of the people posting comments on the CBC's website, following airing of the documentary:

squibs: I disagree that reading by oneself is going to be a thing of the past. We can only read by ourselves. sharing the experience (as with discussing stories with others) is an event that happens after the fact.

on your 6: i guess we're not supposed to be doing anything alone anymore. i don't care what others are reading, nor do i care what they think of my reading choices. i wonder if it's all part of some plan to make us more accepting of big brother when he finally tightens the digital noose.

BOOK BLOG NATION

We have been talking about destinations readers can seek out for a variety of book-related functions. Another important force in the online social reading universe is independent book bloggers. You say, "Sure, anyone is free to talk about books on a personal blog," and you're right. But book blogging turns out to be a larger enterprise than you might imagine, complete with entire directories of book bloggers.[52]

Book bloggers come in all varieties, from traditional and buttoned-down (like those writing the blog of the *London Review of Books*) to people who blog under such names as "Smart Bitches, Trashy Books" or "Book Slut." Some book blogs are perceptive and well crafted. Others are smarmy, sophomoric, or even scatological. It is the virtual public square—Speaker's Corner online. As in most instances when there is more on offer than one person can possibly consume, readers pick and choose whom to listen to.

WHAT'S THE SCORE?

So how social is reading? And if the internet is increasing the social dimension, is that a good thing? The answers are a blend of personal taste, timing, genre, motivation for reading socially, and custom.

As we saw in responses to Bob Stein's declaration that private reading is headed for the literary landfill, there are those who prefer to do their own reading, thank you. Writer Judith Shulevitz pithily summed up the sentiment in her closing line of a piece in the *New York Times Book Review*: "You read your book and I'll read mine."[53]

As many writers observe, it is fine to discuss your reading with others after you have encountered a book on your own. Recall Proust's warning that when we talk about a book with a friend, our personal conversation with the author (albeit in absentia) "dissipates immediately." I am sure Proust discussed books with friends, but presumably only after he and the author had concluded their initial dialogue.

Even builders of online social reading sites acknowledge the need to distinguish between individual and social reading experiences. As the creators of the online social reading site BookGlutton explain,

Our goal in building a reading system was to address two modes of reading: the solitary mode, which required focus, concentration, and lack of distractions, and the social mode, in which interactions with the text and with other people are key requirements.[54]

Patricia Spacks reminds us that if you have read a book in a social context (such as in a book group or a college course), it is valuable to reread the work for yourself to figure out your own perspectives and opinions.[55] It's all too easy to assume we agree with the interpretations of whoever was dominating the conversation. Only by returning to the book in solitude do we have a clear shot at holding our own conversation with the author.

Some books are better suited for solitary reading than others, at least the first time around. If you're reading *Twilight*, will you likely be distracted by other readers' annotations showing up on your eBook? What about by Kobo's social reading tool, "Pulse Indicator," which "gets larger and brighter as you reach pages with more comments and reader activity"?[56] Perhaps not. But I would hope readers initially discovering Sherlock Holmes might be left in peace to experience for themselves the language, the story line, and the way Arthur Conan Doyle builds suspense. I would also hope that students would relish the opportunity to decide independently what is important, curious, or even wrong in the texts they read for courses, rather than having some prior reader (a previous owner, online social reader, or SparkNotes) make those decisions for them.

What is most attractive about social reading: the "reading" part or the "social"? For millions of people, the social connection dominates, and the reading part essentially provides an excuse for meeting up. Remember museum nights for singles? Shopping nights for singles? Book clubs for singles? Which function had the upper hand is pretty clear.

Today, the vast majority of people coming together for the purpose of reading—in face-to-face reading groups or online—are women. And the books they're reading, overwhelmingly, are fiction.

Fiction invites us to slip inside other people's skin and model the world through their eyes. But it also helps us escape our own lives. So do conversations with friends, where we can complain about our spouses, bad-mouth our bosses, condemn to purgatory the inept electrician who had to return three times before getting the new dryer to work. Books can help us fight loneliness—yes, by reading them when we are alone, but also by reading them in the company of others. Just as social networking and its precursors—email and IM, blogging and texting—have enabled individuals to create or maintain social ties, social reading online uses the canvas of books on which to draw interpersonal bonds.

Finally, we have the issue of custom. At the beginning of this chapter, we talked about the practice of putting books on display. Don't look for too many practitioners in Japan. Go into a Japanese bookstore and select a volume you wish to buy.

When you check out, the clerk will invariably offer you a plain white cover for the book, effectively camouflaging the title and author. When you are sitting on the subway or bus with the volume, no one knows what you're reading.

If you are a Kindle reader (or, increasingly these days, a user of almost any eReader), your privacy is compromised at the corporate level. Someone can track every time you open an eBook, every time you turn one of its pages, every time you make an annotation. Here the social reading relationship is not one you asked for but part of the Faustian bargain for reading onscreen.[57]

Hardcopy doesn't come with this particular handicap. And, as we are about to see, reading in print has other advantages as well.

7 "It's Not a Book"

The Physical Side of Reading

Ebooks won't be owned. They'll be accessed.

—*Kevin Kelly*

I wonder if anyone has ever cried reading an e-book.

—*Quoted in the Guardian*

What counts as a book?

For more than 1,500 years, the answer was simple: a collection of pages with writing (or pictures) on them, bound together. A book was always physical. You could smell its binding. Admire it on a shelf. Lend it to a friend. Lose it. Burn it.

A book's tangibility also lets you use it in particular ways. You can stick three fingers into different parts of the volume to easily shuttle back and forth in the text. You can find your way back to a passage by remembering it's about a quarter way through, on the upper left-hand side, just before the end of a chapter. You can leave it on your bedside table, where seeing the cover might entice you into staying up late to discover how the story ends.

Is an eBook actually a book? It does weigh something—sort of. John Kubiatowicz, a computer scientist, calculated that a 4GB ebook reader filled with 3,500 books weighs a billionth of a billionth of a gram more than if it were empty of data—a difference that is approximately the same weight as a molecule of DNA.[1]

But surely that weight rounds to zero.

IMPRESSIONS FROM BOOK EXPO AMERICA

The issue of a book's tangibility came into sharp focus for me on a recent trip to the Big Apple. I had gone to New York to attend the International Digital Publishing Forum, a conference geared toward demonstrating that eBooks should rule the publishing world. The two-day meeting piggybacked on the behemoth Book Expo America (BEA), which sprawled across the Javits Center for its annual showcasing, schmoozing, and deal-making extravaganza.

In one sector of the BEA book fair, booths displayed the latest wares in digital publishing. After having my fill, I wandered off to explore the rest of the exhibition. I found myself crossing an invisible divide, a national border, with different languages, different cultures, different attendees, and very different notions of what constituted a book. Everywhere I turned I saw free books—physical books—on offer. They were overwhelmingly paperbound uncorrected proofs of soon-to-be-published works. The idea was to encourage booksellers, who attended the conference in droves, to place orders, as well as create a buzz among the avid solo readers who also flocked to BEA.

Sometimes authors were ensconced in their publisher's booth, signing books for those who came by. For a number of the authors, there were long lines in the rear of the hall, where you could patiently wait to have your copy autographed.

Autographs? Print books? Weren't those supposed to be disappearing? Apparently not quite yet.

Another cultural conundrum awaited me at the booth of Open Road. This newish eBook publishing venture is the creation of Jane Friedman, former publisher and CEO of HarperCollins. Having just heard Friedman enthuse at an American Booksellers Association session about why independent booksellers should be selling more eBooks rather than so much "p" (as in "print"), I was perplexed to see stacks of print books piled up, with Open Road representatives offering passers-by their pick ("Do you like mystery? You might want to try …").

Helping myself to a few titles, I politely inquired, "Isn't Open Road a digital-only publisher?" "Oh, yes," I was told, but the company had done up some print-on-demand copies for people wanting to get their hands on the books right now. I was also welcome, they continued, to a coupon whose code would give me access to the eVersion.

Was the issue only immediate convenience—or maybe that some in the crowd actually liked reading "p"?

THE PHYSICALITY OF BOOKS

These days, publishers of all stripe (and probably most readers) assume that eBooks are books. Indeed, there is a strong family resemblance. Both physical and virtual books generally contain the same words, are laid out on pages, and can be book-marked or annotated.

Yet there are subtle—though important—differences. One of my undergraduates explained her rejection of digital text this way:

> It's not a book. It doesn't have a smell, you don't touch it…, you're plugged into the internet, you can't concentrate, it hurts your eyes, and you lose the beauty of the words behind this screen. Life itself is in hard copy. Not this treacherous digitalism which has permeated our lives and our reality.

A strong statement, but one we heard echoing in our earlier discussion of university students' preference for print. Or, as we quoted Michael Dirda in our opening chapter, "E-books resemble motel rooms—bland and efficient. Books are home—real physical things you can love and cherish."

Other differences involve the ways in which we mentally engage with what is inside. The starkest disparity between traditional books and eBooks is whether their innards are physically at hand or whether they remain buried out of sight. Even a closed book insinuates its way into our thinking by displaying its cover, its heft, its shape. A *New Yorker* cartoon reminds us how powerful the physical presence of a book can be. Two men are sitting at the beach. One turns to the other and says, "I got tired of 'Moby-Dick' taunting me from my bookshelf, so I put it on my Kindle and haven't thought of it since."[2]

The cartoon leads me to what I call the "stumble-upon test": Is the likelihood of stumbling upon digital texts (literally or figuratively) the same as for print versions? Will Schwalbe describes the difference this way:

> Electronic books live out of sight and out of mind. But printed books have body, presence. Sure, sometimes they'll elude you in improbable places: in

a box full of old picture frames, say, or in the laundry basket, wrapped in a sweatshirt. But at other times they'll confront you, and you'll literally stumble over some tomes you haven't thought about in weeks or years.[3]

What is true of eBooks can apply to any digital files—magazine articles, *Wall Street Journal* stories, personal correspondence. In the print world, you can spread out all your unpaid bills on the dining room table, affording you full measure of your fiscal straits. Bills viewed on your computer or tablet appear one at a time. Seen piecemeal, the damage doesn't look so bad.

THE STUMBLE-UPON TEST: WHEN FILES GO VIRTUAL

These days we file away all manner of virtual documents that we rarely if ever revisit. If we do happen upon some virtually dusty file names, it becomes tedious opening each entry to rediscover what is inside. To get a sense of the real-world implications of written materials being physical or virtual, let's see what happens when we "file away" a physical text—and how that activity compares with using today's digital filing cabinets.

In the mid-1950s, my father received a letter from the US Congress. He hadn't won an award, and no one was asking his opinion on pending legislation. No, the letter was written on behalf of the House Un-American Activities Committee. The committee wanted to know about a meeting my father was alleged to have attended in New York City in the late 1930s, while an undergraduate at CCNY (the City College of New York). The meeting, as the letter ominously explained, had been arranged by a local Communist cell.

Had he attended the gathering? Quite possibly. To be a student at CCNY in the late 1930s all but guaranteed you talked leftist politics. Did that make you an enemy of America? Hardly. As long as you weren't organizing strikes or planting bombs, people were generally left to their own ideological musings. But twenty years later, the political climate had drastically changed. Anyone who lived through the McCarthy Era knows how one man's accusations could ruin careers, dash reputations, and drive victims to depression or suicide. At the time the letter arrived, my father held an innocuous position as an economist at the US Department of Labor. Yet since he was a government employee, the reality was that his job could be at stake and he could be blacklisted from finding another.

Somehow he dodged the bullet. How he responded to the charges in that letter when summoned for an interview, I never learned. But I did know that until he died a decade later, he would not tolerate the color red. No red clocks or upholstery in the house. I even learned to avoid red dresses. The Communist Red Scare transformed his personality—and our household.

How did I learn of my father's brush with McCarthyism? From the gray metal file cabinet that stood in our dining room. When my mother was preparing to move from the house some years after his death, we sorted through the papers my parents had accumulated over time. Thanks to that physical document, which I now saw for the first time, I was able to identify the source of some of the demons haunting my father through much of my childhood.

Fast-forward several decades. In 1987, I arrived at American University in Washington, DC, to assume the position of associate dean in the College of Arts and Sciences. What exactly did the job entail? Good question. During the interviews, I had learned I would be responsible for undergraduates, but not knowing anything of how the institution worked, I had no sense where to start. My predecessor had been fired three months earlier, so I couldn't ask her. The dean told me the equivalent of "figure it out."

My salvation was three large file cabinets, chock full of documents. The files were in disarray, but following several weekends of sorting I was able to figure out what an associate dean of undergraduate affairs was supposed to do.

A decade later, I wasn't so lucky. I had been asked to chair an academic department, and this time I knew my predecessor. However, by 1996, office records had largely migrated from tangible documents to computer files. The administrative handover included the presentation of one computer disk, but it was formatted for a Macintosh, and my PC kept choking on its contents. (The days of smooth cross-platform compatibility were still in the future.) After many frustrating calls to the university's information technology office, it ended up being simpler to start new files from scratch.

In my current university position, I recently found myself in a similar quandary. A key office staff member resigned after several months of tussle and refused to give us the password to her Mac. Thanks to Apple's security-mindedness, it seems there was no reasonable way to break into this model to retrieve its contents. The only option, I was told, was to wipe the hard drive clean. There were no physical backup files, and so again I needed to rebuild from the ground up.

I missed that gray file cabinet.

The way we store documents has an intriguing history. In early modern times, as the print revolution gained steam and literacy rates crept upward, the sheets of paper (printed or handwritten) that needed to be kept—and which their owners had to locate again—began multiplying. If you simply piled everything in one stack,

"Portrait of a Merchant," c. 1530. Jan Gossaert. National Gallery of Art, Washington, D.C.

finding just the document you wanted could be time-consuming. One ingenious solution was to group together similar items and attach them to a wall with hanging strings. This technique is depicted in the Flemish artist Jan Gossaert's "Portrait of a Merchant," painted around 1530. On either side of the merchant's head is a hanging sheaf of papers, one labeled "letters" and the second identified as "drafts."

More practical were the pigeonhole cabinets that became common by the seventeenth century, into which you sorted your papers. In the mid-nineteenth century, a variety of letter and filing drawers appeared, but you generally had to fold the documents to fit the papers in. Edwin G. Seibels solved that problem in 1898 by creating the vertical file cabinet. The twentieth-century office—with its serried ranks of desks occupied by clerks and typewriters—generated a volume of paper unfathomable even a few decades earlier. The vertical file made it possible to easily locate (literally put your finger on) what you were looking for.

The idea of a computer file traces back to the original days of mainframe computers. Even the notion of organizing computer files into hierarchies is half a century old. Yet it was not until 1983, with the release of Apple's visionary but overpriced

Lisa computer (in some ways a precursor to the Macintosh), that the term "folder" was introduced. The idea of a computer "folder" was an analogy with the file folders ubiquitous in American offices.[4] Computer documents (files) could be clustered into computer folders—represented onscreen by rectangular icons, complete with a familiar protruding tab. Thirty years on, folders remain the coin of the realm for most computer users.

Undoubtedly, computer folders are invaluable for organizing documents or, for that matter, sound files, photographs, or videos. Not surprisingly, if you check out what many offices look like today, whether in corporations or personal space, you find the physical file cabinets of yesteryear gone. Increasingly, "physically native" documents are scanned rather than kept as paper copies.

But often out of sight, out of mind. Ask yourself, why do you leave some papers out on a desk or table rather than putting or throwing them away? Often because you want to stumble upon them again. Not necessarily use them right away, but be reminded of their existence by their tangible presence. Jan Gossaert's merchant could see at a glance (from the clumps of documents dangling at either side of his head) the contents of his correspondence.

If out of sight can be out of mind, aren't those papers in physical cabinets also out of mind? Perhaps, but not nearly as far off the radar screen as the files and folders on a computer. It is faster to thumb through tangible files in a drawer than to open dozens of computer files to find what you are looking for. Electronic search tools can be useful but sometimes take more time than they're worth.

Another challenge with digital files is that they lack some of the distinctive properties of paper. Electronic documents give you no tangible feel for their length or age. Yes, computer files will tell you how many bytes they occupy, along with when they were created and last modified. But these numbers and dates have none of the nuance of a two-inch-thick file filled with yellowed pages. Yes, you can use Microsoft's Track Changes to edit documents or insert comment bubbles. But do these electronic markings carry the same semantic force as doodles you left in the margins of the physical document or your inch-high scrawled complaint of "BORING!"?

Finally, there's the question of transferring access. If we up and leave with our computers (and digital storage devices) or refuse to divulge passwords to people with a right to know, the files and folders cease to exist for anyone else. Twice I have been saddled with this burden, and each time I would have given a tidy sum to have access to my office's historical records.

I think back to the gray file cabinet in my childhood dining room. Had the technology of the time been different, had the House Un-American Activities Committee emailed their letter to my father, had he later deleted the file, I never would have unearthed a vital clue to his past. Unlike a leatherbound copy of *Through the Looking Glass* (complete with John Tenniel's drawings), that file cabinet had no aesthetic appeal. It did, though, have a "Drink me" quality. Accessibility was simple: Pull open a physical drawer and look inside.

WHAT COUNTS AS PHYSICAL?

We keep using the word "physical," but what does it actually mean in the case of books?

EX LIBRIS: THE OWNERSHIP TEST

It used to be that if you owned something, you could physically touch it. This physicality was embodied in the Anglo-Saxon procedure for deeding land. Back in the days before Chaucer or *Sir Gawain and the Green Knight*, the written word had little legal standing. If you wanted to transfer land, the act was accomplished by having the current owner hand over a piece of sod from the property in question to the new owner.[5]

Over the centuries, some aspects of ownership have become less tangible. Now that monetary systems have gone off the gold standard, what do you own when you own a dollar bill? With stocks, what belongs to you when you buy 100 shares of Google, especially in light of constant price fluctuations? You may think you own the software on your computer, but actually you are licensing it from the company that made or distributed it. And as we've said, you don't actually own those eBooks for which you paid legal tender.

Kevin Kelly wrote in 2011 that in the future, eBooks won't be owned but rather accessed. Leaving aside the fact we don't actually own eBooks now, Kelly's point is that in the world he envisions emerging in the next decade or so, people won't be building book collections (even virtual ones) but rather will be accessing content through online streaming services, maybe through monthly or annual subscriptions. Think of movies on demand, where you grab what you want, when you want it.

But is Kelly's vision missing an important aspect of what it means to read a book? To own a book and for ownership to be bound up with the very notion of "bookness"?

We cannot put our own marks on books that are accessed rather than owned. I'm not talking here about annotations. Instead I mean the ways in which we lay down our scent, saying, "This is mine." Some of us do this with physical books by writing our names in the front, perhaps with the date we acquired the book or maybe the day we started reading it. There is also the long tradition of bookplates that you affix to the inside front cover, then adding your own name.

Traditional printed book plate.

Ex libris: from the library of. If it's in your library, you own it, at least for now.

If the idea of bookplates is foreign to you, I'll bet you're under thirty. To check them out, try browsing the shelves of a used bookstore. Look at older books in libraries (which used to insert plates rather than using their drab stamped replacements). Or visit the stationery area of your local bookshop.

THE AUTOGRAPH TEST

Did you ever collect autographs? Maybe you made it backstage after an opera and got your program signed by the diva. Perhaps you were at a political event or baseball game. Think about your high school yearbook or, if you are old enough, your autograph book at summer camp.

Another way of collecting autographs is to purchase them. While you can't snag John Hancock's signature on the Declaration of Independence (the National Archives in Washington actually lowers the document into a high-security vault each night), you can buy autographs of many famous personages. If you go on eBay, you will find signatures of one and the same John Hancock, some nicely framed, in a range of prices.

Autographs also commonly go in the fronts of books. My trip to BEA confirmed that physical books are still alive and well—and highly signable by authors. What happens to the physicality of autographs in the eBook world? Both authors and publishers have recognized the value of signatures in books and, not surprisingly, people have concocted digital solutions.

We now have digital autographs, courtesy of businesses bearing names like My-Write, AuthorGraph, and Autography.[6] With AuthorGraph, for instance, readers make online requests for signatures and receive a signed document back by email. In the case of Autography, the author signs a page that is placed inside the cover of an eBook, through cooperation with the publisher. The signed eBooks are then delivered to readers directly by Autography.

Why digital autographs? Because of needs felt by both authors and readers. At bookstore author events, if customers purchase eBooks, the author has nothing to sign. And as I confirmed at BEA, many readers continue to crave these signatures.

SENSING BOOKS

Andrew Piper, author of *Book Was There*, reminds us that "reading isn't only a matter of our brains; it's something that we do with our bodies."[7] Piper goes on to argue that since eBooks lack the tangible presence of print—no body of work you can hold in your hand, no physical pages to turn, no spatial sense of where you are in a book—reading in hardcopy is a very different experience from reading on-screen. Writing nearly a decade earlier (before the Kindle and tablet revolutions), book conservator Gary Frost asked whether the real difference between reading on screens versus in print was less about the quality of textual image and more about the ways our hands navigate in the respective formats.[8]

Reading is obviously predominantly about content. Yet when we read, we don't just decipher words on pages. We also sense them.

Taste. Sound. Smell. Sight. Touch. What does each of the five senses have to do with reading?

TASTE, SOUND, AND SMELL

Taste and books mix only when we are speaking metaphorically ("Betty has a taste for first editions"). Sound comes into play when we listen to audiobooks, though other than being free to replay the book or listen on your own schedule, the sensory experience isn't markedly distinct from attending a live reading.

Smell is different. Physical books have a smell to them, and with a surprising degree of frequency, readers comment on it. There's the musty smell of old books; the paper, glue, and binding smell of freshly minted ones. Kathleen Parker writes in the *Washington Post* that "I belong to that subgroup of individuals who smell a book before reading. (If you are not a book-smeller, we have nothing to discuss.)"[9]

Abe Books, which sells many used volumes, produced a video on findings from chemists at University College London as to why old books smell the way they do. The secret lies in the way the volumes' components (including the ink and chemicals used in their production) interact with light, moisture, and heat, causing the organic ingredients to decompose. The result, says the lead scientist in the study, is "a combination of grassy notes with a tang of acids and a hint of vanilla over an underlying mustiness."[10]

In my research with undergraduates in the United States, the smell of physical books sometimes came up. My favorite was this answer in response to the question of what the student liked least about reading on screens: "You feel disconnected from the work, and they do not smell of rich leather binding." Whether this respondent actually owned books with rich leather bindings, I cannot say. But clearly smell is part of booklore. It was also on the minds of university students in other countries, observed by my colleagues:

> "I have a passion for books (their smell and their touch is incomparable)."
> (Portugal)
> "I like to read on paper as I enjoy the smell of paper and ink." (Russia)

The importance of smelling books has not been lost on at least one entrepreneur. DuroSport Electronics offers an aerosol eBook enhancer called Smell of Books that can add "classic musty smell" or "new book smell" to your tablet or smartphone.[11] Your local carwash probably offers "new car smell" deodorizer. Why not the same principle for eReading devices?

SEEING BOOKS

Unless our vision is impaired, sight is a vital sense for experiencing the physicality of books. Much of our aesthetic appreciation of tangible books comes from the way they look. Book cover design is an art, as is bookbinding. Even those who foresee eBooks largely edging out print find room in their forecasting for "boutique" books, in which paper quality, binding, and overall aesthetics take their place in defining what a book is, alongside the written or graphic content.[12] Writing in the *New York Times*, Charles McGrath complains about the sameness of pages on eBooks: "You can't help missing the pleasing variety and design of books, the dust jackets, the illustrations, the layout of the page."[13] Shades of Michael Dirda's eBooks-as-motels.

Yet when it comes to books (or other printed material, for that matter), sight isn't just about aesthetics. It is also an important tool for finding our way in a text. Yes, there are chapters and page numbers. However, readers orient spatially in other ways as well. As one student in my studies put it, "What I like the most about hard copy is that my spatial memory works best so I remember material [by]...where it was." There is evidence in the psychological literature corroborating readers' perceptions that their memory of a printed text includes not just content but location in the larger work.[14]

On a more whimsical note, the role of sight in reading physical books forms the basis for a commercial experiment in Argentina. The publisher Eterna Cadenica released an anthology of current Latin American fiction under the title *El Libro Que No Puede Esperar* (*The Book That Can't Wait*). Once you open the shrink wrap, the book really can't wait, since the ink is designed to disappear after about two months. The object: to light a fire under well-meaning readers who start reading a book but tend to lose track of the undertaking partway through.[15]

Smell and sight are relevant senses when it comes to reading. But touch may well be the most important.

PLEASE TOUCH: THE HAPTICS OF WRITING AND READING

Literacy has two sides: what we produce (writing) and what we perceive (reading). Touch, more technically known as haptics, plays a role in both. While this book centers on reading, thinking about the connection between touch and writing helps us understand both the physical experience and the mind-set we bring to the perception side.

Writing is a tactile activity. For millennia, we have held some implement—a brush, a chisel, a stylus, a quill—enabling us to make marks on a surface. (Many among us still insist we compose best with a favorite brand or model of pen.) Since the commercial success of typewriters, starting in the 1890s, fingers tapping on keys became another way of generating text. Computer keyboards, tablets, and mobile phones follow in the same tradition.

It is hardly surprising that writers using keyboards can be fussy about the feel of their fingers on the letters and numbers. Manual typewriters "felt" different from electric typewriters (remember the IBM Selectric?) or computers. When tablets with their virtual keys came along, many users complained. "I'm not enamoured with typing on glass," wrote one contributor to a thread on the listserv of the Association of Internet Researchers. As he pointed out, "Many times I know instinctively I've made a typo by feel as opposed to seeing the letter appear," a feat possible on a computer but not a keyboardless tablet. Or maybe it is. Technologies are now emerging that will let users "feel" textures on their screens, using electrostatic charges. There are even designs for pop-up keys that retract when not in use.[16]

Writing by hand seems to have cognitive advantages over using a typewriter or computer, where we select symbols that are pre-formed. A study of first-graders found that children's spelling performance was better when they practiced writing the words themselves than when practice entailed typing on a computer or selecting the letters in the word from a group of plastic tiles.[17] In another study, preschool children who were asked to recognize letters after either producing them by hand or typing them performed better in the handwriting condition.[18] A third study asked adults to memorize characters that were adapted from the Bengali and Gujarati alphabets, either by writing the characters by hand or by finding (and then typing) them on a keyboard. The handwriting training yielded better long-term memory. What is more, brain scans indicated that when the subjects who did their training by hand were asked to remember the characters, the motor function area of the brain became active, which was not the case for those who trained on computers.[19]

Neuroimaging data also suggest that handwriting gives pre-literate children a leg up when it comes to reading acquisition. Research by Karin James and Laura Engelhardt found that when five-year-olds were asked to identify letters, those who had practiced printing out letters by hand had different brain activation patterns from those who had typed or traced the same letters.[20]

Besides formal research, we find personal accounts of pen-in-hand trumping fingers-on-keyboard. The poet Pablo Neruda wrote that "the typewriter separated me from a deeper intimacy with poetry, and my hand brought me closer to that intimacy again."[21] Dennis Baron observed that when the typewriter came into its own, "poets were the last to shift to typing, just as they've been slower to take up composing at the computer."[22] You don't need to be a full-blown poet to appreciate the importance of medium. Sixth-grader Nina Jenkins, who attended a technology-saturated private school, was described as "[unable to] remember the last time she wrote more than two paragraphs by hand." Yet when it came to writing poetry, she wanted pen and paper. "I guess you can say it's more special," she explained.[23]

More observations from writers about their writing medium: Author Iris Murdoch described a word processor as "a glass square which separates one from one's thoughts and gives them a premature air of completeness."[24] Anthropologist Joshua Bell offers a kindred argument for taking field notes by hand rather than using a computer:

My field notebooks have become artifacts of my time in Papua New Guinea not only through what I wrote in them, but also through their materiality—the smudge of dirt, the hurried writing. Looking at these notebooks, these traces are aide-mémoires of what else was happening around me at the time, and my own feelings, which I was too caught up in the moment to write down. These traces are never captured in the digital white of a computer screen and in my view are unique to the written page.[25]

What about haptics and reading?

Undoubtedly, reading is sometimes a hands-off affair. Think of those explanatory panels next to paintings at an art exhibition or the Magna Carta on display at the British Library. Yet much of the time when we read, our hands get involved. Even before development of the codex, you needed to carry scrolls to some flat surface and then unroll and reroll in order to read. We carry books from shelves in much the same way and then hold them in our hands or use our hands to keep them propped open to the right page. Speaking of pages, we turn them with our hands, maybe using our thumb to "fast-forward." When the iPad was designed, naturalistic page turning was one of its selling points.

Touch matters in reading. Here is how David Ulin, author of *The Lost Art of Reading*, describes the feelings he used to have browsing the shelves at Spring Street Books in lower Manhattan:

It's the same feeling I have sometimes in my own home, looking for a book on the shelves, tracing my finger along all those spines, all those reflections, all those stories that both add up and never add up, all the refraction and the residue.[26]

You don't need literary credentials to care about touch when you read. Here's what college students in my studies said they liked most about reading in hardcopy:

"I just like the feel of books."
"Can have it in my hands."
"Tactile interaction with reading material."
"Being able to physically handle the text myself, and see in paper how much I have read or have left to read."
"Turning the pages."

Or in the words of one German student in the COST Action study,

"Reading [books gives] you the feeling that the content is more tangible."

The weight of objects (which we often judge by feel) can influence how we judge their relative importance. Everyday language reflects the bias: We speak of "weighty" problems or of a person being "a lightweight." At MIT, Joshua Ackerman, a business professor, had subjects hold clipboards containing resumés of people presumably applying for a job. Some of the clipboards were physically heavier than others. Candidates whose resumés were on the heavier clipboards were rated more highly than those with resumés on the lighter-weight boards.[27]

Touch is obviously a critical component of reading for people using Braille. Those raised dots representing letters of the alphabet have an interesting backstory. While it was Louis Braille who in 1824 created the system currently used for making written text accessible to those with visual impairment, we have a French army captain to thank for the idea. In response to a demand from Napoleon to devise a system enabling soldiers to read messages in the dark without needing light, Charles Barbier de la Serre invented "night writing," a system based on twelve raised dots.[28]

As we saw earlier, following World War I, audio recordings were introduced—initially for soldiers whose vision had been damaged while fighting, but then extended to anyone with visual impairment. Over the years, tension has developed between those who want to read using Braille and those who prefer audio access to written work.[29]

The debate has both a cultural and cognitive side. Culturally, are you part of the blind community if you don't know Braille? As for cognition, some of those who study and teach visually impaired students suggest that individuals who access texts only auditorily are prone to be disorganized in their writing. In the words of Doug and Diana Brent, compositions written by such students sometimes look "as if all of their ideas are crammed into a container, shaken and thrown randomly onto a sheet of paper like dice onto a table."[30]

A number of developments have updated reading technology for the visually impaired. The Digital Accessible Information System (DAISY) enables users to search, bookmark, and otherwise navigate through audio text.[31] TactoBook translates the digital materials in eBooks into Braille, which then can be read on a portable Braille reader.[32] It will be interesting to see whether the affordance of touch helps make TactoBooks a success or whether the majority of visually impaired readers will end up accessing eBooks as audio files.

Returning to the haptic experience for those reading from traditional print books: Touch can also have emotional consequences. In the words of Kathleen Parker, "Part of the pleasure of a real, snail-mail letter isn't only the effort involved...but also the fact of the letter writer having touched the same piece of paper."[33] At auctions, people pay top dollar for apparel celebrities once wore, and the Catholic Church's tradition of revering holy relics (body parts, clothing, even pieces of the True Cross) traces back many centuries.

The importance of touch combined with sight goes a long way toward explaining the work habits of many professionals as they deal with written information. Abigail Sellen and Richard Harper's book *The Myth of the Paperless Office* used a medley of case studies illustrating why physical paper isn't going away anytime soon.[34]

Research by Sellen and her colleagues explored how a sampling of people (including a journalist, a lawyer, and doctoral students) made use of texts whose content they would be drawing upon in producing their own documents.[35] The researchers interviewed the participants but also observed each working at his or her own desk, complete with papers and computers. Because so many writing tasks these days involve a combination of hardcopy and screens (including consulting paper materials but writing on a computer), participants often spoke about comparative advantages of using printed versus electronic documents.

A number of the writers' comments related to visual-spatial issues:

"There are places where I remember what things look like and of course it looks different in a different edition. So I had to get my old book [i.e., the earlier edition] to find [the passage I was looking for]."

"If I'm scrolling around [on a computer screen] I never know where I am starting from....When you've got them onscreen they all look the same, it's just words."

But there were also considerations involving touch. As the researchers watched one participant at work, they observed him using his fingers to point simultaneously to particular spots on two separate paper documents, something many of us do when trying to pinpoint information we need to use in subsequent writing or conversation.

What about when we read for pleasure? Do haptics matter? Two researchers in Germany suggest they do.[36] Jin Gerlach and Peter Buxmann argue that one reason the readers they observed were not embracing eReaders for leisure reading was what the authors call "haptic dissonance"—a mismatch between reader beliefs about what it should "feel like" when you read a "book" and what it feels like to read an eBook. The study asked participants whether they perceived any haptic differences between reading in print versus on an eReader, and which medium they preferred.

A few caveats. Germany has a low rate of eBook adoption. And second, readers in the study were handed a Kindle and shown how to use it, though the participants probably had little or no prior experience with eReaders. Nonetheless, the readers' comments sound familiar:

"I miss the paper while turning the page."
"I miss the nice feel of paper while reading."
"While holding the book, I can't feel the progress I have made."

Haptics—touch—mattered for these readers, much as it does for people with more digital reading experience, such as my students in the United States.

MOVED TO TEARS: EMOTIONS AND PHYSICAL BOOKS

Another way of thinking about the physicality of books is to ask how they affect us emotionally. Emotionally? Isn't that a pretty touchy-feely kind of question? It is, and that's the whole point.

Seth Godin, who writes about technology and change, made a telling observation. While prophesying that "it's inconceivable to me that five years from now, paper is going to be the dominant form for books," he also admitted that "I get more pleasure knowing I sold a hardcover book than knowing I sold a Kindle book. There shouldn't be a difference, but there is."[37]

Religious texts or treasured works of literature are another case in point. At the Abu Dhabi International Book Fair in April 2013, there were lavishly decorated Korans bearing liberal amounts of gold leaf. Dar Al-Baroudi, whose specialty is fine-quality bound books, even brought its gold-blocking machine to demonstrate how such stunning works are created. As Dar Al-Baroudi's managing director said of an expensive edition of writings by Al-Mutanabbi, a famed Arabian poet, "You cannot do this with digital. This is art. You want to see. You want to touch."[38]

Psychologist Philip Zimbardo had this to say about the physical book in a session at the 2007 London Book Fair: "It's something you hold, near to your heart." Why link the book to the heart? Because, wrote Tania Kindersley, summarizing the event in the *Guardian*, the mind responds more viscerally and profoundly to words on paper, it gets an emotional charge, a deep connection with the characters, a yearning desire to know the ending that is not found on the screen.[39]

Yes, Zimbardo's (and Kindersley's) comments were made pre-Kindle. The question is whether those assessments still ring true.

Consider the books we inherit. In a National Public Radio piece, Amanda Katz asked, "What happens to our books when we die?" If we pass them down to future generations, we are transmitting not just boards, binding, and pages but a memory of who we were, especially if we have written—even our names—in the volumes.[40] That physicality of transmission, and the emotions potentially associated with it, remind me of an article on the sentiments that postage stamps can convey, beyond the words contained in the missives to which they're affixed. Placing a stamp upside down on a letter sent to a military person overseas can be used to say "I love you" (perhaps signaling "My world is upside down without you"). In other contexts, as during the Vietnam War, an upside-down flag stamp indicated a protest against the war. If those cards and letters were automatically metered, personal meaning would have been lost.[41]

Librarians and lovers of rare books understand the emotions that holding a precious volume in your hands can generate. Alice Schreyer, a librarian at the University of Chicago's Special Collections Research Center, speaks of the "emotional rapport you get with an era by holding a relic that is hundreds of years old.... Part of the history of a book is—who were the people who touched this book at every stage of its life."[42] Or, in the words of Julia Keller, a writer for the *Chicago Tribune*, "Google can't provide the goose bumps that go along with being in the presence of a 14th Century book."[43]

I'll vouch for these sentiments. Years back, when I was writing a book on the relationship between spoken, written, and signed language, my husband gave me a small paperback entitled *The Codex Nuttall*. (The codex is also known as Zouche-Nuttall: It once was owned by an Englishman named Lord Zouche but was brought to the attention of scholars by Zelia Nuttall.) A Dover publication, the book reproduced an early fourteenth-century book, written in the Central American language Mixtec, that recounted the exploits of 8-Deer Tiger Claw, who ruled in the eleventh century.[44]

To the untrained eye, the pages seemed to be filled with cartoon-like drawings of people and animals, with a few decorative ball-like objects thrown in. However, Mesoamerican scholarship has established that those decorative figures (including the balls) are actually a form of writing, as also proved to be the case with Mayan hieroglyphs.

I was enthralled by the work's strange beauty. So enthralled that on a trip to London, I set out to see the original, housed in the Museum of Mankind. After presenting my academic credentials and carefully explaining why seeing the original was critical to my work, I was ushered into the manuscript viewing area.

The codex was breathtaking—a work of art. The colors were dazzling, the writing surface far whiter than I had imagined. I could not believe I was actually cradling this treasure in my hands. When I returned home and looked again at the reproduction, it bore at best a family resemblance to what I had held and beheld. In the intervening years, libraries and museums around the world have rendered a vital service to scholars by making digital reproductions of old manuscripts and important objects of art available online. Yet however valuable these digital renderings are for the purpose of study, the originals are often magical.

Which brings us back to eBooks. In her piece on the London Book Fair, Tania Kindersley quotes "my friend the Man of Letters" as saying, "I wonder if anyone has ever cried while reading an e-book."[45] Since 2007, millions of readers have read yet more millions of eBooks. At conferences, I have cited Kindersley's quotation about not crying when reading an eBook. Generally I get nods and smiles from the audience. But when the quotation was tweeted out at one meeting, a Danish researcher responded that when reading for pleasure, she gets as emotionally involved when accessing an eBook as when reading print.

The person who had done the initial tweeting, a Swede, emailed me later that he also becomes emotionally involved when reading eBooks but that "there is some sort of emotional disconnect in relation to this content carrier [that is, a digital device]."[46] What did these Scandinavians mean by "emotional involvement"? Hard to say. A distinction we might think about is between becoming engrossed in a plot (which could happen on any reading platform) and being emotionally transported. Being moved by the death of the heroine. Unable to sleep because of the unbearable suspense in a thriller or horror story.

I don't know of any "tears" or "terror" research, comparing the responses of, say, readers of Daphne du Maurier's *Rebecca* or Ira Levin's *Rosemary's Baby* in hardcopy versus on an eReader. I can't even prove that anyone cries anymore when reading books that brought tears to the eyes of previous generations, or loses sleep over a book (though I surely hope so). My wager is that physical books more easily afford us a freedom—freedom from other distractions, space to ponder the hero's plight, time to emote (even catch our breath) before moving on—than do tablets or mobile phones.

What about eReaders without active internet connections? Because they are standalone devices that don't ring or beep (like phones) or let us toggle elsewhere (like tablets), they may turn out to be more like print. It would be useful to do a real study.

YOU MAKE YOUR NOTES AND I'LL MAKE MINE

If physical books can generate emotional connections, they also can reinforce a sense of privacy. Years ago, if you wanted to order a sex manual, the ads promised it would arrive in "a plain brown paper wrapper," protecting you from the prying eyes of the mailman or your spouse.

Before the coming of Amazon's and Google's all-seeing eyes, and before computerized purchase records at bookstores, what books we chose to read were largely our own business. D. T. Max raised an interesting point of American legal practice in his discussion of books and the Bill Clinton presidential impeachment hearings. Independent counsel Kenneth Starr attempted to subpoena Monica Lewinsky's personal account from Kramerbooks, a well-frequented Washington independent bookstore. Starr's goal was to get a list of the titles Lewinsky had given to Clinton. The federal court said no, "pointing out that the confidentiality of the books we buy is protected by a higher standard than that of ordinary purchases."[47]

American libraries have often taken similar positions when the government has demanded to know what books particular patrons have checked out. Those of us who lived through the end of the Cold War and the heat of protests against the war in Vietnam recall the FBI's interest in the activities (and reading habits) of scores of college students, resulting in demands for lists of books they had checked out from the library. Honorably, my own university addressed this challenge by promptly expunging borrowing records from its system the moment books were returned.

What privacy do today's readers have? Given the ubiquity of credit cards, few of us think twice when we swipe our plastic at the physical or virtual register. For print books, at least we retain the option of using cash in a face-to-face transaction (assuming we have the time and shoe leather to track down what we are looking for in a brick-and-mortar store). With eBooks, all privacy bets are off. Someone knows everything you have bought. Amazon and its competitors also have a pretty good sense of what you've read, since they can trace each page you access. And if you take advantage of such handy features as highlighting, underlining, and jotting notes, every mark you make is likely in their database.

Do we care if our personal annotations are available to others? We've talked about how physical books (including the marks we make in them) remind us of our individual journeys—who we used to be, what we used to think. When we sell books or give them away, or when our heirs inherit them, others are able to glimpse our personal journeys, but these are individual transactions, not public displays.

I think of the annotations—or the pressed flowers or ticket stubs—that have found their way into physical books I own. I may be able to get a digital book autographed, but is there a satisfying way of storing that stub from a performance of *King Lear* at the Globe? And do I really want the digital world at large to have access to my literally sophomoric comments on Chomsky's *Aspects of the Theory of Syntax*, now that I have thought so much more about linguistic theory in the intervening decades?

In the last chapter, we heard Judith Shulevitz declare, "You read your book and I'll read mine."[48] Except in special circumstances, such as letting Samuel Coleridge mark up books lent by friends, here is my working principle: You make your notes, and I'll make mine.

Does this principle make me an antisocial reader? No. It's that as a university teacher, I believe it is critical that students approach texts with fresh eyes, deciding for themselves what they deem worthy of comment—even if they're wrong. Ready-made notes from others could score you more points on exams, but they do little to feed your intellect.

READING ON CRUISE CONTROL

What else can physical books do that eBooks can't (or at least seem to do less well)? They allow us to slow down when we read. No one is making us zip along without stopping when reading on a screen, but since the medium was designed for rapid access (especially of the searching and skimming variety), readers tend to follow suit.

Think about driving along a highway that runs through the mountains. One option is to head straight for your destination. A second is to slow down when you see those signs for scenic overlooks, pull off the main road, and enjoy the natural surroundings. eReading is more like driving on cruise control; print invites stopping.

David Mikics puts the distinction between types of reading this way: "E-books ... promote forward motion rather than slow, considered reading." By contrast, "a print book is designed to aid slow reading, by making it easy for you to look back at what you've already read."[49] Anne Mangen, a professor of reading at the University of Stavanger in Norway, argues that reading on the two platforms offers different kinds of mental orientation. With screens, there isn't a sense of the wholeness of the work, since we only encounter its parts piecemeal. By contrast, says Mangen, because the text on a printed page doesn't move, it offers a kind of tranquility. Print also provides the mental space to slow down and focus on what you are reading. In

Mangen's words, "Learning requires time and mental exertion and the new media do not provide for that."[50]

For another take on the speed issue, consider this 2002 Canadian study. Two university librarians wanted to gauge how undergraduates approached research assignments in terms of the resources they chose: print or online. The researchers had nearly 400 students answer questions about the types of sources they used—print books, print journals, or online materials of any sort—as well as which type they went to first.

Even in the early 2000s (when fewer books and journals were available digitally, internet search engines were far less sophisticated, and networks were slower and less reliable), there was substantial use of electronic sources. Why go for print instead of screens? It turned out that the more intellectually demanding the assignment, the more students relied on hardcopy:

> The use of print books was typically associated with the production of high-quality work, whereas use of online sources was invariably associated with the need to just get things done quickly and easily.[51]

Students said they preferred reading print books if they were going to tackle substantial undertakings. Online materials were fine for grabbing specific pieces of information but not for in-depth study that required comparing across sources and arguments. Print gave a sense of the whole, while online counterparts tended to be read in a more fragmented way.

Thomas Mann, a reference librarian at the Library of Congress in Washington, has worried about the consequences of replacing books with digital sources. He suggests that the move toward wholesale digitization, where electronic files replace (rather than complement) books, is misguided because it assumes that libraries are essentially in the information business, not the book business. Echoing the perception of students in the Canadian study, Mann argues that "if we make only electronic forms available, *we will be undercutting students' ability to understand lengthy works as connected wholes.*"[52]

Screens hasten us along. Print invites us to linger.

Before continuing, I owe it to my digiphile friends and colleagues to remind you that we each have our own reading practices and preferences, and that anyone is capable of lingering over eText and skimming print. My point is that, all things considered, the two media intrinsically invite opposite approaches.

WHAT IF PHYSICAL LONG-FORM VANISHED?

In a nutshell—and to generalize—print

- Enables us to stumble upon works, reminding us of things we've read before or have meant to read
- Gives us a tangible sense of ownership (of both the physical book and its contents)
- Offers a sensory experience—of smell, of sight, of touch
- Is conducive to generating emotional engagement
- Affords us personal space for recording responses to what we read (though, granted, mobile reading affords a different sort of privacy, as for erotica)
- Encourages us to slow down when we are reading, clearing time for understanding or reflection

Since the rise of reading on digital platforms, both writers and scholars (especially those whose expertise involves language or literature) have pondered what a post-print world might look like. Some of the early musings include Sven Birkerts' *The Gutenberg Elegies*, Geoff Nunberg's *The Future of the Book*, William Gass' "In Defense of the Book," and D. T. Max's "The Electronic Book."[53] While Birkerts, Gass, and Max largely offered cautionary tales, Nunberg's collection of essays had a more positive take on the move from print to screens. With the growing profusion of digital materials over the past decade, the "what is the future of print" oeuvre has vastly multiplied.

The main purpose of this book is to move beyond arguments of nostalgia and habit to figuring out what it is about print and digital platforms that leads us to read on them in particular ways. But another goal is to understand the potential consequences of driving reading from print to screens. As we have seen, one effect seems to be privileging the search for data or information over reading for continuity of argument and reflection. In the process, we steer readers (and authors) away from long-form writing to shorter pieces. And we replace the notion of owned, tangible documents with ephemeral access.

What happens when we gravitate toward data and short-form, toward accessed rather than owned, as reading destinations? The question propels us to think on a much broader plane than individual reading choices. It drives us to think about culture.

Consider Max's concern: "What is a culture if the information that forms it never stands still?"[54] You don't have to believe in an eternal canon of great books that every educated citizen should read (such lists rightly change over time) to know that culture entails passing from one generation to the next a society's sense of practices important for living. These may involve the language or dialect we speak, taste in architectural style, food customs, social manners, religious beliefs, and, yes, written works.

Haiku comes in short-form, but most of what constitutes the written heritage of cultures does not—whether we are talking about the *Mahabharata* or *Macbeth*, writings of Aristotle or those of James Joyce. SparkNotes don't substitute for the works themselves. And as for the full-length versions, unless you are reading them the same way you would the latest James Patterson thriller, you might not want to try it on your mobile phone.

THE HUMANITIES CRISIS AND EREADING

There's a flurry of discussion these days about the future of the humanities. Look at graduate degrees granted in the United States. The proportion of master's degrees in the humanities dropped from 15 percent in 1970–1971 to 8 percent in 2009–2010. During the same period, humanities doctoral degrees slipped from 7 percent to 5 percent.[55] A recent report from Harvard documented a decline in undergraduate concentrations (majors) in the humanities—from 36 percent of all Radcliffe and Harvard upper-class students in 1953–1954 to 20 percent in 2011–2012.[56]

Playing the numbers game to measure interest in a subject area can be tricky. After the American Academy of Arts & Sciences issued a report in late spring 2013 on the state of the humanities and social sciences,[57] a bevy of responses popped up, some defending the concerns of the report but others suggesting the Jeremiahs were playing fast and loose with statistics.[58] What is more, what counted as the humanities forty or fifty years ago doesn't cleanly line up with disciplines that might be included today, plus there is much variation from school to school in what students choose to study.

We do know that if you ask undergraduates what they want to get out of college, responses have shifted dramatically over time. UCLA's Higher Education Research Institute has been surveying college freshmen in America since the 1960s, and the data provide a window on students' changing values. Presented in 1967 with a list of possible "life goals," 83 percent of incoming freshman said "developing a meaningful philosophy of life" was important to them. By 1987, that number had dropped to 39 percent. By contrast, while in 1970 only 39 percent of respondents said "being very well-off financially" was a life goal, that number rose to 76 percent by 1987.[59]

Students' reasons for attending college continue to trend toward the pragmatic. In the 2011 UCLA survey, 50 percent of freshman said a very important reason for going to college was "to make me a more cultured person" and 72 percent indicated that college was very important "to gain a general education and appreciation of ideas." However, topping the list of reasons in 2011 at 86 percent was "to be able to get a better job" (up from 70 percent in 2006).[60]

Understandably, downturns in the economy can drive students—and school administrators—to seek ways of connecting higher education with future employment. Given continual rises in tuition, along with the debt so many students face after graduation, we can hardly blame them. But the state of Florida crossed the line when Governor Rick Scott's task force on higher education reform recommended in 2012 that students enrolled in majors for which there wasn't an immediate job payoff ("non-strategic" majors) should be charged higher tuition rates than those selecting job-oriented areas of concentration. Needless to say, the humanities are generally deemed "non-strategic."[61]

There is another factor contributing to this gravitation away from the humanities. And that is the move away from reading long, connected, complex texts in favor of short excerpts and destinations that focus more on search rather than contemplation. As we progressively redefine "society" to mean "information society," as we move cultural artifacts (written or visual) online, as we shift our notion of knowledge to what we can look up, we pursue a path that may lead us to reworking the cultural glue that has historically bound people together.

Can culture reside overwhelmingly online? That is hardly a question to be answered in a couple of paragraphs. In fact, it may take further maturation of the digital world before we even have the concepts needed to respond meaningfully. I do, however, have some premonitions. Let me share an example.

Anyone who teaches today understands the challenge of holding students' attention when the room is filled with mobile phones and laptops or tablets. Some of us declare our classrooms "personal technology-free zones," which seems oddly counterintuitive when we think about how much money our institutions invested to create first wired and now wireless campuses. Others permit students to use their devices for relevant educational purposes, though students themselves will tell you how hard it is to resist the temptation to check Facebook or respond to a text message.

A couple of years ago, I was teaching an undergraduate course on technology, language, and culture. One day in class discussion, the issue came up of whether social networking was actually making us feel less connected rather than more so. In framing my response, I decided to introduce David Riesman's notion of inner-directed versus other-directed societies, which he had laid out more than half a century ago in *The Lonely Crowd*.[62] I started by writing Riesman's name on the board.

I admit to not being the world's most expert on-the-fly speller, particularly when it comes to names. Was it *R-i-e* or *R-e-i*? Was there one *n* at the end or were there two? I correctly chose *R-i-e* but mistakenly put in two *n*'s. As I wrote, I told my students we could confirm the spelling later. What I wanted us to focus on was Riesman's sociological distinction.

Halfway through my explanation, a hand shot up: "Professor, there's one *n*, not two." In her other hand, the student was grasping her mobile phone, whose use was banned in my classroom. Whether the student meant well or was showing off, I didn't care. What mattered was that she demonstrated a bigger appetite for data than for understanding. In hindsight, I'm warmed, in a bittersweet kind of way, by an incident Sherry Turkle relates of a 14-year-old girl trying to talk with her device-happy father during dinner: "Dad, stop Googling. I don't care about the right answer. I want to talk to you."[63]

Classroom rules aside, could I really blame my mobile-phone-wielding student? Lower and higher education alike have been beating the digital technology drum louder and louder each year. We train students how to do searches, how to access readings online. We assign shorter and shorter texts in the hope that students will actually read them. And we accept the fact that many of our students will be renting digital texts that disappear at the end of the term.

But, you say, couldn't students later access those texts online, should they need them? Probably yes, though what's the likelihood they ever will?

A culture lived predominantly online has the danger of becoming a culture out of sight and out of mind. The consequences of rejecting print in favor of digital screens are far greater than whether we will miss the smell and feel of paper.

Culture is an abstract concept, admittedly hard to wrap our heads around. (We'll have more to say about culture in a later chapter.) More concrete is the question of how our brains process what we read in hardcopy versus onscreen—the topic we turn to next.

8 | Your Brain on Hyper Reading

> We know...the brain is...very adaptable but at the same
> time there are built-in fundamental limits to the kind of
> information the brain can process...it may be that the
> ability to really do multiple things at once might be one
> of those built-in limits.
>
> —*Russell Poldrack*

"This is your brain on Jane Austen."

The SuperShuttle was due in a few minutes, taking me back to the San Francisco airport. As I waited at the Stanford Guest House, nestled just above the university on the Stanford Linear Accelerator Campus, I wandered over to the small lounge that housed a few chairs and a computer sporting Stanford's homepage. A headline about Jane Austen caught my eye.[1]

The story featured work by Natalie Phillips, a specialist in eighteenth-century English literature, who had become intrigued with what neuroscience could tell us about how we read literary texts. Teaming up with the Stanford Center for Cognitive and Neuro-biological Imagining, she conducted studies demonstrating that our brains function differently when we leisurely skim a book by Austen than when we carefully reading the same novel. Phillips' work prompted me to explore what we could learn from reading experts, cognitive psychologists, and neuropsychologists about how the brain reads.[2]

I had been at the Stanford Center for Advanced Study in the Behavioral Sciences, working on this book. There was a lingering buzz about Nicholas Carr's 2008 article "Is Google Making Us Stupid?" and his subsequent book *The Shallows: What the Internet Is Doing to Our Brains*.[3] Ambient questions about multitasking—is it really possible?—filled the air. Particularly troubling was the growing disconnect between research confirming the dangers of using a mobile phone while driving and car manufacturers' ever more ingenious tools for, yes, using your phone while driving.

Connecting the dots between the driving problem and Carr's concerns was easy. If your mind is trying to focus on multiple activities, does it function as well as when undertaking those tasks *seriatim*? Since the internet lures us into multitasking (called "dual tasking" in the psychological literature), it takes discipline to stay on track when using a digital technology connected to the internet. If we are reading on a screen, we risk being distracted by the sites and people out there.

The siren call of internet distractions comes with an extra twist. Each time we hear our mobile phone or email client ping to say we have a message waiting, our brain delivers a squirt of dopamine, an addictive neurotransmitter that keeps us returning for more. Which would you prefer: staying glued to Plato's *Apology* or having a shot of dopamine?

Can we really answer email, watch Netflix, and draft a complicated report at the same time? Might it turn out that today's tech-saturated adolescents actually can successfully juggle tasks that older generations can't?

The prospects for an affirmative answer largely hinge on how plastic the brain is. We have known for over a half a century that physical brain development doesn't have to stop when we become adults. Instead, areas of the brain can change their size, depending on how we use them.[4] Take the famous case of London taxi drivers. The streets of London are an intricate maze. If you want a taxi license, you must demonstrate having "the knowledge" (as it's known) of the city's layout. Brain researchers from University College London have shown that the posterior hippocampus (which plays an important role in spatial navigation) is physically larger in highly experienced London taxi drivers than in new drivers or a control group.[5]

Or consider musicians. Regardless of whether you are right- or left-handed, if you play a stringed instrument like the violin, cello, or guitar, you do the fingering with your left hand. The hard work is performed by four fingers (the thumb largely serves as an anchor). Research has demonstrated that the cortical area representing the fingers of the left hand is larger among string players than among control subjects, with the effect being smallest for the thumb.[6]

If experienced taxi drivers and string players can grow their brains through practice, why not multitaskers? Before seeing what the research says, let's get straight on some terminology.

Philosophers have long talked about the relationship between mind and body. In Descartes' time, knowledge of how the "wetware" under our skulls functioned was paltry. Obviously our brains are part of our bodies, but the only evidence we could adduce of what was going on up there was cognitive acts such as memory or mental analysis. When philosophers talk about "mind," they mean the products of our brains.

By the late nineteenth century, we had made some inroads into how the brain enables feats of mind. We learned, for instance, that particular parts of the brain control specific language functions. Paul Broca and Carl Wernicke studied patients whose language deficits resulted from trauma to the head, often during war. (Seeing where the bullet went in helped enormously in drawing connections between brain location and language deficits.) Throughout the twentieth century, our understanding of the brain continued to expand, thanks largely to development of neuroimaging techniques that allowed us to see (without making a hole in someone's head) which parts of the brain were active during mental activities such as reading nonsense words or doing math problems.

Modern neuroimaging tools include PET (positron emission tomography), fMRI (functional magnetic resonance imaging), and MEG (magnetoencephalography). In each case, the level of the subject's activity in different parts of the brain is monitored, typically while performing a mental task. PET scans do this by measuring glucose metabolism, and require use of radioactive isotopes. Both PET scans and fMRI scans measure shifts in blood flow. MEG works by tracking magnetic activity. With PET and fMRI scans, testing is done by moving the subject's entire body into the scanner. In the case of MEG imaging, subjects are seated and insert the tops of their heads into the device, with the scanner looking something like an elaborate hair dryer from a traditional women's beauty salon.[7]

The mental workings of the brain are now studied in two allied fields: cognitive psychology and neuroscience. What is the difference? Simplistically, cognitive psychology studies the mental functioning of people (say, when you ask them to remember a list of words). Neuroscience looks either at what the brain is physically doing during those cognitive tasks or, as with London taxi drivers or string players, how the brain changes as a result of practice. It is the same brain at work in cognitive and neuroimaging studies, regardless of how we measure its activity.

READING AND THE BRAIN

Chimpanzees don't read. Humans do. Considering that we share 96 percent of our DNA with the great apes,[8] something must have happened when our ancestors made their way out of the trees.

Maryanne Wolf explains that the human brain was not built for reading. Instead, through a complex process of patching together the cognitive tools humans did possess, we developed the ability to create symbols we could etch on stone, in wax, or in clay, leaving a durable record for others to decode. Just how this neurological wizardry actually took place is anyone's guess, but happen it did.

Reading isn't done in a vacuum. Since the neural tools for reading are cobbled together from structures designed for other purposes, it is not surprising that reading activates areas related to what the text is about. Say you are reading a scene in a novel in which the hero is running to escape the villain. As you read, the motor area of your brain lights up—even though you're curled up in a chair, not moving. Research done at Washington University in St. Louis, using neuroimaging, concluded that "readers understand a story by simulating the events in the story world and updating their simulation when features of that world change."[9] The link between reading and motor activity extends to clinical areas as well. Researchers have long recognized that children diagnosed with dyslexia also tend to have difficulty with physical coordination.[10] In fact, therapies for dyslexics often include practicing motor skills. The roots of this linkage may be traceable to our genetic makeup. It turns out that the same genes responsible for dyslexia also control traits such as an awkward gait.[11]

WHAT AND HOW WE READ

In 2006, a professor of English at the University of Minnesota wrote an article with the improbable title "Cognitive Science and the History of Reading."[12] Why improbable? The job of people in literature used to be making sense of what we read, not asking how we do it. But of late, disciplines have been adding "cognitive" to their kit bag. We now have the International Cognitive Linguistics Association, along with cognitive cultural studies.[13] Why not the psychology of literature?[14]

How reading literature (especially fiction) affects our brains is intriguing many researchers. Besides motor area activity associated with action stories, there's evidence that the olfactory area of the cortex lights up when you see words like "perfume" or "coffee," and that when you read metaphors involving texture such as "He had leathery hands," the sensory cortex is activated.[15] There is even evidence that when reading about the lives of others (real or imagined), the brain neurologically registers our attempts to figure out what characters think and feel, and to identify with them. Psychologist Raymond Mar and his colleagues argue that avid fiction readers are better at understanding (and empathizing with) others in real life than those reading little or no fiction.[16] (In the opening paragraphs of this book, we saw that reading serious fiction seems to make you more empathic and socially perceptive than reading light fiction.)[17]

We can also chart brain differences reflecting mode of reading. Using cognitive testing methods, Paul van den Brock's research group compared results from college students reading a text for study purposes or for entertainment. Students reading in study mode were better at making inferences, generating paraphrases, and remembering the text's content.[18]

What happens when you switch from cognitive tests to neuroimaging? The question circles us back to Natalie Phillips' work.

Using an fMRI scanner, Phillips and her colleagues had subjects read a chapter of Jane Austen's novel *Mansfield Park*, with words projected onto a mirror inside the scanner. At various points during the experiment, subjects (local PhD students in literature) were instructed either to read for enjoyment or to read in study mode (known in the field as "close reading"). Close reading generated increased blood flow in areas of the brain responsible for executive functions, along with notable brain activity in areas associated with touch and movement.

AND THE INTERNET BEGAT HYPER READING

Sometimes we read "on the prowl," skimming or scanning to get the gist of things or grab specific information. Other times our reading is continuous. We might read continuously for entertainment (think of two Scott Turow thrillers for the long-haul flight from New York to Tokyo). We also might do continuous intensive reading (like those doctoral candidates doing close reading in Phillips' study). The internet entices us to skew the balance away from continuous reading, much less close reading, and toward reading on the prowl.

It is one thing to observe shifts in the balance between reading modes. It's another to wager that the internet and tools we use for navigating it are redefining what it means to read. But that is precisely the possibility worrying a growing number of writers and researchers.

YOUR BRAIN (AND SOUL) ON THE INTERNET

When Nicholas Carr asked whether Google was making us stupid, he wasn't fingering Sergey Brin and Larry Page's company as much as asking how digital communication technologies affect the ways we think and act. Carr argued that explosive use of computer searching, coupled with multitasking (not to mention video gaming and social networking), were making us shallower people.

Critics were quick to pounce. The *Atlantic* ran a counter-piece called "Get Smarter," arguing the internet actually upped our brain power. Writing in the *New York Times*, psychologist Steven Pinker, while not identifying Carr by name, accused him of stirring up a pointless moral panic. Carr retorted that the facts were on his side.[19] A few days later, Steven Johnson, author of *Everything Bad Is Good for You* (a book about the mental virtues of contemporary popular culture), conceded he is "slightly less focused" when virtually dashing about on email, Twitter, or the blogosphere. But then Johnson continued:

> Frankly, most of what we do during the day doesn't require our full powers of concentration.... We are marginally less focused, and exponentially more connected. That's a bargain all of us should be happy to make.[20]

Happy? I'm not. "Marginally less focused" when? It is bad enough that students are increasingly too busy tweeting to hear what professors are saying in class. Besides faculty concerns about a decline in civility (and maybe bruised egos), the main damage is typically points lost on an exam. What about when the stakes are higher?

Consider these scary findings from a study of operating room personnel during cardiopulmonary bypass surgery. The staff in question were perfusionists, the ones who operate the heart-lung machine that keeps you alive during the operation. Of 439 perfusionists who responded to a 2010 survey, 56 percent admitted using their mobile phones during surgery, while 49 percent confessed to texting. Ironically, 78 percent said they were concerned that perfusionists who used their phones during surgery might jeopardize patients' well-being.[21] If you were having bypass surgery, how would you feel knowing the person keeping your heart and lungs functioning was also busy ordering pizza?

Nicholas Carr is hardly alone in his concerns about the human impact of digital communication technologies. Another outspoken voice is that of Susan Greenfield, a professor of pharmacology at the University of Oxford. Greenfield asks, "Does the mind have a future?"[22] Her answer: no, not if we keep using these technologies so extensively. Greenfield contends that screen culture is shortening our attention span, making us more literal-minded, and reducing opportunities to engage with abstract content. She is also worried that so many fundamental aspects of human communication—eye contact, body language, tone, timbre, and bodily contact—are missing from interactions via online social networking.

Greenfield acknowledges that at least one technology might result in selective cognitive gains. Research suggests that playing video games can have positive mental outcomes in visual-spatial representation (including short-term memory thereof) and maybe in our ability to track multiple objects simultaneously (a form of multitasking).[23] Linguist James Gee argues that if designed and used productively, video games have the potential to foster literacy and learning more generally.[24]

That said, are there cognitive downsides? Take off the table whether violent games lead to aggressive behavior and sexism. Our question is what effects video games (along with other visual media) may be having on higher-level cognition. In the words of psychologist Patricia Greenfield,

> Although the visual capabilities of television, video games, and the Internet may develop impressive visual intelligence, the cost seems to be deep processing: mindful knowledge acquisition, inductive analysis, critical thinking, imagination, and reflection.[25]

Susan Greenfield worries about the same cognitive conundrum: While video games may enhance speed of mental processing, they do little for cognitive depth.

Today's concerns about effects of the internet (and its hardware companions) extend to social and personal well-being. Sherry Turkle's book *Alone Together* struck a collective nerve when she wrote that building virtual personae, spending time with robotic pets rather than people, and replacing face-to-face communication with social networks are leading us to care more about our technologies than about one another.[26]

Other research confirms Turkle's fears. A study at the University of Essex found the mere presence of a mobile phone in the social space where two people were talking led subjects to judge the conversation less close, to assess the relationship as being of lower quality, and to have less empathy for the other person than when researchers instead placed a pocket notebook on the same table. The mobile phone wasn't turned on, wasn't vibrating, wasn't beeping. Its sheer physical presence reminded subjects that someone or something else might be waiting to grab their attention. Comparable results have been reported in a subsequent study of similar design.[27]

A spate of books have been probing the same concerns. One of the most eloquent, William Powers' *Hamlet's BlackBerry*, crafts historical vignettes to suggest that if in the past people could overcome the pressures of too much informational or social "noise," we can as well. A journalist, Powers relies upon the internet. However, he reached the point of feeling overwhelmed by too much connectivity. His solution was to move his family to Cape Cod (within reach of Boston, but psychologically distanced from the bustle) and shut off the computers, video games, and even smartphones from Friday evening through Sunday night.[28]

Writers have been particularly vocal about the need to disconnect in order to focus. Cory Doctorow describes his writing practice: Set a modest goal for each day, but while you are writing, "get the world to go away." It's fine to have electronic communication when you really need it, but "leaving your IM running is like sitting down to work after hanging a giant 'DISTRACT ME' sign over your desk."[29] Other authors rely on a software application called Freedom, which accomplishes what users lack the willpower to do themselves: turning off the internet connection.[30] Pico Iyer has a different strategy. Iyer owns no mobile phone, doesn't use Facebook or Twitter, and tries to avoid going online until he has finished writing for the day.[31]

Iyer cherishes quiet, doing nothing ("the only time when I can see what I should be doing the rest of the time"). But even just slowing down, pausing between bursts of activity, can have salutary effects. Researchers at the University of California, San Francisco, found that if you let rats pause while exploring a new physical space, they do better at remembering where they have been than if you keep them barreling ahead.[32]

Rats don't read—but people do. It turns out that even the pauses we make when reading contribute to our comprehension. Scholars at the University of Reading explored how both reading speed and the scrolling patterns subjects used when reading on a computer screen affected their ability to answer questions about the text. Those who did best on comprehension tests were the ones who read short chunks of stationary text at a time (pausing to absorb what they were reading) before scrolling down to the next chunk. Reading while scrolling led to worse comprehension.[33]

ATTENDING TO READING

How much attention do we pay to what we are reading? We've already seen Jakob Nielsen's data on reading web pages (he says we don't actually read them, but only browse selectively). We also mentioned the University College London study analyzing how academics read on digital screens. In sync with Nielsen's findings, the UCL researchers described these academics' behavior as not reading but "power browsing."[34]

Other studies report similar findings. Using log reports from libraries offering access to online journals, scholars from UCL and the University of Tennessee examined the viewing habits of users who downloaded full-text versions of articles. How long did they look at each article? An average of 106 seconds.[35]

The reading medium contributes to how much time we spend with text. Ziming Liu at San Jose State University compared reading behavior onscreen versus in hardcopy. Study participants (graduate students and working professionals) devoted more time to browsing and scanning, and to reading selectively, when working onscreen than when reading print. Subjects also reported that their onscreen reading was less in-depth than with hardcopy.[36]

Even writers who embrace digital media are worried about the effects of eReading on people's willingness to engage with involved ideas. German fiction writer Katharina Hacker is concerned that authors' "writing and thinking is being marginalized" because onscreen readers have trouble concentrating on long, complex texts.[37]

How we read on digital devices is doubtless influenced by the amount of content relentlessly hurled at us. Much like the Red Queen's warning to Alice that "it takes all the running you can do, to keep in the same place," it seems to be taking all our "power browsing" capacity to keep up with the onslaught of digital messages. A study commissioned by Time Inc., called "A Biometric Day in the Life," found that subjects in their twenties switched media sources 27 times an hour—barely two minutes per landing.[38] While advertisers may take such data as a clarion call to ramp up the graphics if they want to hold eyeballs, those of us losing sleep over the diminishing attention spans of digital natives become increasingly uneasy.

There's a name for this kind of mental flitting: hyper attention. And those who engage in hyper attention are primed and ready to be hyper readers.

HYPER ATTENTION AND HYPER READING

How long is your attention span? A 2008 study commissioned in the UK by Lloyds TSB Insurance concluded it averages 5 minutes and 7 seconds—less than half the amount reported ten years earlier.[39] Why does an insurance company care about attention? Think of all those claims for water damage from bathtubs left to overflow or fires caused by pans forgotten on the stove. On the other side of the Atlantic,

Yale graphic design critic Jessica Helfand uses the term "short attention span theater" to describe the younger generation's demand for instant access to streaming video. Helfand wonders to what extent young people are "actually assimilating anything."[40] To accommodate shrinking attention spans, even commercials are getting shorter, now averaging 15 seconds, down from an earlier 30 (in turn retreating from an entire minute, years before).[41]

Does reading stand a chance in a short-attention-span world?

Enter Katherine Hayles, professor of literature. Hayles is a pragmatist, negotiating her way in a world bookended by Cassandras and Pollyannas. While concerned about the growing resistance of college students to reading entire books, she strives to understand where students "live" these days and find ways of capitalizing upon the media-nurtured strengths they possess.

Hayles contrasts the deep attention required for deep reading with "hyper attention." (As we explained earlier, deep reading relies on "inferential and deductive reasoning, analogical skills, critical analysis, reflection, and insight.")[42] While deep attention entails prolonged concentration and ability to shut out external distractors, hyper attention involves rapid task switching, desire for a high level of stimulation, and a low threshold for boredom.[43]

Granted, hyper attention might show up in anyone or probably at any point in history. Yet the digital media revolution has multiplied opportunities for young people now coming of age. Logically, a generation characterized by hyper attention can be expected to carry over these habits of mind when it comes to reading.

The notion of hyper reading was introduced in the late 1990s by James Sosnoski to characterize "reader-directed, screen-based, computer-assisted reading" that includes "searching, skimming, hyperlinking, and extracting fragments from longer texts."[44] In her own analysis, Hayles describes hyper reading as

a strategic response to an information-intensive environment, aiming to conserve attention by quickly identifying relevant information, so that only relatively few portions of a given text are actually read.[45]

That is, she sees it as an efficient strategy for coping with a media-rich world, not a default to laziness. The contrast between deep attention (or deep reading) and hyper attention (or hyper reading) raises two critical questions. The first is cultural; the second is cognitive.

Modern education, especially higher education, is grounded on the assumption that taking your time—with thinking, with reading—is essential for intellectual development. Today's university faculty (particularly the ones who have been around for a while, and significantly in the humanities) are steeped in these assumptions. Frustration arises on both sides when students fail to meet these expectations and even question their contemporary relevance.

What happens to our minds if deep attention and deep reading become the preserve of only a handful of people? Eric Schmidt, then CEO of Google, lamented that with the proliferation of digital devices, "you spend less time reading all forms of literature, books, [and] magazines.... That probably has an effect on cognition, probably has an effect on reading."[46] Maryanne Wolf wonders

> whether the time-consuming demands of the deep-reading processes will be lost in a culture whose principal mediums advantage speed, multitasking, and processing the next piece of information.[47]

Concentrated reading takes concentrated work. The lingering question is whether today's readers feel the payoff is worth the effort. In Wolf's words,

> confronted with a digital glut of immediate information that requires and receives less and less intellectual effort, many...readers will have neither the time nor the motivation to think through the possible layers of meaning in what they read.[48]

Hayles remains optimistic. Her strategy is to find ways of getting students to balance hyper reading with deep reading. Part of her approach is to build upon students' media-based experience (including concentrating on video games for hours on end) and to energize faculty in finding new ways of teaching texts:

> The problem...lies not in hyper attention and hyper reading as such but rather in the challenges the situation presents for parents and educators to ensure that deep attention and close reading continue to be vibrant components of our reading cultures and interact synergistically with the web and hyper reading in which our young people are increasingly immersed.[49]

Yet Hayles also questions the relative importance of deep attention (and, derivatively, deep reading) in universal education. She proposes that "[a] case can be made that hyper attention is more adaptive than deep attention for many situations in contemporary developed societies," listing air traffic control, fast-food restaurants, and currency trading as domains where hyper attention is a valuable skill.[50]

Hayles' argument reminds me of Alan Jacobs' comment that most college students don't find "extensive" (that is, continuous, and sometimes deep) reading attractive, and that the kind of attentiveness necessary in school is closer to hyper attention than deep. Jacobs goes on to posit that

> even reading for information—reading textbooks and the like—does not require extended unbroken focus. It requires discipline but not raptness.[51]

I am all in favor of a modern approach to curricular design, incorporating the technological expertise students increasingly bring to the table. And of course not all reading is tackling *Finnegan's Wake*. Yet I'm not ready to throw in the towel and say, "This is how our students learn and therefore we need to dial down the complexity of reading assignments we believe in." If we want students to be responsible voting citizens, they must be able to grapple with the issues, not just press an electronic lever. If we want them to be active participants in society, they have to understand its cultural and historical underpinnings, including its nuances. And for that, you need to do serious, roll-up-your-sleeves, focus-on-what-you're-doing reading.

Whatever the virtues of hyper reading as an ancillary skill, and whatever the challenges in maintaining the practice of deep reading, this much is clear: Hyper reading is an activity largely practiced onscreen, while deep reading is a child of print.

And so we are back to comparing how we read onscreen versus in hardcopy, but this time with a brain-based focus. We will start with studies that measure reading in the two media. Then we'll turn to research on mental focus (specifically distraction and hypertext), which leads to the 500-pound distractor in the room: multitasking.

MEASURING READING: SIGHT, COMPREHENSION, PREFERENCES

We have more than twenty years of research comparing how people read in print versus digitally.[52] Over time, the quality of screens has vastly improved, and people's everyday experience has increased many fold. So has the sophistication of the research questions we ask.

EYES ON TEXT

Start with a physiological measure: eye tracking. When we read, our eyes move. Within a line of text, they can proceed forward or backward. They also need to transition from the end of one line to the start of the next. Collectively, these movements are known as saccades: progressive, regressive, and line sweeps. Generally speaking, the more difficult the text, the greater the number of regressive saccades we make. People with poorer reading skills tend to make a larger number of regressive saccades as well.

Between saccades, our eyes fixate, and so a second measurement of how we read is the length of our fixations. Eye tracking studies (which have been used for over a century) can measure saccades and fixations. We can also use eye tracking to document how readers navigate an entire page. In his work on reading web pages, Jakob Nielsen used the technique to deduce his F-pattern model.[53]

Several studies have compared eye movement when reading on digital screens versus in print. Despite some differences across digital reading platforms (say, computer screens versus tablets), subjects' amount of onscreen reading experience, or age, the research all points to the same conclusion: Reading patterns in the two media are highly similar. Regressive saccades are the same, with some variation in the number and length of fixations.[54]

Besides doing eye tracking studies, researchers have explored other measures of how we use our eyes when reading onscreen or in print. For example, is the amount of blinking the same when reading in each medium? Answer: yes.[55] There are, however, differences in readers' level of visual comfort, and screens come out on the short end of the stick. Under controlled testing conditions, subjects had more complaints about blurred vision when reading from a screen than from print.[56] My own studies confirmed that eyestrain and legibility were significant problems with reading digitally.

COMPREHENSION

Shifting from the eyes to the brain, what about comprehension? When it comes to adults, medium may not matter. That is the conclusion from studies done in the United States, Germany, Austria, and Israel.[57]

The Israeli study reveals an interesting twist. When subjects were given a set amount of time to complete the reading tasks, their comprehension scores were comparable. However, when free to decide how long to spend on the readings, subjects devoted less time—and had poorer comprehension—in the onscreen condition.[58] Since very little of the reading we do in everyday life is timed, the results lend credence to many people's perceptions that printed text is taken more seriously.

Anne Mangen, the reading specialist whose work emphasizes the physicality of reading (and writing), has a different take on the comprehension question. Her subjects were tenth-grade Norwegian students. (The other comprehension studies used young adults or working professionals.) In Norway, an increasing amount of school testing has students read PDFs on computers. Should it turn out that comprehension is superior when reading from print, computer-based testing may underestimate students' knowledge.

Mangen's study found better comprehension scores for students who did their reading in print.[59] Why? Mangen suggests that part of the problem with reading continuous text onscreen (her samples were 1,400–1,600 words long) is difficulty in constructing a mental map of the entire passage. As a result, it is hard to navigate spatially if you want to look back at something you previously read. Navigation is simpler on paper—a point students in my own studies confirmed. One participant in the United States said she likes the fact that with print she can "easily go back to something I'd already read," while a Japanese student complained that with screens, "it's not easy to locate where I was."

Which comprehension findings should we trust? Maybe all of them—or none. The studies differ in subject age, reading material, testing methodology, and users' prior experience with reading onscreen, making comparison difficult. Another problem may be that comprehension measures were not sufficiently nuanced.

Research by Jan Noyes and Kate Garland also found that the level of correct answers was about the same when subjects were asked questions about a passage read onscreen or in hardcopy. Yet the manner in which subjects recalled what they had read was different. Psychologists distinguish between "remember" responses (commonly associated with the learning episode) and "know" responses (which are recalled without conscious recollection). In Noyes and Garland's experiment, screen reading led to higher "remember" responses and lower "know" responses, while print reading yielded comparable levels of both types. The study concluded that if we really want to understand differences between the two reading media, we need to "find out about the individual's cognitive processing."[60]

Does medium matter for young children? Research with three-to-six-year-olds, carried out at the Joan Ganz Cooney Center in New York, looked at what happens when parents and children "co-read" print books, basic eBooks, or enhanced eBooks. Children remembered more details of the stories they encountered on paper than in enhanced eBooks. It seems that all those enhancements detracted kids from following the story line.[61]

Work by Julia Parish-Morris and her colleagues yielded similar results. When parents read either print or eBooks to their children, preschoolers had more trouble following the narrative line in the digital condition, in part because conversation tended to shift away from the story to trying to get the kids to stop focusing on the device itself.[62] There is also the issue of whether handing young children digital devices rather than talking with them hampers development of their communication skills.[63]

Like many attempts to replicate real-life reading conditions in the laboratory, all the studies we have been talking about (at least those involving adults) share a major shortcoming: The investigations involve relatively brief readings followed by some version of comprehension or memory questions. What we don't have—but sorely need—are data on what happens when people are asked to do close reading of continuous text. In short, we need studies comparing deep reading onscreen versus in print.

The difficulty, of course, is that these sorts of studies are incredibly challenging to design. You might try measuring how often readers break their concentration while reading Gogol's *Dead Souls* in hardcopy and onscreen, comparing the number of times they shift to another focused activity (checking text messages, looking up airfares on Kayak) versus breaks involving limited calls on attention (getting something to eat, stretching). But what would you do with this count? Alternatively, you might test for memory of plot or members of the dramatis personae. Yet producing a SparkNotes version of the story line or knowing the names is not why we read Gogol. Some of the benefits of literature come from discussions with others or personal reflection at quiet moments. Payoffs may not surface until years later when, having lived and experienced more, we discover the relevance of Gogol's world to ours.

Try measuring that.

USER PREFERENCE

There is far less debate about which platform many users prefer. We've already cited a variety of studies that uniformly reached the same conclusion. To recap: Students in my own research strongly preferred reading in print, for both academic work and pleasure. Many parents of young children would rather their children read (or be read to) in print. A sheaf of other reports indicate similar preference for print, even as the volume of eBooks continues to grow.[64]

What is especially interesting is that these same choices show up in studies reporting no comprehension differences between print and screen reading. Austrian researchers found that the hospital clinicians they worked with "distinctly preferred to read on paper, independent of the type of text…, independent of their age, their expertise level and domain of knowledge." German investigators, whose subjects ranged from university students to senior citizens, reported "an overwhelming preference for the paper page in terms of pleasantness ratings and (to somewhat lesser degree) readability."[65]

Yet probably the biggest reason print is so often preferred is that compared with reading onscreen, print tends to limit distraction. As a result, it encourages mental focus.

MENTAL FOCUS AND DISTRACTION

Marie Curie was renowned for her ability to concentrate. As a student in Paris, she read for hours at a stretch, despite the lack of creature comforts such as ample food or heat. Later, in conducting research with her husband, Pierre, that led to the discovery of radium, she frequently labored through the night.

Few of us can match Madame Curie's ability to focus. The question is, how far off the mark are we? Putting aside lack of commitment or boredom, the problem is that most of us tend to get distracted: by the fly buzzing in our ear, by the voice down the hall, and now by the hum of our mobile phone or temptation to look something up on the internet.

Devoting full attention to a single activity takes effort. For the moment, put aside the diversions that lead us off-topic when we read onscreen. Look instead at distractors, designed for our benefit, which are embedded within the texts themselves. Enter hyperlinks and hypertexts.

THE HYPERTEXT TRADE-OFF

The concept of hypertext goes back to work by the information technology pioneer Ted Nelson in the mid-1960s. However, it didn't enter the popular realm until 1987, with creation of the HyperCard program for the Apple Macintosh. The principle is this: Hyperlinks enable readers to access related content that resides elsewhere. Initially, that content was somewhere in the same hypertext file (letting you skip from, say, a chapter heading in the Table of Contents directly to the chapter itself). Over time, as the internet grew, links began pointing readers to a wealth of sites elsewhere on the web. An initial motivation for creating hyperlinks was to add interactivity, hopefully making reading more interesting. Increasingly, another impetus has been to expand access to ancillary educational material.

More interesting? Maybe. But more educationally effective? It's not clear. A meta-study (reviewing many other studies) looked at how people navigate online and how much they comprehend when following hyperlinks (as opposed to reading linear prose). The authors found that hypertext tended to make for worse reading performance. The extra decision making and visual processing involved in navigating from link to link increased the "cognitive load" on readers and "may have required working memory capacity that exceeded readers' capabilities." Readers who had little prior knowledge of the subject matter and whose working memory levels in general were low showed particular problems with the hypertext task.[66]

As usual, reality may be more complex than even well-designed studies can model. Sometimes the goal in reading hypertext is to find what lies down the road less traveled or to just have fun, not to get high scores on a short-term memory comprehension test. Reality checks also need to ask what kind of reading genre we are talking about: Factual information? Literature? It is also possible (though I'm not putting money on it) that our task-switching skills will improve with continued practice.

The literature question is particularly intriguing because one of the early genres incorporating hypertext was fiction. In the late 1990s, literary scholars such as George Landow encouraged writers to explore the new freedom readers could experience with hypertext, since hyperlinks empowered them to "follow links wherever they please."[67]

Not everyone was as enthusiastic as Landow. The problem? Hypertext is disruptive. Jumping about in a text breaks the reader's concentration. Two English professors from the University of Alberta compared how readers approached the hypertext version and the linear version of the same short story. The hypertext readers took longer to go through the story than those with the linear text. More important, hypertext readers reported feeling confused. As one subject put it,

> The story was very jumpy. I don't know if that was caused by the hypertext, but I made choices and all of a sudden it wasn't flowing properly, it just kind of jumped to a new idea I didn't really follow.[68]

"Jumpy" or "wasn't flowing properly" doesn't make for absorbed reading. If we are distracted from the natural logic of the work itself, it is hard to reflect on what the author is trying to say and construct our own responses, even if only in our mind's eye.

Is distraction ever a desirable state when encountering literature—or, for that matter, when writing it? Sometimes the answer is yes, but we are talking about a very particular kind of distraction. Not about shifting focus from reading Molière to checking soccer World Cup scores on your mobile phone and then back to Molière. Rather, what we mean is allowing your mind to meander.

Before studying brain activity in people reading Jane Austen, Natalie Phillips earlier worked on a different question: What kinds of distraction did readers (and writers) of fiction encounter two centuries ago, and did anything beneficial come of it?[69] Phillips argues that the Enlightenment introduced a positive side to the notion of distraction. To quote (in English translation) Diderot's entry for the word "distraction" in the *Encyclopédie*,

> Distraction has its source in an excellent quality of the understanding, an extreme facility in allowing the ideas to strike against, or reawaken one another. It is the opposite of that stupor which rests on the same idea.[70]

In other words, distraction gets us out of our mental ruts and opens up an opportunity for thinking.

Phillips reminds us that eighteenth-century London was bursting with sensory overload: masses of humanity (given the soaring population), new forms of print to choose from (novels, essays, anthologies), taverns and coffeehouses, and streets filled with everything from prostitutes to bear-baiting and puppet shows. It was easy to get distracted—including when reading—however much people tried to focus. One Elizabeth Gurney confessed in her journal in 1799, "I seldom attend sufficiently to what I am reading, to remember at all accurately what I have been reading about."[71] Practically speaking, authors needed to grab their readers' attention. Phillips argues that writers of eighteenth- and early nineteenth-century fiction understood the role distraction played in their readers' lives and actively incorporated the trope of distraction into their works.

There are many ways in which we can become distracted. Phillips talks about four. Two (scattered focus and divided attention) involve the mind hopping from one mental focus to another. The other two (lapses of concentration and wandering attention) are more in the spirit of Diderot, where the mind is released from its current focus and allowed to drift along new currents. Recently, psychologists have begun studying experimentally the creative advantages of letting the mind wander.[72]

But let's not fool ourselves: Not all distraction is constructive. If I stop reading to walk the dog, my mind is still free to think (consciously or unconsciously) about what I have been reading. However, the chances of continuing to mull over that reading diminish if my mind becomes actively engaged in the distracting activity, such as starting up a conversation with a friend who sees me sitting alone at Starbucks, reading.

Recognizing what is productive distraction and what is not can be tricky. Writer Hanif Kureishi suggests that

> a person...must be able to distinguish between creative and destructive distractions by the sort of taste they leave, whether they feel depleting or fulfilling.[73]

His is an excellent metric, but one that requires a level of honesty with ourselves that we all too often don't possess.

THE DISRUPTIVE SIDE OF DISTRACTION

Correlation, as David Hume reminded us, does not imply causation. Yet if we are trying to figure out whether contemporary distractions affect the way we read, correlation is a reasonable place to start.

In 2007, a team of psychologists asked whether the amount of time college students spent on instant messaging correlated with the students' own assessment of how easily they became distracted when doing academic work. The researchers also investigated whether students' levels of distractibility were related to how much time they spent reading hardcopy books. Results? The more time students reported using IM, the higher they indicated their general level of distraction was when doing academic reading. And the more distractible they were, the less time they spent reading print books.[74]

Maybe people who are highly distractible are less likely to be serious readers than those less easily distracted. Perhaps we are really looking at a personality type. But I don't think so. Modern communication technologies beckon us to drop what we are doing, even momentarily, and get sidetracked. Alan Jacobs personalizes the challenge facing today's readers:

> Like Nicholas Carr, I get twitchy within just a few minutes of sitting down with a book.... About two years ago, I realized that I was reading fewer books than I had since age ten, and reading them less well—with less attention—and therefore getting less pleasure from reading.[75]

If professional writers have difficulty warding off distractions, it's understandable that the rest of us struggle.

MULTITASKING: THE ÜBER-DISTRACTOR

There are scores of ways to get distracted while reading: "I'll watch this one television program and then get back to my book" or "A quick trip for ice cream and then I'll finish the reading assignment." However, in a digital world with instant access to other people ("Just one text message…") or other places to park your mind ("I wonder how many "likes" my new Facebook group has scored?"), the biggest challenge comes from thinking we can handle two things at once. That we can multitask. That we can read (whether for work or pleasure) and at the same time be doing something else.

Underlying this attitude is the implicit assumption we can do as well on those multitasked activities as if we had performed each individually. Coupled with this belief is the supposition that since the brain is plastic (remember those string players and London taxi drivers?), if we work at it, we can train ourselves to be good multitaskers. Since young people are getting more practice than their parents or grandparents, successive generations should (so the logic goes) be able to handle multiple tasks successfully, including while reading.

With a limited number of exceptions, these beliefs turn out to be wrong. Yes, organists multitask when they read different lines of music for each hand, plus move their feet. And yes, we can successfully hold a conversation while shelling peas or crocheting. But the list of viable options is restricted. Experts tell us—even warn us—that successful multitasking is essentially a myth.[76] Nowhere is this myth more ubiquitous and more dangerous than when it comes to driving.

THE DRIVING SCENE

I'm in a taxi, heading from my hotel in Prague to the airport, and fearing for my life. The driver speaks no English. I speak no Czech. He's careening down the highway at nearly 140 kilometers an hour, chatting away on his mobile phone. My decades of driving experience tell me when he should be braking, when it's not safe to pass, what it means to stay in your lane. The driver is oblivious to all this. We reach the airport, but my nerves are a puddled mess.

My fears are hardly unfounded. In early 2010, the National Safety Council announced that 28 percent of all traffic accidents in the United States occurred when people were talking or texting on mobile phones. The vast majority of the 1.4 million crashes annually were caused by voice conversations, with 200,000 accidents attributed to texting while driving.[77] And here is a really frightening fact: You are 23 times more likely to crash while driving if you are texting than if you're not.[78]

Moving past the highway statistics, let's get to the science. We can measure the relationship between keeping our eyes on the road and such critical components of driving as reaction time and unintended lane departure. It stands to reason that the more you look at the road (and the cars ahead of you), the faster you will be able to brake when necessary and the less likely you will be to drift into another lane. Researchers in Indiana put subjects into a driving simulator to see what happened when the drivers had to cope with the distraction of being asked to read words on a peripheral display. An eye tracking system measured what the subjects were looking at during the test drive. Not surprisingly, the additional reading task led to decreased performance: slower reaction time for braking, more lane drifts, and less time looking at the road.[79] This scenario is hardly a recipe for safe driving.

We also have self-reported data on how many people (in the United States) talk or text on mobile phones when they drive. The Pew Internet & American Life Project did a pair of studies on driving behavior and mobile phone use of teenagers and adults. Of the 16- and 17-year-old drivers who owned mobile phones, 52 percent admitted to having talked on their mobile while driving. Of those teens who more generally used their phones for texting, 34 percent reported they had texted while driving.[80] Other research on 16-to-18-year-old drivers in America found 26 percent texting "at least once every time they drive."[81] And a worrisome study of college students reported many texting (while driving) without even being aware of doing so.[82]

Among the adults Pew surveyed, 75 percent said they spoke on their phones while driving. For those who more generally did text messaging, 47 percent indicated they had either sent or read a text while behind the wheel.[83] No wonder so many young people assume it's OK to use their phones while driving, given the behavior they see modeled by adults.

Automobiles and phones have a long-standing connection. The first mobile phone, developed in Sweden in the 1950s, was a "car phone," run off the car's battery. In the 1980s, a European consortium called Groupe Spécial Mobile (these days known simply as GSM) brought together eight countries to share a mobile communication network. GSM service went live in 1992. Sweden was among the eight.[84]

Fittingly, some of the earliest research on mobile phone use while driving was done in Sweden. In the study, subjects "drove" using a simulator. A hands-free mobile phone was mounted to the right of the steering wheel. While subjects in the control group were simply asked to drive, people in the experimental group were also instructed to answer the phone and follow instructions for performing various verbal tasks. Those who were multitasking between driving and responding to telephone instructions had slower reaction times.[85]

The study's authors commented that since mobile phones were new devices at the time the research was conducted (in the mid-1990s), "it can be argued that people in general have not had time to learn its effects on their driving behavior."[86] Regrettably, two decades later, drivers still haven't learned.

The findings keep pouring in. Research at the University of Utah showed that drivers (again in simulators) who engaged in hands-free phone conversations took longer to react to a car in front of them that was braking than a control group. The dual-taskers also had worse memory for reading roadside billboards. Eye tracking equipment further revealed that subjects paid less attention to peripheral visual information.[87] A second University of Utah study yielded chilling results: Use of mobile phones (both handheld and hands-free) compromised subjects' driving as much as if they were intoxicated, with a blood alcohol level of .08 percent.[88]

Marcel Just and his colleagues at Carnegie Mellon University used an fMRI scanner to examine what happens in the brain when subjects are asked to simultaneously drive and comprehend spoken language. It turns out that if you are trying to judge whether sentences are true or false at the same time you're driving, you pull mental resources away from the driving task, despite the fact you are not holding a phone and not even conversing. The listening task reduces activation in the bilateral parietal and superior extrastriate secondary visual areas (which are associated with driving) by a whopping 37 percent. In addition, your ability to drive straight down the road (in a simulator) is compromised.[89]

YOUR BRAIN ON MULTITASKING

Very few of us are as good at doing two things at once as when we perform each task separately. So why do we multitask?

The most common answer is something like "I'm busy, and multitasking lets me accomplish several things at once." But when you probe a bit more, you often hear a deeper motivation: "I'm bored." In a study I did on instant messaging, I asked college students why they held concurrent IM conversations. Why not just one at a time? As one student proclaimed, "That would be too weird."[90] There is more potential action if you are tied in to multiple channels.

Ask a neuroscientist why we multitask, and you will hear a more nuanced answer: The human brain seeks novelty.[91] The more new stimuli, the more we satisfy that quest. The real question, of course, is how much our brains can actually handle. Advances in neuroimaging have enabled us to study the brain's wetware as we try to understand the reasons behind these limitations.

The answer seems to lie in an intuitively obvious fact: Our brain can only process so many streams of information at the same time. While not all researchers agree on the neurological explanation behind this limitation, the most prevalent candidate is what's known as the central processing bottleneck.[92] Even if two tasks (say one visual and the other auditory) largely call on different parts of the brain, there is a point in cognitive processing where both tasks converge at the same physical location.

Since only one task can get processed at a time, the result is a slowdown. Sometimes the result is reduced reaction time in one of the tasks, as we saw in the driving studies. Other times the issue is the total amount of brain activity involved. Using fMRI technology, Marcel Just and his colleagues examined the amount of neural activation (measured in voxels) when subjects performed a language task and a mental rotation task individually. They compared those numbers with total activation when the tasks were carried out together. Performed individually, the language task and the mental rotation task each involved 37 voxels. When the tasks were combined, subjects only exerted a total of 42 voxels—sizably less than $37 + 37 = 74$. The authors concluded "there may be biological mechanisms that place an upperbound on the amount of cortical tissue that can be activated at any given time."[93]

Psychologist Russell Poldrack's research reveals how subtle—but important—the effects of multitasking can be. Using an fMRI scanner to monitor brain activity, Poldrack and his colleagues had students learn a weather prediction task using cue cards. With some trials, there were no distractions, but with others, participants simultaneously listened to a series of beeps and had to count how many were high-pitched. Students successfully learned the task under both conditions, though the fMRI results revealed different areas of the brain being activated. This variance was reflected in subsequent cognitive testing, when subjects were asked to articulate the underlying "rules" of prediction in the weather game. Students did much better at this conceptual task when they hadn't heard the distracting tones.[94]

Why? Because the multitasking condition involved procedural memory (also sometimes called habit memory), which we use for learning things like riding a bicycle. This memory is located in the brain's striatum. By contrast, declarative memory (which supports "flexibly accessible knowledge") is located in the medial temporal lobe system. It is declarative memory that lets us generalize our learning to new situations, and it was declarative memory that was compromised in the multitasking condition.

Another way of measuring the effects of multitasking is to calculate how much we remember of information presented in television news programs when multiple messages are presented on the same screen. Take CNN Headline News. The anchor speaks, but a written trailer at the bottom displays different content. A study by journalism researchers has shown that young adults—the generation that often claims to be good at multitasking—missed 10 percent of the factual information in the spoken news story when they also coped with other messages on the screen.[95]

IS ANYONE GOOD AT MULTITASKING?

You'd better hope your pilot is. Odds are he or she is up to the task, given all those hours of training in handling multiple streams of information. The same, incidentally, seems to be true of experienced video gamers, who (as we've seen) may have heightened visual-spatial abilities. It has been suggested that both seasoned pilots and high-level gamers make more efficient uses of their cortical resources—at least in their respective domains—than novices.[96]

Before you get your hopes up about driving and texting (or reading and playing *Angry Birds*) if you just practice enough, look at the odds. Studies at the University of Utah suggest that only about 2½ percent of the population qualifies as what the researchers call supertaskers. These supertaskers were actually adept at doing stop-and-go driving (in a simulator) while successfully completing an auditory task administered through a hands-free headset.[97]

How do you know if you are in that 2½ percent? Don't trust your own judgment. As the late Clifford Nass and his students at Stanford have demonstrated, people who think they are successful multitaskers do worse on standard dual-task experiments than those who are less confident about their multitasking abilities.[98] We would also do well to remember the famous "invisible gorilla" experiment demonstrating what is called inattentional blindness. Subjects were shown a video less than a minute long in which some people wearing white shirts and others wearing black shirts tossed basketballs to one another. The subjects were asked to keep track of the number of passes made by those wearing white shirts, not black ones. In the background of the video, someone in a gorilla suit strolled through the scene, spending nine seconds onscreen. Hardly any of the subjects watching the video noticed. They were too busy counting passes.[99]

MULTITASKING AND READING

It is time to take what we have learned about the cognitive challenges of multi-tasking and return to reading. If you are checking Twitter while reading in the library, you are not going to rear-end a car in front of you. Yet popping onto the internet when your interest wanes takes its own toll on your understanding. More subtly—but sometimes even more significantly—it reduces the likelihood you will reflect on what you're reading or your chances of becoming engrossed in the text.

If young people are a nation's future, we need to keep tabs on what else they are doing while reading. The Kaiser Family Foundation observed in 2006 that 62 per-cent of the 8-to-18-year-olds they surveyed reported multitasking when they read. These same young people were substantially less likely to multitask when playing video games or watching TV (or videos).[100] American adolescents are clearly voting with their minds on what activities merit their full attention.

Why multitask while reading? A familiar rationale is to save time. But does it? In a Connecticut study, one group of college students was asked to reply to a number of questions via instant messaging and then read a passage on whose contents they were later tested. A second group also did the reading and comprehension tasks, but the IM messages were interspersed within the reading. Completing the IM task first and then doing the reading saved time. When you subtract the amount of time the multitasking group spent answering questions on IM, they took significantly longer to read the passage than subjects who polished off the IMs before moving to the reading.[101]

So much for the efficiency argument for multitasking.

We have already seen evidence that college students have different multitasking practices when reading in hardcopy versus onscreen. Among the American stu-dents in my 2013 study, 74 percent reported they only "occasionally" or "never" multitask when reading in print, compared with just 15 percent who only occa-sionally or never multitask when reading onscreen. Of the same group, 92 percent said they concentrate best when reading in hardcopy. (The Japanese and German participants overwhelmingly agreed.) Given these findings, I can only wonder why the educational establishment is pushing students toward digital reading.

HOW MUCH IS TOO MUCH?

It's a no-brainer that using a phone while driving is almost never a good idea. In other cases (like the reading and IMing scenario), the main victim is us—both in extra time spent and, in all probability, in reduced concentration on what we are reading. Given the mounds of data indicating that in most cases the ability to multitask successfully really is a myth, why can't we stop ourselves?

When it comes to resisting the temptation to sneak in a quick hit (remember the dopamine squirt?) by checking voicemail or cruising the internet for a movie review when we are reading, most of us fail as models of self-control. I can't say whether people who take a second helping of chocolate cake are the same ones who can't resist one more Google search. But we do know the internet can be a huge time sink and, depending upon whom you ask, addictive.

DOES INTERNET ADDICTION EXIST?

The *Diagnostic and Statistical Manual of Mental Disorders* (*DSM*) is a cross between a reference guide and a bible in the world of psychiatric medicine. Once a condition is listed, it is felt to be "real." It's like the makers of the *Merriam-Webster Dictionary* elevating a neologism to the status of a word in American English.

In preparing the 2013 version of the manual (*DSM-5*), there was considerable discussion about whether to include "Internet Use Disorder" in Section III. (Section III is the part of the *DSM* that recognizes emerging diagnoses requiring further study before getting incorporated within the official list of mental disorders.) While that diagnosis did not make the final cut (though "Internet Gaming Disorder" did), researchers and even national governments are now talking actively about internet addiction.

FROM INTERNET ADDICTION TO CULTURE

Take China. The Chinese Academy of Social Sciences reported in 2010 that roughly 14 percent of Chinese internet users under age 29 were addicted to the web. That percentage translates into at least 33 million young Chinese.[102] In 2011, a team of Chinese researchers demonstrated structural changes in the brains of adolescents diagnosed with internet addiction disorders. They found reduced gray matter volume, along with white matter abnormalities. These changes increased with the number of months subjects had been suffering from internet addiction. The researchers hypothesized that the alterations may be associated with impairment in cognitive control.[103]

Then there is South Korea. Koreans are particularly heavy users of digital devices, including those connected to the internet. Broadband access is inexpensive, and there's a strong gaming culture.[104] In my own cross-cultural research on mobile phone use, Korean college students far outstripped Swedes, Americans, Italians, and Japanese in their amount of both texting and talking. Koreans were also the most likely to find it acceptable to use mobiles during family dinners and least likely to be disturbed by other people's phone conversations.[105]

The Korean government has been launching several bold educational initiatives. Convinced of the need to make its citizens fluent in English, back in 1977 the Ministry of Education began requiring English-language teaching from third grade onward.[106] Equally convinced of the importance of Korea being at the technological cutting edge, the government declared that by 2015, classrooms would go entirely digital, committing $2.3 billion to the project. All school reading would be onscreen.[107]

But there was a major bump in the road. Like China, South Korea was experiencing a serious internet addiction problem. In response, Korea established the Jump Up Internet Rescue School for treating young internet addicts. A study in 2007 suggested that as many as 30 percent of South Koreans under the age of 18 were at risk of internet addiction, with up to a quarter million of them actually displaying signs of the problem.[108] The affliction wasn't limited to adolescents. The Ministry of Public Administration and Security concluded in a later study that nearly 8 percent of children between ages 5 and 9 already suffered from internet addiction.[109] In late 2013, legislation was introduced into South Korea's parliament to classify online gaming as an addiction, joining ranks with alcohol, drugs, and gambling.[110]

The Korean government pulled back from its all-digital educational strategy. Instead, there would be a combination of both print and digital texts, with the youngest children probably sticking with hardcopy.[111] In a country with hundreds of internet addiction treatment centers and in which 2.6 million people are estimated to be addicted to smartphones (using them eight hours a day or more),[112] the psychological and social health of the next generation was at stake.

Western countries are not immune from excessive internet use. In 2010, the *AAP News* (an official publication of the American Academy of Pediatrics) reported that about 8 to 12 percent of children in the United States had problems with overuse of the internet.[113] London's Capio Nightingale Hospital runs a Technology Addiction Service as part of its larger menu of addiction treatment programs.[114]

Is "addiction" the right word? Maybe it is more like "dementia." South Korean doctors coined the term "digital dementia" to describe people in their late 20s or early 30s who display symptoms such as lack of concentration, memory loss, and inability to sleep—caused by excessive amounts of time spent using digital communication devices. In Germany, neuroscientist Manfred Spitzer has written a book, *Digitale Demenz* (*Digital Dementia*), laying out evidence that overuse of digital devices is undermining the way the brains of today's children are developing.[115]

While there are no international criteria for what constitutes internet addiction or digital dementia among the young, it's likely that any country with inexpensive internet access experiences some level of these problems. But what level? It doesn't follow that availability always correlates with excessive usage. While Sweden had easy access to texting on mobile phones about a decade earlier than the United States, American college students do far more texting than Swedish counterparts.[116] German personal computer culture is as old as America's, but as we will see in the next chapter, there are vastly different attitudes toward eBooks in the two countries.

International comparisons of media choices and reading habits are both fascinating and fraught with challenges. Are we comparing cultures or nations? How do national laws (especially tax structures) affect digital or hardcopy book sales? How are cultural practices impacted when Amazon or Kobo targets a country for eBook expansion?

It's time to delve into these questions.

Edmonton Public Library
Clareview
Express Check #1

Customer ID: ××××××××××8844

Items that you checked out

Title:
Words onscreen : the fate of reading in a
digital world
ID: 31221147505503
Due: April-16-18

Total items: 1
Account balance: $0.00
March-26-18 2:37 PM
Checked out: 1
Overdue: 0
Hold requests: 0
Ready for pickup: 0

Thank you for visiting the Edmonton
Public Library
www.epl.ca

9 Faxing Tokyo

When Cultures and Markets Meet

It's an important part of our national culture, those
bookshops.

—*Tim Waterstone*

The tsunami hit the coast of Miyagi prefecture, near Sendai, on March 11. Boats
and people were hurled about like ping-pong balls. The yet more horrific challenge
would be to the southwest, at Tokyo Electric Power Company's Fukushima Daiichi
nuclear power plant. As the scope of the disaster became clear, officials in Fukushima moved to inform Tokyo.

Not by phone. Not by email. By fax.[1] In the year 2011, in a country known for
technological innovation, this critical message was faxed, and presumably handwritten.

Why?

Handwriting has long held a special place of honor in Japan. The art of callig-
raphy aside, schoolchildren devote countless hours learning to form the *kanji* (Chinese characters), along with two sets of *kana* (syllabic systems) that collectively
make up the core Japanese writing system. (There are also *romaji*—letters of the

Roman alphabet.) Learning to write Japanese understandably takes years, and mastering the roughly 2,000 essential *kanji* has been part of the process of becoming Japanese. The importance of handwriting doesn't cease when you reach adulthood. Even though word processing and email have became increasingly common in Japan, many resumés submitted for jobs (especially when mailed or delivered in person) continued to be written by hand.

The Chinese characters originated as pictures: The character for "man" looks like two legs walking, and so on. Japan continues its graphics tradition, as evidenced these days in anime films and manga comics. In fact, the strongest Japanese interest in eBooks has been in digital manga, not electronic versions of printed text. About 80 percent of eBook sales in Japan are of comics, mostly read on mobile phones.[2]

What about typing in Japan? Don't the Japanese do word processing on computers? And aren't the Japanese frequently texting on mobile phones (known as *keitai*)? Yes, and yes. But producing text on both computers and *keitai* is an intricate process. Writers first input the *kana* that sound like the word to be represented. Either users select the *kana* directly onscreen or they type in the Roman characters representing the syllables, and the computer or phone automatically converts the Roman letters into Japanese *kana*.

The next job is to convert the relevant *kana* into *kanji*. Japanese has many homonyms. (In English, think of the word "bank," which might refer to the edge of a river, a financial institution, or an airplane maneuver.) And so the electronic device brings up a number of choices: Did you mean this *kanji* or that one? When you type in か み (ka-mi), do you mean "hair," "paper," "god," or "up"? (There are other possibilities, but you get the idea.) Make your selection, add on any necessary grammatical endings, and move on to the next word. Mechanical production of words in Japanese is no walk in the park.

Many older Japanese don't know how to use computers or how to text on mobile phones (*keitai meiru*). Younger people have the skills but often find it a hassle. The alternative? Everyone knows how to write by hand. And so the fax machine continues to flourish. Japan's Cabinet Office estimated that as of March 2012, almost 60 percent of Japanese homes had fax machines.[3] Essentially all businesses do. Writing out their messages by hand, people fax invitations to parties, takeout orders to restaurants, and apparently news of nuclear disasters.

CULTURAL PREDILECTIONS

Culture shapes our lives in ways large and small. The twenty-first-century Amish continue to eschew cars in favor of horses and buggies. Swedes and Japanese remove their shoes immediately upon entering the house. It was an Italian, valuing the leisurely communal meal, who launched a protest when McDonald's opened shop in Rome. Try imagining such a crusade in Hong Kong.

Cultural practices sometimes figure in potential international incidents, such as the dustup in 2010 that nearly wrecked talks between the UK and China. David Cameron, leading a trade delegation on his maiden trip to Beijing as prime minister, came sporting a poppy on his jacket lapel. It was early November, with Remembrance Day soon approaching. In the British Commonwealth, everyone dons a red poppy in honor of the World War I dead. But for Brits to wear poppies in China was a cultural faux pas, given Britain's devastating role during the Opium Wars a century and a half earlier.

How we read and write also has a cultural side. The French screenwriter and actor Jean-Claude Carrière poses a perceptive question about whether the physical direction in which a country's language is written affects the way movies there are shot:

When I think of how we read books [in the West], our eyes go from left to right and top to bottom. In Arabic, Persian and Hebrew, it's the other way round; the eye travels from right to left. I wonder what impact this has had on camera movements in film. Most tracking shots in Western cinema move from left to right, whereas I have often noticed the opposite in Iranian films, for example.

As Carrière asks, "And why shouldn't our reading habits influence our ways of seeing?"[4]

Umberto Eco—whose conversations with Carrière were edited into a volume called *This Is Not the End of the Book*—reminds us that even people from western European backgrounds don't all have the same reading habits. Many of us know Eco from his blockbuster (though arcane) medieval whodunit *The Name of the Rose*. Himself an Italian, Eco writes:

The English mostly prefer to borrow their books from libraries. As for Italy, sales [of *The Name of the Rose*] are probably slightly higher than in Ghana. Instead of books, Italians read a lot of magazines—many more than the French.[5]

Now I better understand why a dear Italian colleague of mine always has a stack of newspapers and magazines, not books, stuffed into her ample purse.

It turns out that culture also shapes attitudes toward eBooks. Sales figures show stark differences in uptake between countries. But how much of that variance derives from cultural preference and how much from business practices and even legal regulations? To help unpack that question, consider a familiar cultural icon.

I'D LIKE TO BUY THE WORLD A COKE: BUSINESS MEETS CULTURE

American advertisers decided years ago that if you want to sell a product, it may help to sing. One verse from back in 1971 keeps rattling around in my head, courtesy of the Coca-Cola Company:

> I'd like to teach the world to sing
> In perfect harmony
> I'd like to buy the world a Coke
> And keep it company
> That's the real thing.[6]

A Coke? Surely a pair of shoes or access to clean drinking water would have been more beneficial. What's more, judging from international sales, the world has been buying its own Cokes for some time, thank you.

Business interests have a history of insinuating themselves into cultural practices. There would have been fewer opium dens in nineteenth-century China if the British had not promoted sale of the drug to increase its coffers. London, a city initially identified with coffeehouses, began switching to tea after Thomas Twining bought Tom's Coffee House on the Strand in 1706 and changed brews.[7] The tables turned once more by the end of the twentieth century, when Costa Coffee and then Starbucks started up in England, increasingly making an espresso or latte the hot drink of choice.[8] Similarly, the world's continuing hunger for fast food was driven by American business interests.

What do Cokes and coffee, opium and Chicken McNuggets have to do with eReading?

WHO WANTS eBOOKS?

Where you stand on the question of who wants eBooks really does heavily depend upon where you sit. Those with commercial interests in the production and sale of eReaders and eBooks envision billions of potential customers. Those from cultures cherishing independent bookstores, fine paper quality, and personal libraries have often been less enthusiastic.

As the publishing and distribution industries plow massive resources into internationalizing their eReading base, we need to be asking questions such as:

- How much of the expansion is filling an existing appetite and how much is seeding new markets?
- Where is there cultural resistance?
- Are business practices reshaping cultural reading practices—and if so, with what consequences?

Calvin Coolidge aptly observed in 1925 that "the chief business of the American people is business."[9] Throughout the twentieth century, commercial schemes have redefined the way Americans live. It is said that Henry Ford priced his Model Ts so that autoworkers—along with the general public—could afford them. Ford's pricing worked, contributing to the decline not only of horse-drawn vehicles but eventually of many city public transportation systems. American business (starting with the General Motors Acceptance Corporation for car loans) introduced the installment plan, the layaway plan, the home mortgage, and the credit card, all designed to increase consumption.[10] And increase consumption they did. By the end of 2013, the outstanding balance for just auto loans in the United States was $860 billion.[11]

Americans have also gotten used to tossing out older products when new ones come along. With the advent of cassette tapes, collections of long-playing records gathered dust or maybe ended up in the trash. Next came CDs (time to dump the cassettes), and then iPods and iTunes (so much for those CDs).

Are eBooks like songs on iTunes? Is it time to say goodbye to print and buy only "e"? Unlike music, which was traditionally heard live, books have had a physical, durable presence since the inception of clay and waxed tablets, scrolls, and codexes. But like tastes in music, our reading practices—what we read, why we read, and how we read—tend to be culturally marked.

WHO WANTS YOU TO WANT eBOOKS?

eBooks got off to a halting start in the early years of the new millennium. Sony introduced its eReader in Japan in 2003 (where it has retained some traction) and in the United States in 2004 (where it essentially fizzled). Amazon's Kindle revolutionized reading in the United States and, with Amazon's international spread, has been shifting reading patterns around the globe. Kobo, a newer but aggressive competitor, has been nipping at Amazon's heels.[12]

To understand global eBook adoption rates, we cannot simply look at country-by-country statistics. If there aren't many eBooks available in Italian, we can't expect Italy to embrace eReading. If no one is supplying eBooks to Latin America, why bother talking about low eBook adoption in Brazil? Many discussions of international resistance to eBooks invoke only culture-based themes like reverence for bookstores, ignoring the supply chain.

Since the Kindle appeared in America in 2007, Amazon has dominated the marketplace, with its international push ginning up in 2011. Besides launching Kindle stores in other countries, Amazon continues expanding language platforms through which authors and publishers can sell digital materials. There are 34 languages to choose from, ranging from Afrikaans to Welsh.[13] Kobo, which got its start in Canada in 2009, entered the American market in 2012. On December 5, 2012—a red-letter day for eBooks—Kobo launched in Brazil on precisely the same date as Amazon and Google. I happened to be in Rio de Janeiro, and the collective hoopla was impressive, even if you didn't know Portuguese.

Competing with the international giants are an ever-growing number of homegrown enterprises. The French supermarket chain Carrefour has introduced Nolimbook and Nolimbook+. In India, there's Attano (an eBook store). Russia sells Qumo eReaders, South Africa's Kalahari is a general online store (in the style of Amazon), Australia's retail chain Big W now sells eBooks, and South Korea has Sam (an eBook service from Kyobo Bookstore), which provides downloads on Kyobo's own eReader. It is anyone's guess what the local landscape for eReaders and eBooks will look like even a few years hence.

eBOOK READERSHIP STATS

The publishing industry is keen to track the global marketplace, sniffing out target growth opportunities. It was in late spring 2012, sitting in a conference room in New York, that I became intrigued with the cultural side of eReading. The presentation on international eBook trends was from Bowker Market Research. Bowker's data, collected earlier that year, revealed stark national differences. (Yes, "culture" and "nation" hardly mean the same thing, but since the book industry collects data nationally and the press files national stories, we will have to live with the fudged equivalence.) Some findings particularly struck me:

- 20 percent of the people surveyed in the United States who had internet access had purchased an eBook in the past six months. The comparable number in Japan was 8 percent. In France, it was 5 percent.

- In the United States, the UK, France, and Germany, the top eBook sellers were fiction. In India, Brazil, and South Korea, people were largely buying business or professional books.
- PCs and laptops were the devices most often used for reading eBooks in India, Japan, France, and Brazil. In the United States and UK it was eReaders, while in South Korea smartphones reigned.[14]

A Bowker follow-up study, using data collected in fall 2012, focused on a somewhat different set of questions and reconfigured group of countries.[15] The highest adoption rates continued to be in the United States and UK, with Amazon remaining the major vendor of eBooks (74 percent of eBook sales in the UK and 59 percent in the United States). Adult fiction remained the top seller in the UK and the United States, with business and professional works again topping the list in India. eReading in the UK was still heavily done on eReaders, while in the United States, eReaders had been edged out by tablets. India continued to rely on PCs and laptops.

Another way of measuring eBook penetration is to ask what percentage of all book sales are eBooks. These are tricky numbers to pin down, for a couple of reasons. For starters, Amazon doesn't release its sales figures. For another, sometimes figures represent percentage of revenues and other times percentage of copies sold. These numbers can be widely divergent, particularly because a large portion of self-published eBooks (and there are thousands of them) carry very low price tags. Yet even rough country comparisons are useful for getting a sense of the disparity in national eBook adoption. Here are some approximate figures for book market share in 2012:[16]

United States	c. 20% of the trade market
United Kingdom	c. 13% (January–June)
Germany	c. 2½%
France:	c. 3%
Italy	c. 2%
Sweden	negligible

eBook penetration of markets in most other parts of the world has also hovered in the low single digits. In Taiwan, for instance, eBooks constitute only about 2 percent of book sales.[17] In the Czech Republic, it is less than ½ percent.[18] These numbers bounce around, sometimes from season to season and sometimes depending upon whether there is a best-selling title. Germany has showed some growth, while other numbers have tended to be rather flat.

Living in the United States, I already had a pretty good feel for what was happening with eBooks on my home turf (aided by reports from the Pew Internet & American Life Project).[19] But what was going on in places like Japan and France? And how about Germany, where Bowker's initial study reported 13 percent of those with internet access had bought an eBook in the last six months but in terms of revenue, eBooks represented a very small percent of the market? My search for answers led not only into cultural crannies but also into the worlds of profit and governance.

BUSINESS MEETS LAW

Most Americans (including, until recently, me) know little about how book sales work elsewhere in the world. We walk into the local Barnes & Noble in Augusta, Maine, and anticipate getting a discount on bestsellers. We go online to Amazon and are disappointed if we don't find the cost of the book we are about to order slashed from list price. About the only fiscal issue we might be aware of is whether online purchases are taxed.

Then I started talking with Europeans.

FIXED PRICES

It was late afternoon at Stanford's Center for Advanced Study in the Behavioral Sciences (affectionately known as CASBS). I'd been chatting with colleagues about my research on eBooks in global context, and Marlis Buchmann invited me to her study. A professor of sociology in Zurich and native speaker of German, she often ordered books from Amazon in Germany, since there is no Swiss Amazon .co.ch. She had also spent large stretches of time in the States and was no stranger to Amazon.com.

We sat down at her computer and began some online comparative shopping for print books. First the German site, Amazon.co.de: Each book showed one price—the same price charged by the publisher, the same amount you would pay in a bookstore in Germany. Then the American site, Amazon.com: Almost all the books displayed an "original" price with a red line through it, followed by the bargain price Amazon was charging—less than the publisher would ask and generally less than at my nearest independent bookstore.

Fixed pricing versus unfettered capitalism.

The idea behind fixed pricing is to preserve independent bookstores. A number of European countries have some version of fixed pricing on books. So does Japan.

The United States obviously does not. Neither does the UK (which abandoned fixed pricing in the 1990s).[20] Free marketeering in both countries has unquestionably contributed to the demise of smaller bookstores, which lack Amazon's bargaining power with publishers and ability to operate on razor-thin margins.[21] This economic reality is not lost elsewhere. The Canadian province of Québec spent months debating whether to establish fixed book pricing for new titles. The minister of culture and communications finally announced a plan that will limit discounts on new books to 10 percent for the first nine months following their release.[22]

The spirit of supporting community-based bookstores is also important to some Americans, including blockbuster author James Patterson, whose thrillers have sold 280 million copies. Patterson has donated $1 million to help independent bookstores.[23] (He even placed full-page ads in places like the *New York Times Book Review*, advocating for the sort of governmental support of the book industry found in Europe.)[24] And as we have mentioned, Zola.com welcomes brick-and-mortar booksellers to establish storefronts on the Zola site and share in profits.[25]

Most talk of fixed book pricing is directed at print sales. What about eBooks?

No surprise that in the United States and the UK, it's the Wild West, with sellers charging what the market will bear. Pricing of eBooks on the Continent is more complex. France, where fixed pricing on print books was established in 1981 under the Lang law, added fixed pricing to eBooks in 2011.[26] In Germany, there is fixed pricing on eBooks, with sticker prices averaging about 20 percent less than print.[27] But costs don't stop there. Customers purchasing a book (print or electronic) must also pay tax. And taxes on different forms of books are not the same.

VAT

Walk into a grocery store in the United States. Suppose you're buying a gallon of milk, a bottle of aspirin, and a bag of potatoes. You also pick up a potato peeler. When you go to check out, chances are you will pay tax on the peeler but not the milk, aspirin, or potatoes. Taxation policies differ from state to state (even county to county and city to city), though the principle remains roughly the same. Generally there is no tax on food items or drugs purchased in a grocery store, but you are likely to be taxed on things you won't be putting into your mouth—or maybe shouldn't, like soda and candy bars (at least in my state). Assuming there is tax on that potato peeler, it's at the same rate as for a pair of shoes, a new refrigerator, or a Mercedes.

Now go online to Amazon. If you're shipping to California (one of the states currently collecting sales tax on purchases made online), you will pay tax on a potato peeler and on the hardcopy of Malcolm Gladwell's *David and Goliath*, as well as on the eBook. Same tax rate for everything.

If you live within the European Union, once again not all taxes on goods are equal. What is taxed, and at what rate, is substantially set by the EU.[28] Say you live in Germany. If you go to purchase the milk and the potatoes, you pay 7 percent VAT (value-added tax). The aspirin and the potato peeler? It's 19 percent. Why the difference? Because while the standard tax is 19 percent in Germany, there are reduced taxes for some items: foodstuffs, water supplies, medical equipment for the disabled, passenger transport, newspapers and periodicals, and admission to cultural and entertainment events.

Print books also get the reduction. But eBooks don't. The reason is Council Directive 2002/38/EC, which sets the higher tax on "radio and television broadcasting services and certain electronically supplied services."[29] An eBook counts as an "electronic service." Print books obviously do not. There is some wiggle room on the eBook VAT, with the official EU minimum set at about 14 percent and the maximum around 20 percent, with considerable variation across countries. In addition, the numbers keep fluctuating. But there's a huge difference between 7 percent and even 14 percent.

There are EU countries that follow the policy and those that don't. While Germany charges 7 percent VAT on print and 19 percent on eBooks, in France the VAT on both print and digital is 5.5 percent. Italy's rates are 4 percent VAT on print and 22 percent on eBooks. Luxembourg charges a flat 3 percent tax on both formats.[30] In an interesting recent legal twist, the European Court of Justice found Sweden guilty of charging too high a VAT (25 percent instead of 6 percent) on printed works, resulting in a massive amount of money that must be repaid.[31]

The UK has no VAT on print, but there has been a 20 percent VAT on eBooks. However, since there is no fixed pricing on eBooks in the UK and price wars sometimes drive eBook sticker costs to ridiculously low levels, that VAT sometimes turns out to be less burdensome than in, say, Germany or Italy.

The EU's differential taxation policies for print versus digital books are based upon a social assumption: Print matters, and so do the establishments that sell it. Therefore the tax rate on hardcopy is relatively low. eReading has a place at the table, but only alongside hardcopy. At the same time, it is clear that the high VAT on eBooks is hurting the European economy, since savvy readers figure out how to purchase eBooks from sellers in countries that don't have the steep VAT. (In Japan, residents also know how to purchase digital downloads from outside the country, thereby avoiding paying the Japanese consumption tax.)[32]

In March 2013, Neelie Kroes, vice president of the European Commission for the EU Digital Agenda, delivered a provocative speech at the Paris Book Fair. Her title was "Making Europe the Home of eBooks." Here is part of what she said:

> We are not taking enough risks. In the US, eBooks are about one quarter of book sales; in only one European country does that figure go above 2 percent.... I know that tax can make a difference.... [I]n Europe we continue, for the most part, to charge the higher rate of VAT for eBooks.... The EU Commission is obliged to enforce EU law. But that does not mean we all agree with it, or think it needs to stay as it is.[33]

Change is in the offing. The European Parliament has been reviewing the VAT on eBooks.

LEGAL ENTANGLEMENTS

The economics of eBooks in Europe don't stop with regulations on fixed pricing and taxation. You need to add in business maneuverings designed to reduce costs. Some are technically legal, but others end up in court.

It's no secret that Luxembourg is a tax haven. Amazon shrewdly based its European operations there. Why? Because in Luxembourg, the effective taxation rate on corporate profits for foreign businesses is around 12 percent (compared with almost 40 percent in the United States), and the VAT on eBooks is only 3 percent.

The European Commission sued Luxembourg in the European Court of Justice, saying the VAT rate on eBooks needed to be increased to 15 percent. The Commission also requested that France raise its eBook VAT back up to 19.6 percent (where it once stood). In both cases, the argument was that the reduced rates provided an unfair advantage in the EU eBook market.[34] The EC took the further step of drawing up new legislation, effective January 1, 2015, whereby "non-resident traders" (like Amazon) will be required to pay the full EU-mandated VAT on "e-services" (like eBooks) in the country in which those services are used.[35] And so, for instance, if Amazon (whose European headquarters are located in Luxembourg) sells an eBook to a customer in Italy, Amazon needs to charge the Italian VAT (22 percent) and send that money to Italian tax collectors.

From its still-friendly VAT tax base in Luxembourg, Amazon managed a negotiating sleight of hand that has continued to reap the company strong profits in the UK. In selling eBooks in the UK (where the VAT is 20 percent) from Luxembourg (with its 3 percent tax), the question was how to comply with British law. Amazon's solution: Pass the tax burden on to publishers. As the *Guardian* reported, "Amazon starts negotiations with its publishers on the basis that the UK VAT rate of 20% must be knocked off the cost price."[36]

British booksellers—and the British reading public—were not amused. In 2013, booksellers Frances and Keith Smith collected 170,000 signatures on a petition against Amazon, which they delivered to 10 Downing Street.[37] In the Smiths' words, "As independent booksellers, we are happy with competition...but it must be on level terms....Amazon starts with an unfair advantage."[38] Or, in a memorable comment by Margaret Hodge, chair of a parliamentary committee investigating tax practices for sales in the UK by Amazon, Google, and Starbucks, "We're not accusing you of being illegal, we are accusing you of being immoral."[39]

The threat to British booksellers is real. In 2013, there were 1,028 independent booksellers in the UK, down from 1,535 in 2005. The UK has been eyeing the French government's recent commitment of €9 million to assist French booksellers.[40] Philip Jones, editor of the *Bookseller* (a British online publication about the book business), went a step further, hoping that the British secretary of state for culture, media and sport would speak up for the importance of books, as governments have on the Continent. As Jones put it, "Books are thought of as high culture in France and Germany, they're not really here."[41]

France continues to have its own legal battles with Amazon. Thanks to the Lang law, the maximum that a seller can discount a book is 5 percent. Amazon was offering the 5 percent price cut but also throwing in free shipping. The French parliament protested, arguing that the two discounts constituted unfair competition. In June 2014, the parliament unanimously adopted what promptly came to be known as the "Anti-Amazon Law," which forbade free shipping on books ordered online and mailed to France. Amazon.co.fr promptly countered by imposing a one-penny shipping charge.[42]

To sum up how commercial and legal forces influence eBook pricing and adoption: It seems reasonable to conclude there is an effect, but it's hard to measure directly, since the regulatory maze keeps shifting pathways. The cultural side of eBook adoption—which we turn to now—is at least less of a moving target.

THE CULTURAL TURN

Books are cultural artifacts, sometimes treasured ones. You find them housed in museums and special collections—like the *Book of Kells* in the Old Library at

Trinity College, Dublin, or Leonardo da Vinci's notebook known as the *Codex Leicester*, which Bill Gates owns but lends out for exhibitions. Books are also embedded within national histories. In Mainz, Johannes Gutenberg produced the first printed codex in the early 1450s. The legendary Frankfurt Book Fair began soon thereafter. Contemporary Germans tend to feel more attachment to printed books than Americans, for many of whom books are primarily associated with required schooling, not with aesthetics or national culture.

Let me share a personal example of what I mean about American attitudes. When my son was in middle school about fifteen years ago, a number of his friends were having bar or bat mitzvahs. What to give as a present? Parents usually did the choosing, and many of us made the "safe" choice of a gift card from Barnes & Noble. ("Let the recipients select the books they really want," we reasoned.) We had not anticipated what actually happened once the ceremony was over, the celebration had wound down, and it was time to organize the loot. I barely have enough fingers to tally the times I heard about savvy 13-year-olds trading those well-intentioned gift cards with their parents for cold hard cash so that the newly anointed men and women could buy the video games or clothing they actually fancied. So much for book culture among the rising generation of people of the book.

When you ask people which countries have strong book cultures (however that gets measured), France is often high on the list. Visitors returning from Paris fondly remember those green bookstalls lining the Seine. Inquire of a Frenchman, and you might hear words such as these, coming from Bernard Fixot, owner and publisher of a small publishing house:

> There are two things you don't throw out in France—bread and books.... In Germany the most important creative social status is given to the musician. In Italy it's the painter. Who's the most important creator in France? It's the writer.[43]

The French book business doesn't go it alone. Besides fixed prices on books (print and electronic) and that promise of a €9 million infusion, people looking to open bookstores are eligible for direct government support.

Germany is another top contender for the country with the strongest book culture. Besides Gutenberg and the Frankfurt Book Fair, there is a pervasive belief in books—particularly hardcopy ones. In a country of 82 million people, there are about 3,500 physical bookstores and over 13 million inhabitants report reading books at least once a week.[44]

As Barbara Pfetsch, a professor of communication in Berlin, explained to me, when you move to a new town in Germany, you need to settle on a place of worship, a doctor, and a bookshop. (The tradition of fixed prices on books, which helps keep those bookstores in business, dates back to 1888.)[45] Barbara went on to underscore Germans' affinity for print by recounting a tale of two subway rides—one from Frankfurt am Main Flughafen and the other from San Francisco International Airport. Riding the S-Bahn from the Frankfurt airport into the city, my colleague observed her fellow travelers reading their paper newspapers, much as she would expect. But a cultural disconnect came when she returned to California and settled into a BART train. No print newspapers; only electronic devices. Sure, there are exceptions on both ends, but as a German, she was immediately struck by the contrast.

How important are books in German culture? Michael Naumann, former CEO of Henry Holt in New York but also former publisher at the German company Rowohlt as well as minister of culture in his native Germany, put it this way:

> In Germany the cultural definition of the "book" as a major source of intellectual, scientific, economic and aesthetic self-improvement has carried the day over the capitalist notion that a book is a commodity and therefore deserving of no special considerations. The book as such is sacred. One does not throw books away.[46]

"One does not throw books away" in Germany, and the French "don't throw out... bread and books." The gap between European and American values when it comes to books sometimes feels as wide as the Atlantic Ocean.

Naumann went on to point out that Germany publishes about four times as many new books per capita as the United States (though I suspect the recent surge of indie self-publishing and the likes of Kindle Singles in the United States might rejigger the ratio). Germany also has a plentitude of local bookstores to sell those titles. Unlike the United States, where downloading an eBook to your Kindle or Kobo is often done as a time-saver, in Germany, chances are you can pick up the printed book with just a short walk.

THE PHYSICAL SIDE OF BOOKS

During my time at CASBS I met another German, this time a philosopher named Konstantin Pollack. Konstantin has taught in both Germany and the United States.

He spoke passionately about how attitudes toward books differ in the two countries. Much of our conversation centered on the physical properties of books themselves.

The issue largely came down to quality of manufacture. When his German students worked through a German-language, sold-in-Germany work, they marked up the book and, when the course was done, placed the volume on their bookshelf. In the United States, when his students purchased the English-translation, sold-in-America version of the same text, there was little to keep, since after a term's worth of close reading, the cheaply made physical book quite often literally fell apart.

Beyond the binding, paper quality matters in Germany. It also matters in Japan. When I travel to either of these countries, a prime souvenir for me is a stack of notebooks. Yes, I commonly write at a computer, but when I set a favorite pen to smoothly crafted paper, I find myself caring more about the words I record, even about my penmanship. When I am writing by hand on a legal pad purchased in the United States, the middling paper quality has no such charm.

The physicality of books takes on additional meaning in Japan thanks to size. Most Japanese books are small by Western standards: small in height, small in width, and thin. While some American books can make for a hefty carry, their Japanese counterparts (known as *bunko*) easily slip into an interior jacket pocket. For those long subway and bus rides in cities like Tokyo, it is easy to whip out your *bunko*, read for a bit, and then stow the book once more. As for digital devices, most Japanese (excluding a number of the elderly) carry mobile phones, which are handy for anything needing an internet connection. They are also convenient for reading *keitai* novels—short novels written to be accessed on a phone during those lengthy commutes.[47] Between your *keitai* and the lightweight *bunko*, who needs to lug an additional device like an eReader or tablet, holding dozens of books you won't be reading right now anyway?

Looking at the prospects for eReading in any country, it helps to check how much reading—on any platform—people say they are doing. In my studies, I asked university students how many hours a week they read for schoolwork or for pleasure. Looking at the lower and upper extremes, here is what they said:

	United States	Japan	Germany
Reading for schoolwork			
Between 0 and 2 hours per week	9%	71%	5%
At least 7 hours per week	43%	8%	54%
Reading for pleasure			
Between 0 and 2 hours per week	45%	62%	23%
At least 7 hours per week	17%	7%	38%

For both schoolwork and personal enjoyment, the Germans are clearly the heavy readers (at least for students in my samples). Next come university students in the United States, with the Japanese bringing up the rear. When they did read, what kind of mobile device did these Japanese students choose? One-quarter said they primarily did academic reading on their *keitai*, and almost three-quarters relied on their *keitai* for pleasure reading.

Tablets may also have a niche among the Japanese eReading public. Beginning in 1997, a project known as Aozoru Bunko ("Blue Sky Library") followed in the spirit of Project Gutenberg: free digital access to books that are out of copyright. Aozoru Bunko attracted volunteers who scanned and digitized books, which were initially accessed on computers. I am told that when tablets were introduced in Japan, one of the selling points was using them to read Aozoru Bunko.[48]

Tablets bring another advantage in Japan they don't tend to have elsewhere. We have already mentioned the wide local popularity of manga. You could read them on your *keitai*, but the screen real estate is too small for appreciating the intricate graphics. A tablet's screen size is ideal.

GENDER AS A CULTURAL ISSUE

When we talk about cultural variation, we tend to think about people who live in different countries or maybe in the same country but use different languages (like the Swiss, who might speak French, German, Italian, or Romansh). Yet gender is another dimension of culture. You don't have to be sexist or even mildly judgmental to acknowledge that gender differences exist (at least statistically) in musculature, temperament, and language. They also may be relevant in people's approaches to reading online.

In my own studies, I didn't have enough of a gender balance to look for variation in usage or preference. But some Chinese data from the University of Guangzhou are intriguing.[49] Females had a stronger preference for print than males. Not surprisingly, females were more likely to print out electronic documents. They were also heavier annotators of printed materials, indicating (in the words of the study's authors) "that females are likely more serious readers than males."[50] Males were happier with online reading than with print. They reported doing more browsing, scanning, and nonlinear reading when online, compared with females.

The Chinese data were collected in 2006—when "screen" meant "computer screen." Would these gender distinctions hold today? And what about in other countries? Good questions, awaiting good studies. The first step will be to control for students' seriousness of educational purpose, level of academic success, and degree of comfort using digital technologies. As gender studies elsewhere continue to show, experience and socialization (along with personality) are at least as important in predicting behavior patterns as genes.

THE HANDWRITING ON THE WALL

However entrenched cultural practices may be, technology can redefine traditional behaviors and values. Handwriting is a good example.

In Japan, when children learn to write *kanji*, neatness is not the only thing that counts. So does stroke order. Just ask any *gaijin* (foreigner) who is studying Japanese. The *kanji* lessons come complete with little numbers next to the strokes, indicating the order in which to form the characters.

Now along come word processing programs and *keitai*, on both of which you produce the *kanji* not by drawing the strokes but by selecting from a variety of pre-formed options. This technological turn may end up dismantling an essential component of what it has meant to educate children to be Japanese. The issue boils down to relevance. If you are not going to use that painstakingly acquired knowledge of stroke order, why bother learning it? Several of my Japanese colleagues who went through the Japanese schooling system and now are language teachers in the United States tell me they are having a hard time remembering stroke order. Outside of when they are teaching, they simply aren't getting much practice.

Relevance and practice are also major considerations in a debate currently raging in America over cursive writing: Should we still teach it?[51] A growing number of schools don't. (At last count, 41 states out of 50 no longer require it.) The arguments go like this.

In the "ditch cursive" camp, the major rallying cry is that everyone types anyway. Why waste time teaching children a skill they will almost never use, except maybe to sign their name? Even the signature issue is questionable, as payments move from checks to credit cards, and no one looks at the scrawl you produce on a charge slip or charge machine anyway. As for losing handwriting as a window onto our character and personality (until recently a valued practice in Europe and America),[52] we may need to just let go. Think of the benefits. If physicians typed rather than handwrote prescriptions, maybe pharmacists could read them. And if students typed all their exams rather than writing them by hand, think how much less strain there would be for teachers struggling to decipher chicken scratch.

On the "keep" side, we hear about the virtues of improving eye-hand coordination, of nurturing an aesthetic sense, and of having the necessary tools for reading cursive writing both modern (my grocery list) and vintage (like the Declaration of Independence). A major argument in Japan against replacing its writing system with the Roman alphabet has been insistence on the populace being able to read historical documents written in *kanji* and *kana*.[53]

Given the continuing growth of mechanical writing tools (computers, tablets, mobile phones), if cursive goes, will handwritten print letters be far behind?

DIGITS TO THE RESCUE

At the same time, the digital world has many virtues, including cultural ones. Think about the challenge of rejuvenating endangered languages. Of the roughly 6,000 languages in use today, half are expected to die out by the end of the twenty-first century.[54] Dozens of local efforts are underway to document these threatened tongues before the last native speaker is no more and his or her children know only English, Spanish, Russian, or some other majority language. Equally impressive are attempts to bring endangered languages back into active community use. Here is where tools like the internet are invaluable. Facebook pages and blogs in languages like Cymraeg (aka Welsh), established in an attempt to support the language, are attracting young users.

When it comes to cultural artifacts such as original manuscripts or rare printed books, the internet offers invaluable digital access to scholars and the general public. If you can't make it to Dublin, the entire *Book of Kells* is available online.[55] So is Gutenberg's Bible.[56] Digital materials—including in multimedia formats—are also aiding cultural preservation in countries beyond the European sphere. One example is the United Arab Emirates, where there is a concerted effort to preserve not just texts but the sounds of regional dialects, along with videos of long-standing rituals (be they around the camel track or at weddings) that are integral parts of the social fabric.[57]

THE ORAL SIDE OF BOOKS

Earlier we talked about audiobooks—their emergence, their popularity, and whether purists actually consider them "books." The conversation has a cultural side, and you can hear it in countries with strong oral traditions. In an interview, Nigerian author Ekenyerengozi Michael Chima described the rather rudimentary state of reading in his homeland. But Chima reminds us that

> Nigerian literature is largely based on our oral culture before the advent of English Literature in the South around the 17th century and Arabic Literature in the North in the 15th century.

Acknowledging this oral heritage, Chima suggests that audiobooks rather than print or eBooks may be the best avenue for book development in Nigeria.[58]

ECONOMICS MEETS CULTURAL PRACTICE

Chima makes an excellent case for matching book access to cultural practice in Nigeria. But another reality in Africa shapes the kind of reading technologies likely to take off soon, and that is money. In Nigeria, most people live on less than $2 a day.[59] Much of the rest of sub-Saharan Africa isn't any better off. Internet connections are often iffy at best, and book piracy is rampant. There also isn't a strong book culture. In South Africa, half of households don't contain a single book, only about 1 percent of the populace buys books, and roughly 14 percent read them. Plus the VAT on eBooks is 14 percent.[60]

One solution, the brainchild of Arthur Attwell, is an enterprise called Paperight. In South Africa, where more than half the population has no internet access, Attwell set up a service in local photocopy shops (which do have internet) where customers can download print copies of books. The company now has more than 200 locations in South Africa and is expanding to other African countries.[61]

An alternative solution has been to bypass laptops and tablets (which most Africans can't afford) and go straight for eBooks on mobile phones. Mobile phone adoption in the developing world has already profoundly benefited people's working lives.[62] It may also be poised to increase the amount that Africans read. In Nigeria, there are almost 67 mobile phone subscriptions for every 100 people.[63] In Kenya, with about 71 mobile subscriptions for every 100 people, the Kwani Trust is undertaking to bring works of literature (commonly short stories, but also graphic novels) to the tiny screen.[64]

Others looking to spread reading in Africa are expanding their reach to mobile phones as well. Earlier we talked about Worldreader, the organization distributing Kindles (and eBooks) to children in sub-Saharan Africa. Worldreader has now broadened its distribution network to include mobile phones. Using an app called biNu, millions of mobile phone subscribers in Africa can download Worldreader books, along with other content.[65]

Economics and culture intersect in yet other ways. Take credit cards and online purchases. In countries where people feel comfortable shopping online using credit cards, purchasing eBooks is as natural as ordering a parka from LLBean.com. However, in areas largely operating on cash economies or where the trust level regarding online purchases is low, the eBook trade can be expected to feel the pinch.[66]

ENTRENCHMENT OR MOVING WITH THE TIMES

As part of Roosevelt's New Deal in the 1930s, an act was passed creating the Tennessee Valley Authority. The TVA was designed to control floods on the Tennessee River, improve agriculture, and provide electricity to the rural South. Worthy goals—but not many who lived along the river and were being relocated, often against their will. The government's challenge was to get them to move, abandoning not just hearth and home but decades of memories and family history. Anyone who has seen Elia Kazan's 1960 movie *Wild River* has witnessed the resolve—and pain—of one of the last holdouts, an old woman who refused to leave.[67]

The case of the TVA relocating people for a public works project is hardly unique. Think of Egypt's Aswan High Dam, whose construction displaced not just people but the ancient temples at Abu Simbel, which were relocated to save them from being flooded. A more bitter case is China's continuing ejection of landowners in the name of urban expansion. Some, reluctantly, agree to leave. Others resort to more heartbreaking measures, including suicide.[68]

Personal history. Custom. Culture. We are all products of our past. Giving up pieces of it is often troubling, even when there's no threat to life and limb. I witnessed this lesson firsthand during travels to Greece.

Years back, I was in Athens on vacation. These were the days before ATM machines or even common use of credit cards, at least in Greece, so I needed to find a bank to change my US dollars into drachmas. Knowing there was a large bank in Syntagma Square, I made my way there at about one o'clock in the afternoon. Of course it was closed. As any self-respecting citizen of the Mediterranean knows, businesses—even churches—conventionally open in the morning, close for an extended lunch, and reopen in late afternoon. I resigned myself to a long (but necessarily frugal) lunch.

When I returned to Athens several years later, Greek banks were under cultural siege. Greek "bankers' hours" weren't the same as in northern Europe (only one time zone away), much less in North America. If Greece wanted to be part of the international economic community, it was told it needed to eliminate its lunchtime closure. This time my challenge wasn't trying to change money in the early afternoon. (I had already learned that lesson.) Now the banks were shut down, on strike, protesting the demand to change their ways.

Eventually, the Greeks capitulated—sort of. Now the main banks open at 8:00 a.m. but close for the day at 2:30 p.m., with an earlier closing on Friday. (By contrast, in the United States, banks have extended hours on Friday.) We might call this a cultural draw.

Digital technologies offer up their own challenges to tradition and culture. Take mobile phones. They are incredibly handy tools for communicating with friends, family, or business associates. But how do we behave toward people who are physically in our midst? Sherry Turkle asked this question a few years back in *Alone Together*.[69] Now so has Catherine Steiner-Adair, a clinical psychologist at Harvard Medical School. In *The Big Disconnect*, Steiner-Adair documents the unhealthy effects we are having on children through our mobile phone practices, often privileging conversation with unseen others over talking with the young son or daughter sitting across from us.[70]

And now take eReading. Businesses (such as Amazon and Kobo) and educational establishments (whether CourseSmart or state boards of education) are working to change the culture of reading by replacing print with screens. I am not against the profit motive, and I'm hardly averse to change. The issue is simply, who benefits? Will France, Germany, and Japan be well served culturally if their level of eBook adoption reaches that of the United States? Will the university students in my three-country study, who generally expressed a strong preference for print, simply need to adapt to new ways, as have Greek bankers?

Ten years from now, will we have fundamentally redefined our notion of what it means to read? Sure, some people will still seriously grapple with Montaigne and Marx. Some will continue to be engrossed in long-form fiction. But maybe the new normal will be writing that is more straightforward and shorter. Maybe schools and parents will emphasize smart search techniques rather than knowledge we hold in our heads, and promote reading strategies compatible with multitasking and other digital distractions.

Or perhaps not. Maybe ten years from now, we will look back and laugh at the resistance put up in some quarters to eReading. Digitally native books (which we haven't really talked about) will have evolved into an entirely new genre of reading. Perhaps we will have learned to monitor our behavior when reading continuous text on digital devices, so we'll naturally keep distraction and multitasking to a minimum. More and more young people might be emulating Patricia Hamilton Dowrie, a member of Stanford's class of 1937 who is now in her 90s. As the *Stanford Alumni Magazine* recently described her, "An avid reader, Pat spends hours glued to her Kindle."[71]

Practices—and cultures—change. The Chinese no longer bind women's feet. Women's suffrage is a reality in much of the world. And yes, an African American was elected president of the United States. Just so, literacy is now nearly universal in many countries. Millions of children in Africa and India have a chance to own books because of the availability of eReaders and mobile phones. Pat Dowrie had no Kindle for more than 80 years of her life but made a successful transition from hardcopy.

What the world of reading will look like a decade from now is impossible to know. What we can do is weigh the pros and cons of different possibilities. We can also offer suggestions on how to shape that future.

10 The Future of Reading in a Digital World

The Age of Print is passing.

—Katherine Hayles

The Internet makes words as cheap and as significant as Chee[z] Doodles.

—David Gelernter

In the midst of a revolution, it's tricky calling a winner. One side is ahead, but then the weather turns and so does the outcome. Technological developments (and public uptake) aren't physically bloody uprisings. Yet predicting victory during the turmoil of innovation can be every bit as challenging.

Will babies born today ever read anything in print? Yes, but how much? After several years of triple-digit growth in eBooks, the numbers are settling down. By mid-2013, the share of eBook sales compared with overall book numbers in the United States was pretty flat: about 30 percent of units sold and a bit under 15 percent of revenues.[1] For the first half of 2013, sales of children's and young adult eBooks plunged 46 percent from the previous year-to-date, due largely to lack of blockbusters like *The Hunger Games*.[2] The Association of American Publishers reported that by year's end, overall eBook sales for 2013 had risen only 3.8 percent.[3] Maybe we will see a new spike as more people acquire tablets and smartphones. Or maybe not.

At the same time, the data suggest that people who read on digital devices tend to do more reading overall than those only reading print. A poll by *USA Today* and Bookish found that adults with eReaders or tablets average 18 books a year, compared with hardcopy-only readers, who average 11.[4] And as we have seen, the number of people owning and using mobile reading devices continues to grow. To recap: By early 2014, more than 40 percent of Americans owned a tablet, while one-third owned an eReader. What's more, 28 percent said that they had read at least one eBook over the past year.[5]

When I began studying the rise of eBooks and its consequences for reading, I kept hearing an array of different voices. One set warned it was too soon to know how the battle would play out or what the consequences would be for education or personal satisfaction. Another reminded me that if I had concerns about the downside of eReading, I needed to speak up—if you see something, say something. I remembered the pronouncement made in 1971 by Alan Kay, inventor of the computer language Smalltalk and of the early Apple graphical user interface:

> Don't worry about what anybody else is going to do.... The best way to predict the future is to invent it.[6]

And so my dilemma. First computers, then eReaders, and now tablets and mobile phones are shaking up the world of reading to a degree not seen for centuries. As ownership of devices proliferates and publishers (along with independent authors) spin out eBooks to fill them, it's uncertain how the story will end. Equally unclear is how digital reading is changing us as readers. Should I bide my time until more data are available?

I followed Kay and started writing.

SIZING UP DIGITAL READING

At my university, faculty are encouraged to do midsemester teaching evaluations. Rather than waiting until the end of the term to hear what students liked or disliked about the course (when it's too late to make changes), many of us poll our classes about seven weeks in.

It is hard to judge how far into the digital reading revolution we are at this point. However, if we want the chance to do course correction, now's the time to take stock.

PROS

No one questions that eReading is convenient. Grab your phone or tablet or eReader, and leave the pile of books behind.

The week it came out, I bought Jhumpa Lahiri's new book, *The Lowland*. I looked forward to savoring Lahiri's nuanced prose during an upcoming transatlantic flight. If I wanted print (which I did), it was only available in hardcover. As I packed, I stowed my conference materials, unlocked GSM phone, and Macbook Air. Was reading Lahiri's book right now worth the extra weight and bulk? Could I even wedge it into my backpack? And if so, should I abandon the volume when I arrived in Sweden, like those visitors to Brighton Beach more than a century ago? Not a good plan, I decided, since my husband would need to purchase another copy to read himself.

I settled on a David Baldacci thriller—a small, lightweight paperback—which I polished off during the flight and then ditched at my Stockholm hotel. Had I gone with *The Lowland* in eBook, the problem would have vanished.

Part of the convenience of eReading is being able to search the text. Much as I believe in continuous reading, I share my students' frustration when I can't locate the specific passage I am looking for. I worry about students being tempted to use the FIND function, zero in on a snippet, and ignore what the larger reading is about. Yet surely the answer is to teach people appropriate uses of search tools, not to brand FIND as evil.

And eReading encourages reading extensively. The *USA Today*/Bookish survey described one respondent's reading pattern this way: "He raced through all 14 books in Jim Butcher's fantasy/mystery series, *The Dresden Files*," most of which he downloaded from a public library. Said the Butcher fan: "As soon as I finish one, I download the next."[7] It is hard not to be reminded of Robert Darnton's description of the switch from intensive to extensive reading during the second half of the eighteenth century:

[Men] read all kinds of material, especially periodicals and newspapers, and read it only once, then raced on to the next item.[8]

Another obvious advantage of digital reading platforms is their invaluable contribution in democratizing access to the written word. The more archives, research findings, news, and works of literature we can make available to the public, the better off we are as individuals, cultures, and nations. Democratizing access is rooted in a social agenda. Particularly in the developing world, millions of children have never owned a book, and millions of adults cannot read. Projects such as Worldreader provide a vital humanitarian service that often would be more challenging with print.[9]

Admittedly, this kind of access is not on most people's radar screen, including that of college students. Their digital access question is more often "Can I get the book for free?" or "Does my library have an electronic subscription to that journal?" But these same students continue to have clear views about the pros and cons of eTextbooks.

Market research confirms that students find eTextbooks convenient to carry around and easy to search. Plus there's a general perception that eTextbooks cost less than print and are environmentally friendly. Yet there is also continuing resistance to eTextbooks. Recall that for fall 2013, the Book Industry Study Group reported that 71 percent of the students they surveyed preferred hardcopy textbooks over digital.[10]

The full student eReading story is, of course, more complicated. Digital activity is increasingly woven into students' educational lives. Online learning management systems such as Blackboard or Canvas are widely used. Journal articles have significantly migrated from library stacks to digital access. The number of online courses (with online readings) continues to soar, and mobile learning tools are finding their way into ever more face-to-face classrooms. Yet textbooks seem to be a different matter. In the words of Carl Kulo, director of Bowker Market Research in the United States, "Students aren't resisting digital.... But they are seeing more learning and monetary value in print textbooks."[11]

Remember that respondent from the *USA Today*/Bookish poll who zipped through Jim Butcher's fantasy/mystery series on a digital reader? It turns out that his 17-year-old son prefers print, saying he finds it easier to focus on what he is reading. Plus, he says, he likes the way the book feels in his hands.

CONS

The French writer Anatole France, winner of the 1921 Nobel Prize in literature, identified these as the three most important qualities in a writer: lucidity first, lucidity second, lucidity third. What are the three most critical drawbacks to reading onscreen? Distraction first, distraction second, distraction third.

Study upon study confirms that if your digital device has an internet connection enabling you to do more than just download books, it is likely more challenging to read onscreen than in hardcopy. Whether you ask people about distraction, concentration, or multitasking, the result is always the same. Continuous, absorbed reading can be a struggle when the medium you are using beckons you elsewhere.

Writers—even those who love digital devices—continue to report the challenges they face when trying to do focused reading on a screen that proffers additional options. David Ulin reports that while he reads eBooks on his tablet, "there's no question that I read less closely, less immersively . . . or perhaps it's more accurate to say that my diversions are always close to hand."[12] Even Steven Johnson, who extols the virtues of video games and social reading, writes that "print books have remained a kind of game preserve for the endangered species of linear, deep-focused reading" and that as we read more online, "I fear that one of the great joys of book reading—the total immersion in another world, or in the world of the author's ideas—will be compromised."[13]

To be fair, it's hard to blame readers. Computers and now tablets and mobile phones were not designed for lengthy, focused reading. Searching, skimming, polishing off short texts. Only reading something once. Sure. But Goethe? Yes, you could read *The Sorrows of Young Werther* on your mobile, but to do so meaningfully requires more discipline than in print. Some readers might rise to the occasion, but probably not most.

A colleague of mine noted an interesting social dimension to the distraction question. Say you are reading a print book. While you might stop reading to talk with someone (face-to-face, on the phone, through a text message), the book itself doesn't inherently invite such conversation. By contrast, when you read on a digital device with a full-fledged internet connection, your social network is just a click (or press or swipe) away.

Another colleague pointed out an additional social factor involving interruption. If you see someone looking at printed text, you can reasonably assume he or she is actually reading, and you may hesitate to intrude. But what about when you see someone gazing at a digital screen whose content you're not privy to? Who knows what that person is actually doing on the device? It's easier to start talking under these circumstances, since there is a lower probability you are interrupting someone's act of reading.[14]

Digital devices inherently provoke distraction, whatever else you are trying to do. At the University of Canberra, Sora Park collected revealing data in a study of students who were given iPads as part of a larger educational experiment. One of

Park's questions was how students perceived their tablets: as productive tools or distractions? The answer was some of both. But listen to how students struggled not to yield to temptation and use the iPad for R&R when they should have been studying or paying attention in class. Among their strategies:

"Simply not leaving it on the desk when studying."
"Requires a lot of self-control."
"Deleting all of my distracting apps but finding myself pulling out my phone with the same apps."[15]

Then there are mobile phones. How many times do you see people (yourself included) tapping away during a meeting? The lure is just too great. And heck, everyone's doing it anyway.

Students share your sentiment. A recent study tallied how often university students use their mobiles during class for non-class-related purposes. Ready? On a typical day, the average for undergraduates is 11 times daily. More than 90 percent did so at least once daily, with 15 percent reporting more than 30 daily uses in class. With this kind of mind-set, does concentrated intellectual activity of any sort stand a chance?[16]

Many of us lack the self-control to step away from our mobile phones, even when we are on holiday. I am reminded of a story about Sharon Ringley, the co-founder of a major government relations company in Washington that deals with technology and new media. When on the clock, she is noted for emailing colleagues late into the night. Even on vacation, Ringley couldn't stop checking email on her iPhone, continually interrupting her attempt to read an eBook on that same device. Finally, she admits, she "went to go buy a 'real' book so I would stop."[17]

Just as there is more to good writing than lucidity, distraction isn't the only challenge when reading onscreen. We have considered a number of issues throughout the book, but here's a quick refresher on the most pressing.

Cognitive and Emotional Prospects

We don't all read the same way. Some sit upright at desks, while others like to lounge on a couch. There are those who only read digitally (if they can help it), people who stick with print, and lots of us in between. One colleague, a philosopher, assures me he can follow intricate logical arguments when reading on his mobile phone, while another, also a philosopher, scoffs at the notion.

Whatever our predilections, when you listen to what large numbers of readers—and reading experts—have to say, a list emerges of the kinds of reading that digital devices generally discourage:

- Reading longer texts
- Rereading
- Deep reading
- Memory of what you have read (which is often aided by handwritten annotation)
- Individual (rather than primarily social) encounters with books
- Stumble-upon possibilities
- Strong emotional involvement

On the issue of emotions: We have talked about the difference between being moved to tears (a high level for setting the bar) and becoming absorbed in what you're reading (a notch or two down). Somewhere along the spectrum lies the traditional notion of becoming lost in a book, being so involved in the content that the world around you fades. As the title figure put it in Elizabeth Barrett Browning's poem *Aurora Leigh*,

> when
> We gloriously forget ourselves, and plunge
> Soul-forward, headlong, into a book's profound,
> Impassioned for its beauty and salt of truth—
> 'Tis then we get the right good from a book.[18]

I strongly suspect it is harder to "plunge soul-forward" into an eBook than into a physical one.

Since we are on the subject of literature, permit me to return to Lahiri's *The Lowland*. I finally read it, in hardcover, when I was back in the States. The book has received resounding praise from the press, so there's no need to recount its virtues. What I would like to do is share a line that made me pause, reread, underline, copy out, and read again. Lahiri is conveying the perceptions of Subhash Mitra, who departed the teeming metropolis of Calcutta in the late 1960s to study in the quaintly rural town of Kingston, Rhode Island. Lahiri writes:

> Here was a place where humanity was not always pushing, rushing, running as if with a fire at its back.[19]

Had I taken the convenience option and loaded the eVersion onto a digital device, would I have breezed by the line, missing the power of Lahiri's imagery?

"It's Not a Book"

For a remarkably large number of readers, the physicality of a print book continues to matter. In my own research, students—especially the Japanese—said that reading books was "real" reading, while eReading was not. In fact, one out of every seven Japanese students volunteered that what he or she liked best about reading in hardcopy was some variation of "able to feel that I am actually reading." Yet another student said that what he liked least about reading onscreen was "I don't feel that I actually read a book."

In the study Ricoh commissioned comparing American attitudes toward print versus eBooks, the findings closely tracked with my own:

- College students reported it was easier to concentrate on print than on eBooks.
- Two of the top reasons consumers preferred print were the look and feel of the paper, and the fact you could add a print book to your library or bookshelf.[20]

Another survey, this one done by Voxburner in the UK, reported that 62 percent of 16-to-24-year-olds preferred reading in print. While "value for the money" was one top reason, an emotional connection with hardcopy was another. Fully 51 percent gave explanations relating to physicality (such as "I like to hold the product"). Others mentioned liking the smell of books and being able to fill bookshelves.[21]

Reading the Ricoh and Voxburner studies, I couldn't help reflecting on Jabr Ferris' comment in his piece "Why the Brain Prefers Paper," in *Scientific American*: "Paper's greatest strength may be its simplicity."[22] Or on Umberto Eco's declaration in *This Is Not the End of the Book*: "The book is like the spoon, scissors, the hammer, the wheel. Once invented, it cannot be improved."

Devices and Downloads

Digital platforms carry some structural baggage. A major source of users' complaints involves eyestrain, especially when reading on computer screens. I was surprised to see how pervasive the problem is. Responses to my survey question "What is the one thing you like least about reading onscreen?" tell the tale. In the American data, 30 percent of the answers related to eyestrain. Studies done by colleagues for the COST Action FP1104 project regularly mentioned eyestrain as well. And eyestrain from reading on a screen was also among the top three reasons in the Ricoh study for why people preferred print.

A second drawback—this time with the software—is ownership. You paid good money for all those books you downloaded from Amazon (and other vendors) but don't really own them: You can't sell them, and you can't even give them away, though now there are at least some ways to lend them.

While the ownership issue will probably sort itself out, it's less clear that we will reach consensus on cost and environmental impact. Yes, list price for digital is generally less than for hardcopy—but only in certain countries. Governmental tax structures, along with regulations on fixed prices for books, quickly muddy the comparisons. In Singapore, eBooks account for at most 5 percent of the book market. An eBook explosion waiting to happen? Not necessarily, since there is little price difference between digital and print copies.[23] In Finland, which also has a low eBook adoption rate, high taxes mean the cost of eBooks sometimes exceeds that of print.[24]

In thinking about cost, we need to ask what consumers consider to be value for their money. Would you rather pay less but not own the book? Used print books typically cost less than digital. And while saving money may be appealing, university students in all three countries I surveyed said that if the price were the same for print or digital, they preferred print.

Assessing environmental costs of digital versus print is equally complicated. How do you balance the amount of fossil fuels used to produce and transport reams of paper against health hazards in recycling digital devices? Or the bill for air-conditioning a physical bookstore versus driving fans to cool server farms? Now that paper production and recycling are becoming more efficient, we can hope parallel improvements will come in the manufacture, use, and recycling of digital devices.

When Talk Is Cheap

As an author, I take words seriously. Readers (so authors hope) do as well. So when I came upon David Gelernter's comment that "the Internet makes words as cheap and as significant as Chee[z] Doodles," I sat up.

If Jakob Nielsen is right about how little we read on a web page; if the University College London study is correct in characterizing academics as doing power browsing, not reading; if students whom my colleagues and I have surveyed are accurately reporting that they don't remember as much when they read onscreen as when reading in hardcopy—is the significance of words consumed on digital devices being reduced to that of snack food?

Words are not the only thing at stake. The value of works in which they appear is also challenged. If readers believe they get what they pay for, and the price of at least many eBooks is low—or free—do electronic productions garner the same respect as their print counterparts? When an eBook that took the author years to write costs less than a doughnut, how much lasting worth is the work perceived to have?

To be fair, we can ask a similar question about print. Once inexpensive versions of books became available (think of nineteenth-century penny dreadfuls, of today's "quality" paperbacks, or even of mass-market books), are readers as invested in the text as when they pay more dearly for a hardback?

In the current publishing climate, many authors who care about the elegance of their prose, about paying the rent, or both, are concerned. There is even the fundamental question of whether they will get paid at all.

Copyright law in both England and the United States has long recognized the need for a balance between authors' rights and the public good, which requires access to the fruits of other people's intellectual labors. In the words of the US Constitution, Congress shall have the right

> to promote the Progress of Science and useful Arts, by securing for limited Times to Authors and Inventors the exclusive Right to their respective Writings and Discoveries.[25]

An "exclusive Right" but "for limited Times." Once that time runs out, the populace gets to enjoy such works for free.

Public access is a double-edged sword: beneficial to the common good but not always in the interest of the producer. Judge Denny Chin's November 2013 ruling in the suit against Google Books is a case in point.[26] The underlying issue was whether Google had the right to display significant portions of books still under copyright without paying royalties to authors. Google said yes. Publishers and the Authors Guild said no. While the publishers had earlier settled, the Authors Guild held out—and lost.

In his decision, Judge Chin stressed the public benefits of fair use. He also observed that authors profit through sales of their books, which Google facilitates by including links to sites from which the works can be ordered. Presumably users are led to purchase the actual books (generating royalties for authors), since the online versions in Google Books typically display only a limited number of pages.[27]

An interesting argument, but I would like to see the sales figures. As a frequent user of Google Books, I often get lucky and find the passage or reference I'm looking for in pages that are displayed. No need, then, for me to buy the book—and I generally don't.

DIGITAL FUTURES

We can count on the world of reading onscreen to look very different tomorrow from the way it does today. It doesn't take a soothsayer to predict that a number of our current challenges with digital reading will sort themselves out. Here are some developments already emerging or in the pipeline.

DEVICES AND DOWNLOADS

Digital reading devices will continue to get lighter. Their storage capacity and battery life will grow, and annotation tools will improve. It is also a good bet that new screen types will reduce eyestrain. What is more, it is likely that eBook distributors and lawyers will resolve the ownership question, though we may need some major lawsuits to get there.

Another challenge of digital reading has been screen real estate. Try comparing the number of pages in the print version of a novel with pages in an eBook. The eBook might have three or four times as many, even if you don't increase font size.

Given average-sized eReaders, tablets, or mobile phones (models vary, but imagine an average), an important challenge has been the need for continual scrolling or frequent shifting from page to page. In comparing the cognitive dimensions of reading onscreen versus in hardcopy, we have seen that physical landscape of pages matters, at least for many readers and many kinds of reading. Print books let you easily see two full pages at once. You can use your fingers to hold your place for others. The topography of the text helps you remember where you read something. Anne Mangen's research suggests that when students don't need to be scrolling or clicking through so many pages—that is, when they read in print—their comprehension improves.

Sony has taken a stab at addressing the scrolling/swiping problem by engineering a new large tablet for use in Japan. Designed for the student textbook market, the 13.3-inch eInk reader offers the equivalent of an A4-sized piece of paper (the standard in many countries outside the United States).[28] Amazon's Kindle DX, introduced in 2009, was also designed for the textbook market but failed miserably. To be fair, 2009 is antediluvian in the eReading world. We will see if Sony's new design takes off.

An important new feather in digital's cap came in late 2013, when the US Federal Aviation Administration relaxed its rules on use of portable electronic devices on airplanes. Now it's OK during takeoff and landing, as long as your device is in airplane mode.[29] More convenience for users, as one of the previous advantages of hardcopy bites the dust.

There are even initiatives to make electrical charging and batteries unnecessary on eReaders. A joint project of Disney Research and Carnegie Mellon University is creating "Paper Generators" that create the energy needed to power an eReader through the natural human motions of touching, tapping, or swiping on the device.[30]

PUBLIC ACCESS

It is uncertain how the story of authors' rights to payment for material available on the web will end. Much clearer is the growing trend toward increased public access, even if someone is bankrolling it behind the scenes.

Public digital libraries (such as the Digital Public Library of America) and open-access journals (like those published by PLoS) will continue serving the population at large, assuming there is financial backing to underwrite the endeavors. American publishers are finally making larger numbers of eBook titles available to public libraries, though the pricing structure continues to need work. (One publisher was charging three times the cost of the highest priced edition available in print.)[31] Since taxpayers ultimately foot the bill for volumes circulated digitally, we can hope public libraries will increasingly be able to afford making a wide selection of eBooks available.

TEXTBOOKS REVISITED: LEGISLATING OPEN ACCESS

We know that textbooks, especially in higher education, are often quite costly. Earlier we talked about university-based initiatives to create open-access textbooks. While such works are often faculty labors of love, sometimes they are supported through grants or institutional funding. In November 2013, US Senators Dick Durbin and Al Franken introduced the Affordable College Textbook Act, which would provide government backing for creating and distributing open-access textbooks.[32]

What format would these textbooks assume? While the early part of the bill refers only to "education material that can be used in postsecondary instruction, including textbooks and other written or audiovisual works," a later paragraph on "access and distribution" is unambiguous:

The full and complete digital content of each educational resource created or adapted...shall be made available free of charge to the public...on an easily accessible and interoperable website...[and] in a machine readable, digital format that anyone can directly download, edit, and redistribute.[33]

In other words, the texts will be electronic. Whatever faculty members' (or students') feelings about reading onscreen versus in hardcopy, selecting these books will potentially save students hundreds of dollars a year, with the national total annually running into the millions.

The United States is not alone in addressing the access issue. In Europe, there is a massive project, the EU's Digital Agenda for Europe, designed to "help digital technologies, including the Internet, to deliver economic growth." It goes without saying that education is a key pillar of the agenda, and that expanding access to digitally based learning resources is a central component of the initiative.[34] Meanwhile, as a way of reducing textbook costs for primary school children, Hungary has nationalized its textbook market. Poland and South Africa are considering similar moves.[35]

REDEFINING THE READING EXPERIENCE

A major development we can anticipate over the next few years is the growth of digitally native books, what we might call eBooks 2.0. Instead of being essentially PDFs or slightly gussied-up versions of print works, these are books designed digitally from the ground up. eBooks 2.0 are already appearing in educational contexts and as children's books. Since they tend to be expensive to produce, the market is emerging slowly compared with eBooks 1.0. Educational technologists who understand curricula and curricular design are voicing much enthusiasm about these ventures. And rightly so. They are highly interactive by nature and have very different intended learning outcomes than a straight digital rendering of *Wuthering Heights* or *The Critique of Pure Reason*.

More initiatives are emerging as well. One is a cross between a video game and a book. Device 6 (a "metaphysical thriller" developed in Sweden and sold as an app) is a text-heavy game that works like this:

Playing it is like reading a book—except, in this book, the words veer off in unexpected directions, rather than progressing in orderly fashion down the page. When Anna, the game's protagonist, turns a corner in the narrative, the text does too, swerving off to one side at a right angle, forcing the player to rotate the screen.

Other book-games-as-apps include Type:Rider ("the first game played from the point of view of a punctuation mark") and Stride and Prejudice (wherein "an animated Elizabeth Bennet runs and leaps over the text of *Pride and Prejudice*").[36] There's even a digitally interactive version of John Buchan's classic *The Thirty-Nine Steps*.[37]

Here's another project: a wearable book, created at the MIT Media Lab as part of a project called Sensory Fiction. Here is the idea: Instead of the reading process being strictly an interaction between you and the text, digital gadgetry is used to activate physical reactions, based on what the characters in the story are up to. You, the reader, wear a kind of vest that essentially does your emoting for you:

> There are air pressure bags in the vest that will constrict and make the reader feel tighter, if the protagonist is depressed. Excitement will be accompanied by vibration patterns to make your heart race faster. Similarly, a heating device on the vest can change your skin temperature to augment the sense of embarrassment felt while reading the book.[38]

Inventive technology, yes, but what happens to your own ability to think and feel? Does it atrophy? Psychologists have demonstrated what lovers of literature have known all along: that serious reading of serious fiction helps us make sense of other people's thoughts and feelings. (As author Ann Patchett put it, "Reading fiction...is a vital means of imagining a life other than our own, which in turn makes us more empathetic beings.")[39] If I am rigged up to a vest that makes my heart race faster just before Anna Karenina jumps in front of the oncoming train, does it make much difference that I am reading Tolstoy?

Years ago there was a machine called a RelaxAcizor, which had a reasonable sales run in the United States. Essentially the RelaxAcizor did your exercising for you. You placed some pads at strategic spots on your body and connected them with leads to a box about the size of a briefcase—something like the setup for doing an EKG of your heart. But this time, when you flipped on the switch and adjusted the dial, your muscles would contract automatically. You didn't need to budge from your easy chair.

In the end, automated exercise didn't pan out. We recognized that we should be doing the work ourselves (whether or not we actually follow through). I hope the same recognition will prove true when it comes to reading books worthy of a personal mental and emotional workout.

What might be next in redefining what it means to read a book in a digital world? To help keep up with new ideas and innovations, have a look at what's happening at the Books in Browsers annual conferences, held in San Francisco each fall, and the annual International Digital Publishing Forum in New York in late spring.

ACCULTURATION

In projecting the future of digital reading technologies, it is a reasonable guess that over time, people will become increasingly comfortable reading on mobile digital devices. Many (though hardly all) readers report that if you try it, you'll like it.

While my family of three owns four eReaders, I haven't managed to derive pleasure from reading even light fiction on any of them. I do bring up the *New York Times* on my phone while waiting in airports or standing in line, though I still relish spreading out real newsprint when I can. Maybe I need to try harder. Maybe my habit strength (as John Dewey would say) for reading print is too strong. Or, given the fondness for print expressed by so many of the young adults I surveyed, perhaps it's a case of *chacun à son goût.*

BATTLING DISTRACTION

Distraction while reading on digital devices is one of the hardest nuts to crack. But tools designed to help us resist temptation are already appearing. We have mentioned software programs like Freedom that sever your internet connection for the time period you select. Now Kobo has a feature called Reading Mode, enabling users to silence notifications from other apps living on their tablet. Amazon has followed suit, with a Quiet Time feature on its Kindle Fire HDX. Another technique is using different devices (say a computer and a tablet) for different tasks. Some people report this solution helps them focus on one thing at a time.[40]

Will these strategies actually help readers block out distractions? I remember when seat belts were introduced into cars in the United States. Almost no one used them. (They still don't in many parts of the world.) Americans seriously started buckling up only when use of seat belts was legally mandated and anyone failing to comply risked a fine. Since there is no legal stick driving us to embrace the likes of Reading Mode, large-scale adoption seems less likely.

SPOTIFYING EREADING

One trend we don't need to wait on is selling subscriptions to eBooks. The Book-of-the-Month Club, aptly enough, mails its members one selection each month. What if you want to read more?,

Enter the eBook analogue of Spotify, the online music site enabling users to download (legally) as much music as they would like for a set monthly fee. The number of eBook purveyors lining up to capitalize on the model is growing. For $9.95 a month—4 cents less than the original cost of one book for your Kindle—Oyster offers unlimited access to more than half a million eBooks. More subscription services include Scribd (allowing you for $8.99 monthly to download whatever you wish from its own vast supply), and Entitle (offering tiered pricing for varying numbers of eBooks per month). For readers who partake of the plentitude of offerings on these sites, eBook costs become yet more favorable in comparison with print.

The subscription model continues to grow. (In the words of Tim O'Reilly, an industry leader in digital reading technology, "Anybody who is not looking at subscription models is foolish.") Amazon, being no fool, introduced its own eBook subscription service, Kindle Unlimited, in July 2014.[41]

JOINING FORCES: DIGITAL PLUS PRINT

The future of publishing seems headed for a hybrid model. One possibility is that fiction, or at least light fiction, will become heavily digital, while nonfiction and maybe fiction classics stay largely print. American print sales for 2013 (in retail outlets and book clubs) showed a drop of 2½ percent compared with 2012. That drop was almost entirely due to more than an 11 percent slump in sales of adult fiction, whose readership is increasingly utilizing digital books.[42]

A promising scenario is increasingly combining print and digital options.[43] Think about QR codes. They appear on printed surfaces but then lead viewers to more information accessed on mobile screens. Or consider offers of free apps complementing the content sold in print books. The HarperCollins Unbound app for smartphones recognizes special symbols in the print version that connect to added digital content.[44] The same underlying concept is used in many print newspapers providing story teasers for full content only available digitally. And Scholastic Book Fairs has a mobile app enabling attendees to point at the cover of a (physical) book and immediately see on their phone the target age and reading level for which the book is intended.[45]

What if readers could easily choose when to read a particular piece in which format? Better still, what if publishers bundled together the digital and print versions for a reasonable price?

The market is already experimenting with this concept. In fall 2013, Amazon introduced its Kindle MatchBook program, offering digital copies of eBooks (for free or a low price) to customers who had purchased the print version as far back as 1995, when Amazon first opened shop. (Earlier in 2013, Amazon introduced AutoRip, a program giving free MP3 files to customers who had purchased the CD.)[46] Research by the Book Industry Study Group found that 48 percent of those surveyed were willing to pay more for bundled print plus digital versions.[47]

University presses are stepping up to the plate. My favorite is the University Press of Kentucky, which provides (for free) eBook versions of volumes readers already purchased in hardcopy. Proof of ownership comes through a creative twist: Owners post on Tumblr a picture of themselves holding the print version.[48]

Some authors are lobbying for the bundled model, with the goal of supporting print. As Bill Bryson said at a Booksellers Association conference in the UK,

> I've nothing against digital books but I want both. I'm being forced to make the choice and I feel that by buying a digital book I'm not supporting a bookshop, I'm not supporting the physical book and that makes me feel guilty.[49]

For those committed to digital reading but still wanting flexibility in how they access written words, there's technology enabling you to switch between reading on your tablet, eReader, or mobile phone and hearing the audiobook version. Amazon bought a company called Audible, whose Whispersync for Voice program lets you toggle between any book in the Kindle library and the audiobook. Stop listening at one point in the audio version. When you switch to eReading, you pick up right where you left off in the audiobook.[50]

Prospects for moving between print and digital versions of a book may be complicated by copyright issues. Earlier we talked about Alex Halavais, who guillotined the spines off much of his print book collection and digitized the pages, partly for personal convenience but also to save space in his apartment. The Japanese have started doing the same, but by enlisting help from commercial enterprises. The service, known as *jisui* (literally "cooking for oneself"), takes a print book that the owner has already purchased and converts it into an eBook. The problem, or so a number of Japanese writers have charged, is that reproducing the works digitally violates Japanese copyright law. Tokyo District Court ruled in favor of the authors, ordering the *jisui* companies to close operations and pay damages.[51]

MOVING ONTO PRINT'S TURF

Remember when the iPad was introduced and Apple boasted about how the tablet simulated physical page turning? Digital manufacturers and eBook distributors continue looking for electronic equivalents of functions we typically associate with hardcopy.

Consider Amazon's digital literary journal, *Day One*. When I think about literary journals, publications such as *The Partisan Review* or *Antioch Review* come to mind. Of course, their audience has always been fairly exclusive. Amazon's venture is aimed at a broader readership. Taking a page from its Amazon Singles playbook, *Day One* is short: one piece of prose and one poem per issue, along with an introduction from the editor and maybe some bonus content such as interviews with the authors or illustrations.[52]

Another example of bringing digital features to a traditionally print domain is a product called the Sparkup Magical Book Reader. We've seen that many parents of young children believe that reading aloud to kids is preferable to presenting them with digital reading devices. The Sparkup Reader offers a compromise: You attach the device to a hardcopy book and record yourself reading the story aloud. The child can then press the playback button and hear you reading, but on demand.[53]

PRINT FUTURES

What about the future of print? Those of us living in the Nation's Capital are particularly sensitive to the question, now that Jeff Bezos has bought the *Washington Post*. Will the print edition continue? If so, in what form? And what might the fate of the *Post* presage for print more generally?

As we try to read the tea leaves, it may be instructive to hear Bezos' take:

> The tail of these things tends to be very long lived; [the transition to e-books] will go on for a very long time.... Our heaviest Kindle e-book buyers also buy lots of paper books.... For many people, it's not an either-or choice. If you go out into the future far enough, paper books will be luxury items, but that's quite a distance.[54]

Thus spake the world's largest retailer of print books. What else do we need to know as we polish our crystal balls?

JUST-IN-TIME PRINTING

A technological innovation whose time may finally have come is print-on-demand. American editor and publisher Jason Epstein, longtime editorial director at Random House and co-founder of the *New York Review of Books*, turned his attention in the late 1990s to a contraption that would allow readers to order up a book of their choosing with nearly the same ease as asking a barista for a macchiato. Known as the Espresso Book Machine, the device debuted in 2006, with an installation in Washington at the World Bank.[55]

For all the initial hoopla, Espresso print-on-demand had a rocky start. The machine was expensive and unreliable, and quality control was sometimes iffy. But times have changed, and print-on-demand has taken the place of a good chunk of offset printing of books around the world.

The World Bank now distributes all of its books as eBooks through commercial retail and wholesale channels and through its Open Knowledge Repository. However, regional print-on-demand and distribution hubs enable the Bank to continue to serve the remaining market for hardcopies. The bank has hubs in India, Singapore, England, and the United States. As a result, international shipping costs are greatly reduced, and customers around the world receive their orders much faster, thanks to printing closer to the final destination. There is also an environmental benefit, since the pollution generated by international air freight for shipping books is worse than what is caused by paper production.[56]

As for print-on-demand, the Espresso Book Machine is now available at a growing number of libraries and bookstores, and even in such unexpected sites as drugstores. At Bartell Drugs in Seattle, you can both pick up your prescription and order up a bound book, choosing from over 7 million titles or self-publishing anything from an academic project to your collection of family recipes.[57]

Print-on-demand has other uses as well. It is becoming a staple in the world of commercial publishing. Rather than doing large print runs and hoping books will sell, publishers are increasingly printing copies as sales or publicity warrants. (Recall those paperbacks I picked up at the booth of all-digital publisher Open Road at Book Expo America.) Open-access textbooks, while distributed digitally, can also be printed on demand—hopefully at cost—for those wanting hardcopy. The bottom line is that a number of the traditional publishing challenges that came with print, including running out of copies or needing to stockpile unsold ones, can be solved through print-on-demand technology. Publishers are also using print-on-demand to make available books in their backlist that are long out of print. Princeton University Press' Princeton Legacy Library is one such example.

CONTAINERS MATTER

For many readers, the sheer physicality of a book continues to matter. Even if they have read the eVersion, they still want a copy they can hold in their hands, put on their shelves. This sentiment is hardly restricted to digital immigrants (aka older readers). A secondary school student from Singapore had this to say about Erin Morgenstern's fantasy novel *The Night Circus*: "I loved it so much I had to save up and buy this [hardcopy].... Holding it makes it more real."[58]

Speaking of younger readers, I was roundly surprised by the number of university-age people in my studies (and those of European and Asian colleagues) who waxed eloquent over the properties of physical books. I received abundant comments about the smell of a book, how it feels in your hands, and the joy of navigating your way through the pages. With just one or two exceptions, the comments were not about centuries-old books, crafted productions of the Folio Society, first editions, or coffee-table offerings. No, just normal books.

For all the convenience of eBooks and for all their potential to save readers money, young adults—tomorrow's primary consumers—are declaring in sizable numbers that they value the affordances of print. Personal choice doesn't always drive the market, but it is a factor not to be ignored.

BOOKSTORES AS PHYSICAL PLACES

One harbinger of the future may be the bookstore. Despite the demise of Borders Books, despite the Great Recession, and despite the explosive growth of online shopping and eBooks, many independent booksellers are proving resilient. In countries such as France, government support surely helps, but even in the UK and the United States—where you're on your own—a sizable number of independents continue to thrive, and new ventures are sprouting up. Membership in the American Booksellers Association (home of independent booksellers) is up from 1,600 in 2008 to 2,022 in the year 2013. And in many cases, sales are up as well.[59]

What do brick-and-mortar bookstores potentially have to offer that the online competition can't? On the quirky side, one option is the smell of chocolate. A Belgian study reported that when chocolate scent is piped into a bookstore, shoppers are more likely to linger, potentially leading to higher book sales than in scent-free stores.[60] A fascinating prospect, though I wonder if you need world-renowned Belgian chocolate for the technique to succeed.

At a meeting of the Booksellers Association, UK owners and key personnel met to brainstorm ways of building on their physical footprint. Many of the suggestions sound familiar: a terrific café, play space for children, authors' events, and concerts. (In Italy, Feltrinelli is opening RED stores—as in "Read, Eat, Dream"—that take these concepts to new heights.)[61] Other UK ideas looked to enterprises such as creating pop-up stores at cultural events or printing customized editions of special books.[62]

Two of the suggestions at the London gathering had a particular resonance. The first was to build relationships with customers by training staff who make recommendations readers can trust—as Bill Bryson put it (with an apparent dig at Amazon), recommendations by human beings, not algorithms. Traditionally, small bookstores have played this role, and online-weary customers might be ready for more live contact.

The second idea centered on individual readers themselves and how they navigate through a bookstore. Foyles, long a landmark on London's Charing Cross Road, was moving to new premises, offering the chance to rethink how books are laid out in the store. Miriam Robinson, Foyles' head of marketing, explained:

What good bookshops do well is...encourage...serendipity, this stumbling onto something that you never thought you would find.

Robinson went on:

Those are the moments that we all cherish...when you found that book that you didn't know you wanted and that changed your life.[63]

Such optimism about the future of bookstores is refreshing, especially in light of broader trends. On one side of the Atlantic, members of the American Booksellers Association were operating around 7,000 stores in 1995,[64] a far cry from the more recent 2,022. On the other side of the Pond, 98 publishers in the UK (mostly in the book business) closed up shop in a year's span.[65] Amazon remains the elephant in the room, threatening the existence of booksellers. For independent purveyors, the keys to success are creativity, business savvy, and eternal vigilance.

CHANTERELLES AT JULIJA'S OR A NEW NORMAL?

Ljubljana is a picturesque city, cozily laid out along both sides of the Ljubljanica River. While visiting Slovenia's capital for a conference, I had several opportunities to explore the local cuisine. The day before the meetings began, a colleague and I settled in for lunch at Most, a traditional restaurant close by the river in central Ljubljana. Our waiter reviewed the specials of the day, highly recommending the grilled chanterelles as an appetizer. Yes, please! Sadly, the waiter returned a few minutes later, apologizing: We needed to make another choice. The mushrooms in the kitchen had been delivered yesterday (probably picked the day before), so they weren't fresh enough to serve.

Not fresh enough? I thought of the chanterelles I buy at my local Whole Foods in the States. I'm lucky if they were picked two weeks ago.

Another restaurant, this one named Julija's, located across the river in Old Town. Again chanterelles were on the menu, and this time the order was filled. The recipe was simple: sautéed, with a touch of salt. The taste: otherworldly. My Slovenian companions were pleased by my enjoyment but said, in essence, that's how chanterelles normally taste.

What counts as normal? In the United States, I would need to pay dearly—and get lucky—to find this quality fare. In Slovenia, Julija's was merely providing the expected level of freshness. I pondered immigrating.

A vital trait of human beings is our adaptability to new circumstances. Sometimes the shift proves beneficial, but not always. Over the millennia, we have learned to wear shoes, though many podiatrists will tell you we would be better off barefoot. The developed world now largely sits on chairs rather than on the ground, though we pay the price in back ailments. On a more positive note, outside of a few traditional societies (and traditionalists), we have gone from eating with our hands to using cutlery or chopsticks, generally leading to improved health and less mess. In the world of politics, regime change has led populations to adapt to new governmental realities—some more democratic, but others harsher. And on the culinary front, Europeans who have settled in America commonly resign themselves to lower standards of freshness in "fresh" food.

Many adjustments are psychological. Take privacy. The first closed-circuit television cameras set up in London were for Elizabeth II's coronation in 1953. Since then the number has mushroomed, with cameras sprouting up on lampposts and trees across Britain. By 2006, there were over 4 million cameras in the United Kingdom, with individuals being viewed up to 300 times a day.[66]

Americans who began hearing about all those cameras were initially dumb-founded at how a population could allow its every move to be monitored. But over the years, the same Americans (now older and wiser) have come to have few illusions about their actual privacy, online or off. Whether it's Google, subway stations, department stores, speed cameras, or the National Security Agency, lack of privacy has become the new normal, alongside weeks-old mushrooms.

Is there a new normal for reading? As we have seen, current trends include letting digital technologies nudge us away from continuous reading to reading on the prowl, losing patience with complicated texts or even long ones, and paying less attention to the cognitive and aesthetic affordances of physical print. If these trends are signs of a new normal, are readers losing out on some of the long-standing personal delights and intellectual rewards of the uniquely human enterprise we know as reading?

When I teach, I often survey my undergraduates to help me keep a finger on the pulse of the personal and social lives of young adults in America. I ask questions such as "When was the last time you were lonely?" or "When was the last time you were bored, and what did you do to relieve the boredom?"

My most recent recruits were 22 sophomores in a class where I was giving a guest lecture. They had all completed a brief online survey prior to my visit. Each one reported experiencing boredom relatively recently (no surprise), but it was their sources of respite that troubled me. Seventeen had turned to a digital technology (watching a movie on Netflix, checking out Instagram, doing something with their phone or laptop). Three sought out social interaction (visiting a friend down the hall, hanging out). One slept, while another thought about "other stuff."

Not one mentioned reading a book.

Boredom used to be a reason many people turned to books. Given alternative options these days (especially choices that have on-off switches), reading isn't getting much traction as a personal refuge. In fact, as I found in my own studies, several undergraduates complained that reading in hardcopy was itself boring and took too much effort:

"It's boring."
"Just boring material and hard to read."
"it takes time to sit down and focus on the material."

Understandably so, if you are used to interspersing reading with tweets, vacation pricing, and YouTube.

The Harry Potter series sold millions of books. So did *The Hunger Games* and *Twilight*. Many of those readers were adolescents and young adults, presumably to-morrow's mature reading public. Goodreads has millions of members. It's not that no one is reading. But what kinds of writing is the general populace consuming, and how much?

On Goodreads, there were (when I last counted) 2,184 different groups tagged as "Romance," including 123 marked "Erotic Romance." ("Science Fiction" clocked in at 775 groups.) The latest study from the National Endowment for the Arts indicates that in 2012, the number of Americans who were reading books of any sort was on par with 2008: almost 55 percent. But the count of adults who had read at least one work of literature had fallen to 2002 levels—which wasn't so impressive to begin with, with fewer than 47 percent having read one literary work (a novel, short story, poem, or play) in the past year. In 1982, that number had been 56 percent.[67] These days, not exactly a nation of readers.

How do American reading habits compare with those in the rest of the world? NOP, a London-based market research company, released results of its Culture Score media habits index in June 2013. While Americans watched a fair amount of television (averaging 19 hours a week), the United States ranked 23rd in reading, with fewer than 6 hours weekly. In the reading part of the survey, India came in first (almost 11 hours on average), followed by Thailand (over 9) and China (at 8).[68]

When blogs and then social networking became wildly popular, there was much talk about how beneficial all this writing experience would be. Yet I've seen no ev-idence that the prose skills of amateur bloggers, Facebookers, and tweeters have improved as a result of online activity. I will never knock writing practice, whatever the outcome, and I am pleased to see people reading on a variety of platforms. But I worry that digital technologies are contributing to lowered expectations from parents and teachers. It is increasingly difficult for us to get young people to read the "hard stuff."

Reading—whether in print or onscreen—faces other challenges in a media-rich world in which people seem to have ever-lower boredom thresholds. As those 22 students reported, if you are bored, you can watch television or a movie, or amuse yourself online. Who needs books? And as we have seen, those who do read out of choice are increasingly gravitating to shorter pieces. Short attention span and yielding to distraction are in; mental discipline is an increasingly hard sell.

Only a wide-eyed dreamer would assume the average reader scoops up Proust's *À la recherche du temps perdu* or Tocqueville's *Democracy in America* before heading for the beach or an airport. And no, I don't pine for a world in which every college graduate rereads *King Lear* multiple times. My concern is that deep reading and rereading, uninterrupted reading, and tackling longer texts are seen by fewer and fewer people as part of what it means to read.

I said at the outset that I'm a linguist by training. Fairly early in his career, Noam Chomsky, the man who came to dominate the field for several decades, wrote a book called *Aspects of the Theory of Syntax*.[69] *Aspects* stirred up considerable discussion, mostly about the language model proposed therein. But others were taken aback by Chomsky's hubris: "*the* theory of syntax"? No other possibilities?

The worlds of reading, technology, business, education, and personal taste are too varied and unpredictable for me to recommend *the* way in which we might forge a productive alliance between print and digital reading in the coming years. But I do have some recommendations—*a* way forward.

A WAY FORWARD

"Keep your options open." The phrase resonates in so much of our lives. In choosing a career, keep your options open. Don't buy the first car you look at; visit other dealers for comparison. Rather than race to divorce court, try marriage counseling; keep your options open.

The same goes for reading. Think through whether your reading patterns expand or restrict the value you derive from the experience, and keep your options open. Marlene England, co-owner of The Curious Iguana, a new bookstore in Frederick, Maryland, put it this way: "You don't have to be an either-or. You don't have to feel guilty for buying e-books."[70]

Yet in modeling reading habits for the young, we also need to set appropriate goalposts and hold our ground. Commercial products—hardware and reading materials—are sure to shift, and rapidly. We should not be surprised if many educational institutions continue following business trends, even when the educational consequences are unclear. With forethought, we can minimize the risk of losing some of the rich possibilities reading can provide. We can avoid being blindsided by our very human quest for the next new thing. That said, we can embrace the genuine advantages of digital technologies.

FORM FOLLOWS FUNCTION

It was the legendary Chicago architect Louis Sullivan who coined the phase "form follows function" back in 1896, in an article on designing what we now call skyscrapers.[71] Leaders of the Bauhaus movement would embrace the concept, which now permeates our thinking beyond the confines of architectural structures.

The principle also applies to reading. The reason newspapers are printed on, well, newsprint is that we generally read them once and move on. Printing an art book on acid-free paper makes sense, as does reading the *Huffington Post* online.

Thus far, people have proven fairly savvy about recognizing reading platforms that suit their needs. College students in my surveys indicated that eReading is often fine when the text is short, but print is the better way to go for longer works. Studies by Abigail Sellen's group confirm that professionals naturally find a balance between print and digital that is consonant with both their own work patterns and their interactions with colleagues.

Those reading for pleasure are making their own "form follows functions" decisions. Data collected in mid-2013 by the Book Industry Study Group turned up clear evidence of genre shaping choice for reading medium. For romance, erotic fiction, and mysteries or thrillers, eBooks were strongly preferred over print. The reverse was true for travel and cookbooks.[72] Readers are aware that both print and digital screens have a place in their lives. In the words of one of the Japanese students in my study,

> Since both have merits and demerits, the ideal for me is that both are available for use and I can choose one depending on the need.

Historian Anthony Grafton, in a discussion of the future of reading—and in particular, its relation to libraries—had this to say about reading in hardcopy versus onscreen:

> For now and for the foreseeable future, any serious reader will have to know how to travel down two very different roads simultaneously.

What are those roads? The digital one makes a cornucopia of texts and information available to all via the internet. But, continues Grafton, those

> streams of data, rich as they are, will illuminate, rather than eliminate, books and prints and manuscripts that only the library can put in front of you.

Referring to the New York Public Library and its famed entrance on Fifth Avenue, Grafton counsels:

> If you want deeper…knowledge, you will have to take the narrower path that leads between the lions and up the stairs.[73]

AN R~x~ FOR READING IN A DIGITAL WORLD

It is always dangerous offering advice to a general audience. Particularly for an activity as precious—and personal—as reading, objectors have every right to ask, "What business do you have telling me what to do?" I hope that the cumulative analyses I've laid out in this book have at least earned me the credibility to offer suggestions, which readers may deal with as they see fit.

The symbol for a medical prescription, R_x, comes from a medieval abbreviation for the Latin *recipe*, the imperative form of the Late Latin verb *recipere*. The verb meant "to receive." Think of what follows as the kind of prescription your doctor might hand you with the advice "I think this medicine will do you good, but you decide if you want to take it."

And so, my R_x for reading in a digital world:

- Make room for both eReading and print (let form follow function).
- Find effective ways to read without distraction when reading for academic or professional purposes, as well as when reading for pleasure.
- Model focused face-to-face activity for students and progeny. (If you do personal texting while sitting in meetings, young people will assume it's OK for them to follow suit in class or at the dinner table.)
- Foster respect for print and for authorship in any medium.
- Make the effort to read works that are continuous, long, or complex (deep reading matters).
- Examine and share facts about the environmental costs of digital devices versus paper.
- When shaping educational policy regarding reading platforms, don't abandon learning outcomes for the sake of cost.
- Don't presuppose that students know how to do meaningful reading on-screen. We need to teach them how. (The same goes for reading in print.)
- Don't assume we know learners' reading preferences just because they own and use many digital devices.

INVENTING THE FUTURE

Just beyond the suburbs of Ljubljana lies an area known as Ljubljansko barje. This marshy plain was once home to so-called pile dwellers, who used posts to elevate their houses, protecting them from the watery surrounds. In 2002, an archaeological

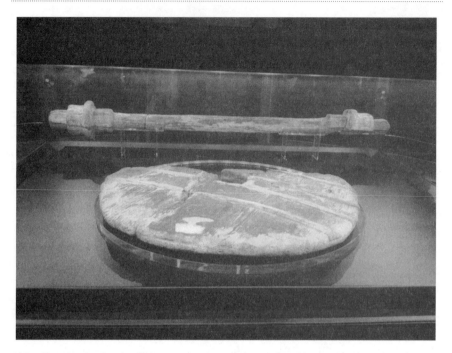

Oldest known wheel and axle, c. 3200 BC. City Museum of Ljubljana, Slovenia. Photo by author.

treasure was unearthed there: the oldest known wheel and axle in the world, dating from about 3200 BC.[74]

During my time in Ljubljana, I made a pilgrimage to the City Museum, where the find is now housed. As I stood peering through the glass display case, my mind ran through the centuries and millennia.

The basic wheel was probably invented about 6,000 years ago. Someone figured out that by putting holes in the centers of two wheels, you could insert the ends of a length of wood into the holes, making it possible to harness an animal and drag heavy items, plow fields, or be carried about. With the coming of spokes instead of a solid disk, the wheel became lighter. Water wheels could turn, Romans could run chariot races, bicycles became popular, and today we can drive Toyotas or Teslas. Wheels have evolved.

Just so, reading has evolved. Some of the change has been driven by technology. Paper made manuscripts more affordable than when written on parchment. Printing drove down the price of books and pamphlets further still, enabling more people to become literate. New literary genres—novels, short stories, detective stories, penny dreadfuls—expanded the audience of readers. Intensive reading was joined by extensive reading. Anthologies, serializations, and condensations offered shortcuts to working through longer complete texts. Something for everyone or every circumstance.

Today's digital technologies place no limits on text length or complexity. Richardson's complete *Clarissa* is available as an eBook from Amazon, keeping company with Kindle Singles. You can read Aristotle on your mobile phone if you choose, and no one is stopping you from rereading *Pride and Prejudice* on your tablet as many times as you please.

The real question is whether the affordances of reading onscreen lead us to a new normal. One in which length and complexity and annotation and memory and rereading and especially concentration are proving more challenging than when reading in hardcopy. One in which we are willing to say that if the new technology doesn't encourage these approaches to reading, maybe these approaches aren't so valuable after all.

Is this the new normal we want? In case not, the ball is in your court.

Acknowledgments

"Thanks."

As so many authors know, that monosyllable doesn't approach the level of appreciation we feel for all the help we receive in birthing a book. To everyone mentioned below (plus anyone I have forgotten), my genuine gratitude. (At least that's seven syllables.)

Mazneen Havewala and Rachelle Calixte gave invaluable assistance in gathering and analyzing the data on university student reading habits. Other crucial partners were Noriko Ishihara, Tsuyoshi Ishihara, and Kumiko Akikawa (for the Japanese survey), along with Joachim Höflich and Afifa El Bayed (for the German sample). Thanks as well to the US, Japanese, and German students who participated in the surveys, and to colleagues from COST Action FPS 1104 for sharing their international data with me: Nie Yao (China); Sakari Taipale (Finland); Joachim Höflich, Juliane Kirchner, and Julia Roll (Germany); Chung-tai Cheng and Pui-lam Law (Hong Kong); Leopoldina Fortunati and Jane Vincent (Italy); Pedro Isaías, Paula Miranda, and Sara Pífano (Portugal); Olga Vershinskaya (Russia); Vladislav Kaputa (Slovakia); and Chris Lim and Jane Vincent (UK).

Colleagues near and far enlightened me about cultural reading practices, especially Marlis Buchmann, Barbara Pfetch, and Konstantin Pollack (for Switzerland and Germany) and Miyaka Inoue and Noriko Ishihara (regarding Japan). For their gracious provision of background information and references, plus access to materials not yet published, thank you to—in alphabetical order—Joshua Bell (on anthropological field work in Papua New Guinea), John Hyman (on the Citation Project), Jonas Larsen (on digital photos), David Mikics (on reading in an age of distraction), Julia Parish-Morris (on storybook reading), Randi Park (on World Bank ePublishing), Kathleen Smith (on medieval manuscript compilations), Birgitte Stougaard Pedersen (on audiobooks), and Heather Wolfe (on the history of filing systems).

This book also benefited greatly from the generosity of people and organizations that shared with me their newest data relating to university student and consumer reading practices. These include Eric Weil at Student Monitor, Jo Henry and Nadine Vassallo at the Book Industry Study Group, and—though we have never corresponded—Jeremy Greenfield, editor of Digital Book World.

During the four years I have been actively working on *Words Onscreen*, I have been privileged to share my ideas (and, in Denmark, even a debating stage) with people willing to hear me out and to tell me where they disagree. These include—again, alphabetically—Leopoldina Fortunati, Rich Ling, the late Cliff Nass, and Will Schwalbe. They also include Todos 2012–2013 (aka the scholars and fellows at the Stanford Center for Advanced Study in the Behavioral Sciences for that academic year), especially our "new media language group," which included Cynthia Gordon, Susan Herring, Michael Marcovski, and Deborah Tannen. Thank you, Deborah, for bringing us together.

My time at CASBS proved a scholar's dream, in no small part because of the excellent staff, not to mention the tranquil natural surroundings. A special mention to the two CASBS librarians, Tricia Soto and Amanda Thomas, who magically produced whatever research materials I needed. My gratitude as well to Laurel Leone and Steve Bellamy, and their son Danny, whose nearby accommodations and friendship were appreciated in equal measure.

Colleagues at American University afforded me the flexibility I needed to make this book happen. Phyllis Peres, senior vice provost and dean of academic affairs, along with Peter Starr, dean of the College of Arts and Sciences, agreed to my crazy plan to essentially commute between Washington and Palo Alto. Members of my staff at AU's Center for Teaching, Research, and Learning put up with Skype meetings and unusual schedules. Sara Dumont and Lynne Feely, the harpsichordist and flautist in our baroque trio, forgave me when I didn't practice my violin part enough and offered cherished friendship.

Once the draft of the book was done, Rich Ling and Kathy Ruckman, along with Peter Ohlin, worked through the manuscript, pointing out where I was unclear or unconvincing. Rachelle Calixte saved me from dozens of embarrassments by double-checking all the footnotes. I take full blame for any remaining errors—or for sometimes ignoring these readers' good advice.

In putting together the illustrations for the book, I was fortunate in receiving much-appreciated assistance. Graphic designer Lori Milani worked her magic by creating some images anew and rendering others into high-resolution black and white. Lisa Occhipinti and Lilian Sutton were instrumental in securing the image from *The Repurposed Library*. Corey Fein from Litographs and American University's photographer Jeff Watts facilitated reproduction of the company's literary T-shirt version of Alice falling down the rabbit hole. Margaret Tenney, head of the Reading Room at the Harry Ransom Center at the University of Texas at Austin, made it possible for me to include the annotated page from the Gutenberg Bible. And Peter Huestis at Washington's National Gallery of Art steered me to public access of Gossaert's "Portrait of a Merchant."

Felicia Eth, my literary agent, deserves abundant credit for inspiring and coaxing me all along the way. Peter Ohlin, my editor at Oxford, was a constant source of ideas and much-appreciated advice. It has also been a joy working with editor Hallie Stebbins. Joellyn Ausanka (the production editor), along with Sue Warga (copy editor), partnered with me to transform the manuscript into a book.

Finally, there's my family, who tolerated my absence (across the country or ensconced in my study) for months on end. For his steadfast support and endurance as I have written books, now eight times over, I say to my husband, Nikhil, *"Lajabab!"*

Notes

PREFACE

1. Pam Belluck, "For Better Social Skills, Scientists Recommend a Little Chekhov," *New York Times*, October 3, 2013. Available at http://well.blogs.nytimes.com/2013/10/03/i-know-how-youre-feeling-i-read-chekhov/?_r=0. For the actual study, see Kidd and Castano 2013.

CHAPTER 1

The epigraph is from Todd Kliman, " 'Washington Is a Terrific Place if You're a Serious Reader': An Interview with Book Reviewer Michael Dirda," *Washingtonian*, January 10, 2012, 40. Available at http://www.washingtonian.com/articles/people/washington-is-a-terrific-place-if-youre-a-serious-reader.

1. Jeremy Greenfield, "E-Retailers Now Accounting for Nearly Half of Book Purchases by Volume, Overtake Physical Retail," Digital Book World, March 18, 2013. Available at http://www.digitalbookworld.com/2013/e-retailers-now-accounting-for-nearly-half-of-book-purchases-by-volume.

2. Alastair Jamieson, "Oxford English Dictionary 'Will Not be Printed Again,' " *Telegraph*, August 29, 2010. Available at http://www.telegraph.co.uk/culture/books/booknews/7970391/Oxford-English-Dictionary-will-not-be-printed-again.html; Britannica Editors, "Change: It's Okay. Really," Encyclopedia Britannica blog, March 13, 2012. Available at http://www.britannica.com/blogs/2012/03/change; "Macmillan Stops the Presses on Dictionaries, Goes All Digital,"

New York Business Journal, November 6, 2012. Available at http://www.bizjournals.com/newyork/news/2012/11/06/macmillan-stops-the-presses-on.html.

3. Ralph Blumenthal, "College Libraries Set Aside Books in a Digital Age," *New York Times*, May 14, 2005. Available at http://www.nytimes.com/2005/05/14/education/14library.html?pagewanted=all. The volumes were dispersed to other campus collections.

4. "A Texas Library Without Books," *New York Times*, September 18, 2010. Available at http://www.nytimes.com/2010/09/19/weekinreview/19grist.html?_r=0.

5. BiblioTech website, http://bexarbibliotech.org.

6. Brian Fung, "A U.S. Ambassador Was Just Sworn in on a Kindle," *Washington Post*, June 2, 2014. Available at http://www.washingtonpost.com/blogs/the-switch/wp/2014/06/02/a-u-s-ambassador-was-just-sworn-in-on-a-kindle.

7. Nunberg 1996; Institute for the Future of the Book, http://www.futureofthebook.org; website for the May 2012 symposium "Unbound: Speculations on the Future of the Book," http://futurebook.mit.edu.

8. Not to be confused with "digital natives," meaning users who have grown up with digital technology.

9. Megan McArdle, "E-Donnybrook," *Atlantic*, April 2010. Available at http://www.theatlantic.com/magazine/archive/2010/04/e-donnybrook/307985; Richard Adams, "Amazon's eBook Sales Eclipse Paperbacks for the First Time," *Guardian*, January 27, 2011. Available at http://www.guardian.co.uk/world/richard-adams-blog/2011/jan/28/amazon-kindle-ebook-paperback-sales.

10. "AAP Estimates: E-Book Sales Rose 117% in 2011 as Print Fell," *Publishers Weekly*, February 27, 2012. Available at http://www.publishersweekly.com/pw/by-topic/industry-news/financial-reporting/article/50805-aap-estimates-e-book-sales-rose-117-in-2011-as-print-fell.html; John Soares, "2010 Book and E-Book Sales Data for the United States," Productive Writers, February 16, 2011. Available at http://productivewriters.com/2011/02/16/book-e-book-sales-data-united-states-2010; Jim Milliot, "E-Book Sales Jump 176% in Flat Trade Year," *Publishers Weekly*, February 22, 2010. Available at http://www.publishersweekly.com/pw/by-topic/digital/content-and-e-books/article/42173-e-book-sales-jump-176-in-flat-trade-year.html.

11. Jeremy Greenfield, "Ebooks Account for 23% of Publisher Revenue in 2012, Even as Growth Levels," Digital Book World, April 11, 2013. Available at http://www.digitalbookworld.com/2013/ebooks-account-for-23-of-publisher-revenue-in-2012-even-as-growth-levels; Jeremy Greenfield, "Ebook Growth Slows to Single Digits in U.S. in 2013," Digital Book World, April 1, 2014. Available at http://www.digitalbookworld.com/2014/ebook-growth-slows-to-single-digits-in-u-s-in-2013.

12. "Print Units Fell 9 Percent in 2012," *Publishers Weekly*, January 4, 2013. Available at http://www.publishersweekly.com/pw/by-topic/industry-news/publisher-news/article/55357-print-units-fell-9-percent-in-2012.html.

13. Rüdiger Wischenbart et al., *The Global eBook Market: Current Conditions & Future Projections*, Fall 2013, 39, 30. Available at http://www.wischenbart.com/upload/Global-Ebook-Report2013_final03.pdf.

14. Kathryn Zickuhr and Lee Rainie, "E-Reading Rises as Device Ownership Jumps," Pew Internet & American Life Project, January 16, 2014. Available at http://www.pewinternet.org/2014/01/16/e-reading-rises-as-device-ownership-jumps.

15. Quoted in John Markoff, "The Passion of Steve Jobs," *New York Times*, January 15, 2008. Available at http://bits.blogs.nytimes.com/2008/01/15/the-passion-of-steve-jobs.

16. Jen Doll, "Are Tablets Killing Our Attention Span for Books?," *The Wire*, March 5, 2012. Available at http://www.thewire.com/entertainment/2012/03/are-tablets-killing-our-attention-span-books/49504.

17. Jacobs 2011, 81.

18. Kevin C. Tofel, "Five Reasons E-Reader Sales Will Nearly Triple by 2016," *Bloomberg Businessweek*, November 15, 2011. Available at http://www.businessweek.com/technology/five-reasons-ereader-sales-will-nearly-triple-by-2016-11152011.html.

19. Greg Bensinger, "The E-Reader Revolution: Over Just as It Has Begun?" *Wall Street Journal*, January 4, 2013. Available at http://online.wsj.com/article/SB10001424127887323874204578219834160573010.html?mod=WSJ_Tech_LEFTTopNews.

20. Zickuhr and Rainie, "E-Reading Rises as Device Ownership Jumps" (see note 14).

21. Comments made at a Digital Book World conference, reported in Jeremy Greenfield, "iPad E-Reading Market Share Stagnates as Tablet E-Reading Rises," Digital Book World, May 7, 2012. Available at http://www.digitalbookworld.com/2012/ipad-e-reading-market-share-stagnates-as-tablet-e-reading-rises.

22. "Webcast: Designing E-Books for the New Tablet Reality, Fighting Distraction and Delivering Quality" (promotional material for a webcast), Digital Book World, June 22, 2012. Available at http://www.digitalbookworld.com/2012/webcast-designing-e-books-for-the-new-tablet-reality-fighting-distraction-and-delivering-quality.

23. Amy Mitchell, Tom Rosenstiel, Laura Houston Santhanam, and Leah Christian, "Future of Mobile News," Pew Research Center's Project for Excellence in Journalism, October 1, 2012. Available at http://www.journalism.org/analysis_report/future_mobile_news.

24. "Latest IDC Data Spotlights a Billion Smartphones Shipped in 2013," TeleRead, January 28, 2014. Available at http://www.teleread.com/smartphones/latest-idc-data-spotlights-a-billion-smartphones-shipped-in-2013.

25. Kathryn Zickuhr, Lee Rainie, Kristen Purcell, Mary Madden, and Joanna Brenner, "Younger Americans' Reading and Library Habits," Pew Internet &American Life Project, October 23, 2012. Available at http://libraries.pewinternet.org/2012/10/23/younger-americans-reading-and-library-habits.

26. Zickuhr and Rainie, "E-Reading Rises as Device Ownership Jumps" (see note 14).

27. National Endowment for the Arts, *Reading at Risk: A Survey of Literary Reading in America*, NEA Research Division Report #46, 2004. Available at http://arts.gov/publications/reading-risk-survey-literary-reading-america-0.

28. National Endowment for the Arts, *To Read or Not to Read: A Question of National Consequence*, NEA Research Division Report #47, 2007. Available at http://arts.gov/publications/read-or-not-read-question-national-consequence-0.

29. National Endowment for the Arts, *Reading on the Rise: A New Chapter in American Literacy*, Office of Research Analysis, 2009. Available at http://www.arts.gov/research/ReadingonRise.pdf.

30. "Teens Don't Read for Fun Anymore, New Data Says," Digital Book World, January 13, 2014. Available at http://www.digitalbookworld.com/2014/teens-dont-read-for-fun-anymore-new-data-says/?et_mid=656063&rid=241005576; US Bureau of Labor Statistics, "Table 11. Time Spent in Leisure and Sports Activities for the Civilian Population by Selected Characteristics, 2013 Annual Averages," Economic News Release, June 18, 2014. Available at http://www.bls.gov/news.release/atus.t11.htm.

31. Alex Madrigal, "The Next Time Someone Says the Internet Killed Reading Books, Show Them This Chart," *Atlantic*, April 2012. Available at http://www.theatlantic.com/technology/archive/2012/04/the-next-time-someone-says-the-internet-killed-reading-books-show-them-this-chart/255572; David W. Moore, "About Half of Americans Reading a Book," Gallup, June 3, 2005. Available at http://www.gallup.com/poll/16582/about-half-americans-reading-book.aspx.

32. Lee Rainie, Kathryn Zickuhr, Kristen Purcell, Mary Madden, and Joanna Brenner, "The Rise of E-Reading," Pew Internet & American Life Project, April 4, 2012. Available at http://libraries.pewinternet.org/2012/04/04/the-rise-of-e-reading.

33. David Streitfeld, "As New Services Track Habits, the E-Books Are Reading You," *New York Times*, December 24, 2013. Available at http://www.nytimes.com/2013/12/25/technology/as-new-services-track-habits-the-e-books-are-reading-you.html?_r=0.

34. Zickuhr et al., "Younger Americans' Reading and Library Habits" (see note 25).

35. Jason Boog, "Adult Hardcover Revenues Down Nearly 7% in 2012," GalleyCat blog, Media Bistro, April 11, 2013. Available at http://www.mediabistro.com/galleycat/adult-hardcover-revenues-down-nearly-7-in-2012_b68524.

36. Cited in Quentin Fottrell, "Half of Bedtime Stories Now Read on E-Books," MarketWatch, July 17, 2012. Available at http://blogs.marketwatch.com/realtimeadvice/2012/07/17/half-of-bedtime-stories-now-read-on-e-books/?mg=blogs-sm.

37. Jeremy Greenfield, "Two-Thirds of Kids Now Reading Digitally, New Study Shows," Digital Book World, January 13, 2014. Available at http://www.digitalbookworld.com/2014/two-thirds-of-kids-now-reading-digitally-new-study-shows/?et_mid=656063&rid=241005576.

38. Rainie et al., "The Rise of E-Reading" (see note 32); Kathryn Zickuhr, "In a Digital Age, Parents Value Printed Books for Their Kids," Pew Internet & American Life Project, May 28, 2013. Available at http://www.pewresearch.org/fact-tank/2013/05/28/in-a-digital-age-parents-value-printed-books-for-their-kids.

39. Matt Richtel and Julie Bosman, "For Their Children, Many E-Book Fans Insist on Paper," *New York Times*, November 20, 2011. Available at http://www.nytimes.com/2011/11/21/business/for-their-children-many-e-book-readers-insist-on-paper.html?pagewanted=print.

40. Matt Richtel "A Silicon Valley School That Doesn't Compute," *New York Times*, October 22, 2011. Available at http://www.nytimes.com/2011/10/23/technology/at-waldorf-school-in-silicon-valley-technology-can-wait.html?pagewanted=all.

41. Bowker, "Understanding the Children's Book Consumer in the Digital Age: Wave 4: Fall 2012," PowerPoint presentation at Digital Book World, New York, January 15, 2013. Available at http://www.slideshare.net/PublishersLaunch/sizing-up-the-kids-book-market.

42. Harris Interactive, "State of Bedtime Stories Survey," report commissioned by Reading Is Fundamental and Macy's, 2013. Executive summary available at http://www.scribd.com/doc/148798776/Harris-Interactive-Executive-Summary-of-Survey-Commissioned-by-RIF-and-Macy-s.

43. Scholastic, "Kids & Family Reading Report, 4th Edition," prepared by Harrison Group, 2013. Available at http://mediaroom.scholastic.com/files/kfrr2013-noappendix.pdf.

44. William Gleason, "Goodnight, iPad? Children's Literature in a Digital Age," *Princeton Alumni Weekly*, October 10, 2012. Available at http://paw.princeton.edu/issues/2012/10/10/pages/1091; Hanna Rosin, "The Touch-Screen Generation," *Atlantic*, April 2013. Available at http://www.theatlantic.com/magazine/archive/2013/04/the-touch-screen-generation/309250; Jabr 2013a.

45. American Academy of Pediatrics 2011; Zimmerman quoted in Cecilia Kang, "Kid Apps Explode on Smartphones and Tablets. But Are They Good for Your Children?" *Washington Post,* November 17, 2011. Available at http://articles.washingtonpost.com/2011-11-17/business/ 35281254_1_app-stores-smartphone-samsung-galaxy. More recently, Dimitri Christakis, co-author of the American Academy of Pediatrics' 2011 policy statement, has suggested that "judicious use of interactive media [roughly 30–60 minutes per day] is acceptable for children younger than the age of 2 years" (Christakis 2014).

46. Paul Theroux, "Fiction in the Age of E-Books," *Atlantic,* April 2010. Available at http:// www.theatlantic.com/magazine/archive/2010/08/fiction-in-the-age-of-e-books/308041.

47. Mohsin Hamid and Anna Holmes, "How Do E-Books Change the Reading Experience?" *New York Times,* December 31, 2013. Available at http://www.nytimes.com/2014/01/05/books/ review/how-do-e-books-change-the-reading-experience.html.

48. Farhad Manjoo, "I'm Through with Paper," *Slate,* May 17, 2012. Available at http://www .slate.com/articles/technology/technology/2012/05/ipad_retina_display_thanks_to_my_new_ tablet_i_don_t_read_anything_on_paper_.html.

49. William H. Gass, "In Defense of the Book," *Harper's,* November 1999; David Streitfeld, "A Champion of the Book Takes to the iPad," *New York Times,* August 17, 2012. Available at http:// bits.blogs.nytimes.com/2012/08/17/a-champion-of-the-book-takes-to-the-ipad.

50. Hillel Italie, "Booksellers Talk Big, Act Quietly at Convention," *USA Today,* June 1, 2008. Available at http://usatoday30.usatoday.com/money/economy/2008-06-01-1819108364_x. htm; Jennifer Steinhauer, "A Literary Legend Fights for a Local Library," *New York Times,* June 19, 2009. Available at http://www.nytimes.com/2009/06/20/us/20ventura.html?_r=2&.

51. Alison Flood, "Ray Bradbury's Work Finally Available Digitally in the UK," *Guardian,* November 30, 2011. Available at http://www.guardian.co.uk/books/2011/nov/30/fahrenheit-451- ebook-ray-bradbury.

52. Stanhope 1968, 1291.

53. L. Price 2012, 4–5, 7.

54. O'Leary 2012, 7.

55. See articles by Brett Sandusky (177–183), Ron Martinez (185–189), Peter Brantley (191–198), and Neal Hoskins (221–228) in McGuire and O'Leary 2012.

56. Cressy 1986. Cressy took the story about the woman eating her New Testament from *Notes and Queries,* 9th series, 8 (1901).

57. "Furniture Books," *Fraser's Magazine* 59, no. 349 (January 1859): 95. Cited in Dettmar 2005, 5.

58. Cited in L. Price 2011, 2. See Price's "Introduction" for more stories about books as decor.

59. Defoe 1890, 135–136.

60. http://www.bookdecor.com (emphasis in original); http://www.booksbythefoot.com.

61. Examples include Thompson 2011 and Hueston 2006.

62. *Red Badge of Courage:* http://www.doylenewyork.com/content/more.asp?id=227; Fourth Folio: http://www.abebooks.com/servlet/SearchResults?an=Shakespeare&fe=on&prl=10.00&re centlyadded=all&sortby=1&sts=t&x=43&y=11.

63. Cara Barer's website is http://www.carabarer.com/portfolio/sculpture; Kara Witham offers her products at http://www.etsy.com/shop/SecretSafeBooks?ref=l2-shopheader-name#.

64. The Litographs T-shirts can be found at http://www.litographs.com.

65. Gibson 1977; Hutchby 2001; Ling and Donner 2009.

66. Jennifer Howard, "Digitizing the Personal Library," *Chronicle of Higher Education*, September 28, 2010. Available at http://chronicle.com/blogs/wiredcampus/digitizing-the-personal-library/27222.

67. Andrew Piper, "Out of Touch: E-Reading Isn't Reading," *Slate*, November 15, 2012. Available at http://www.slate.com/articles/arts/culturebox/2012/11/reading_on_a_kindle_is_not_the_same_as_reading_a_book.html.

68. See "Lending Kindle Books," http://www.amazon.com/gp/help/customer/display.html?nodeId=200549320.

CHAPTER 2

The epigraph is from Darnton 1991, 161. For a brief overview of contemporary work on reading and its history, see L. Price 2004.

1. Jawaharlal Nehru, "Prison Diary," 1935. Cited in Iyengar 2007, 678.

2. Halsey 2011.

3. Augustine's *Confessions*, Book 6, Chapter 3.

4. Saenger 1997.

5. Recounted in Manguel 1996, 112–114.

6. Described in Blair 2010, 60.

7. University College London, "Information Behaviour of the Researcher of the Future," CIBER Briefing Paper, January 11, 2008. Available at http://www.jisc.ac.uk/media/documents/programmes/reppres/ggworkpackagei.pdf.

8. Wolf and Barzillai 2009, 33.

9. Wharton 1903, 513.

10. Stallybrass 2002, 46–47.

11. Cited in Wittmann 1999. 293.

12. Blair 2012.

13. Useful references on the history of writing include Sampson 1990, Coulmas 1996, and Gaur 1987.

14. Schmandt-Besserat 1992.

15. For more on Egyptian pyramid texts, see Allen and Der Manuelian 2005.

16. Chadwick 1959.

17. On the history of early Chinese writing, see Boltz 2003.

18. Pohl, Pope, and von Nagy 2002.

19. Charpin 2010.

20. For riddles, see Alexander 2007. On medicinal recipes, see Van Arsdall 2002.

21. My summary draws upon Cohn 1979 and Gilmont 1999.

22. Cited from Luther's works in Gilmont 1999, 220.

23. Cited from Luther's works in Gilmont 1999, 220.

24. William Boyd, "A Short History of the Short Story," *Prospect*, July 10, 2006. Available at http://www.prospectmagazine.co.uk/magazine/william-boyd-short-history-of-the-short-story.

25. Murasaki Shikibu's *Tale of Genji*, written in Japan between A.D. 1008 and 1020, is sometimes called the world's first novel.

26. Wittmann 1999, 302. For more on the history of reading, see Manguel 1996, Cavallo and Chartier 1999, and Lyons 2010.

27. Jackson 2001. For displays of marginalia in the early centuries of printing, see http://annotatedbooksonline.com.

28. By recent estimates, a complete copy of Gutenberg's Bible would fetch at least $25 million. See Philipp Harper, "In the Book World, the Rarest of the Rare," in the "Books" section of the *Today* show website, http://www.today.com/id/6124643#.UXRPURzUq2l.

29. Sometimes notes are written as marginalia in books, other times on separate paper. For more on the past and future of note taking, see the November 2012 conference "Take Note," held at the Radcliffe Institute for Advanced Study, Harvard University, http://www.radcliffe.harvard.edu/event/2012-take-note-conference.

30. The opening paragraph of Edgar Allan Poe, "Marginalia," *United States Magazine and Democratic Review,* November 1844, 484–499.

31. Jacobs 2011, 67.

32. Jackson 2001, 7. Chapter 5 in Jackson's book offers an extended discussion of Coleridge's annotation practices.

33. John Brinsley, *Ludus Literarius: Or, the Grammar Schoole.* London: Thomas Mann, 1612), 46, 42. Cited in Sherman 2002, 121.

34. Adler 1940, 110–111.

35. Dirk Johnson, "Book Lovers Fear Dim Future for Notes in the Margins," *New York Times,* February 20, 2011. Available at http://www.nytimes.com/2011/02/21/books/21margin.html.

36. John Dickerson, quoted in John Swansburg, "I Hate My iPad," *Slate,* February 18, 2011. Available at http://www.slate.com/articles/news_and_politics/im/2011/02/i_hate_my_ipad.2.html.

37. Book Industry Study Group, *Student Attitudes Toward Content in Higher Education,* vol. 4, no. 1 (New York: BISG, 2013).

38. From Amazon's FAQ entry on "Public Notes": "With Public Notes, our Kindle customers can choose to make public their highlights and notes. Once a customer enables Public Notes for one of their books, then any other customer who follows them will be able to see their Public Notes."

39. David Streitfeld, "Teacher Knows if You've Done the E-Reading," *New York Times,* April 8, 2013. Available at http://www.nytimes.com/2013/04/09/technology/coursesmart-e-textbooks-track-students-progress-for-teachers.html?pagewanted=all.

40. See Roberts and Skeat 1983, chapter 9.

41. Febvre and Martin 1976, 84–85.

42. For historical details on indexing, see Wellisch 1991.

43. Parsons 1952, 205.

44. For the history of alphabetization, see Daly 1967.

45. Cited in Wells 1973, 17.

46. Saenger 2010, 403.

47. Saenger 2010, 405.

48. Another "the heck with it" confession: Titles appearing in print copies of newspapers or periodicals are often changed in the online versions. Worse still, sometimes the online titles themselves change. Since I haven't a clue how to handle the discrepancy properly, I made an executive decision. In these notes, I have included the title appearing in the version I actually read.

49. Blair 2010. Also see Yeo 2002 and Rosenberg 2003.

50. Chartier 1989.

51. Raven 1998, 275.

52. For the classic discussion of the growth of the novel, see Watt 1957. For a more recent study, see Seager 2012.

53. Gerard 1980, 214.

54. Watt 1957, 36.

55. Darnton 1991, 148. One of the classic citations for Engelsing's work is Engelsing 1974.

56. Hall 1983.

57. Vauhini Vara, "Project Gutenberg Fears No Google," *Wall Street Journal*, December 10, 2005. Available at http://online.wsj.com/public/article/SB113415403113218620-U_OqLOmApoaSvNpy5 SjNwvhpW5w_20061209.html.

58. The Project Gutenberg website is http://www.gutenberg.org.

59. Philips 2007.

60. Cited in Rubery 2011, 1.

61. Besides Rubery's collection (2011), see, for example, Pedersen and Have 2012.

62. From Rubery 2011, "Introduction." For discussion of the "bookness" of audiobooks, see Irwin 2009 and Olga Khazan, "Is Listening to Audio Books Really the Same as Reading?" *Forbes*, September 12, 2011. Available at http://www.forbes.com/sites/olgakhazan/2011/09/12/is-listening-to-audio-books-really-the-same-as-reading.

63. Varao Sousa, Carriere, and Smilek 2013.

64. Quoted in James Parker, "The Mind's Ear," *New York Times Book Review*, November 25, 2011. Available at http://www.nytimes.com/2011/11/27/books/review/the-minds-ear.html?pagewanted=all.

65. Hats off to Sue Warga, who later unearthed the reference in a newer edition on Google Books.

66. "Research Questions," The Citation Project, http://citationproject.net/Research-questions.html.

67. Alber and Miller 2012, 158–159.

CHAPTER 3

1. "January 2013: Top US Entertainment Sites and Web Brands," Nielsen, March 22, 2013. Available at http://www.nielsen.com/us/en/newswire/2013/january-2013--top-u-s--entertainment-sites-and-web-brands.html.

2. Weinreich et al. 2008.

3. Jakob Nielsen, "How Users Read on the Web," October 1, 1997. Available at http://www.nngroup.com/articles/how-users-read-on-the-web.

4. Jakob Nielsen, "How Little Do Users Read?," May 6, 2008. Available at http://www.nngroup.com/articles/how-little-do-users-read. Nielsen draws upon work by Weinreich et al. 2008.

5. Jakob Nielsen, "F-Shaped Pattern for Reading Web Content," April 17, 2006. Available at http://www.nngroup.com/articles/f-shaped-pattern-reading-web-content.

6. Yahoo! and others report similar results, though the actual scan pattern is influenced by individual differences, as well as by the kind of material and layout, such as photos or single versus multiple columns.

7. Jakob Nielsen, "Scrolling and Attention," March 22, 2010. Available at http://www.nngroup.com/articles/scrolling-and-attention.

8. Cipolla 1978; Landes 1983.

9. Blaise 2000.

10. Carey 1983.

11. Linton Weeks, "The No-Book Report: Skim It and Weep," *Washington Post*, May 14, 2001.

12. Burchfield and Sappington 2000.

13. Daniel de Vise, "Is College Too Easy? As Study Time Falls, Debate Rises," *Washington Post*, May 21, 2012. Available at http://articles.washingtonpost.com/2012-05-21/local/35456815_1_ college-students-study-time-students-report. A study by Student Monitor conducted in fall 2013 reports a very similar figure, 14.9 hours weekly. This average is further confirmed by the National Survey of Student Engagement for 2013. See Allie Grasgreen, "New Survey, Same Engagement," *Inside Higher Ed*, November 14, 2013. Available at http://www.insidehighered. com/news/2013/11/14/nsse-2013-measure-student-engagement-and-learning-outcomes.

14. Robert Douglas-Fairhurst, "*The Anatomy of Influence: Literature as a Way of Life* by Harold Bloom: Review," *Telegraph*, June 30, 2011. Available at http://www.telegraph.co.uk/ culture/books/bookreviews/8608875/The-Anatomy-of-Influence-Literature-as-a-Way-of-Life-by-Harold-Bloom-review.html.

15. Assuming a reading rate of about 250–300 words per minute.

16. Brett Nelson, "Do You Read Fast Enough to Be Successful?," *Forbes*, June 4, 2012. Available at http://www.forbes.com/sites/brettnelson/2012/06/04/do-you-read-fast-enough-to-be-successful.

17. World Speed Reading Council website, http://www.mentalworldrecords.com/world speedreadingcouncil/index.asp.

18. Angela Chen, "Speed Reading Returns," *Wall Street Journal*, March 26, 2014. Available at http://online.wsj.com/news/articles/SB10001424052702303779504579463210145917986.

19. "Keeping an Eye on Recruiter Behavior," The Ladders website, March 26, 2012. Available at http://cdn.theladders.net/static/images/basicSite/pdfs/TheLadders-EyeTracking-StudyC2.pdf.

20. Neuburg 1989.

21. "Tatler," Condé Nast International, http://www.condenastinternational.com/country/ united-kingdom/tatler.

22. Newman 2005, 12.

23. "The Online Books Page Presents Serial Archive Listings for The Gentleman's Magazine," http://onlinebooks.library.upenn.edu/webbin/serial?id=gentlemans.

24. Johnson 1755, 1240–1241.

25. "About Us," *Saturday Evening Post* website, http://www.saturdayeveningpost.com/about.

26. Leibniz 1951, 29.

27. Estimates vary, though see, for example, Lynn Karpen, "In Short: Nonfiction," *New York Times*, September 11, 1994. Available at http://www.nytimes.com/1994/09/11/books/in-short-nonfiction-192406.html.

28. Richardson 1804, vol. 1:100.

29. L. Price 2000a.

30. Tennenhouse 1998, 184–185.

31. See, for example, Batt 2012.

32. Patterson 1968.

33. L. Price 2000b.

34. Publisher's description for *The Norton Anthology of American Literature*, 8th ed., http:// books.wwnorton.com/books/The-Norton-Anthology-of-American-Literature.

35. This discussion of the history of book reviews draws upon Forster 2001 and Gael 2012.

36. This declaration appeared in an advertisement for the *Quarterly Review*. Cited in Forster 2001, 171.

37. Cited in Forster 2001, 177–178.

38. See Wiles 1957, chapter 1.

39. For more on the rise of the serial, see Law 2000 and Lund 1993.

40. *Scribner's Monthly* 17, no. 1 (November 1878): 146.

41. For more on *The Mystery of Edwin Drood*, see Forsyte 1980.

42. Hagedorn 1988, 6–7.

43. My discussion of *Reader's Digest* and Reader's Digest Condensed Books draws from Volkersz 1995 and Schreiner 1977.

44. Even when original pieces were composed in-house, writers were instructed to draft their prose without considering length. These drafts were then handed over to the editing staff, which performed the kind of condensation they were doing on previously published works.

45. Schreiner 1977, 35.

46. Schreiner 1977, 50.

47. Volkersz 1995, 58.

48. Quoted from Volkersz 1995, 59–60.

49. "About SparkNotes," http://www.sparknotes.com/about.

50. Quoted in Kate Zernike, "Book-Club Smarts in a Nutshell: Get Notes," *New York Times*, June 19, 2002. Available at http://www.nytimes.com/2002/06/19/us/book-club-smarts-in-a-nutshell-get-notes.html?pagewanted=all&src=pm.

51. See "About CliffsNotes," http://www.cliffsnotes.com/about-cliffsnotes.html.

52. Description of No Fear Shakespeare series from SparkNotes, http://nfs.sparknotes.com.

53. Craig Timberg, "News App Summly's Blockbuster Sale to Yahoo Shows How the Smartphone Rules," *Washington Post*, March 27, 2013. Available at http://articles.washingtonpost.com/2013-03-27/business/38071760_1_marissa-mayer-mobile-users-google-colleague.

54. Roger E. Bohn and James E. Short, "How Much Information? 2009 Report on American Consumers," Global Information Industry Center, University of California, San Diego, 2009. Available at http://hmi.ucsd.edu/howmuchinfo_research_report_consum.php.

55. "Kindle Serials," Amazon.com, http://www.amazon.com/b?ie=UTF8&node=5044445011. In spring 2013, Amazon also launched a pilot online "television" series, available in installments; see Verne Gay, "'Alpha House' Review: Amazon Series Is Bitter but Funny," *Newsday*, April 23, 2013, http://www.newsday.com/entertainment/tv/alpha-house-review-amazon-series-is-bitter-but-funny-1.5127834.

56. Julie Bosman, "E-Books Expand Their Potential with Serialized Fiction," *New York Times*, September 30, 2012. Available at http://mediadecoder.blogs.nytimes.com/2012/09/30/e-books-expand-their-potential-with-serialized-fiction; David Streitfeld, "Web Fiction, Serialized and Social," *New York Times*, March 23, 2014. Available at http://www.nytimes.com/2014/03/24/technology/web-fiction-serialized-and-social.html?_r=0.

57. "Kindle Singles," Amazon.com, http://www.amazon.com/b?ie=UTF8&node=2486013011.

58. "Best-Selling Author Stephen King Publishes Kindle Single 'Guns,' Available Exclusively in the Kindle Store—You Won't Find It Anywhere Else," BusinessWire, January 25, 2013. Available at http://www.businesswire.com/news/home/20130125005110/en/Best-Selling-Author-Stephen-King-Publishes-Kindle-Single#.UvY-c3lelKM.

59. "Nook Snaps," Barnes & Noble website, http://www.barnesandnoble.com/u/eBook-NOOK-Snaps-Short-Content-Quick-Reads/379003386.

60. "Amazon Publishing Launches StoryFront," BusinessWire, December 4, 2013. Available at http://www.businesswire.com/news/home/20131204005689/en/Amazon-Publishing-Launches-StoryFront.

61. SnackReads website, http://www.snackreads.com.

62. John Harris, "Tim Waterstone: 'If Reading Is Going [to] Be All Digital in 50 Years, So Be It,'" *Guardian*, April 9, 2013. Available at http://www.guardian.co.uk/books/2013/apr/09/tim-waterstone-reading-entirely-digital.

63. Robert Budden, "Waterstone's Founder Joins Read Petite," *Financial Times*, April 12, 2013.

64. "TED Books," http://www.ted.com/pages/tedbooks.

65. Vicesimus Knox, "Of Essay Writing," in *Essays: Moral and Literary* (1778), 3. Cited in Phillips 2010, 20.

66. Quoted in Scott Heller, "The Shrinking Scholarly Book," *Chronicle of Higher Education*, February 26, 1999. Available at http://chronicle.com/article/The-Shrinking-Scholarly-Book/6219.

67. Heller, "The Shrinking Scholarly Book."

68. See Jennifer Howard, "Ditch the Monograph," *Chronicle of Higher Education*, October 14, 2012. Available at http://chronicle.com/article/Ditch-the-Monograph/135108.

69. "Princeton Shorts," Princeton University Press, http://press.princeton.edu/PrincetonShorts.

70. "Introducing UNC Press E-Book Shorts," University of North Carolina Press, http://www.uncpress.unc.edu/browse/books?page_type=series&page_type_id=38.

71. "'Bite-Sized' Reading from SUP," The Dish, Stanford University, May 17, 2012, http://news.stanford.edu/thedish/?p=19315.

72. Kristi McGuire, "Introducing Chicago Shorts," University of Chicago Press, February 1, 2013, http://pressblog.uchicago.edu/2013/02/01/introducing-chicago-shorts.html.

73. "Very Short Introductions," Oxford University Press USA, http://global.oup.com/academic/content/series/v/very-short-introductions-vsi.

74. Howard, "Ditch the Monograph" (see note 68).

75. "Bookstore," *New York Times* website, http://www.nytstore.com/ebooks.

76. Laura Hazard Owen, "The Atlantic Launches a New eBook Division; Will Sell e-Singles and Curated Collections," Gigaom, May 1, 2013. Available at http://gigaom.com/2013/05/01/the-atlantic-launches-a-new-ebook-division-with-e-singles-and-curated-collections.

77. Tenopir et al. 2009.

78. M. Price 2011.

79. Ledgerwood and Sherman 2012; Marco Bertamini and Marcus R. Munafò, "The Perils of 'Bite Size' Science," *New York Times*, January 28, 2012. Available at http://www.nytimes.com/2012/01/29/opinion/sunday/the-perils-of-bite-size-science.html?_r=0.

80. Evans 2008.

CHAPTER 4

The epigraph is the caption of a YouTube video. Available at http://www.youtube.com/watch?v=aXV-yaFmQNk.

1. Quentin Fottrell, "Why Sex Sells Better on E-Books," MarketWatch, June 24, 2012. Available at http://blogs.marketwatch.com/paydirt/2012/06/24/why-sex-sells-better-on-e-books/?mg=blogs-sm.

2. Lewis 2012, 291.

3. Results of the study were presented at a conference in February 2013. See "What's Going On with Readers Today? Goodreads Finds Out," Goodreads, February 25, 2013, http://www.goodreads.com/blog/show/410-what-s-going-on-with-readers-today-goodreads-finds-out.

4. Lyall 1989, 11.

5. Anne Trubek, "How the Paperback Novel Changed Popular Literature," *Smithsonian Magazine*, March 31, 2010. Available at http://www.smithsonianmag.com/arts-culture/How-the-Paperback-Novel-Changed-Popular-Literature.html.

6. Alison Flood, "Ebook Price War Sees Discounts Reach 97%," *Guardian*, September 18, 2012. Available at http://www.guardian.co.uk/books/2012/sep/18/ebook-price-war-discounts.

7. Paul Bentley, "How a Third of Bestselling eBooks Cost *More* than the Same Title in Hardback," *Daily Mail*, September 30, 2012. Available at http://www.dailymail.co.uk/sciencetech/article-2211022/How-bestselling-ebooks-cost-MORE-title-hardback.html.

8. Thomas Catan, Jeffrey A. Trachtenberg, and Chad Bray, "U.S. Alleges E-Book Scheme," *Wall Street Journal*, April 11, 2012. Available at http://online.wsj.com/article/SB10001424052702304444604577337573054615152.html.

9. "What Is 'Agency Pricing'?," *Wall Street Journal*, April 11, 2012. Available at http://blogs.wsj.com/digits/2012/04/11/what-is-agency-pricing.

10. Jeremy Greenfield, "Macmillan Settles with DOJ over Ebook Price-Fixing, Leaving Apple Alone to Face Lawsuit," Digital Book World, February 8, 2013. Available at http://www.digitalbookworld.com/2013/macmillan-settles-with-doj-over-ebook-price-fixing-leaving-apple-alone-to-face-lawsuit; *United States v. Apple Inc. et al.*, Nos. 12 Civ. 2826 (DLC), 12 Civ. 3394 (DLC) (July 10, 2013). Available at http://www.justice.gov/atr/cases/f299200/299275.pdf.

11. Trena White, "Canadian Competition Bureau Limits Agency eBook Pricing," Digital Book World, February 7, 2014. Available at http://www.digitalbookworld.com/2014/canadian-competition-bureau-limits-agency-ebook-pricing.

12. Chris Foresman, "Apple, Publishers Settle EU e-Book Investigation with No Fines," Ars Technica, December 13, 2012. Available at http://arstechnica.com/apple/2012/12/apple-publishers-settle-eu-e-book-investigation-with-no-fines.

13. Jeremy Greenfield, "Simon & Schuster Joins Other Big Six Publishers with Library Ebook Pilot," Digital Book World, April 15, 2013. Available at http://www.digitalbookworld.com/2013/simon-schuster-joins-other-big-six-publishers-with-library-ebook-pilot.

14. Quoted in Flood, "Ebook Price War Sees Discounts Reach 97%" (see note 6).

15. Kudos to Anna Olsson (a Swede) for creating American University's Green Teaching Program. For more information, see http://www.american.edu/ctrl/green.cfm.

16. Book Industry Study Group, *Student Attitudes Toward Content in Higher Education*, vol. 4, no. 1 (New York: BISG, 2013).

17. Daniel Goleman and Gregory Norris, "How Green Is My iPad?," *New York Times*, April 4, 2010. Available at http://www.nytimes.com/interactive/2010/04/04/opinion/04opchart.html?_r=0.

18. James Glanz, "Power, Pollution and the Internet," *New York Times*, September 22, 2012. Available at http://www.nytimes.com/2012/09/23/technology/data-centers-waste-vast-amounts-of-energy-belying-industry-image.html?pagewanted=all.

19. Åsa Moberg, Martin Johansson, Göran Finnveden, and Alex Jonsson, "Screening Environmental Life Cycle Assessment of Printed, Web Based and Tablet e-Paper Newspaper," report from the KTH Centre for Sustainable Communications, Stockholm, 2007. Available at http://www.infra.kth.se/fms/pdf/Report_epaper_final.pdf.

20. Jennifer Schwab, "E-Readers Versus Old-Fashioned Books—What Is Greener?," *Huffington Post*, December 9, 2010. Available at http://www.huffingtonpost.com/jennifer-schwab/ereaders-vs-old-fashioned_b_794634.html.

21. Thomas F. Gattiker and Scott E. Lowe, "Can E-Textbooks Help Save the Planet? It Depends on You," *Chronicle of Higher Education*, October 1, 2012. Available at https://chronicle.com/article/Can-E-Textbooks-Help-Save-the/134680.

22. For more recent developments, see European Commission, "Recast of the WEEE Directive," last updated July 2, 2014, http://ec.europa.eu/environment/waste/weee/index_en.htm.

23. Sunil Herat, "Major Threats from E-Waste: Current Generation and Impacts," *ChemViews Magazine*, April 5, 2011. Available at http://www.chemistryviews.org/details/ezine/1037973/Major_Threats_From_E-Waste_Current_Generation_And_Impacts.html.

24. Mark Glaser, "5Across: Environmental Impact of Newspapers, Books, e-Waste," Media Shift, PBS.org, January 22, 2010. Available at http://www.pbs.org/mediashift/2010/01/5across-environmental-impact-of-newspapers-books-e-waste022.

25. COST Action FPS 1104, "New Possibilities for Print Media and Packaging—Combining Print with Digital." See http://www.cost.eu/domains_actions/fps/Actions/FP1104.

26. Sessa 1980.

27. Harrison 1961.

28. See Hamilton 2004.

29. Creative Commons, http://creativecommons.org.

30. "History," PLoS website, http://www.plos.org/about/plos/history.

31. "Google Books History," http://books.google.com/intl/en/googlebooks/about/history.html.

32. Matthew Saltmarsh, "Google Loses in French Copyright Case," *New York Times*, December 19, 2009. Available at http://www.nytimes.com/2009/12/19/technology/companies/19google.html?_r=0.

33. Claire Cain Miller and Julie Bosman, "Siding with Google, Judge Says Book Search Does Not Infringe Copyright," *New York Times*, November 14, 2013. Available at http://www.nytimes.com/2013/11/15/business/media/judge-sides-with-google-on-book-scanning-suit.html?_r=0.

34. See, for example, Robert Darnton, "Google and the Future of Books," *New York Review of Books*, February 12, 2009. Available at http://www.nybooks.com/articles/archives/2009/feb/12/google-the-future-of-books/?pagination=false.

35. The Digital Public Library of America's website is http://dp.la. See discussion of the launch in Robert Darnton, "The National Digital Public Library Is Launched!," *New York Review of Books*, April 25, 2013. Available at http://www.nybooks.com/articles/archives/2013/apr/25/national-digital-public-library-launched/?pagination=false.

36. Library of Congress, American Memory, "Mission and History," http://memory.loc.gov/ammem/about/index.html.

37. Europeana website, http://www.europeana.eu.

38. National Library of Norway, "Digitizing Policy," http://www.nb.no/English/The-Digital-Library/Digitizing-policy.

39. Worldreader website, http://www.worldreader.org.

40. See Geoffrey A. Fowler, "Nonprofit Tries One-Kindle-Per-Child in Ghana," *Wall Street Journal*, August 5, 2010. Available at http://blogs.wsj.com/digits/2010/08/05/nonprofit-tries-one-kindle-per-child-in-ghana.

41. Bruce Watson, "The High Cost of Higher Education Explained in One Simple Graphic," Power of Planning blog, AOL Money and Finance, March 15, 2013. Available at http://www.dailyfinance.com/on/college-costs-tuition-rising-student-debt-infographic.

42. College Board Advocacy and Policy Center, "Trends in College Pricing 2012," http://trends.collegeboard.org/sites/default/files/college-pricing-2012-full-report_0.pdf.

43. Government Accountability Office, "College Textbooks: Students Have Greater Access to Textbook Information," June 6, 2013. Available at http://www.gao.gov/products/GAO-13-368.

44. Institute for College Access and Success, "Student Debt and the Class of 2012," December 2013. Available at http://projectonstudentdebt.org.

45. Tyler Kingkade, "Rising Costs Force Students to Skimp on Textbooks," *Huffington Post*, August 11, 2011. Available at http://www.huffingtonpost.com/2011/08/11/student-advocates-sound-alarm-on-textbooks_n_924536.html. A study conducted in fall 2013 confirms these findings: Ethan Senack, "Fixing the Broken Textbook Market: How Students Respond to High Textbook Costs and Demand Alternatives," US PIRG Education Fund and the Student PIRGs, January 2014, http://uspirg.org/sites/pirg/files/reports/NATIONAL%20Fixing%20Broken%20Textbooks%20Report1.pdf.

46. Zack Budryk, "Rights Reserved," *Inside Higher Ed*, March 4, 2013. Available at http://www.insidehighered.com/news/2013/03/04/colleges-try-beat-textbook-costs-book-reserves.

47. Steve Kolowich, "e-Reservations," *Inside Higher Ed*, May 15, 2012. Available at http://www.insidehighered.com/news/2012/05/15/court-ruling-landmark-e-reserve-leaves-unanswered-questions.

48. Tom Chorneau, "California Faces Potential $11 Billion Deficit in Budget Next Year," *San Francisco Chronicle*, November 7, 2007. Available at http://www.sfgate.com/bayarea/article/California-faces-potential-11-billion-deficit-in-3237025.php; Kristin Kloberdanz, "The Great California Fiscal Earthquake," *Time*, January 8, 2009. Available at http://www.time.com/time/nation/article/0,8599,1870299,00.html.

49. Arnold Schwarzenegger, "Digital Textbooks Can Save Money, Improve Learning," *San Jose Mercury News*, June 7, 2009. Available at http://www.mercurynews.com/opinion/ci_12536333.

50. Megan Garber, "California Takes a Big Step Forward: Free, Digital, Open-Source Textbooks," *Atlantic*, September 30, 2012. Available at http://www.theatlantic.com/technology/archive/2012/09/california-takes-a-big-step-forward-free-digital-open-source-textbooks/263047.

51. European Commission, "Digital Agenda for Europe: A Europe 2020 Initiative," http://ec.europa.eu/digital-agenda.

52. Jordan Usdan and Josh Gottheimer, "FCC Chairman: Digital Textbook to All Students in Five Years," FCC Blog, February 3, 2012. Available at http://www.fcc.gov/blog/fcc-chairman-digital-textbooks-all-students-five-years.

53. See, for example, the report "Out of Print: Reimagining the K-12 Textbook in a Digital Age," issued by the State Educational Technology Directors Association. Available at http://www.setda.org/c/document_library/get_file?folderId=321&name=DLFE-1587.pdf.

54. Jeremy Greenfield, "When Will We See Mass Adoption of Digital Classrooms? September 2014," Digital Book World, September 4, 2013. Available at http://www.digitalbookworld.com/2013/when-will-we-see-mass-adoption-of-digital-classrooms-september-2014.

55. "Textbook Rentals: Frequently Asked Questions," Amazon.com, http://www.amazon.com/b?ie=UTF8&node=5657188011#highlight/ref=txtb_rent_faq_highlight.

56. Courseload website, http://www.courseload.com.

57. EDUCAUSE, "E-textbooks," http://www.educause.edu/library/e-textbooks. For an analysis of progress, see the Roundtable on eContent (eText) from the Internet2 Annual Meeting, April 24, 2013, available at http://events.internet2.edu/2013/annual-meeting/program.cfm?go=session&id=10003011.

58. See OpenStax CNX website, http://cnx.org, and OpenStax College website, http://openstaxcollege.org.

59. Nick DeSantis, "Temple U. Project Ditches Textbooks for Homemade Digital Alternatives," *Chronicle of Higher Education*, February 7, 2012. Available at http://chronicle.com/blogs/wiredcampus/temple-project-ditches-textbooks-for-homemade-digital-alternatives/35247; Mitch Smith, "Textbook Alternative," *Inside Higher Ed*, May 10, 2012. Available at http://www.insidehighered.com/news/2012/05/10/university-minnesota-compiles-database-peer-reviewed-open-source-textbooks.

60. Student Monitor LLC, fall 2013 survey.

61. Student Monitor LLC, "Lifestyle & Media—Spring 2013."

62. Bowker, "Student Response to Digital Textbooks Climbs, Says New BISG Research," press release, January 25, 2013 (results from *Student Attitudes Toward Content in Higher Education*, vol. 3, first installment), http://www.bowker.com/en-US/aboutus/press_room/2013/pr_01252013.shtml.

63. Book Industry Study Group, *Student Attitudes Toward Content in Higher Education*, vol. 4, no. 1 (New York: BISG, 2013).

64. Hyung Lee, "Kindles Yet to Woo University Users," *Daily Princetonian*, September 28, 2009. Available at http://dailyprincetonian.com/news/2009/09/kindles-yet-to-woo-university-users. On the Reed experiment, see Trina Marmarelli and Martin Ringle, "The Reed College Kindle Study," http://web.reed.edu/cis/about/kindle_pilot/Reed_Kindle_report.pdf.

65. Alan Dennis, Anastasia Morrone, and Binny Samuel, "eTexts at Indiana University: Fall 2011 Update," March 2012. Available at http://etexts.iu.edu/files/etextbook%20research%20fall%202011.pdf.

66. "Internet2 eTextbook Spring 2012 Pilot: Final Project Report," August 1, 2012. Available at http://www.internet2.edu/media/medialibrary/2013/10/07/eText-Spring-2012-Pilot-Report.pdf.

67. "EDUCAUSE and Internet2 E-Content Pilot Series," EDUCAUSE, http://www.educause.edu/focus-areas-and-initiatives/policy-and-security/educause-policy/issues-and-positions/e-content-pilot-series.

68. For example, Jennifer Howard, "For Many Students, Print Is Still King," *Chronicle of Higher Education*, January 27, 2013. Available at http://chronicle.com/article/For-Many-Students-Print-Is/136829.

69. "9 out of 10 Students Find Textbooks Too Expensive—The Big Bookboon Textbook Survey," Bookboon.com, September 11, 2012. Available at http://bookboon.com/blog/2012/09/the-big-bookboon-textbook-survey-read-the-opinion-of-almost-10-000-students.

70. For results from the first two studies, see N. Baron 2013a, 2013b.

71. For the German data, there were practically no differences between the collective responses of 18-to-24-year-olds and 18-to-26-year-olds, and so we included the handful of 25- and 26-year-olds in the study.

72. Similarly, see Student Monitor LLC, "Lifestyle & Media—Spring 2013."

73. Cited in Louise Gray, "Authors Stand Up for Traditional Books over e-Books," *Telegraph*, July 21, 2013. Available at http://www.telegraph.co.uk/culture/books/10193467/Authors-stand-up-for-traditional-books-over-e-books.html.

74. The Japanese and German analyses weren't complete when I finished this book.

75. Student Monitor LLC, "Lifestyle & Media—Spring 2013."

76. These examples are drawn from materials distributed in November 2013 at the fall meetings of the COST Action FPS 1104 in Ljubljana, Slovenia. Two of the studies are published: Fortunati and Vincent 2014; Taipale 2014.

CHAPTER 5

1. Schwalbe 2012, 280–281.

2. Cited in Jabr 2013a.

3. Jhumpa Lahiri, "My Life's Sentences," *New York Times*, March 17, 2012. Available at http://opinionator.blogs.nytimes.com/2012/03/17/my-lifes-sentences/?_r=0.

4. Henkel 2014.

5. Odom et al. 2012.

6. Larsen 2005, 2014.

7. Elisabeth Bumiller, "We Have Met the Enemy and He Is PowerPoint," *New York Times*, April 26, 2010. Available at http://www.nytimes.com/2010/04/27/world/27powerpoint.html.

8. Gaskins 2012. For highlights of the history, see Gaskins' web page, http://www.robertgaskins.com.

9. Tufte 2003.

10. From the Slow Food website, http://www.slowfood.com.

11. Honoré 2004.

12. Quoted in Honoré 2004, 4.

13. "The Slow Media Manifesto," posted by Bruce Sterling to *Wired*'s Beyond the Beyond blog, June 28, 2010 (http://www.wired.com/beyond_the_beyond/2010/06/the-slow-media-manifesto); Ellen Cushing, "The Slow-Beer Movement," *East Bay Express*, October 26, 2011. Available at http://www.eastbayexpress.com/oakland/the-slow-beer-movement/Content?oid=3025006.

14. Nietzsche 1982, 5.

15. Adler 1940.

16. Brower 1961.

17. Birkerts 1994, 146.

18. Birkerts 2010.

19. Stephanie Harvey and Harvey "Smokey" Daniels, *Comprehension and Collaboration: Inquiry Circles in Action* (2009), 93; cited in Mikics 2013, 94.

20. Harvard Library Research Guides, "Interrogating Texts: Six Reading Habits to Develop in Your First Year at Harvard," last updated October 23, 2013. Available at http://guides.library.harvard.edu/sixreadinghabits.

21. Howard Gardner, "Test for Aptitude, Not for Speed," *New York Times*, July 18, 2002. Available at http://www.nytimes.com/2002/07/18/opinion/test-for-aptitude-not-for-speed.html.

22. Miedema 2008, 7, 42–43, 3.

23. The website from which these quotations were drawn is no longer active.

24. Newkirk 2012, 2.

25. "The Slow Reading Manifesto," available at http://www.slowreading.org.

26. Mikics 2013, 40. For more on slow reading, see Love 2012; Maura Kelly, "A Slow-Books Manifesto," *Atlantic*, March 26, 2012. Available at http://www.theatlantic.com/entertainment/archive/2012/03/a-slow-books-manifesto/254884.

27. Quoted in Patrick Kingsley, "The Art of Slow Reading," *Guardian*, July 14, 2010. Available at http://www.theguardian.com/books/2010/jul/15/slow-reading.

28. Just and Carpenter 1987.

29. Dillon 1992.

30. Jeff Bezos, Amazon.com, "Letter to Shareholders," April 2008. Available at http://www.sec.gov/Archives/edgar/data/1018724/000119312508084145/dex991.htm.

31. "About Longform," http://longform.org/about.

32. See, for example, comments by Gerald Marzorati, then editor of the *New York Times Magazine*, on the future of long-form journalism: "Talk to the Times: Assistant Managing Editor Gerald Marzorati," *New York Times*, August 24, 2009. Available at http://www.nytimes.com/2009/08/24/business/media/24askthetimes.html?pagewanted=all&_r=0.

33. Quoted in Jason Fry, "Does Long-Form Journalism Work Online?," Reinventing the Newsroom blog, August 25, 2009. Available at http://reinventingthenewsroom.wordpress.com/2009/08/25/does-long-form-journalism-work-online.

34. National Endowment for the Arts, *Reading on the Rise: A New Chapter in American Literacy*, Office of Research Analysis, 2009. Available at http://www.arts.gov/research/ReadingonRise.pdf.

35. Quoted in Tim Parks, "Why Finish Books?," *New York Review of Books* blog, March 13, 2012. Available at http://www.nybooks.com/blogs/nyrblog/2012/mar/13/why-finish-books.

36. Quoted in Heidi Mitchell, "Guilt Complex: Why Leaving a Book Half-Read Is So Hard," *Wall Street Journal*, June 5, 2013. Available at http://online.wsj.com/article/SB10001424127887323469804578525354146879558.html.

37. "Reading Statistics," Statistic Brain, http://www.statisticbrain.com/reading-statistics.

38. David Streitfeld, "As New Services Track Habits, the E-Books Are Reading You," *New York Times*, December 24, 2013. Available at http://www.nytimes.com/2013/12/25/technology/as-new-services-track-habits-the-e-books-are-reading-you.html?pagewanted=all&_r=0.

39. Amory 1996, 55.

40. IT Strategies and the University of Colorado, "The Evolution of the Book Industry: Implications for U.S. Book Manufacturers and Printers," commissioned by Ricoh Americas Corporation, 2013. Available at http://www.infoprint.com/internet/comnelit.nsf/Files/ITStrategies_FINAL/$File/ITStrategies_FINAL.pdf.

41. Nabokov 1980, 3.

42. Spacks 2011, 12.

43. Spacks 2011, 9.

44. Verlyn Klinkenborg, "Some Thoughts on the Pleasures of Being a Re-Reader," *New York Times*, May 29, 2009. Available at http://www.nytimes.com/2009/05/30/opinion/30sat4.html?_r=0.

45. Danny Heitman, "Encounters with Biblio-Amnesia," *Washington Post*, June 10, 2011. Available at http://articles.washingtonpost.com/2011-06-10/opinions/35233892_1_poetry-and-prose-new-books-memory.

46. Fadiman 2005, xiii.

47. Fadiman 2005, xiv.

48. Spacks 2011, 273.

CHAPTER 6

The Hitchings epigraph is quoted from Patrick Kingsley, "The Art of Slow Reading," *Guardian*, July 14, 2010. Available at http://www.theguardian.com/books/2010/jul/15/slow-reading. The Chandler epigraph is from "What's Going On with Readers Today? Goodreads Finds Out," February 25, 2013, http://www.goodreads.com/blog/show/410-what-s-going-on-with-readers-today-goodreads-finds-out.

1. Darnton 1991, 150.

2. "Frequently Asked Questions" for Amazon Kindle, https://kindle.amazon.com/faq. Other eReader companies offer comparable tools.

3. Steven Johnson, "Yes, People Still Read, but Now It's Social," *New York Times*, June 19, 2010. Available at http://www.nytimes.com/2010/06/20/business/20unbox.html?_r=0.

4. Cynthia Ozick, "Where to Connect to the Inner Hum," *New York Times Magazine*, May 7, 2000. Available at http://www.nytimes.com/2000/05/07/magazine/where-to-connect-to-the-inner-hum.html?pagewanted=all&src=pm.

5. Proust 1971, 31.

6. Proust 1971, 35.

7. Proust 1971, 53, 55.

8. Spacks 2011, 9.

9. L. Price 2011, 1.

10. "New Kindle Helps Readers Show Off By Shouting Title of Book Loudly and Repeatedly," *Onion*, July 30, 2014. Available at http://www.theonion.com/video/new-kindle-helps-readers-show-off-by-shouting-titl,36568.

11. LibraryThing website, http://www.librarything.com.

12. Ferguson 2001.

13. Alex Clark, "The New Wave of Literary Events," *Guardian*, July 30, 2010. Available at http://www.guardian.co.uk/books/2010/jul/31/bookslams-literary-events-books.

14. Literary Death Match website, http://www.literarydeathmatch.com.

15. Kevin Smokler, "Virtual Book Touring," http://www.kevinsmokler.com/virtual_book_tour.html. Other options include TLC Book Tours, Virtual Author Book Tours, and Historical Fiction Virtual Book Tours.

16. "NYC Start-Up, Shindig, Hosts Grandmasters in First Ever Online Video Chat Chess Tournament," PR Newswire, June 16, 2011. Available at http://www.prnewswire.com/news-releases/nyc-start-up-shindig-hosts-grandmasters-in-first-ever-online-video-chat-chess-tournament-124038899.html.

17. Shindig website, http://shindigevents.com.

18. Douglas Corleone, "Author Tour: An Essential Part of the Writer's Journey or Just Another Ego Trip?," posting on Algonquin Redux, July 14, 2013. Available at http://algonquinredux.com/author-tour-an-essential-part-of-the-writers-journey-or-just-another-ego-trip.

19. Desmond 1978, 27.

20. Barzun 2001, 49.

21. Darnton 1991, 151. For discussion of continental reading societies, see Wittmann 1999, 306 ff.

22. Kaufman 1964.

23. See Nathan Heller, "Book Clubs: Why Do We Love Them So Much? Is It the Zucchini Bread?" *Slate*, July 29, 2011. Available at http://www.slate.com/articles/news_and_politics/assessment/2011/07/book_clubs.html.

24. Franklin 2004, 164–166, 48–49.

25. For discussions of men's self-betterment organizations, see Harrison 1961; Rice 2004, chapter 2.

26. Ray 2005.

27. See, for example, the history of the Providence Athenaeum at http://www.providence athenaeum.org/history/history.html and that of the Boston Athenaeum in Story 1975.

28. On the history of the Chautauqua movement, see Gould 1961.

29. Renaissance Institute, "Illustrative Lists of Past Participants," http://www.renaissanceweekend .org/participants/illustrativelists.htm.

30. Long 2003, 31.

31. Long 2003, 227–228 n. 3.

32. Putnam 2000, 149. For a study of the relationship between highbrow reading groups and community involvement, see Davis 1961.

33. Long 2003, 37–38.

34. Adele Briscoe Looscan, reporting for the Houston Ladies Reading Club in 1890. Cited in Long 2003, 40.

35. Long 2003, 40.

36. US Census Bureau, *Statistical Abstracts of the University States: 2012*, Table 226, "School Enrollment by Sex and Level: 1970 to 2009." Available at http://www.census.gov/prod/ 2011pubs/12statab/educ.pdf.

37. For discussion of the history of the Book-of-the-Month Club, see Rubin 1985 and Radway 1997.

38. Rubin 1985, 790.

39. Barzun 2001.

40. Aswini Anburajan, "Breaking Down Oprah's Numbers," NBC News, December 7, 2007, http://firstread.nbcnews.com/_news/2007/12/07/4425062-breaking-down-oprahs-numbers?lite.

41. Quoted in Farr 2005, 9.

42. In 2012, Oprah launched Oprah's Book Club 2.0, a joint project of the Oprah Winfrey Network and her magazine *O*.

43. Cade Metz, "LibraryThing," *PC Magazine*, July 21, 2006. Available at http://www.pcmag. com/article2/0,2817,1992863,00.asp. For an analysis of LibraryThing, see Pinder 2012.

44. Shelfari website, http://www.shelfari.com.

45. Jeremy Greenfield, "Goodreads CEO Otis Chandler on the Future of Discoverability and Social Reading," Digital Book World, November 8, 2012. Available at http://www .digitalbookworld.com/2012/goodreads-ceo-otis-chandler-on-the-future-of-discoverability-and-social-reading; "Goodreads Grows to 20 Million Readers," July 23, 2013, Available at http:// www.goodreads.com/blog/show/425-goodreads-grows-to-20-million-readers.

46. Rob Spillman, "Amazon Buys Goodreads: We're All Just Data Now," *Salon*, March 31, 2013. Available at http://www.salon.com/2013/03/31/amazon_buys_goodreads_were_all_ just_data_now.

47. For an overview of Zola's early development, see Rachel Deahl, "New Retailer Zola Premieres, Softly, at BEA," *Publishers Weekly*, June 8, 2012. Available at http://www.publishersweekly.com/ pw/by-topic/industry-news/bea/article/52475-new-retailer-zola-premieres-softly-at-bea.html. On publishing digital editions of Didion's work, see Julie Bosman, "Start-Up to Offer Didion E-Books," *New York Times*, November 3, 2013. Available at http://www.nytimes.com/2013/11/04/ business/media/ZolaBooks-start-up-will-offer-didion-e-books.html?_r=0.

48. For a description of Librify's plans as of mid-2013, see Judith Rosen, "Librify: The BOMC for E-Books?," *Publishers Weekly*, June 22, 2013. Available at http://www.publishersweekly.com/ pw/by-topic/digital/retailing/article/57941-librify-the-bomc-for-e-books.html.

49. Bob Stein, "The Future of the Book Is the Future of Society," if:book, A Project of the Institute for the Future of the Book, March 18, 2013. Available at http://futureofthebook.org/ blog/2013/03/18/the_future_of_the_book_is_the.

50. "Social Book," Open Utopia, http://theopenutopia.org/social-book.

51. Quoted in Sean Prpick, "'Social Reading' the Next Phase of e-Book Revolution," CBC News, February 25, 2013. Available at http://www.cbc.ca/news/canada/story/2013/02/22/f-prpick-ebook.html. CBC's 2013 documentary *Opening the Book* is available at http://www.cbc.ca/ideas/episodes/2013/02/25/opening-the-book.

52. For example, Book Blogger Directory, http://bookbloggerdirectory.wordpress.com.

53. Judith Shulevitz, "The Close Reader; You Read Your Book and I'll Read Mine," *New York Times Book Review*, May 19, 2002. Available at http://www.nytimes.com/2002/05/19/books/the-close-reader-you-read-your-book-and-i-ll-read-mine.html.

54. Alber and Miller 2012, 163.

55. Spacks 2011, 19.

56. "Kobo Reading Life," http://www.kobobooks.com/readinglife.

57. The Electronic Frontier Foundation has produced a fascinating "E-Reader Privacy Chart," indicating the kinds of information that a variety of digital book platforms have about your reading patterns. See https://www.eff.org/pages/reader-privacy-chart-2012.

CHAPTER 7

The first epigraph is from Kevin Kelly, "What Books Will Become," The Technium, April 15, 2011. Available at http://www.kk.org/thetechnium/archives/2011/04/what_books_will.php. The second is from Tania Kindersley, "BooksBlog: The Death of the Book, Again," *Guardian*, April 17, 2007. Available at http://www.guardian.co.uk/books/booksblog/2007/apr/17/thedeathofthebookagain.

1. Andrew Losowsky, "Why EBooks Are Inspiring a New Age of Print," *Huffington Post*, October 29, 2012. Available at http://www.huffingtonpost.com/2012/10/29/ebooks-new-age-print_n_2040602.html. Also see C. Claiborne Ray, "The Weight of Memory," *New York Times*, October 24, 2011. Available at http://www.nytimes.com/2011/10/25/science/25qna.html?_r=0.

2. Cartoon by William Haefeli, *New Yorker*, September 3, 2012, 51.

3. Schwalbe 2012, 42–43.

4. In some European countries, filing is done differently, relying on hole-punched paper in binders, along with slim file boxes.

5. Clanchy 1993, 36.

6. Maryann Yin, "HarperCollins and Autography Partner for Author Signings," GalleyCat blog, Media Bistro, July 16, 2013. Available at http://www.mediabistro.com/galleycat/harpercollins-autography-partner-for-author-signings_b74265; also see Beth Bacon, "Digital Book Signings Help Grow Authors' Careers," May 16, 2013, and "Digital Book Signings: A Range of Technologies and Services," May 21, 2013, Digital Book World. Available at http://www.digitalbookworld.com/2013/digital-book-signings-help-grow-authors-careers.

7. Piper 2012. The quotation is from an excerpt that appeared under the title "Out of Touch: E-Reading Isn't Reading" in *Slate*, November 15, 2012. Available at http://www.slate.com/articles/arts/culturebox/2012/11/reading_on_a_kindle_is_not_the_same_as_reading_a_book.html.

8. Gary Frost, "Haptics and Habitats of Reading," Future of the Book blog, August 9, 2003. Available at http://futureofthebook.com/storiestoc-5/haptic.

9. Kathleen Parker, "The Hard Truth: How Human Touch Influences Our Emotions," *Washington Post*, July 7, 2010. Available at http://www.jewishworldreview.com/kathleen/parker070710.php3#.Uv_RXXlelKM.

10. "Why Do Old Books Smell So Good?," *Huffington Post*, April 11, 2012. Available at http://www.huffingtonpost.com/2012/04/11/old-book-smell_n_1415275.html.

11. See Smell of Books website at http://smellofbooks.com.

12. For wonderful examples of fine-edition books (in this case, produced by Andrew Hoyem, who runs Arion Press), see Nathan Heller, "A Nearly Perfect Book," *Harvard Magazine*, October 2013, 34–39. Also see Klanten, Hübner, and Losowsky 2013.

13. Charles McGrath, "By-the-Book Reader Meets the Kindle," *New York Times*, May 28, 2009. Available at http://www.nytimes.com/2009/05/29/books/29kind.html?pagewanted=all.

14. Rothkopf 1971.

15. "Disappearing Ink Book: 'The Book That Can't Wait' Fades Away After Two Months," *Huffington Post*, June 29, 2012. Available at http://www.huffingtonpost.com/2012/06/29/disappearing-ink-book-the_n_1637388.html.

16. For examples, see the Senseg website at http://senseg.com and video of Tactus Technology's morphing touchscreen keyboard at https://www.youtube.com/watch?v=nNnGpIEa3AU.

17. Cunningham and Stanovich 1990.

18. Longcamp, Zerbato-Poudou, and Velay, 2005.

19. Longcamp et al. 2008. For more on the haptics of writing, see Mangen and Velay 2010.

20. James and Engelhardt 2012. Also see Maria Konnikova, "What's Lost as Handwriting Fades," *New York Times*, June 2, 2014. Available at http://www.nytimes.com/2014/06/03/science/whats-lost-as-handwriting-fades.html?_r=0.

21. Cited in Chandler 1992.

22. D. Baron 2009, 157.

23. Cecilia Kang, "High-Tech vs. No-Tech: D.C. Area Schools Take Opposite Approaches to Education," *Washington Post*, May 12, 2012. Available at http://www.washingtonpost.com/business/technology/high-tech-vs-no-tech-dc-area-schools-take-opposite-approaches-to-education/2012/05/12/gIQAv6YFLU_story.html.

24. Cited in Chandler 1992.

25. From an email (December 12, 2013) from Joshua Bell, curator of globalization at the Smithsonian's National Museum of Natural History, Washington, DC.

26. Ulin 2010, 19.

27. Ackerman, Nocera, and Bargh 2010.

28. Sadato 2005.

29. Rachel Aviv, "Listening to Braille," *New York Times*, December 30, 2009. Available at http://www.nytimes.com/2010/01/03/magazine/03Braille-t.html?pagewanted=all&_r=0.

30. Quoted in Aviv, "Listening to Braille" (see note 29).

31. "DAISY Playback Devices," Vision Australia website, 2012, http://www.visionaustralia.org/living-with-low-vision/learning-to-live-independently/using-technology-and-computers/technology-overview/ebook-readers-and-daisy/daisy-playback-devices.

32. Velázquez, Hernández, and Preza 2012.

33. Parker, "The Hard Truth" (see note 9).

34. Sellen and Harper 2002.

35. O'Hara et al. 2002, 282, 281.

36. Gerlach and Buxmann 2011.

37. Avi Solomon, "Interview: Seth Godin," Boing Boing, May 16, 2011. Available at http://boingboing.net/2011/05/16/interview-seth-godin.html.

38. Quoted in Roger Tagholm, "Is a Digital Book as Devout as a Physical Copy?," *Publishing Perspectives*, April 26, 2013. Available at http://publishingperspectives.com/2013/04/is-a-digital-book-as-devout-as-a-physical-copy.

39. Tania Kindersley, "BooksBlog: The Death of the Book, Again," *Guardian*, April 17, 2007. Available at http://www.guardian.co.uk/books/booksblog/2007/apr/17/thedeathofthebookagain.

40. Amanda Katz, "Will Your Children Inherit Your E-Books?," National Public Radio, June 21, 2012. Available at http://www.npr.org/2012/06/21/155360197/will-your-children-inherit-your-e-books.

41. Ian Urbina, "From Love to Longing to Protest, It's All in the Tilt of the Postage," *New York Times*, August 15, 2005. Available at http://www.nytimes.com/2005/08/15/national/15stamps.html?hp&oref=login.

42. Julia Keller, "Relevance of the Book Questioned in Internet Age," *Chicago Tribune*, April 20, 2008. Available at http://articles.chicagotribune.com/2008-04-20/news/0804180493_1_book-sales-galileo-book-s-end.

43. Keller, "Relevance of the Book" (see note 42).

44. *The Codex Nuttall* 1975.

45. Kindersley, "BooksBlog: The Death of the Book, Again" (see note 39).

46. My thanks to Torill Mortensen (the Dane) and Mathias Klang (the Swede) for their observations.

47. Max 2000, 26.

48. Judith Shulevitz, "The Close Reader: You Read Your Book and I'll Read Mine," *New York Times Book Review*, May 19, 2002. Available at http://www.nytimes.com/2002/05/19/books/the-close-reader-you-read-your-book-and-i-ll-read-mine.html.

49. Mikics 2013, 46.

50. Quoted in University of Stavanger, "Storybooks on Paper Better for Children than Reading Fiction on Computer Screen, According to Expert," *Science Daily*, December 22, 2008. Available at http://www.sciencedaily.com/releases/2008/12/081219073049.htm.

51. Dilevko and Gottlieb 2002, 391.

52. Mann 2001, 270. The emphasis is Mann's.

53. Birkerts 1994; Nunberg 1996; William H. Gass, "In Defense of the Book," *Harper's*, November 1999, 45–51; Max 2000.

54. Max 2000, 18.

55. National Center for Education Statistics, *Digest of Education Statistics: 2011*, Table 289: "Bachelor's, Master's, and Doctor's Degrees Conferred by Degree-Granting Institutions, by Field of Study: Selected Years, 1970–71 Through 2009–10." Available at http://nces.ed.gov/programs/digest/d11/tables/dt11_289.asp?referrer=list.

56. Harvard University, "The Teaching of the Arts and Humanities at Harvard College: Mapping the Future," May 2013. Available at http://artsandhumanities.fas.harvard.edu/files/humanities/files/mapping_the_future_31_may_2013.pdf.

57. American Academy of Arts & Sciences, Commission on the Humanities and Social Sciences, "The Heart of the Matter," 2013. Available at http://www.humanitiescommission.org/_pdf/hss_report.pdf.

58. Compare Verlyn Klinkenborg, "The Decline and Fall of the English Major," *New York Times*, June 22, 2013 (available at http://www.nytimes.com/2013/06/23/opinion/sunday/the-decline-and-fall-of-the-english-major.html) with Nate Silver, "As More Attend College, Majors Become More Career-Focused," FiveThirtyEight blog, *New York Times,* June 25, 2013 (available

at http://fivethirtyeight.blogs.nytimes.com/2013/06/25/as-more-attend-college-majors-become-more-career-focused/?pagewanted=print) and with Michael Bérubé, "The Humanities, Declining? Not According to the Numbers," *Chronicle of Higher Education*, July 1, 2013 (available at http://chronicle.com/article/The-Humanities-Declining-Not/140093).

59. Eric L. Day, Alexander W. Astin, and William S. Korn, "The American Freshman: Twenty-Five Year Trends, 1966–1990," Higher Education Research Institute, Graduate School of Education, University of California, Los Angeles, September 1991. Available at http://www.heri.ucla.edu/PDFs/pubs/TFS/Trends/Monographs/TheAmericanFreshman25YearTrends.pdf.

60. John H. Pryor, Linda DeAngelo, Laura Palucki Blake, Sylvia Hurtado, and Serge Tran, "The American Freshman: National Norms Fall 2011," Higher Education Research Institute, Graduate School of Education & Information Studies, University of California, Los Angeles, 2011. Available at http://heri.ucla.edu/PDFs/pubs/TFS/Norms/Monographs/TheAmericanFreshman2011.pdf.

61. Colleen Flaherty, "Pricing Out the Humanities," *Inside Higher Ed*, November 26, 2012. http://www.insidehighered.com/news/2012/11/26/u-florida-history-professors-fight-differential-tuition.

62. Riesman 1950.

63. Sherry Turkle, "The Documented Life," *New York Times*, December 15, 2013. Available at http://www.nytimes.com/2013/12/16/opinion/the-documented-life.html?_r=0.

CHAPTER 8

The epigraph is from an interview with Lynn Neary, "How Multitasking Affects Human Learning," National Public Radio, March 3, 2007. Available at http://www.npr.org/templates/story/story.php?storyId=7700581.

1. Corrie Goldman, "This Is Your Brain on Jane Austen, and Stanford Researchers Are Taking Notes," *Stanford University News*, September 7, 2012. Available at http://news.stanford.edu/news/2012/september/austen-reading-fmri-090712.html.

2. Good places to start are Wolf 2007, Dehaene 2009, and Klingberg 2009.

3. Nicholas Carr, "Is Google Making Us Stupid?," *Atlantic*, July-August 2008. Available at http://www.theatlantic.com/magazine/archive/2008/07/is-google-making-us-stupid/306868; Carr 2010. More recently, see Wegner and Ward 2013.

4. For a highly readable discussion of brain plasticity, see Doidge 2007.

5. Maguire et al. 2000.

6. Elbert et al. 1995.

7. For discussion of brain imaging techniques used in studying reading, see Breznitz et al. 2012.

8. Stefan Lovgren, "Chimps, Humans 96 Percent the Same, Gene Study Finds," *National Geographic News*, August 31, 2005. Available at http://news.nationalgeographic.com/news/2005/08/0831_050831_chimp_genes.html.

9. Speer et al. 2009.

10. For an overview of the connection, see Koning 2012.

11. Juha Kere, "Dyslexic Candidate Genes and Cognitive Ability," paper presented at the Child and Adolescent Mental Health conference, Royal Swedish Academy of Sciences, Stockholm, Sweden, October 22–23, 2013.

12. Elfenbein 2006.

13. See, for instance, Zunshine 2010.

14. One example appears in *OnFiction*, "An Online Magazine on the Psychology of Fiction," http://www.onfiction.ca.

15. Annie Murphy Paul, "Your Brain on Fiction," *New York Times*, March 17, 2012. Available at http://www.nytimes.com/2012/03/18/opinion/sunday/the-neuroscience-of-your-brain-on-fiction.html. For the original studies, see González et al. 2006; Lacey, Stilla, and Sathian 2012.

16. Mar 2011; Mar et al. 2006.

17. Kidd and Castano 2013.

18. van den Broek et al. 2001.

19. Jamais Cascio, "Get Smarter," *Atlantic*, July 1, 2009. Available at http://www.theatlantic.com/magazine/archive/2009/07/get-smarter/307548; Steven Pinker, "Mind over Mass Media," *New York Times*, June 10. 2010. Available at http://www.nytimes.com/2010/06/11/opinion/11Pinker.html?_r=0; Nicholas Carr, "Steven Pinker and the Internet," Rough Type, June 12, 2010. Available at http://www.roughtype.com/?p=1392.

20. Johnson 2005; Steven Johnson, "Yes, People Still Read, but Now It's Social," *New York Times*, June 19, 2010. Available at http://www.nytimes.com/2010/06/20/business/20unbox.html.

21. Smith, Darling, and Seales 2011.

22. Susan Greenfield, "Does the Mind Have a Future?," Oxford Internet Institute webcast, April 7, 2011. Available at http://webcast.oii.ox.ac.uk/?view=Webcast&ID=20110407_350.

23. Green and Bavelier 2003, 2006.

24. Gee 2005.

25. Greenfield 2009.

26. Turkle 2011.

27. Przybylski and Weinstein 2013; Misra et al. 2014.

28. Powers 2011.

29. Cory Doctorow, "Writing in the Age of Distraction," *Locus Magazine*, January 7, 2009. Available at http://www.locusmag.com/Features/2009/01/cory-doctorow-writing-in-age-of.html.

30. Freedom app website, http://macfreedom.com.

31. Pico Iyer, "The Joy of Quiet," *New York Times*, December 29. 2011. Available at http://www.nytimes.com/2012/01/01/opinion/sunday/the-joy-of-quiet.html?pagewanted=all&_r=0.

32. Matt Richtel, "Digital Devices Deprive Brain of Needed Downtime," *New York Times*, August 24, 2010. Available at http://www.nytimes.com/2010/08/25/technology/25brain.html?pagewanted=all.

33. Dyson and Haselgrove 2000. Also see Piolat, Roussey, and Thunin 1997.

34. Jakob Nielsen, "How Users Read on the Web," October 1, 1997. Available at http://www.nngroup.com/articles/how-users-read-on-the-web; University College London, "Information Behaviour of the Researcher of the Future," CIBER Briefing Paper, January 11, 2008. Available at http://www.jisc.ac.uk/media/documents/programmes/reppres/ggworkpackagei.pdf.

35. Nicholas et al. 2008.

36. Liu 2005.

37. Joy Hawley, "In Germany Digital Publishing Is No Longer Satan, but Savior," Publishing Perspectives, November 12, 2013. Available at http://publishingperspectives.com/2013/11/in-germany-digital-publishing-is-no-longer-satan-but-savior.

38. Emily Anne Epstein, "The Digital Generation: How Twenty-Somethings Scan 27 Different Media Sources an Hour—Ten Times More than Older People," *Mail Online*, April 9,

2012. Available at http://www.dailymail.co.uk/news/article-2127403/People-20s-switch-media-venues-27-times-nonworking-hour--10-times-older-counterparts.html.

39. "'Five-Minute-Memory' Costs Brits £1.6 Billion," Lloyds TSB Insurance, November 27, 2008. Available at http://www.insurance.lloydstsb.com/personal/general/mediacentre/homehazards_pr.asp.

40. "The Future of 'Short Attention Span Theater,'" *Morning Edition*, National Public Radio, October 26, 2012. Available at http://www.npr.org/2012/10/26/163649283/the-future-of-short-attention-span-theater.

41. Emily Fredrix, "TV Commercials Shrink to Match Attention Spans," *USA Today*, October 30, 2010. Available at http://usatoday30.usatoday.com/money/advertising/2010-10-30-shorter-v-commercials_N.htm.

42. Wolf and Barzillai 2009, 33.

43. Hayles 2007, 187.

44. Sosnoski 1999, 167.

45. Hayles 2012, 12.

46. Eric Schmidt at the World Economic Forum in Davos, Switzerland, January 29, 2010. Cited in Nicholas Carr, "Second Thoughts on Reading and Technology by Google's Eric Schmidt," *Encyclopedia Britannica* blog, February 23, 2010. Available at http://www.britannica.com/blogs/2010/02/second-thoughts-on-reading-and-technology-by-googles-eric-schmidt.

47. Maryanne Wolf, "Will the Speed of Online Reading Deplete Our Analytic Thought?," *Guardian*, August 14, 2011. Available at http://www.theguardian.com/commentisfree/2011/aug/14/marshall-mcluhan-analytic-thought.

48. Maryanne Wolf, "Our 'Deep Reading' Brain: Its Digital Evolution Poses Questions," Nieman Reports: Nieman Foundation for Journalism at Harvard, summer 2010. Available at http://www.nieman.harvard.edu/reports/article/102396/Our-Deep-Reading-Brain-Its-Digital-Evolution--Poses-Questions.aspx.

49. Hayles 2012. 69.

50. Hayles 2007. 194.

51. Jacobs 2011, 107–108, 115.

52. One of the earliest studies was Dillon 1992.

53. Jakob Nielsen, "F-Shaped Pattern for Reading Web Content," April 17, 2006. Available at http://www.nngroup.com/articles/f-shaped-pattern-reading-web-content.

54. Siegenthaler et al. 2011; Zambarbieri and Carniglia 2012; Kretzschmar et al. 2013.

55. Koslowe et al. 2011.

56. Chu et al. 2011.

57. Green et al. 2010; Kretzschmar et al. 2013; Holzinger et al. 2011; Ackerman and Goldsmith 2011.

58. Ackerman and Goldsmith 2011.

59. Mangen, Walgermo, and Brønnick 2013.

60. Noyes and Garland 2003, 421.

61. Cynthia Chiong, Jinny Ree, Lori Takeuchi, and Ingrid Erickson, "Comparing Parent-Child Co-Reading on Print, Basic, and Enhanced e-Book Platforms," Jane Ganz Cooney Center, Spring 2012. Available at http://www.joanganzcooneycenter.org/wp-content/uploads/2012/07/jgcc_ebooks_quickreport.pdf. For similar findings with children in kindergarten through sixth grade, see Schugar, Smith, and Schugar 2013.

62. Parish-Morris et al. 2013.

63. "'Babysitter' Gadgets Up Speech Problem in Kids," *Times of India*, December 29, 2012; Nick Bilton, "The Child, the Tablet and the Developing Mind," *New York Times*, March 31, 2013. Available at http://bits.blogs.nytimes.com/2013/03/31/disruptions-what-does-a-tablet-do-to-the-childs-mind/?_r=0.

64. N. Baron 2013a; Kristen McLean and James Howitt, "Understanding the Children's Book Consumer in the Digital Age," Bowker Market Research, 2013 Available at http://www.slideshare.net/BKGKristen/understanding-the-childrens-book-consumer-in-the-digital-age-toc-bologna-2013; Scholastic, *Kids and Family Reading Report*, prepared by the Harrison Group, 4th ed., 2013. Harrison Group. Available at http://mediaroom.scholastic.com/files/kfrr2013-noappendix.pdf; Book Industry Study Group, *Student Attitudes Toward Content in Higher Education*, vol. 3, no. 1, February 2013; Internet2, "Internet2 eTextbook Spring 2012 Pilot: Final Project Report," August 1, 2012. Available at http://www.internet2.edu/media/medialibrary/2013/10/07/eText-Spring-2012-Pilot-Report.pdf; Moyer 2011; Liu 2006; Annand 2008; Fortunati and Vincent 2014.

65. Holzinger et al. 2011, 569; Kretzschmar et al. 2013, 7.

66. DeStefano and LeFevre 2007, 1636.

67. Landow 1997, 273.

68. Miall and Dobson 2001.

69. Phillips 2010.

70. Denis Diderot and Jean D'Alembert, eds., *Encyclopédie, ou dictionnaire raisonné des sciences, des arts et des métiers*, vol. 4 (1754), quoted in Phillips 2010, 5.

71. Quoted in Phillips 2010, 21.

72. Baird et al. 2012.

73. Hanif Kureishi, "The Art of Distraction," *New York Times*, February 18, 2012. Available at http://www.nytimes.com/2012/02/19/opinion/sunday/the-art-of-distraction.html?pagewanted=all&_r=0.

74. Levine, Waite, and Bowman 2007.

75. Jacobs 2011, 79.

76. For example, Loukopoulos, Dismukes, and Barshi 2009.

77. Reported in Ashley Halsey III, "28 Percent of Accidents Involve Talking, Texting on Cellphones," *Washington Post*, January 13, 2010. Available at http://articles.washingtonpost.com/2010-01-13/news/36800274_1_focusdriven-cellphone-hands-free-devices.

78. "Official U.S. Government Website for Distracted Driving," NHTSA and US Department of Transportation, http://www.distraction.gov.

79. Zhang, Smith, and Witt 2006.

80. Mary Madden and Amanda Lenhart, "Teens and Distracted Driving," Pew Internet & American Life Project, November 16, 2009. Available at http://pewinternet.org/Reports/2009/Teens-and-Distracted-Driving.aspx.

81. Toyota/University of Michigan Transportation Research Institute, "Driver Distraction Study from the University of Michigan Transportation Research Institute and Toyota Shows Significant Correlation Between Parent and Teen Distractions," press release, November 27, 2012. Available at http://pressroom.lexus.com/releases/toyota+teen+driver+study+text+distracted+nov27.htm.

82. Bayer and Campbell 2012.

83. Mary Madden and Lee Rainie, "Adults and Cell Phone Distractions," Pew Internet & American Life Project, June 18, 2010. Available at http://pewinternet.org/Reports/2010/Cell-Phone-Distractions.aspx.

84. For a history of early mobile telephony, see Agar 2003.

85. Alm and Nilsson 1995.

86. Alm and Nilsson 1995, 713.

87. Strayer, Drews, and Johnston 2003.

88. Strayer, Drews, and Crouch 2006.

89. Just, Keller, and Cynkar 2008.

90. N. Baron 2008, 41.

91. Russell Poldrack, "Multitasking: The Brain Seeks Novelty," *Huffington Post*, October 28, 2009. Available at http://www.huffingtonpost.com/russell-poldrack/multitasking-the-brain-se_b_334674.html.

92. See, for example, Sigman and Dehaene 2006.

93. Just et al. 2001.

94. Foerde, Knowlton, and Poldrack 2006.

95. Bergen, Grimes, and Potter 2005.

96. Bavelier et al. 2012.

97. Watson and Strayer 2010.

98. Ophir, Nass, and Wagner 2009. Also see Sanbonmatsu et al. 2013.

99. Chabris and Simons 2009.

100. Ulla G. Foehr, *Media Multitasking Among American Youth*, Henry J. Kaiser Family Foundation, December 2006. Available at http://kff.org/other/media-multitasking-among-american-youth-prevalence-predictors.

101. Bowman et al. 2010.

102. Mike Clendenin, "Internet Addiction Plaguing Chinese Youth," *Information Week*, June 22, 2010. Available at http://www.informationweek.com/security/government/internet-addiction-plaguing-chinese-yout/225700969.

103. Yuan et al. 2011.

104. Carolyn Sun, "Online Cravings," *Newsweek*, October 17, 2011. Available at http://mag.newsweek.com/2011/10/16/south-korea-s-video-game-addiction.html.

105. Baron and Campbell 2012.

106. Kang 2012.

107. Husna Haq, "In South Korea, All Textbooks Will Be e-Books by 2015," *Christian Science Monitor*, July 6, 2011. Available at http://www.csmonitor.com/Books/chapter-and-verse/2011/0706/In-South-Korea-all-textbooks-will-be-e-books-by-2015.

108. Martin Fackler, "In Korea, a Boot Camp Cure for Web Obsession," *New York Times*, November 18, 2007. Available at http://www.nytimes.com/2007/11/18/technology/18rehab.html?pagewanted=all.

109. "More Young Kids than Adults Addicted to Internet," *Chosun Ilbo*, March 7, 2012. Available at http://english.chosun.com/site/data/html_dir/2012/03/07/2012030700477.html.

110. "South Korean MPs Consider Measures to Tackle Online Gaming Addiction," *Guardian*, December 11, 2013. Available at http://www.theguardian.com/world/2013/dec/11/south-korea-online-gaming-addiction/print.

111. Chico Harlan, "In South Korean Classrooms, Digital Textbook Revolution Meets Some Resistance," *Washington Post*, March 24, 2012. Available at http://articles.washingtonpost.com/2012-03-24/world/35450448_1_textbooks-digital-program-digital-education.

112. Youkyung Lee, "South Korea: 160,000 Kids Between Age 5 and 9 Are Internet-Addicted," *Huffington Post*, November 28, 2012. Available at http://www.huffingtonpost.com/2012/11/28/south-korea-internet-addicted_n_2202371.html?view=print&comm_ref=false.

113. Heather Waldron, "Internet Addiction a Real Problem for U.S. Kids," *AAP News* 31, no. 5 (2010). Available at http://aapnews.aappublications.org/content/31/5/26.5.full.

114. "Technology Addiction," Capio Nightingale Hospital, http://www.nightingalehospital.co.uk/condition/technology-addiction.

115. Charles Recknagel, "Computer Exposure Leads to Fears of 'Digital Dementia,'" Radio Free Europe/Radio Liberty, August 12, 2013. Available at http://www.rferl.org/content/computer-exposure-digital-dementia/25073023.html; Claudia Ehrenstein, "Does the Internet Make You Dumb? Top German Neuroscientist Says Yes—and Forever," Worldcrunch, September 12, 2012. Available at http://www.worldcrunch.com/tech-science/does-the-internet-make-you-dumb-top-german-neuroscientist-says-yes-and-forever/digital-dementia-manfred-spitzer-neuropsychiatry/c4s9550/#.Ur9KbKVTTnY.

116. Baron and Campbell 2012.

CHAPTER 9

The epigraph is from an interview with Tim Harris, "Tim Waterstone: 'If Reading Is Going [to] Be All Digital in 50 Years, So Be It,'" *Guardian*, April 9, 2013. Available at http://www.guardian.co.uk/books/2013/apr/09/tim-waterstone-reading-entirely-digital.

1. Chico Harlan, "In Japan, Fax Machines Remain Important Because of Language and Culture," *Washington Post*, June 7, 2012. Available at http://www.washingtonpost.com/world/asia_pacific/in-japan-fax-machines-find-a-final-place-to-thrive/2012/06/07/gJQAshFPMV_story_1.html.

2. "EPUB3 Key to Growing Illustrated Ebooks Internationally?" Digital Book World, May 29, 2014. Available at http://www.digitalbookworld.com/2014/epub3-key-to-growing-illustrated-ebooks-internationally.

3. Harlan, "In Japan, Fax Machines Remain Important" (see note 1). Also see Martin Fackler, "In High-Tech Japan, the Fax Machines Roll On," *New York Times*, February 13, 2013. Available at http://www.nytimes.com/2013/02/14/world/asia/in-japan-the-fax-machine-is-anything-but-a-relic.html?pagewanted=2.

4. Carrière and Eco 2009, 44–45.

5. Carrière and Eco 2009, 276.

6. For the story behind the commercial, see "The Making of 'I'd Like to Buy the World a Coke'" at http://www.coca-colacompany.com/stories/coke-lore-hilltop-story.

7. See a short history of Twining tea at http://twinings.co.uk/our-stores/twinings,-216,-strand,-london.

8. Guy Adams, "The Man Who Founded Costa Coffee," *Mail Online,* May 2, 2013. Available at http://www.dailymail.co.uk/news/article-2318601/The-man-founded-Costa-Coffee--sold-fraction-value--insists-hes-bitter-So--WHY-does-Mr-Costa-refuse-drink-coffee.html.

9. The comment was part of an address to the American Society of Newspaper Editors on January 17, 1925, in Washington, DC.

10. On the history of the installment plan, see Sharon Murphy, "The Advertising of Installment Plans," 2012, *Essays in History*. Available at http://www.essaysinhistory.com/articles/2012/155.

11. Mark Macesich, "Auto Loans Their Highest in Five Years, Equifax Reports," Santander Consumer USA, February 14, 2014. Available at https://www.santanderconsumerusa.com/blog/auto-loans-highest-five-years-equifax-reports.

12. Given its iffy future, I am omitting Barnes & Noble's Nook from discussion. While Apple and Google are also obviously major players, I will focus on Amazon and Kobo as illustrative of the market.

13. Nate Hoffelder, "Updated: Where Amazon Will Expand the Kindle Store Next," Digital Reader, September 18, 2013. Available at http://www.the-digital-reader.com/2013/09/18/kindle-store-expands-langauge-support-reveals-clues-possible-kindle-store-expansion; "Supported Languages," Kindle Direct Publishing information, Amazon.com, https://kdp.amazon.com/help?topicId=A9FDO0A3V0119.

14. Kelly Gallagher, "The Global eBook Monitor: What About the Global eBook Experience?," Bowker Market Research, June 12, 2012. Available at http://www.slideshare.net/bisg/kelly-gallagher-global-ebook-monitor.

15. Bowker Market Research, *The Global eBook Monitor*, vol. 2 (2012).

16. Rüdiger Wischenbart, *The Global eBook Market: Current Conditions & Future Projections*, October 2013, 17, 22, 27, 32, 39, 43. Available at http://www.wischenbart.com/upload/Global-Ebook-Report2013_final03.pdf.

17. Adam Critchley, "In Taiwan Reading Is Cool, but Lukewarm on EBooks," Publishing Perspectives, December 4, 2013. Available at http://publishingperspectives.com/2013/12/in-taiwan-reading-is-cool-but-lukewarm-on-ebooks/?et_mid=651149&rid=241005576.

18. "Czech Booksellers to Sell Half Million e-Books This Year," *Prague Daily Monitor*, October 4, 2013. Available at http://praguemonitor.com/2013/10/04/czech-booksellers-sell-half-million-e-books-year.

19. Lee Rainie and Maeve Duggan, "E-Book Reading Jumps; Print Book Reading Declines," Pew Internet & American Life Project, December 27, 2012. Available at http://libraries.pewinternet.org/2012/12/27/e-book-reading-jumps-print-book-reading-declines.

20. Angelique Chrisafis, "Why France Is Shunning the eBook," *Guardian*, June 24, 2012. Available at http://www.theguardian.com/books/shortcuts/2012/jun/24/why-is-france-shunning-ebooks.

21. For an analysis of Amazon's business model and its effects on the publishing industry, see George Parker, "Cheap Words," *New Yorker*, February 17, 2014. Available at http://www.newyorker.com/reporting/2014/02/17/140217fa_fact_packer?currentPage=all.

22. Luca Palladino, "Could Book Prices Become Fixed in Québec?," *Publishers Weekly*, August 21, 2013. Available at http://www.publishersweekly.com/pw/by-topic/international/international-book-news/article/58784-quebec-book-industry-considers-price-fixing.html; Luca Palladino, "Fixed Pricing Law Project Gets the Green Light in Québec," *Publishers Weekly*, December 4, 2013. Available at http://www.publishersweekly.com/pw/by-topic/industry-news/publisher-news/article/60247-fixed-pricing-law-project-gets-the-green-light-in-qu-bec.html.

23. Liz Bury, "James Patterson Donates $1m to Independent US Bookshops," *Guardian*, September 17, 2013. Available at http://www.theguardian.com/books/2013/sep/17/james-patterson-one-million-dollars-bookshops.

24. Daniel D'Addario, "James Patterson Speaks Out About His Aggressive 'Book Industry Bailout' Ads," *Salon*, April 24, 2013. Available at http://www.salon.com/2013/04/24/james_patterson_speaks_out_about_his_aggressive_book_industry_bailout_ads.

25. Jeremy Greenfield, "Zola Aims to Replace Google Books, Then Take on Amazon," Digital Book World, July 19, 2012. Available at http://www.digitalbookworld.com/2012/zola-aims-to-replace-google-books-then-take-on-amazon.

26. Robert Andrews, "France Lets Book Publishers Fix Minimum e-Book Prices," Gigaom, May 19, 2011. Available at http://gigaom.com/2011/05/19/419-france-lets-book-publishers-fix-minimum-e-book-prices.

27. Siobhan O'Leary, "E-Book Market in Germany Profitable for 'A Small Minority,'" Publishing Perspectives, July 11, 2012. Available at http://publishingperspectives.com/2012/07/e-book-market-in-germany-profitable-for-a-small-minority.

28. For official VAT rates in the EU as of July 1, 2013, see http://ec.europa.eu/taxation_customs/resources/documents/taxation/vat/how_vat_works/rates/vat_rates_en.pdf.

29. "VAT on Electronic Services," 2013, European Commission Taxation and Customs Union. Available at http://ec.europa.eu/taxation_customs/taxation/vat/how_vat_works/e-services.

30. These numbers were accurate at the end of 2013, but as I said, they keep shifting.

31. Johanna Westlund, "VAT Muddle Threatens Sweden's Publishers," The Bookseller, June 24, 2014. Available at http://www.thebookseller.com/news/vat-muddle-threatens-swedens-publishers.html.

32. "For e-Book Sellers, Tax Hike Distorts Field," Japan Times, December 3, 2013. Available at http://www.japantimes.co.jp/news/2013/12/03/business/for-e-book-sellers-tax-hike-distorts-field/#.UwTC-HlelKM.

33. Neelie Kroes, "Making Europe the Home of eBooks," 2013, speech delivered at the Paris Book Fair, March 25. Available at http://europa.eu/rapid/press-release_SPEECH-13-262_en.htm.

34. Aoife White, "Amazon's European Base Luxembourg Sued by EU on E-Books Tax," Bloomberg.com, February 21, 2013. Available at http://www.bloomberg.com/news/2013-02-21/amazon-s-european-base-luxembourg-sued-by-eu-on-low-e-books-tax.html.

35. "VAT on Electronic Services" (see note 29).

36. Ian Griffiths and Dan Milmo, "Amazon Makes UK Publishers Pay 20% VAT on eBook Sales," Guardian, October 21, 2012. Available at http://www.guardian.co.uk/technology/2012/oct/21/amazon-forces-publishers-pay-vat-ebook.

37. "Amazon Tax Petition Leads to Commons Debate," BBC News, June 27, 2013. Available at http://www.bbc.co.uk/news/uk-england-coventry-warwickshire-23077059.

38. Quoted in Alison Flood,, "Amazon Tax Petition Hits 100,000 Signatures," Guardian, March 22, 2013. Available at http://www.theguardian.com/books/2013/mar/22/amazon-tax-petition-signatures.

39. Quoted in Rajeev Syal, "Amazon, Google and Starbucks Accused of Diverting UK Profits," Guardian, November 12, 2012. Available at http://www.theguardian.com/business/2012/nov/12/amazon-google-starbucks-diverting-uk-profits.

40. Henry Samuel, "Amazon Is 'Destroyer of Bookshops,' Says French Culture Minister," Telegraph, June 4, 2013. Available at http://www.telegraph.co.uk/technology/amazon/10098626/Amazon-is-destroyer-of-bookshops-says-French-culture-minister.html.

41. Quoted in Rupert Neate and Angelique Chrisafis, "British Booksellers Seek Amazon Curb," Guardian, June 4, 2013. Available at http://www.theguardian.com/books/2013/jun/04/british-booksellers-seek-amazon-curb.

42. "French Parliament Passes 'Anti-Amazon Law' for Online Book Sales," French Culture Books, June 26, 2014. Available at http://frenchculture.org/books/news/french-parliament-passes-anti-amazon-law-online-book-sales; "Report: Amazon Offers Ultra-Cheap Shipping in

France, Circumventing No Free Shipping Law," *Digital Book World*, July 11, 2014. Available at http://www.digitalbookworld.com/2014/report-amazon-offers-ultra-cheap-shipping-in-france-circumventing-no-free-shipping-law.

43. Quoted in Elaine Sciolino, "The French Still Flock to Bookstores," *New York Times*, June 20, 2012. Available at http://www.nytimes.com/2012/06/21/books/french-bookstores-are-still-prospering.html?_r=0.

44. "Global Book Market Snapshots: France and Germany," *Publishing Perspectives*, June 10, 2014. Available at http://publishingperspectives.com/2014/06/global-book-market-snapshots-france-and-germany.

45. Michael Naumann, "How Germany Keeps Amazon at Bay and Literary Culture Alive," *The Nation*, May 29, 2012. Available at http://www.thenation.com/article/168124/how-germany-keeps-amazon-bay-and-literary-culture-alive.

46. Naumann, "How Germany Keeps Amazon at Bay" (see note 45).

47. Dana Goodyear, "I ♥ NOVELS," *New Yorker*, December 22, 2008. Available at http://www.newyorker.com/reporting/2008/12/22/081222fa_fact_goodyear.

48. My thanks to Miyako Inoue and Noriko Ishihara for discussing with me Japanese reading practices.

49. Liu and Huang 2008.

50. Liu and Huang 2008, 622.

51. For examples of the keep-it-or-kill-it debate in the United States, see comments by Jimmy Bryant ("A Cultural Tradition Worth Preserving"), Kate Gladstone ("Handwriting Matters; Cursive Doesn't"), Suzanne Baruch Asherson ("Cursive Benefits Go Beyond Writing"), and Morgan Polikoff ("Let It Die. It's Already Dying"), *New York Times*, "Room for Debate: Is Cursive Dead?," April 30 and May 1, 2013. Available at http://www.nytimes.com/roomfordebate/2013/04/30/should-schools-require-children-to-learn-cursive.

52. Thornton 1996.

53. Unger 1996.

54. UNESCO, "Endangered Languages." Available at http://www.unesco.org/new/en/culture/themes/endangered-languages.

55. The *Book of Kells* is available in Trinity College Dublin's digital collection at http://digitalcollections.tcd.ie/home/index.php?DRIS_ID=MS58_003v.

56. The Gutenberg Bible is available in the British Museum's digital collection at http://www.bl.uk/treasures/gutenberg/homepage.html.

57. Anna Zacharias, "Ebooks Crucial in Preserving UAE Heritage, Experts Say," *The National* (Abu Dhabi), November 26, 2012. Available at http://www.thenational.ae/news/uae-news/heritage/ebooks-crucial-in-preserving-uae-heritage-experts-say.

58. Joanna Penn, "Are African Writers and Readers Ready for the eBook Revolution?," The Creative Penn website, March 23, 2013. Available at http://www.thecreativepenn.com/2013/03/23/african-ebook-revolution.

59. Penn, "Are African Writers and Readers Ready" (see note 58).

60. "S Africans Slow to Adopt e-Books," *TechCentral*, January 21, 2014. Available at http://www.techcentral.co.za/s-africans-slow-to-adopt-e-books/45965.

61. Arthur Attwell, "Why I Publish eBooks on Paper for South Africans," *Publishing Perspectives*, May 21, 2013. Available at http://publishingperspectives.com/2013/05/why-i-publish-ebooks-on-paper-for-south-africans.

62. Donner and Escobari 2010.

63. "Statistics," International Telecommunications Union website, http://www.itu.int/en/ITU-D/Statistics/Pages/stat/default.aspx.

64. Donna Bryson, "A 'Novel' Idea for Spreading Literature in Africa: The Cellphone," *Christian Science Monitor*, May 9, 2013. Available at http://www.csmonitor.com/World/Africa/2013/0509/A-novel-idea-for-spreading-literature-in-Africa-The-cellphone.

65. "Mobile Phones as E-Readers," Worldreader, http://www.worldreader.org/what-we-do/worldreader-mobile.

66. On this general point, see Mike Shatzkin, "Things to Think About as the Digital Book Revolution Gains Global Steam," The Shatzkin Files blog, August 27, 2012. Available at http://www.idealog.com/blog/things-to-think-about-as-the-digital-book-revolution-gains-global-steam.

67. In reality, the last holdout was a somewhat younger (but equally feisty) woman named Mattie Randolph, though Mattie's refusal to leave inspired the story depicted in the movie. For archival records of the actual eviction, see Rebecca Onion, "The Tennessee Valley Authority vs. the Family That Just Wouldn't Leave," *Slate*, September 5, 2013. Available at http://www.slate.com/blogs/the_vault/2013/09/05/tennessee_valley_authority_the_agency_s_fight_against_one_family_that_wouldn.html.

68. Ian Johnson, "Picking Death over Eviction," *New York Times*, September 8, 2013. Available at http://www.nytimes.com/2013/09/09/world/asia/as-chinese-farmers-fight-for-homes-suicide-is-ultimate-protest.html?pagewanted=all&_r=0.

69. Turkle 2011.

70. Steiner-Adair 2013.

71. *Stanford Alumni Magazine*, July-August 2013, 74.

CHAPTER 10

The first epigraph is from Hayles 2012, 2. The second is from David Gelernter, "The Book Made Better," in *New York Times*, "Does the Brain Like E-Books?," October 14, 2009. Available at http://roomfordebate.blogs.nytimes.com/2009/10/14/does-the-brain-like-e-books/?_r=0.

1. Jeremy Greenfield, "Study: Ebook Growth Stagnating in 2013," Digital Book World, October 30, 2013. Available at http://www.digitalbookworld.com/2013/study-ebook-growth-stagnating-in-2013.

2. "Trade Ebook Revenue Growth Continues to Slow Through First Half of 2013," Digital Book World, September 19, 2013. Available at http://www.digitalbookworld.com/2013/trade-ebook-revenue-growth-continues-to-slow-through-first-half-of-2013.

3. Jeremy Greenfield, "Ebook Growth Slows to Single Digits in U.S. in 2013," Digital Book World, April 1, 2014. Available at http://www.digitalbookworld.com/2014/ebook-growth-slows-to-single-digits-in-u-s-in-2013.

4. "Survey: Readers Who Read Digitally Read 60% More than Other Readers," Digital Book World, October 7, 2013. Available at http://www.digitalbookworld.com/2013/survey-readers-who-read-digitally-read-60-more-than-other-readers.

5. Lee Rainie and Aaron Smith, "Tablet and E-Reader Ownership Update," Pew Internet & American Life Project Report, October 18, 2013. Available at http://pewinternet.org/Reports/2013/

Tablets-and-ereaders/Findings.aspx; Kathryn Zickuhr and Lee Rainie, "E-Reading Rises as Device Ownership Jumps," Pew Internet and American Life Project, January 16, 2014. Available at http://www.pewinternet.org/2014/01/16/e-reading-rises-as-device-ownership-jumps.

6. Spoken at a meeting held at Xerox PARC, Palo Alto, CA.

7. Bob Minzesheimer, "E-Books Are Changing Reading Habits," *USA Today*, October 7, 2013. Available at http://www.usatoday.com/story/life/books/2013/10/06/e-books-reading/2877471.

8. Darnton 1991, 148.

9. "Worldreader Receives Grant to Pilot E-Reading Program in Africa's Libraries," PRWeb, October 17, 2013. Available at http://www.prweb.com/releases/2013/10/prweb11237526.htm.

10. Book Industry Study Group, *Student Attitudes Toward Content in Higher Education*, vol. 4, no. 1 (New York: BISB, 2013).

11. Jeremy Greenfield, "Students, Professors Still Not Yet Ready for Digital Textbooks," Digital Book World, June 11, 2013. Available at http://www.digitalbookworld.com/2013/students-professors-still-not-yet-ready-for-digital-textbooks.

12. David L. Ulin, "Are Tablets Cutting into E-Book Sales?," *Los Angeles Times*, August 12, 2013. Available at http://articles.latimes.com/2013/aug/12/entertainment/la-et-jc-are-tablets-cutting-into-ebook-sales-20130812.

13. Steven Johnson, "How the E-Book Will Change the Way We Read and Write," *Wall Street Journal*, April 20, 2009. Available at http://online.wsj.com/news/articles/SB123980920727621353.

14. My thanks to Andraž Petrovčič and Sakari Taipale for their insights.

15. Sora Park, "The Process of Adapting to Mobile Tablet Devices by Switching Between Distractive and Productive Multitasking," paper presented at IR 14.0, International Conference of the Association of Internet Researchers, Denver, CO, October 24–26, 2013.

16. McCoy 2013.

17. Cecilia Kang, "Firms Tell Employees: Avoid After-Hours E-Mail," *Washington Post*, September 21, 2012. Available at http://www.washingtonpost.com/business/economy/after-hours-e-mail-companies-are-telling-employees-to-avoid-it/2012/09/21/a95f53b2-fdba-11e1-a31e-804fccb658f9_story.html.

18. *Aurora Leigh,* Book 1, lines 705–709, Cited in Brewer 1998, 1.

19. Lahiri 2013, 34.

20. IT Strategies and the University of Colorado, "The Evolution of the Book Industry: Implications for U.S. Book Manufacturers and Printers," commissioned by Ricoh Americas Corporation, 2013. Available at http://www.infoprint.com/internet/comnelit.nsf/Files/ITStrategies_FINAL/$File/ITStrategies_FINAL.pdf.

21. Liz Bury, "Young Adult Readers 'Prefer Printed to eBooks,'" *Guardian*, November 25, 2013. Available at http://www.theguardian.com/books/2013/nov/25/young-adult-readers-prefer-printed-ebooks.

22. Jabr 2013b.

23. Akshita Nanda, "Re-Read the e-Books Chapter," *Straits Times*, September 30, 2013. Available at http://www.straitstimes.com/the-big-story/case-you-missed-it/story/re-read-the-e-books-chapter-20130930.

24. Personal communication from Sakari Taipale, November 2013.

25. US Constitution, Article 1, Section 8. For an overview of relevant copyright issues, see Woodmansee and Jaszi 1994.

26. Claire Cain Miller and Julie Bosman, "Siding with Google, Judge Says Book Search Does Not Infringe Copyright," *New York Times*, November 14, 2013. Available at http://www.nytimes.com/2013/11/15/business/media/judge-sides-with-google-on-book-scanning-suit.html?_r=0.

27. For the record, some authors negotiate with publishers to have their entire works available on the web as open access.

28. Michelle Starr, "Sony Launching 13.3-Inch E Ink PDF Reader in Japan," CNET, November 8, 2013. Available at http://www.cnet.com/news/sony-launching-13-3-inch-e-ink-pdf-reader-in-japan.

29. "FAA to Allow Airlines to Expand Use of Personal Electronics," press release, October 31, 2013, http://www.faa.gov/news/press_releases/news_story.cfm?newsId=15254.

30. Tom Lombardo, "E-Book Reader: Batteries Not Required," Engineering.com, December 1, 2013. Available at http://www.engineering.com/ElectronicsDesign/ElectronicsDesignArticles/ArticleID/6740/E-book-Reader-Batteries-Not-Required.aspx.

31. "Frequently Asked Questions Regarding e-Books and U.S. Libraries," American Library Association, 2013. Available at http://www.ala.org/transforminglibraries/frequently-asked-questions-e-books-us-libraries.

32. "Durbin, Franken Introduce Legislation to Help Make College Textbooks More Affordable," website for Dick Durbin, US senator for Illinois, November 14, 2013. Available at http://www.durbin.senate.gov/public/index.cfm/pressreleases?ID=26d6b011-b4b3-4fa1-9fea-8b2706026943.

33. Affordable College Textbook Act, S.1704, 113th Congress, http://thomas.loc.gov/cgi-bin/query/z?c113:S.1704.

34. European Commission, "Digital Agenda for Europe: A Europe 2020 Initiative," http://ec.europa.eu/digital-agenda, and its "Education" section, http://ec.europa.eu/digital-agenda/en/education.

35. "Can Textbook Nationalization Curb 'Profiteering Publishers'?," Publishing Perspectives, February 4, 2014. Available at http://publishingperspectives.com/2014/02/can-textbook-nationalization-curb-profiteering-publishers/?et_mid=658936&rid=241005576.

36. Rowland Manthorpe, "This Video Game Could Revolutionize Publishing—and Reading," *Atlantic*, November 26, 2013. Available at http://www.theatlantic.com/entertainment/archive/2013/11/this-video-game-could-revolutionize-publishing-and-reading/281765.

37. Claire Armitstead, "Next-Generation eBooks Introduced at London Book Fair," *Guardian*, April 17, 2013. Available at http://www.theguardian.com/books/2013/apr/17/next-generation-ebooks-london-book-fair.

38. Ajit Jha, "Augmented Reality Books? New 'Wearable Book' Feeds You Its Characters' Emotions as You Read," *International Science Times*, January 28, 2014. Available at http://www.isciencetimes.com/articles/6749/20140128/augmented-reality-wearable-book-mit-sensory-fiction.htm.

39. Ann Patchett, "And the Winner Isn't…," *New York Times*, April 17, 2012. Available at http://www.nytimes.com/2012/04/18/opinion/and-the-winner-of-the-pulitzer-isnt.html?_r=0.

40. "Kobo Launches Fleet of New Devices, Kids Ebook Store, Partnership with Pocket," Digital Book World, August 27, 2013. Available at http://www.google.com/url?sa=t&rct=j&q=&esrc=s&source=web&cd=1&cad=rja&ved=0CDoQFjAA&url=http%3A%2F%2Fwww.digitalbookworld.com%2F2013%2Fkobo-launches-fleet-of-new-devices-kids-ebook-store-partnership-with-pocket%2F&ei=BgCSUvOLINPFsATA4oGIBg&usg=AFQjCNEXmdtB-cWoBWlsueWobeD-

IGRgXw; "Amazon's New Fleet of Tablets: Kindle Fire HDX," Digital Book World, September 25, 2013. Available at http://www.digitalbookworld.com/2013/amazons-new-fleet-of-tablets-kindle-fire-hdx; Clive Thompson, "How Working on Multiple Screens Can Actually Help You Focus," Wired, July 7, 2014. Available at http://www.wired.com/2014/07/multi-screen-life.

41. Quoted in Joshua Brustein, "Amazon Will Probably Dominate Books-by-Subscription, Too," Bloomberg Businessweek, January 15, 2013. Available at http://www.businessweek.com/articles/2014-01-15/new-subscription-model-for-e-books-challenges-traditional-publishers; John Biggs, "Amazon Officially Announces Kindle Unlimited, Offering Endless Reading and Listening for $9.99 a Month," TechCrunch, July 18, 2014. Available at http://techcrunch.com/2014/07/18/amazon-officially-announces-kindle-unlimited-offering-reading-and-listening-for-9-99-a-month.

42. Jim Milliot, "Sales of Print Units Slipped in 2013," Publishers Weekly, January 3, 2014. Available at http://www.publishersweekly.com/pw/by-topic/industry-news/bookselling/article/60529-sales-of-print-units-slipped-in-2013.html.

43. Jim Milliot, "Reinventing Book Printing Toward a Hybrid Market," Publishers Weekly, September 20, 2013. Available at http://www.publishersweekly.com/pw/by-topic/industry-news/manufacturing/article/59191-reinventing-book-printing-toward-a-hybrid-market.html.

44. "HarperCollins Unbound Links Print, Digital," Publishers Weekly, November 4, 2013. Available at http://www.publishersweekly.com/pw/by-topic/industry-news/publishing-and-marketing/article/59840-harpercollins-unbound-links-print-digital.html.

45. Beth Bacon, "Digital App Connects Parents and Book Info at Scholastic Book Fairs," Digital Book World, November 13, 2013. Available at http://www.digitalbookworld.com/2013/digital-app-connects-parents-and-book-info-at-scholastic-book-fairs.

46. "Amazon AutoRip Service Gives Out Free Digital Copies of CDs," BBC News, January 10, 2013. Available at http://www.bbc.co.uk/news/technology-20972027.

47. "Now Available: Report Two of Consumer Attitudes Toward E-Book Reading, Volume 4," Book Industry Study Group, October 29, 2013. Available at https://www.bisg.org/news/now-available-report-two-consumer-attitudes-toward-e-book-reading-volume-4.

48. Megan Rogers, "Buy One, Get One Free," Inside Higher Ed, November 5, 2013. Available at http://www.insidehighered.com/news/2013/11/05/university-press-uses-social-media-increase-brand-loyalty.

49. Ian Youngs, "Bill Bryson Urges e-Book Bundle Tie-up," BBC News, September 24, 2013. Available at http://www.bbc.co.uk/news/entertainment-arts-24222420.

50. "Amazon Upgrades Whispersync to Offer Seamless Ebook to Audio Book Experience," Digital Book World, October 8, 2013. Available at http://www.digitalbookworld.com/2013/amazon-upgrades-whispersync-to-offer-seamless-ebook-to-audio-book-experience.

51. John Hofilena, "Tokyo Court Rules to Stop Companies with Book 'Digitization' Services," Japan Daily Press, October 3, 2013. Available at http://japandailypress.com/tokyo-court-rules-to-stop-companies-with-book-digitization-services-0337091.

52. "Amazon Launches Digital Literary Journal, 'Day One,'" Digital Book World, October 30, 2013. Available at http://www.digitalbookworld.com/2013/amazon-launches-digital-literary-journal-day-one.

53. Beth Bacon, "Personalized Book Reader Follows Kids as They Turn the Pages," Digital Book World, December 2, 2013. Available at http://www.digitalbookworld.com/2013/personalized-book-reader-follows-kids-as-they-turn-the-pages.

54. Sascha Segan, "Bezos: Books Will Live On, So Will DRMed E-Books," *PC Magazine*, September 25, 2013. Available at http://www.pcmag.com/article2/0,2817,2424829,00.asp.

55. "Espresso Printing," The InfoShop, World Bank, April 11, 2006. Available at http://web.worldbank.org/WBSITE/EXTERNAL/PUBLICATION/INFOSHOP1/0,,contentMDK:20884077~pagePK:162350~piPK:165575~theSitePK:225714,00.html.

56. My thanks to Randi Park, publishing officer, Electronic Products and Distribution, at the World Bank in Washington, for talking with me about current Bank distribution practices.

57. "Seattle-Based Drugstore Pilots Espresso Book Machine, On-Demand Printing Center," *Digital Book World*, November 6, 2013. Available at http://www.digitalbookworld.com/2013/seattle-based-drugstore-pilots-espresso-book-machine-on-demand-printing-center.

58. Quoted in Nanda, "Re-Read the e-Books Chapter" (see note 23).

59. Michael S. Rosenwald, "Independent Bookstores Turn a New Page on Brick-and-Mortar Retailing," *Washington Post*, December 15, 2013. Available at http://www.washingtonpost.com/local/independent-bookstores-turn-a-new-page-on-brick-and-mortar-retailing/2013/12/15/2ed615d8-636a-11e3-aa81-e1dab1360323_story.html.

60. Doucé et al. 2013.

61. Roger Tagholm, "In Italy, Feltrinelli's New RED Store Aims at Young Techies," Publishing Perspectives, August 5, 2014. Available at http://publishingperspectives.com/2014/08/in-italy-feltrinellis-new-red-store-aims-at-young-techies.

62. Ian Youngs, "Browsing the Bookshop of the Future," BBC News, September 24, 2013. Available at http://www.bbc.co.uk/news/entertainment-arts-24203287.

63. Quoted in Youngs, "Browsing the Bookshop of the Future" (see note 62).

64. Jeremy Greenfield, "Amazon Courts Local Bookstores with New 'Source' Program," *Forbes*, November 6, 2013. Available at http://www.forbes.com/sites/jeremygreenfield/2013/11/06/amazon-courts-local-bookstores-with-new-source-program.

65. Liz Bury, "Ebooks and Discounts Drive 98 Publishers Out of Business," *Guardian*, November 4, 2013. Available at http://www.theguardian.com/books/2013/nov/04/ebooks-discounts-98-publishers-closure.

66. "How We Are Being Watched," BBC News, November 3, 2006. Available at http://news.bbc.co.uk/2/hi/uk_news/6110866.stm.

67. National Endowment for the Arts, *How a Nation Engages with Art: Highlights from the 2012 Survey of Public Participation in the Arts*, NEA Research Report #27, 2013. Available at http://arts.gov/sites/default/files/highlights-from-2012-SPPA-rev.pdf.

68. "NOP World Culture Score™ Index Examines Global Media Habits…Uncovers Who's Tuning In, Logging On and Hitting the Books," PR Newswire, June 15, 2013. Available at http://www.prnewswire.com/news-releases/nop-world-culture-scoretm-index-examines-global-media-habits-uncovers-whos-tuning-in-logging-on-and-hitting-the-books-54693752.html.

69. Chomsky 1965.

70. Rosenwald, "Independent Bookstores Turn a New Page" (see note 59).

71. Louis H. Sullivan, "The Tall Office Building Artistically Considered," *Lippincott's Magazine* 57, March 1896, 403–409. Available at http://archive.org/details/tallofficebuildi00sull. Sullivan's actual phrase was "form ever follows function," though the phrase has been shortened in common parlance.

72. Jack W. Perry, "BISG Report—A Few More Ebook Stats," Digital Book World, November 14, 2013. Available at http://www.digitalbookworld.com/2013/bisg-report-a-few-more-ebook-stats.

73. Anthony Grafton, "Future Reading," *New Yorker*, November 5, 2007. Available at http://www.newyorker.com/reporting/2007/11/05/071105fa_fact_grafton?currentPage=all.

74. Velušček 2009.

References

This list includes books and academic articles. References to other sources cited appear in the Notes.

Ackerman, Joshua M., Christopher C. Nocera, and John A. Bargh. 2010. "Incidental Haptic Sensations Influence Social Judgments and Decisions." *Science* 328, no. 5986: 1712–1715.

Ackerman, Rakefet, and Morris Goldsmith. 2011. "Metacognitive Regulation of Text Learning: On Screen Versus on Paper." *Journal of Experimental Psychology: Applied* 17, no. 1: 18–32.

Adler, Mortimer. 1940. *How to Read a Book*. New York: Simon and Schuster.

Agar, Jon. 2003. *Constant Touch: A Global History of the Mobile Phone*. Duxford, Cambridge: Icon Books.

Alber, Travis, and Aaron Miller. 2012. "Above the Silos: Social Reading in the Age of Mechanical Barriers." In Hugh McGuire and Brian O'Leary, eds., *Book: A Futurist's Manifesto*, 153–176. Boston: O'Reilly Media.

Alexander, Michael. 2007. *Old English Riddles: From the Exeter Book*. London: Anvil Press Poetry.

Allen, James P., and Peter Der Manuelian. 2005. *The Ancient Egyptian Pyramid Texts: Writings from the Ancient World*. Atlanta, GA: Society of Biblical Literature.

Alm, Håkan, and Lena Nilsson. 1995. "The Effects of a Mobile Telephone Task on Driver Behaviour in a Car Following Situation." *Accident Analysis & Prevention* 27, no. 5: 707–715.

American Academy of Pediatrics. 2011. "Policy Statement: Media Use by Children Younger than 2 Years." *Pediatrics* 128: 1040–1045.

Amory, Hugh. 1996. "The Trout and the Milk: An Ethnobibliographical Talk." *Harvard Library Bulletin* 7, no. 1: 50–65.

Annand, David. 2008. "Learning Efficiency and Cost-Effectiveness of Print Versus e-Book Instructional Material in an Introductory Financial Accounting Course." *Journal of Interactive Online Learning* 7, no. 2: 152–164.

Baird, Benjamin, Jonathan Smallwood, Michael D. Mrazek, Julia W. Y. Kam, Michael S. Franklin, and Jonathan W. Schooler. 2012. "Inspired by Distraction: Mind Wandering Facilitates Creative Incubation." *Psychological Science* 23, no. 10: 1117–1122.

Baron, Dennis. 2009. *A Better Pencil: Readers, Writers, and the Digital Revolution.* New York: Oxford University Press.

Baron, Naomi S. 2008. *Always On: Language in an Online and Mobile World.* New York: Oxford University Press.

Baron, Naomi S. 2013a. "Reading in Print Versus Onscreen: Better, Worse, or About the Same?" In Deborah Tannen and Ann Marie Trester, eds., *Discourse 2.0: Language and New Media,* 201–224. Washington, DC. Georgetown University Press.

Baron, Naomi S. 2013b. "Redefining Reading: The Impact of Digital Communication Media." *PMLA* 128, no. 1: 193–200.

Baron, Naomi S., and Elise M. Campbell. 2012. "Gender and Mobile Phones in Cross-National Context." *Language Sciences* 34, no. 1: 13–27.

Barzun, Jacques. 2001. "Three Men and a Book." *The American Scholar* 70, no. 3: 49–57.

Batt, Jennifer. 2012. "Eighteenth-Century Verse Miscellanies." *Literature Compass* 9, no. 6: 394–405.

Bavelier, D., R. L. Achtman, M. Mani, and J. Föcker. 2012. "Neural Bases of Selective Attention in Action Video Game Players." *Vision Research* 61: 132–143.

Bayer, Joseph B., and Scott W. Campbell. 2012. "Texting While Driving on Automatic: Considering the Frequency-Independent Side of Habit." *Computers in Human Behavior* 28, no. 6: 2083–2090.

Bergen, Lori, Tom Grimes, and Deborah Potter. 2005. "How Attention Partitions Itself During Simultaneous Message Presentations." *Human Communication Research* 31, no. 3: 311–336.

Birkerts, Sven. 1994. *The Gutenberg Elegies: The Fate of Reading in an Electronic Age.* Boston: Faber and Faber.

Birkerts, Sven. 2010. "Reading in a Digital Age." *The American Scholar* 79, no. 2: 32–44.

Blair, Amy L. 2012. *Reading Up: Middle-Class Readers and the Culture of Success in the Early Twentieth-Century United States*. Philadelphia: Temple University Press.

Blair, Ann. 2010. *Too Much to Know: Managing Scholarly Information Before the Modern Age*. New Haven, CT: Yale University Press.

Blaise, Clark. 2000. *Time Lord: Sir Sandford Fleming and the Creation of Standard Time*. New York: Pantheon Books.

Boltz, William G. 2003. *The Origin and Early Development of the Chinese Writing System*. New Haven, CT: American Oriental Society.

Bowman, Laura L., Laura E. Levine, Bradley M. Waite, and Michael Gendron. 2010. "Can Students Really Multitask? An Experimental Study of Instant Messaging While Reading." *Computers & Education* 54, no. 4: 927–931.

Brewer, Kenneth. 1998. "Lost in a Book: Aesthetic Absorption 1820–1880." Doctoral dissertation. Stanford University, Stanford, CA.

Breznitz, Zvia, Orly Rubinsten, Victoria J. Molfese, and Dennis L. Molfese, eds. 2012. *Reading, Writing, Mathematics and the Developing Brain*. Dordrecht: Springer.

Brower, Reuben. 1961. "Reading in Slow Motion." In Reuben Brower and Richard Poirier, eds. *In Defense of Reading: A Reader's Approach to Literary Criticism*, 3–21. New York: E. P. Dutton.

Burchfield, Colin M., and John Sappington. 2000. "Compliance with Required Reading Assignments." *Teaching of Psychology* 27, no. 1: 58–60.

Carey, James W. 1983. "Technology and Ideology: The Case of the Telegraph." In *Prospects: An Annual of American Cultural Studies* 8: 303–325.

Carr, Nicholas. 2010. *The Shallows: What the Internet Is Doing to Our Brains*. New York: W. W. Norton.

Carrière, Jean-Claude, and Umberto Eco. 2009. *This Is Not the End of the Book: A Conversation Curated by Jean-Philippe de Tonnac*. Trans. Polly McLean. Evanston, IL: Northwestern University Press.

Cavallo, Guglielmo, and Roger Chartier, eds. 1999. *A History of Reading in the West*. Trans. Lydia G. Cochrane. Amherst: University of Massachusetts Press.

Chabris, Christopher, and Daniel Simons. 2009. *The Invisible Gorilla: How Our Intuitions Deceive Us*. New York: Broadway Books.

Chadwick, John. 1959. "A Prehistoric Bureaucracy." *Diogenes* 26: 7–18.

Chandler, Daniel. 1992. "The Phenomenology of Writing by Hand." *Intelligent Tutoring Media* 3, no. 2/3: 65–74.

Charpin, Dominique. 2010. *Reading and Writing in Babylon*. Trans. Jane Marie Todd. Cambridge, MA: Harvard University Press.

Chartier, Roger, ed. 1989. *The Culture of Print: Power and the Uses of Print in Early Modern Europe*. Trans. Lydia G. Cochrane. Princeton, NJ: Princeton University Press.

Chomsky, Noam. 1965. *Aspects of the Theory of Syntax*. Cambridge, MA: MIT Press.

Christakis, Dimitri. 2014. "Interactive Media Use at Younger than the Age of 2 Years: Time to Rethink the American Academy of Pediatrics Guidelines?" *JAMA Pediatrics* 168, no. 5: 399–400.

Chu, Christina, Mark Rosenfield, Joan K. Portello, Jaclyn A. Benzoni, and Juanita D. Collier. 2011. "A Comparison of Symptoms After Viewing Text on a Computer Screen and Hardcopy." *Ophthalmic and Physiological Optics* 31, no. 1: 29–32.

Cipolla, Carlo. 1978. *Clocks and Cultures, 1300–1700*. New York: W. W. Norton.

Clanchy, M. T. 1993 [1979]. *From Memory to Written Record: England 1066–1307*, 2nd edition. Oxford: Blackwell.

The Codex Nuttall: A Picture Manuscript from Ancient Mexico. 1975. Edited by Zelia Nuttall with new introductory text by Arthur G. Miller. New York: Dover Publications.

Cohn, Henry J. 1979. "Anticlericalism in the German Peasants' War 1525." *Past & Present* 83, no. 1: 3–31.

Coulmas, Florian. 1996. *The Blackwell Encyclopedia of Writing Systems*. Oxford: Blackwell.

Cressy, David. 1986. "Books as Totems in Seventeenth-Century England and New England." *The Journal of Library History* 21, no. 1: 92–106.

Cunningham, Anne E., and Keith E. Stanovich. 1990. "Early Spelling Acquisition: Writing Beats the Computer." *Journal of Educational Psychology* 82, no. 1: 159–162.

Daly, Lloyd W. 1967. *Contributions to a History of Alphabetization in Antiquity and the Middle Ages*. Brussels: Latomus.

Darnton, Robert. 1991. "History of Reading." In Peter Burke, ed., *New Perspectives on Historical Writing*, 140–167. Cambridge: Polity.

Davis, James. 1961. *Great Books and Small Groups*. New York: Free Press.

Defoe, Daniel 1890 [1729]. *The Compleat English Gentleman*. Edited by Karl D. Bülbring. London: David Nutt. Available at http://www.archive.org/stream/compleatenglishgoodefouoft/compleatenglishgoodefouoft_djvu.txt.

Dehaene, Stanislas. 2009. *Reading in the Brain: The Science and Evolution of a Human Invention*. New York: Viking.

Desmond, Robert W. 1978. *The Information Process: World News Reporting to the Twentieth Century*. Iowa City: University of Iowa Press.

DeStefano, Diana, and Jo-Anne LeFevre. 2007. "Cognitive Load in Hypertext Reading: A Review." *Computers in Human Behavior* 23, no. 3: 1616–1641.

Dettmar, Kevin, J. H. 2005. "Bookcases, Slipcases, Uncut Leaves: The Anxiety of the Gentleman's Library." *NOVEL: A Forum on Fiction* 39, no. 1: 5–24.

Dilevko, Juris, and Lisa Gottlieb. 2002. "Print Sources in an Electronic Age: A Vital Part of the Research Process for Undergraduate Students." *Journal of Academic Librarianship* 28, no. 6: 381–392.

Dillon, Andrew. 1992. "Reading from Paper Versus Screens: A Critical Review of the Empirical Literature." *Ergonomicis* 35, no. 10: 1297–1326.

Doidge, Norman. 2007. *The Brain That Changes Itself*. New York: Viking.

Donner, Jonathan, and Marcela Escobari. 2010. "A Review of Evidence on Mobile Use by Micro and Small Enterprises in Developing Countries." *Journal of International Development* 22, no. 5: 641–658.

Doucé, Lieve, Karolien Poels, Wim Janssens, and Charlotte De Backer. 2013. "Smelling the Books: The Effect of Chocolate Scent on Purchase-Related Behavior in a Bookstore." *Journal of Environmental Psychology* 36: 65–69.

Dyson, Mary C., and Mark Haselgrove. 2000. "The Effects of Reading Speed and Reading Patterns on the Understanding of Text Read from Screen." *Journal of Research in Reading* 23, no. 2: 210–223.

Elbert, Thomas, Christo Pantev, Christian Wienbruch, Brigitte Rockstroh, and Edward Taub. 1995. "Increased Cortical Representation of the Fingers of the Left Hand in String Players." *Science* 270, no. 5234: 305–307.

Elfenbein, Andrew. 2006. "Cognitive Science and the History of Reading." *PMLA* 121, no. 2: 484–502.

Engelsing, Rolf. 1974. *Der Bürger als Leser. Lesergeschichte in Deutschland 1500–1800*. Stuttgart: Metzler.

Evans, James A. 2008. "Electronic Publication and the Narrowing of Science and Scholarship." *Science* 321, no. 5887: 395–399.

Fadiman, Anne, ed. 2005. *Rereadings: Seventeen Writers Revisit Books They Love*. New York: Farrar, Straus and Giroux.

Farr, Cecilia Konchar. 2005. *Reading Oprah: How Oprah's Book Club Changed the Way America Reads*. Albany: State University of New York Press.

Febvre, Lucien, and Henri-Jean Martin. 1976. *The Coming of the Book: The Impact of Printing 1450–1800*. Trans. David Gerard. London: NLB.

Ferguson, Susan. 2001. "Dickens's Public Readings and the Victorian Author." *Studies in English Literature 1500–1900* 41, no. 4: 729–749.

Foerde, Karin, Barbara J. Knowlton, and Russell Poldrack. 2006. "Modulation of Competing Memory Systems by Distraction." *Proceedings of the National Academy of Sciences* 103, no. 31: 11778–11783.

Forster, Antonia. 2001. "Review Journals and the Reading Public." In Isabel Rivers, ed., *Books and Their Readers in Eighteenth-Century England: New Essays*, 171–190. London: Leicester University Press.

Forsyte, Charles. 1980. *The Decoding of "Edwin Drood."* London: Gollancz.

Fortunati, Leopoldina, and Jane Vincent. 2014. "Sociological Insights on the Comparison of Writing/Reading on Paper with Writing/Reading Digitally." *Telematics and Informatics* 31: 39–51.

Franklin, Benjamin. 2004. *Franklin: The Autobiography and Other Writings on Politics, Economics, and Virtue*. Edited by Alan Houston. Cambridge: Cambridge University Press.

Gael, Patricia. 2012. "The Origins of the Book Review in England, 1663–1749." *The Library: The Transactions of the Bibliographical Society* 13, no. 1: 63–89.

Gaskins, Robert. 2012. *Sweating Bullets: Notes About Inventing PowerPoint*. San Francisco: Vinland Books.

Gaur, Albertine. 1987. *A History of Writing*. London: British Museum.

Gee, James Paul. 2005. *What Video Games Have to Teach Us About Learning and Literacy*. New York: Palgrave Macmillan.

Gerard, David. 1980. "Subscription Libraries: Great Britain." In Allen Kent, Harold Lancour, and Jay Daily, eds., *Encyclopedia of Library and Information Science*, vol. 29. New York: Marcel Dekker.

Gerlach, Jin, and Peter Buxmann. 2011. "Investigating the Acceptance of Electronic Books – The Impact of Haptic Dissonance on Innovation Adoption." *ECIS 2011 Proceedings*, Paper 141.

Gibson, James J. 1977. "The Theory of Affordances." In Robert Shaw and John Bransford, eds. *Perceiving, Acting, and Knowing: Toward an Ecological Psychology*, 67–82. Hillsdale, NJ: Erlbaum.

Gilmont, Jean-François. 1999. "Protestant Reformations and Reading." In Guglielmo Cavallo and Roger Chartier, eds., *A History of Reading in the West*, 213–237. Trans. Lydia G. Cochrane. Amherst: University of Massachusetts Press.

González, Julio, Alfonso Barros-Loscertales, Friedemann Pulvermüller, Vanessa Meseguer, Ana Sanjuán, et al. 2006. "Reading *Cinnamon* Activates Olfactory Brain Regions." *NeuroImage* 32, no. 2: 906–912.

Gould, Joseph. 1961. *The Chautauqua Movement: An Episode in the Continuing American Revolution*. Albany: State University of New York Press.

Green, C. Shawn, and Daphne Bavelier, 2003. "Action Video Game Modifies Visual Selective Attention." *Nature* 423, no. 6939: 534–537.

Green, C. Shawn, and Daphne Bavelier. 2006. "Enumeration Versus Multiple Object Tracking: The Case of Action Video Game Players." *Cognition* 101, no. 1: 217–245.

Green, Thomas D., Robert A. Perera, Lauryn A. Dance, and Elizabeth A. Myers. 2010. "Impact of Presentation Mode on Recall of Written Text and Numerical Information: Hard Copy Versus Electronic." *North American Journal of Psychology* 12, no. 2: 233–242.

Greenfield, Patricia M. 2009. "Technology and Informal Education: What Is Taught, What Is Learned?" *Science* 232, no. 5910: 69–71.

Hagedorn, Roger. 1988. "Technology and Economic Exploitation: The Serial as a Form of Narrative Presentation." *Wide Angle: A Film Quarterly of Theory, Criticism and Practice* 10, no. 4: 4–12.

Hall, David. 1983. "The Uses of Literacy in New England, 1600–1850." In William L. Joyce, ed., *Printing and Society in Early America*, 1–47. Worcester, MA: American Antiquarian Society.

Halsey, Katie. 2011. " 'Something Light to Take My Mind off the War': Reading on the Home Front During the Second World War." In Katie Halsey and W. R. Owens, eds., *The History of Reading, Volume 2, Evidence from the British Isles, 1750–1950*, 84–100. London: Palgrave Macmillan.

Hamilton, Nigel. 2004. "Hugh Chisholm. 1866–1924." In H. C. G. Matthew and Brian Harrison, eds., *Oxford Dictionary of National Biography*, vol. 11, 488–490. Oxford: Oxford University Press.

Harrison, J. F. C. 1961. *Learning and Living, 1790–1960: A Study in the History of the English Adult Education Movement*. London: Routledge and Paul.

Hayles, N. Katherine. 2007. "Hyper and Deep Attention: The Generational Divide in Cognitive Modes." *Profession*, 187–199.

Hayles, N. Katherine. 2012. *How We Think: Digital Media and Contemporary Technogenesis*. Chicago: University of Chicago Press.

Henkel, Linda A. 2014. "Point-and-Shoot Memories: The Influence of Taking Photos on Memory for a Museum Tour." *Psychological Science* 25, no. 2: 396–402.

Holzinger, Andreas, Markus Baernthaler, Walter Pammer, Herman Katz, Vesna Bjelic-Radisic, et al. 2011. "Investigating Paper vs. Screen in Real-Life Hospital Workflows: Performance Contradicts Perceived Superiority of Paper in the User Experience." *International Journal of Human-Computer Studies* 69, no. 9: 563–570.

Honoré, Carl. 2004. *In Praise of Slowness: How a Worldwide Movement Is Challenging the Cult of Speed*. San Francisco: HarperSanFrancisco.

Hueston, Marie Proeller. 2006. *Decorating with Books*. New York: Hearst Books.

Hutchby, Ian. 2001. "Technologies, Texts, and Affordances." *Sociology* 35, no. 2: 441–456.

Irwin, William. 2009. "Reading Audio Books." *Philosophy and Literature* 33, no. 2: 358–368.

Iyengar, Uma. 2007. *The Oxford India Nehru*. New Delhi: Oxford University Press.

Jabr, Ferris. 2013a. "The Reading Brain in the Digital Age: The Science of Paper Versus Screens." *Scientific American*, April 11. Available at http://www.scientificamerican.com/article/the-reading-brain-in-the-digital-age-why-paper-still-beats-screens.

Jabr, Ferris. 2013b. "Why the Brain Prefers Paper." *Scientific American* 309, no. 5: 48–53.

Jackson, H. J. 2001. *Marginalia: Readers Writing in Books*. New Haven, CT: Yale University Press.

Jacobs, Alan. 2011. *The Pleasures of Reading in an Age of Distraction*. New York: Oxford University Press.

James, Karin H., and Laura Engelhardt. 2012. "The Effects of Handwriting Experience on Functional Brain Development in Pre-Literate Children." *Trends in Neuroscience and Education* 1, no. 1: 32–42.

Johnson, Samuel. 1755. *A Dictionary of the English Language*. London: W. Strahan.

Johnson, Steven. 2005. *Everything Bad Is Good for You: How Today's Popular Culture Is Actually Making Us Smarter.* New York: Riverhead Books.

Just, Marcel A., and Patricia A. Carpenter. 1987. "Speed Reading." In Marcel Just and Patricia Carpenter, eds., *The Psychology of Reading and Language Comprehension,* 425–452. Newton, MA: Allyn and Bacon.

Just, Marcel A., Patricia A. Carpenter, Timothy A. Keller, Lisa Emery, Holly Zajac, et al. 2001. "Interdependence of Nonoverlapping Cortical Systems in Dual Cognitive Tasks." *NeuroImage* 14: 417–426.

Just, Marcel A., Timothy A. Keller, and Jacquelyn Cynkar. 2008. "A Decrease in Brain Activation Associated with Driving When Listening to Someone Speak." *Brain Research* 1205: 70–80.

Kang, Hyun-Sook. 2012. "English-Only Instruction at Korean Universities: Help or Hindrance to Higher Learning?" *English Today* 28, no. 1: 29–34.

Kaufman, Paul. 1964. "English Book Clubs and Their Role in Social History." *Libri* 14, no. 1: 1–31.

Kidd, David, and Emanuele Castano. 2013. "Reading Literary Fiction Improves Theory of Mind." *Science* 342, no. 6156: 377–380.

Klanten, Robert, Matthias Hübner, and Andrew Losowsky, eds. 2013. *Fully Booked: Ink on Paper.* Berlin: Gestalten.

Klingberg, Torkel. 2009. *The Overflowing Brain: Information Overload and the Limits of Working Memory.* New York: Oxford University Press.

Koning, Sophie de. 2012. "Dyslexia and Early Delayed Motor Development: A Study of Co-Occurring Problems in At-Risk Children." BA thesis. University of Utrecht, The Netherlands.

Koslowe, Kenneth C., Hadas Waissman, and Marta Biner-Kaplan. 2011. "The Blink Frequency Relationship between Reading from a Computer Screen and Reading from a Printed Page." *Optometry & Vision Development* 42, no. 3: 168–171.

Kretzschmar, Franziska, Dominique Pleimling, Jana Hosemann, Stephan Fuessel, Ina Bornkessel-Schlesewsky, et al. 2013. "Subjective Impressions Do Not Mirror Online Reading Effort: Concurrent EEG-Eyetracking Evidence from the Reading of Books and Digital Media." *PLoS ONE,* February 6.

Lacey, Simon, Randall Stilla, and K. Sathian. 2012. "Metaphorically Feeling: Comprehending Textural Metaphors Activates Somatosensory Cortex." *Brain & Language* 120, no. 3: 416–421.

Lahiri, Jhumpa. 2013. *The Lowland.* New York: Alfred A. Knopf.

Landes, David. 1983. *Revolution in Time: Clocks and the Making of the Modern World*. Cambridge, MA: Harvard University Press.

Landow, George. 1997. *Hypertext 2.0: The Convergence of Contemporary Critical Theory and Technology*. Baltimore: Johns Hopkins University Press.

Larsen, Jonas. 2005. "Families Seen Sightseeing: Performativity of Tourist Photography." *Space and Culture* 8, no. 4: 416–434.

Larsen, Jonas. 2014. "The (Im)mobile Life of Digital Photographs: The Case of Tourist Photography." In Jonas Larsen and Mette Sandbye, eds., *Digital Snaps: The New Face of Photography*, 25–47. London: I. B. Tauris.

Law, Graham. 2000. *Serializing Fiction in the Victorian Press*. New York: Palgrave.

Ledgerwood, Alison, and Jeffrey W. Sherman. 2012. "Short, Sweet, and Problematic? The Rise of the Short Report in Psychological Science." *Perspectives on Psychological Science* 7, no. 1: 60–66.

Leibniz, Gottfried Wilhelm. 1951 [1680]. "Precepts for Advancing the Sciences and Arts." In Philip Wiener, ed., *Leibniz Selections*, 29–46. New York: Scribner.

Levine, Laura E., Bradley M. Waite, and Laura L. Bowman. 2007. "Electronic Media Use, Reading, and Academic Distractability in College Youth." *CyberPsychology & Behavior* 10, no. 4: 560–566.

Lewis, Jacob. 2012. "The Forgotten Consumer." In Hugh McGuire and Brian O'Leary, eds. *Book: A Futurist's Manifesto*, 287–295. Boston: O'Reilly Media.

Ling, Rich, and Jonathan Donner. 2009. *Mobile Phones and Mobile Communication*. Cambridge: Polity.

Liu, Ziming. 2005. "Reading Behavior in the Digital Environment: Changes in Reading Behavior Over the Past Ten Years." *Journal of Documentation* 61, no. 6: 700–712.

Liu, Ziming. 2006. "Print vs. Electronic Resources: A Study of User Perceptions, Preferences, and Use." *Information Processing and Management* 42, no. 2: 583–592.

Liu, Ziming and Xiaobin Huang. 2008. "Gender Differences in the Online Reading Environment." *Journal of Documentation* 64, no. 4: 616–626.

Long, Elizabeth. 2003. *Book Clubs: Women and the Uses of Reading in Everyday Life*. Chicago: University of Chicago Press.

Longcamp, Marieke, Céline Boucard, Jean-Claude Gilhodes, Jean-Luc Anton, Muriel Roth, et al. 2008. "Learning through Hand- or Typewriting Influences Visual Recognition of New Graphic Shapes: Behavioral and Functional Imaging Evidence." *Journal of Cognitive Neuroscience* 20, no. 5: 802–815.

Longcamp, Marieke, Marie-Thérèse Zerbato-Poudou, and Jean-Luc Velay. 2005. "The Influence of Writing Practice on Letter Recognition in Preschool Children: A Comparison between Handwriting and Typing." *Acta Psychologica* 119: 67–79.

Loukopoulos, Loukia D., R. Key Dismukes, and Immanuel Barshi. 2009. *The Multitasking Myth: Handling Complexity in Real-World Operations*. Burlington, VT: Ashgate.

Love, Jessica. 2012. "Reading Fast and Slow." *The American Scholar* 81, no. 2: 64–72.

Lund, Michael. 1993. *America's Continuing Story: An Introduction to Serial Fiction, 1850–1900*. Detroit, MI: Wayne State University Press.

Lyall, R. J. 1989. "Materials: The Paper Revolution." In Jeremy Griffiths and Derek Pearsall, eds., *Book Production and Publishing in Britain, 1375–1475*, 11–29. Cambridge: Cambridge University Press.

Lyons, Martyn. 2010. *A History of Reading and Writing in the Western World*. New York: Palgrave Macmillan.

Maguire, Eleanor A., David G. Gadian, Ingrid S. Johnsrude, Catriona D. Good, John Ashburner, et al. 2000. "Navigation-Related Structural Change in the Hippocampi of Taxi Drivers." *Proceedings of the National Academy of Sciences* 97, no. 8: 4398–4403.

Mangen, Anne, and Jean-Luc Velay. 2010. "Digitizing Literacy: Reflections on the Haptics of Writing." In Mehrdad Hosseini Zadeh, ed. *Advances in Haptics*, 385–401. Rijeka, Croatia: InTech.

Mangen, Anne, Bente R. Walgermo, and Kolbjørn Brønnick. 2013. "Reading Linear Texts on Paper Versus Computer Screen: Effects on Reading Comprehension." *International Journal of Educational Research* 58: 61–68.

Manguel, Alberto. 1996. *A History of Reading*. London: HarperCollins.

Mann, Thomas. 2001. "The Importance of Books, Free Access, and Libraries as Places – and the Dangerous Inadequacy of the Information Science Paradigm." *The Journal of Academic Librarianship* 27, no. 4: 268–281.

Mar, Raymond. 2011. "The Neural Bases of Social Cognition and Story Comprehension." *Annual Review of Psychology* 62: 103–134.

Mar, Raymond, Keith Oatley, Jacob Hirsh, Jennifer dela Paz, and Jordan B. Peterson. 2006. "Bookworms Versus Nerds: Exposure to Fiction Versus Non-Fiction, Divergent Associations with Social Ability, and the Simulation of Fictional Social Worlds." *Journal of Research in Personality* 40, no. 5: 694–712.

Max, D. T. 2000. "The Electronic Book." *The American Scholar* 69, no. 3: 17–28.

McCoy, Bernard. 2013. "Digital Distractions in the Classroom: Student Classroom Use of Digital Devices for Non-Class Related Purposes." *The Journal of Media Education* 4, no. 4: 5–14.

McGuire, Hugh, and Brian O'Leary, eds. 2012. *Book: A Futurist's Manifesto*, 7–20. Sebastopol, CA: O'Reilly.

Miall, David S., and Teresa Dobson. 2001. "Reading Hypertext and the Experience of Literature." *Journal of Digital Information* 2, no. 1.

Miedema, John. 2008. *Slow Reading*. Duluth, MN: Litwin Books.

Mikics, David. 2013. *Slow Reading in a Hurried Age*. Cambridge, MA: Belknap Press.

Misra, Shalini, Lulu Cheng, Jamie Genevie, and Miao Yuan. 2014. "The iPhone Effect: The Quality of In-Person Social Interactions in the Presence of Mobile Devices." *Environment & Behavior*, published online before print, July 1, DOI 10.1177/0013916514539755.

Moyer, Jessica. 2011. "'Teens Today Don't Read Books Anymore': A Study of Differences in Comprehension and Interest Across Formats." Doctoral dissertation. University of Minnesota, Minneapolis.

Nabokov, Vladimir. 1980. *Lectures on Literature*. Edited by Fredson Bowers. New York: Harcourt Brace Jovanovich.

Neuburg, Victor. 1989. "Chapbooks in America." In Cathy N. Davidson, ed., *Reading in America*, 81–113. Baltimore: Johns Hopkins University Press.

Newkirk, Thomas. 2012. *The Art of Slow Reading: Six Time-Honored Practices for Engagement*. Portsmouth, NH: Heinemann.

Newman, Donald, ed. 2005. *The Spectator: Emerging Discourses*. Cranbury, NJ: Associated University Presses.

Nicholas, David, Paul Huntington, Hamid R. Jamali, Ian Rowlands, Tom Dobrowolski, and Carol Tenopir. 2008. "Viewing and Reading Behaviour in a Virtual Environment—The Full-Text Download and What Can be Read Into It." *Aslib Proceedings: New Information Perspectives* 60, no. 3: 185–198.

Nietzsche, Friedrich. 1982 [1881]. *Daybreak: Thoughts on the Prejudices of Morality*. Trans. R. J. Hollingdale. Cambridge: Cambridge University Press.

Noyes, Jan M., and Kate J. Garland. 2003. "VDT Versus Paper-Based Text: Reply to Mayes, Sims and Koonce." *International Journal of Industrial Ergonomics* 31, no. 6: 411–423.

Nunberg, Geoffrey, ed. 1996. *The Future of the Book*. Berkeley: University of California Press.

Occhipinti, Lisa. 2011. *The Repurposed Library: 33 Craft Projects That Give Old Books New Life*. New York: Stewart, Tabori & Chang.

Odom, William, Abigail Sellen, Richard Harper, and Eno Thereska. 2012. "Lost in Translation: Understanding the Possession of Digital Things in the Cloud." Paper presented at the ACM SIGCHI Conference on Human Factors in Computing Systems, May 5–10, Austin, TX.

O'Hara, Kenton P., Alex Taylor, William Newman, and Abigail J. Sellen. 2002. "Understanding the Materiality of Writing from Multiple Sources." *International Journal of Human-Computer Studies* 56, no. 3: 269–305.

O'Leary, Brian. 2012. "Context, Not Container." In Hugh McGuire and Brian O'Leary, eds., *Book: A Futurist's Manifesto*, 7–20. Sebastopol, CA: O'Reilly.

Ophir, Eyal, Clifford Nass, and Anthony D. Wagner. 2009. "Cognitive Control in Media Multitaskers." *Proceedings of the National Academy of Sciences* 106, no. 37: 15583–15587.

Parish-Morris, Julia, Neha Mahajan, Kathy Hirsh-Pasek, Roberta Michnick Golinkoff, and Molly Fuller Collins. 2013. "Once Upon a Time: Parent-Child Dialogue and Storybook Reading in the Electronic Era." *Mind, Brain, and Education* 7, no. 3: 200–211.

Parsons, Edward Alexander. 1952. *The Alexandrian Library*. London: Cleaver-Hume Press.

Patterson, L. Ray. 1968. *Copyright in Historical Perspective*. Nashville, TN: Vanderbilt University Press.

Pedersen, Birgitte Stougaard, and Iben Have. 2012. "Conceptualizing the Audiobook Experience." *SoundEffects* 2, no. 2: 79–95.

Philips, Deborah. 2007. "Talking Books: The Encounter of Literature and Technology in the Audio Book." *Convergence* 13: 293–306.

Phillips, Natalie M. 2010. "Narrating Distraction: Problems of Focus in Eighteenth-Century Fiction, 1750–1820." Doctoral dissertation. Stanford University. Stanford, CA.

Pinder, Julian. 2012. "Online Literary Communities: A Case Study of LibraryThing." In Anouk Lang, ed., *From Codex to Hypertext: Reading at the Turn of the Twenty-First Century*, 68–87. Amherst: University of Massachusetts Press.

Piolat, Annie, Jean-Yves Roussey, and Olivier Thunin. 1997. "Effects of Screen Presentation on Text Reading and Revising." *International Journal of Human-Computer Studies* 47: 565–589.

Piper, Andrew. 2012. *Book Was There: Reading in Electronic Times*. Chicago: University of Chicago Press.

Pohl, Mary, Kevin Pope, and Christopher von Nagy. 2002. "Olmec Origins of Mesoamerican Writing." *Science* 298, no. 5600: 1984–1987.

Powers, William. 2011. *Hamlet's BlackBerry: Building a Good Life in the Digital Age*. New York: HarperCollins.

Price, Leah. 2000a. "Reading (and Not Reading) Richardson, 1765–1868." *Studies in Eighteenth Century Culture* 29: 87–103.

Price, Leah. 2000b. *The Anthology and the Rise of the Novel: From Richardson to George Eliot.* New York: Cambridge University Press.

Price, Leah. 2004. "Reading: The State of the Discipline." *Book History* 7: 303–320.

Price, Leah, ed. 2011. *Unpacking My Library: Writers and Their Books.* New Haven, CT: Yale University Press.

Price, Leah. 2012. *How to Do Things with Books in Victorian Britain.* Princeton, NJ: Princeton University Press.

Price, Michael. 2011. "Restoring Glory." *American Psychological Association Monitor* 42, no. 1: 68.

Proust, Marcel. 1971 [1905]. *On Reading.* Trans. and edited by Jean Autret and William Burford. New York: Macmillan.

Przybylski, Andrew K., and Netta Weinstein. 2013. "Can You Connect with Me Now? How the Presence of Mobile Communication Technology Influences Face-to-Face Conversation Quality." *Journal of Social and Personal Relationships* 30, no. 3: 237–246.

Putnam, Robert. 2000. *Bowling Alone: The Collapse and Revival of American Community.* New York: Simon and Schuster.

Radway, Janice. 1997. *A Feeling for Books: The Book-of-the-Month Club, Literary Taste, and Middle-Class Desire.* Chapel Hill: University of North Carolina Press.

Raven, James. 1998. "New Reading Histories, Print Culture, and the Identification of Change: The Case of Eighteenth-Century England." *Social History* 23, no. 3: 268–287.

Ray, Angela G. 2005. *The Lyceum and Public Culture in the Nineteenth-Century United States.* East Lansing: Michigan State University Press.

Rice, Stephen P. 2004. *Minding the Machine: Languages of Class in Early Industrial America.* Berkeley: University of California Press.

Richardson, Samuel. 1804. *The Correspondence of Samuel Richardson, Author of Pamela, Clarissa, and Sir Charles Grandison,* 6 vols. Selections, biography, and observations by Anna Letitia Barbauld. London: Printed for Richard Phillips.

Riesman, David. 1950. *The Lonely Crowd: A Study of the Changing American Character.* New Haven, CT: Yale University Press.

Roberts, Colin H., and T. C. Skeat. 1983. *The Birth of the Codex*. London: Oxford University Press.

Rosenberg, Daniel. 2003. "Early Modern Information Overload." *Journal of the History of Ideas* 64, no. 1: 1–9.

Rothkopf, Ernst Z. 1971. "Incidental Memory for Location of Information in Text." *Journal of Verbal Learning and Verbal Behavior* 10: 608–613.

Rubery, Matthew, ed. 2011. *Audiobooks, Literature, and Sound Studies*. New York: Routledge.

Rubin, Joan Shelley. 1985. "Self, Culture, and Self-Culture in Modern America: The Early History of the Book-of-the-Month Club." *Journal of American History* 71, no. 4: 782–806.

Sadato, Norihiro. 2005. "How the Blind 'See' Braille: Lessons from Functional Magnetic Resonance Imaging." *The Neuroscientist* 11, no. 6: 577–582.

Saenger, Paul. 1997. *Space between Words: The Origins of Silent Reading*. Stanford, CA: Stanford University Press.

Saenger, Paul. 2010. "The Impact of the Early Printed Page on the History of Reading." In Ian Gadd, ed., *The History of the Book in the West: 1455–1700*, vol. II, 385–449. Surrey, UK: Ashgate.

Sampson, Geoffrey. 1990. *Writing Systems: A Linguistic Introduction*. Stanford, CA: Stanford University Press.

Sanbonmatsu, David M., David L. Strayer, Nathan Medeiros-Ward, and Jason M. Watson. 2013. "Who Multi-Tasks and Why? Multi-Tasking Ability, Perceived Multi-Tasking Ability, Impulsivity, and Sensation Seeking." *PLoS ONE* 8, no. 1.

Schmandt-Besserat, Denise. 1992. *Before Writing: From Counting to Cuneiform*, 2 vols. Austin: University of Texas Press.

Schreiner, Samuel A. 1977. *The Condensed World of the Reader's Digest*. New York: Stein and Day.

Schugar, Heather R., Carol A. Smith, and Jordan T. Schugar. 2013. "Teaching with Interactive E-Books in Grades K-6." *The Reading Teacher* 66, no. 8: 615–624.

Schwalbe, Will. 2012. *The End of Your Life Book Club*. New York: Alfred Knopf.

Seager, Nicholas. 2012. *The Rise of the Novel*. New York: Palgrave Macmillan.

Sellen, Abigail J., and Richard H. R. Harper. 2002. *The Myth of the Paperless Office*. Cambridge, MA: MIT Press.

Sessa, Frank B. 1980. "Public Libraries, International: History of the Public Library." In Allen Kent, Harold Lancour, and Jay E. Daily, eds., *Encyclopedia of Library and Information Science*, vol. 24, 267–291. New York: Marcel Dekker.

Sherman, William H. 2002. "What Did Renaissance Readers Write in Their Books?" In Jennifer Andersen and Elizabeth Sauer, eds., *Books and Readers in Early Modern England*, 119–137. Philadelphia: University of Pennsylvania Press.

Siegenthaler, Eva, Pascal Wurtz, Per Bergamin, and Rudolf Groner. 2011. "Comparing Reading Processes on e-Ink Displays and Print." *Displays* 32, no. 5: 268–273.

Sigman, Mariano, and Stanislas Dehaene. 2006. "Dynamics of the Central Bottleneck: Dual-Task and Task Uncertainty." *PLoS Biology* 4, no. 7.

Smith, T., E. Darling, and B. Searles. 2011. "2010 Survey on Cell Phone Use While Performing Cardiopulmonary Bypass." *Perfusion* 26, no. 5: 375–380.

Sosnoski, James. 1999. "Hyper-Readers and Their Reading Engines." In Gail E. Hawisher and Cynthia L. Selfe, eds., *Passions, Politics, and 21st Century Technologies*, 161–177. Logan: Utah State University Press–NCTE.

Spacks, Patricia Meyer. 2011. *On Rereading*. Cambridge, MA: Harvard University Press.

Speer, Nicole K., Jeremy R. Reynolds, Khena M. Swallow, and Jeffrey M. Zacks. 2009. "Reading Stories Activates Neural Representations of Visual and Motor Experiences." *Psychological Science* 20, no. 8: 989–999.

Stallybrass, Peter. 2002. "Books and Scrolls: Navigating the Bible." In Jennifer Andersen and Elizabeth Sauer, eds., *Books and Readers in Early Modern England: Material Studies*, 42–79. Philadelphia: University of Pennsylvania Press.

Stanhope, Philip Dormer, Lord Chesterfield. 1968. *The Letters of Philip Dormer Stanhope, 4th Earl of Chesterfield*, vol. 4. Edited by Bonamy Dobrée. New York: AMS Press.

Steiner-Adair, Catherine, with Teresa H. Barker. 2013. *The Big Disconnect: Protecting Childhood and Family Relationships in the Digital Age*. New York: Harper.

Story, Ronald. 1975. "Class and Culture in Boston: The Athenaeum, 1807–1860." *American Quarterly* 27, no. 2: 178–199.

Strayer, David L., Frank A. Drews, and Dennis J. Crouch. 2006. "A Comparison of the Cell Phone Driver and the Drunk Driver." *Human Factors* 48, no. 2: 381–391.

Strayer, David L., Frank A. Drews, and William A. Johnston. 2003. "Cell Phone-Induced Failures of Visual Attention During Simulated Driving." *Journal of Experimental Psychology: Applied* 9, no. 1: 23–32.

Taipale, Sakari. 2014. "The Affordances of Reading/Writing on Paper and Digitally in Finland." *Telematics and Informatics* 31, no. 4: 532–542.

Tennenhouse, Leonard. 1998. "The Americanization of *Clarissa*." *Yale Journal of Criticism* 11, no. 1: 177–196.

Tenopir, Carol, Donald W. King, Sheri Edwards, and Lei Wu. 2009. "Electronic Journals and Changes in Scholarly Article Seeking and Reading Patterns." *Aslib Proceedings: New Information Perspectives* 61, no. 1: 5–32.

Thompson, Damian. 2011. *Books Make a Home*. London: Ryland Peters & Small.

Thornton, Tamara. 1996. *Handwriting in America*. New Haven, CT: Yale University Press.

Tufte, Edward. 2003. *The Cognitive Style of PowerPoint*. Cheshire, CT: Graphics Press.

Turkle, Sherry. 2011. *Alone Together: Why We Expect More from Technology and Less from Each Other*. New York: Basic Books.

Ulin, David L. 2010. *The Lost Art of Reading: Why Books Matter in a Distracted Time*. Seattle, WA: Sasquatch Books.

Unger, J. Marshall. 1996. *Literacy and Script Reform in Occupation Japan*. New York: Oxford University Press.

Van Arsdall, Anne. 2002. *Medieval Herbal Remedies: The Old English Herbarium and Anglo-Saxon Medicine*. New York: Routledge.

van den Broek, Paul, Robert F. Lorch Jr., Tracy Linderholm, and Mary Gustafson. 2001. "The Effects of Readers' Goals on Inference Generation and Memory for Texts." *Memory & Cognition* 29, no. 8: 1081–1087.

Varao Sousa, Trish L., Jonathan S. A. Carriere, and Daniel Smilek. 2013. "The Way We Encounter Reading Material Influences How Frequently We Mind Wander." *Frontiers in Psychology* 4, Article 892.

Velázquez, Ramiro, Hermes Hernández, and Enrique Preza. 2012. "A Portable Piezoelectric Tactile Terminal for Braille Readers." *Applied Bionics and Biomechanics* 9: 45–60.

Velušček, Anton, ed. 2009. *Stare Gmajne Pile-Dwelling Settlement and Its Era*. Ljubljana, Slovenia: Institute for Archaeology.

Volkersz, Evert. 1995. "McBook: The Reader's Digest Condensed Books Franchise." *Publishing Research Quarterly*, Summer, 52–61.

Watson, Jason M., and David L. Strayer. 2010. "Supertaskers: Profiles in Extraordinary Multitasking Ability." *Psychonomic Bulletin & Review* 17, no. 4: 479–485.

Watt, Ian. 1957. *The Rise of the Novel: Studies in Defoe, Richardson and Fielding*. Berkeley: University of California Press.

Wegner, Daniel M., and Adrian F. Ward. 2013. "How Google Is Changing Your Brain." *Scientific American* 309, no. 6: 58–61.

Weinreich, Harald, Hartmut Obendorf, Eelco Herder, and Matthias Mayer. 2008. "Not Quite the Average: An Empirical Study of Web Use." *ACM Transactions on the Web* 2, no. 1. article #5.

Wellisch, Hans. 1991. *Indexing from A to Z*. New York: H. W. Wilson.

Wells, Ronald A. 1973. *Dictionaries and the Authoritarian Tradition: A Study in English Usage and Lexicography*. The Hague: Mouton.

Wharton, Edith. 1903. "The Vice of Reading." *The North American Review* 177, no. 563: 513–521.

Wiles, R. M. 1957. *Serial Publication in England Before 1750*. New York: Cambridge University Press.

Wittmann, Reinhard. 1999. "Was There a Reading Revolution at the End of the Eighteenth Century?" In Guglielmo Cavallo and Roger Chartier, eds., *A History of Reading in the West*, 284–312. Trans. Lydia G. Cochrane. Amherst: University of Massachusetts Press.

Wolf, Maryanne. 2007. *Proust and the Squid: The Story and Science of the Reading Brain*. New York: HarperCollins.

Wolf, Maryanne, and Mirit Barzillai. 2009. "The Importance of Deep Reading." *Educational Leadership* 66, no. 6: 32–37.

Woodmansee, Martha, and Peter Jaszi, eds. 1994. *The Construction of Authorship: Textual Appropriation in Law and Literature*. Durham, NC: Duke University Press.

Yeo, Richard. 2002. "Managing Knowledge in Early Modern Europe." *Minerva* 40: 301–314.

Yuan, Kai, Wei Qin, Guihong Wang, Fang Zeng, Liyan Zhao, et al. 2011. "Microstructure Abnormalities in Adolescents with Internet Addiction Disorder." *PLoS ONE* 6, no. 6.

Zambarbieri, Daniela, and Elena Carniglia. 2012. "Eye Movement Analysis of Reading from Computer Displays, eReaders, and Printed books." *Ophthalmic and Physiological Optics* 32: 390–396.

Zhang, Harry, Matthew R. H. Smith, and Gerald Witt. 2006. "Identification of Real-Time Diagnostic Measures of Visual Distraction with an Automatic Eye-Tracking System." *Human Factors* 48, no. 4: 805–821.

Zunshine, Lisa, ed. 2010. *Introduction to Cognitive Cultural Studies*. Baltimore: Johns Hopkins University Press.

Index

Note: Page numbers in italics indicate illustrations.

magazines, 46–47, 106
magnetoencephalography (MEG), 159
Mahabharata, 154
Mangen, Anne, 151–152, 169–170, 217
Manjoo, Farhad, 14
Mann, Thomas, 152
Mansfield Park (Austen), 161
Mar, Raymond, 161
Marcos, Imelda, 35
marginalia, 27, 30. *See also* annotations
Max, D.T., 153–154
McCarthy Era, 134
McGinniss, Joe, 57
MEG. *See* magnetoencephalography
memory, 83, 142
mental focus and distraction, 172–176, 221.
    See also concentration
mental wandering, 174–175
Microsoft, 98
Miedema, John, 103
Mikics, David, 104–105, 151
Milton, John, 51
MIT Media Lab, 220
mobile phones, for reading, x
Modern Times (Chaplin), 44
Monarch Notes, 55
Morgenstern, Erin, 226
Morrison, Toni, 93, 109
MS Cotton Vitellius A. xv, 49
Mulcaster, Richard, 32
multitasking, 88–89
    as distractor, 176
    brain on, 158, 159, 178–180
    reading and, 88–89, 181
Murdoch, Iris, 143
Mycenaean Greece, 25
My Life with Martin Luther King, Jr. (Coretta Scott King), 54
The Mystery of Edwin Drood (Dickens), 52
The Myth of the Paperless Office (Sellen, Harper), 146
MyWrite, 140

Nabokov, Vladimir, 110
The Name of the Rose (Eco), 187
Nass, Clifford, 180
National Endowment for the Arts (NEA), ix, 10, 107, 230
National Safety Council, 176
Naturalis Historia (Pliny), 32
Naumann, Michael, 198
NEA. *See* National Endowment for the Arts
Nehru, Jawaharlal, 20, 24
Neruda, Pablo, 143
Netflix, 158
Newkirk, Thomas, 103–104

"New Possibilities for Print Media and Packaging-Combining Print with Digital." *See* COST Action FPS 1104
New School for Social Research, ix
New York Review of Books, 51, 225
New York Times Book Review, 51, 128
Nielsen, Jakob, 42–43, 164–165, 169, 215
Nielsen.com, 42
Nietzsche, Friedrich, 101–102
The Night Circus (Morgenstern), 226
"The No-Book Report: Skim It and Weep," 44
No Fear Shakespeare series, 55
Nook, 8
Nook Media, 57
Nook Snaps, 57
Norman, Donald, 43
Norris, Gregory, 69
Norton Anthology of American Literature, 50
Norway, 74. *See also* Mangen
La Nouvelle Héloïse (Rousseau), 24
novel, historical development of, 35, 48
Noyes, Jan, 170
Nunberg, Geoff, 5, 153

Occhipinti, Lisa, 17
"Of Studies" (Bacon), 35
Olchowski, Alexander, 103
The Old Curiosity Shop (Dickens), 51, 57
Old English, 25
Olmec, 25
One Bite Reads, 57
one-off reading, xiii, 94–95, 99–100, 108–109
"On Reading" (Proust), 115
On Rereading (Spacks), 110
open access, 71–72, 77–78
Opening the Book, 127
Open Knowledge Repository, 225
Open Road, 132, 225
Oprah's Book Club, 123–124
oracle bones, 25
oral side, of books, 202–203
Othello, 55
ownership
    of books, 81–82
    of digital materials, 96, 138, 215
Oxford English Dictionary, 4
Oxford University Press, Very Short Introduction Series, 59
Oyster, 11
Ozick, Cynthia, 114–115

Page, Larry, 73
page numbers, 33–34
Pamela (Richardson), 26, 35, 48, 49
paper
    costs with, 64